Effective Communication in Criminal Justice

This book is dedicated to our grandsons, Benson and Cash—

Benson, you opened our eyes to differences, made us see the world through your lens, and taught us to embrace possibilities we would never have conceived. Never let anyone stand in the way of your goals or keep you from dreaming. Autism does not define you; you are Benson.

Cash, you have an open and loving heart but also a mischievous nature. The Wizard of Oz told the Tin Man, "A heart is not judged by how much you love but by how much you are loved by others." A more apt description of you could not be found. Be who you are for now and for always.

All of our love—

Pop-Pop and GiGi

Sara Miller McCune founded SAGE Publishing in 1965 to support the dissemination of usable knowledge and educate a global community. SAGE publishes more than 1000 journals and over 800 new books each year, spanning a wide range of subject areas. Our growing selection of library products includes archives, data, case studies and video. SAGE remains majority owned by our founder and after her lifetime will become owned by a charitable trust that secures the company's continued independence.

Los Angeles | London | New Delhi | Singapore | Washington DC | Melbourne

Effective Communication in Criminal Justice

Robert E. Grubb

Paradox Enterprises

K. Virginia Hemby

Middle Tennessee State University

Los Angeles | London | New Delhi
Singapore | Washington DC | Melbourne

FOR INFORMATION:

SAGE Publications, Inc.
2455 Teller Road
Thousand Oaks, California 91320
E-mail: order@sagepub.com

SAGE Publications Ltd.
1 Oliver's Yard
55 City Road
London, EC1Y 1SP
United Kingdom

SAGE Publications India Pvt. Ltd.
B 1/I 1 Mohan Cooperative Industrial Area
Mathura Road, New Delhi 110 044
India

SAGE Publications Asia-Pacific Pte. Ltd.
3 Church Street
#10-04 Samsung Hub
Singapore 049483

Printed in the United States of America

Library of Congress Cataloging-in-Publication Data

Names: Grubb, Robert E., author. | Hemby, K. Virginia, author.

Title: Effective communication in criminal justice / Robert E. Grubb, K. Virginia Hemby.

Description: First Edition. | Thousand Oaks : SAGE Publications, [2018] |

Includes bibliographical references and index.

Identifiers: LCCN 2017048166 | ISBN 9781506392134 (pbk. : alk. paper)

Subjects: LCSH: Communication in law enforcement. | Criminal justice, Administration of. | Criminal records—Management.

Classification: LCC HV7936.C79 G78 2018 | DDC 364.01/4—dc23 LC record available at https://lccn.loc.gov/2017048166

Acquisitions Editor: Jessica Miller
Editorial Assistant: Rebecca Lee
Content Development Editor: Adeline Wilson
Production Editor: Laureen Gleason
Copy Editor: Jared Leighton
Typesetter: Hurix Digital
Proofreader: Scott Oney
Indexer: Molly Hall
Cover Designer: Michael Dubowe
Marketing Manager: Jillian Ragusa

This book is printed on acid-free paper.

SFI Certified Sourcing
www.sfiprogram.org
SFI-00453

18 19 20 21 22 10 9 8 7 6 5 4 3 2 1

BRIEF CONTENTS

DETAILED CONTENTS

PART IV • EFFECTIVE COMMUNICATION WITH DIFFERENT POPULATIONS

Chapter 11 • Communication With Diverse Populations: Ethnic/Cultural Groups and Children and Youth 230

Chapter 12 • Communication With Special Groups: Cognitive, Physiological, Psychological, and Emotional Disabilities 249

PREFACE

As university professors, we were aware of issues involving communication skills in our students. So my coauthor and I collaborated on the creation of a text that would address some of them in the belief that we could help our students gain a better understanding of the importance of and the need for effective communication. The first edition of *Effective Communication for Criminal Justice Professionals* was published as a "special publication" by Wadsworth (Cengage) in 2003.

I began using the book in fall 2003 as a supplemental text in several of my criminal justice classes. By doing so, I identified areas that required additional work. I also received information from several law enforcement agencies and corrections personnel about the need for this type of text to assist with developing skills in communication. I conducted numerous report writing and interview and interrogation workshops for the Franklin Police Department (Franklin, TN) and received vast amounts of feedback from various law enforcement and corrections agencies about the need for additional training and education in communication skills.

This edition of the text includes some of the original material from the first edition. However, a majority of the information has been updated and new materials have been added. We are now partnering with SAGE Publications, and the book has been relaunched as a first edition.

Criminal justice agencies' need to better communicate with one another, within agencies (internal), and with their constituents (external) has not changed. As the generations change—and their communication strategies and approaches change—criminal justice agencies must adapt their methods to meet those needs across generations. We can no longer rely on the way "we have always done it" to fight the criminal element or to communicate within our communities. Thus, this edition has a section in the first chapter focusing on communication across generations. This new information addresses the generations (including definitions and characteristics) and the ways in which they desire to receive information—and to process information. As many of today's law enforcement and corrections officers fall within the Generation X and Generation Me (Millennial) designations, their communication strategies differ greatly from their predecessors or superiors, who are part of the Baby Boomer group. The update to Chapter 1 should help make sense of these generational differences and create a dialogue for implementing policies designed to make communication more effective between and among all affected groups.

Another area of importance in drafting a textbook for effective communication skills development is that of digital communication. This edition contains information regarding the use of social networking tools in law enforcement. In addition, the use of smartphones has changed the way law enforcement and corrections officers communicate. They often do not recognize the relationship between digital writing and regular report or "fill-in-the-blank" writing. They are unaware of the ability of legal constituencies to subpoena e-mail messages or text messages because they believe once deleted, these items are no longer available. This edition of the text addresses these types of communication challenges.

Also, with the growth and expansion of technology, criminal justice agencies are more likely to find themselves and their officers in YouTube videos and in social media postings as part of Twitter or Snapchat. Dash cameras, body cameras, and just the pervasiveness of the smartphone have led to readily available video; sometimes, that video may be very one-sided, depending on who or what recorded it. In response to the ubiquitous influence of social media, most criminal justice agencies have created or rely more heavily on chief information officers (CIOs) to address the issues as they arise. The content for Chapter 9, "Technology and Communication: A New Frontier," has been reworked to focus on social media, smartphones, and body and vehicle cameras, as these aspects of the communication process must be addressed. Students or trainees desiring to work in the criminal justice field must be aware of their actions and words, as they will very often find themselves on the Internet and usually not from a flattering perspective.

In addition, Chapter 5, "Preparing to Speak: Presentations and Visual Aids," has been updated to address the televised or recorded presentation (e.g., news reports, televised reports, and updates). The information in this section covers both the non-verbal and verbal aspects of appearing on television or in a recording. People make judgment calls based on the appearance and perceived intellect of an individual speaking as part of a televised or recorded interview. Students and trainees need to know how simple acts of appearance and body language, as well as vocalics (particularly the use of "uh" or "um"), can undermine a positive televised or recorded report or action.

As the grandparents of a child on the autism spectrum, my coauthor and I became vitally interested in how cognitive, physiological, psychological, and emotional disabilities could impact a person when he or she is interacting with criminal justice personnel. Without the understanding that comes from having a family member with autism, Asperger's, Down syndrome, traumatic brain injury, and/or post-traumatic stress disorder, among many others, criminal justice agencies do not see the need to train personnel in how to handle situations involving these individuals. As people age, their hearing diminishes; however, few criminal justice agencies have officers and other personnel attend training sessions designed to help them identify situations where an individual has such a physical disability. Most physical disabilities are visible—can be seen—but psychological, cognitive, and emotional disabilities are invisible. The individual looks "normal" but does not respond properly when questioned. First thoughts usually turn to impairment—alcohol or drugs. This edition has a new chapter on communication with special groups—people who have cognitive, physiological, psychological, and emotional disabilities. Our ultimate goal with the addition of this chapter is to help criminal justice agencies develop more effective training to help personnel recognize people with disabilities and to learn to address the individual and not the disability. The update to this textbook should help students and trainees learn to recognize the signs of disabilities and to learn ways in which to address individuals with disabilities. My coauthor (Hemby) is a traumatic brain injury survivor and has executive function impairment that leads her to curse and to say inappropriate things. How would a criminal justice professional handle an interaction with her? She also suffers from PTSD, and situations involving law enforcement can sometimes lead to a full-blown panic attack. How would they handle that situation? These are questions, among many others, that are addressed in this chapter on communication with special groups.

While no textbook can be the "be all, end all" and contain every fragment of information on a specific topic, my coauthor and I believe this edition of this text has the potential to be a valuable resource for both community college and university programs in criminal justice, as well as for law enforcement and correctional training academies. This text extends the information beyond simply writing reports and offers instructors and trainers a valuable tool in the area of communication skills development.

Robert E. Grubb, PhD
K. Virginia Hemby, PhD

ACKNOWLEDGMENTS

Special thanks are extended to the following individuals:

Chief Tim Potts, Columbia Police Department, Columbia, TN. Chief Potts's participation and guidance in many areas has been a tremendous asset, and I am proud to call him a friend.

Chief Debra Jordan, Bexar County Re-entry Program, San Antonio, TX. Chief Jordan's contribution to this project allowed me to view some aspects of communication in a different light.

Chief Michael Simpson (formerly with Premier Protective Services, Nashville, TN). Chief Simpson's knowledge concerning technology and technology-related issues was an invaluable resource.

I also want to express my gratitude to my coauthor, K. Virginia Hemby. Without her contributions, this edition would not be a reality. Her research, writing, editing, and countless hours of work on this project made everything mesh. I am deeply indebted to her for sharing her skills and talents.

Robert E. "Skip" Grubb

SAGE and the authors would also like to acknowledge the following reviewers whose feedback helped shape the development of this text:

Lauren M. Barrow, Chestnut Hill College

Dianne Berger-Hill, Old Dominion University

James C. Brown, Utica College

Hayley Cleary, Virginia Commonwealth University

Vicky Dorworth, Montgomery College

Katherine J. Ely, Lock Haven University

Diane Evett, Pensacola State College

Brooke Miller, University of North Texas

Johannes P. Oosthuizen, University of Winchester

Norman Rose, Kent State University

Tameka Samuels-Jones, University of Florida

THE BASICS OF EFFECTIVE COMMUNICATION

1

COMMUNICATION
Words Are Not Enough

LEARNING OBJECTIVES

After students have completed this chapter, they will be able to do the following:

1. Identify the importance of communication skills in criminal justice professions

2. Describe the process of communication

3. Distinguish between the verbal and nonverbal components of communication

4. Describe the flow of communication in organizations

5. Explain the impact of generational differences on the communication process

For law enforcement professionals, communication skills are the most important of all the skills necessary to succeed in your profession. Understanding this reality is a must for law enforcement officers.[1]
—Lt. Jim Glennon, Lombard, IL (Ret.), *PoliceOne*

As correctional officers, we owe it to ourselves and our partners to strive for quality leadership in our chosen profession. . . . It's no secret that communication is key to successfully doing this job. Learn how to communicate effectively. . . . Communicate with your peers, whether good or bad in nature, and do so directly but diplomatically.[2]
—Harriet Fox, California correctional officer, *CorrectionsOne*

In the case of security officers, being able to carry out a conversation in a clear and concise manner is a must. It eliminates the risk of getting lost in translation and being misunderstood. On the other hand, an officer's inability to communicate properly can restrict his job performance.[3]
—Jonathan Maliwat, *Security Matters* magazine

The dangers of law enforcement are well documented. The threat of bodily harm is a daily occurrence. However, navigating the obstacles on the path to effective communication can also be particularly hazardous for unprepared or ill-prepared criminal justice professionals. In an era when the law enforcement profession has become identified with racism and racist statements of officers as well as a lack of communication skills—demonstrated via the use of malapropisms of personnel—an effort to train law enforcement personnel to use communication skills effectively to enhance the image created by speech is essential.

Turn on the television, access any radio station or news network, check any social media site, read any newspaper, and you hear about the latest problems in the law enforcement community. A police officer accepts a bribe, a state trooper assaults a speeding motorist, a federal agent supplies sensitive information to a foreign power—mishandled evidence, perjury on the witness stand—the accounts go on and on.

Review the fiascos involving the fatal shooting of Walter Scott in North Charleston, South Carolina; the fatal shooting of Daniel Kevin Harris, a deaf driver, stopped by a North Carolina trooper for speeding; the applying of an improper chokehold to Eric Garner by a New York City police officer that resulted in Garner's death; and the fatal shooting of Oscar Grant III by a BART police officer in Oakland, California—all cases in which law enforcement failed in its attempt to serve the ends of justice. Not only did law enforcement fail, but its image was severely tarnished because of these abysmal events. Can a single cause or a series of causes be identified that resulted in these less-than-successful outcomes? While poor planning and execution might be the explanation offered by law enforcement, more likely than not the proximal cause may be a lack of adequate communication skills on the part of officers, agents, and other personnel.

Communication issues arising in the corrections area occur with regularity, too. Recent occurrences in Cayuga County, New York, at the Auburn Correctional Facility show that corrections officers can find themselves embroiled in investigations in which they are subjects because of misleading or false statements made against inmates. In several cases involving inmates at the Auburn Correctional Facility, Corrections Officer Matthew Cornell fabricated evidence against nine inmates, claiming those inmates possessed contraband that he collected from them. Mr. Cornell went on to testify against these inmates, and they were convicted based almost entirely on his testimony. The Cayuga County district attorney Brian Leeds agreed to dismiss the cases in which Cornell was the complaining witness. However, Mr. Leeds reiterated that the inmates involved in these complaints voluntarily pleaded guilty to the charges—despite Cornell's alleged wrongdoing. He explained that the cases were dismissed as a precautionary measure and that no evidence existed that any wrongdoing or misconduct occurred in these cases.

The defense attorneys representing inmates at the Auburn Correctional Facility disagree with Mr. Leeds's perceptions and explanation. They believe other corrections officers to be involved in these acts. As one attorney pointed out, "As it turns out, the least 'credible' people in our society were telling the truth while trusted officials fabricated evidence."[4]

Private security officers have been embroiled in situations, sometimes as off-duty police officers, in which they have overstepped the bounds of their legally proscribed responsibilities. So all criminal justice agencies have a mandate to better train and equip their personnel to communicate effectively within their jurisdictions—whether a correctional facility, jail, community, or corporation—to avoid bad publicity and perceptions of bias or wrongdoing on their part.

WHAT IS COMMUNICATION?

Communication has been defined in numerous fashions. Notwithstanding the varying definitions, however, the common elements in any communication process are the exchange of information through a shared system of symbols between two or more persons. The essence of communication is conveying a message—a common understanding between the sender and the receiver. This concept is not particularly difficult or abstract when viewed superficially but is one for which the true key to grasping the essence of communication is appreciating all of the nuances involved in this process. When people communicate optimally, both the sender and the receiver can transmit, receive, and process information.

In the communication process, the parties involved engage in certain unconscious behaviors which direct the flow of communication. When we break this process down, we see that it involves a **sender**, a **receiver**, a **message**, a **communication channel**, **encoding**, **decoding**, and **feedback**.[5]

The sender of the message is the party with whom the idea originated. Think of a light bulb being turned on when the switch is flipped, and you have the concept of what the sender experiences when he or she has an idea and wishes to communicate that information to another party or parties. The sender then encodes the message by converting his or her idea into words or gestures that will convey meaning to the receiver. In essence, encoding involves putting the idea into a shared system of language that both parties understand. A major problem can occur at this stage of the communication cycle since words have different meanings for different persons. To avoid this mishap of **bypassing** (a barrier to communication that will be discussed later in the chapter), the sender must choose his or her words carefully, selecting those with concrete meanings that are sure to elicit the same meanings from both sender and receiver. An important point to remember is that since the sender is the person who initiated the communication process, he or she has primary responsibility for its success. Taking care to ensure the selection of the appropriate words or symbols is the first step in successful communication.

The communication channel is the medium by which the message is physically transmitted. Messages may be transmitted by phone (voice or text), e-mail, letter,

TABLE 1.1 ■ Selecting the Appropriate Communication Channel		
Ask yourself these questions:		
Does this message require a written record?	YES	E-mail/memorandum OR Letter OR Report
Do I need immediate feedback?	YES	Phone call OR Personal visit OR E-mail/text message
Does this message require careful organization and supporting documentation?	YES	Long memorandum OR Reports with visuals (charts, graphs, etc.)
How urgent is this message?	URGENT	Personal visit OR Phone call
	ROUTINE	Memorandum OR Letter

memorandum, report, announcement, picture, face-to-face delivery, or some other medium. Senders must choose the communication channel very carefully since situations dictate which method of delivery is most appropriate. Both verbal and nonverbal messages are conveyed through communication channels, and the sender must ensure that both verbal and nonverbal signals are in harmony with each other as well.

Noise is anything that interrupts the communication process. While most people think of noise as physical sounds that are disruptive and prohibit the communication from being heard, things such as typographical or spelling errors in reports, letters, or memoranda may also be damaging to the transmission of a message. Channel noise might also include the annoyance of a receiver at the sender's inappropriate selection of a medium for transmitting the message, such as when a person is fired via a memorandum. The issue of selecting the appropriate medium for sending a message will be discussed later in this chapter.

The individual to whom the message is sent or transmitted is the receiver. The receiver must translate the message from the sender into words or symbols that he or she can understand. This process is called decoding. Communication can only take place when the receiver decodes the message and understands the meaning intended by the sender. Decoding is not a simple process, however. As mentioned previously, many problems exist in communicating between individuals. Since no two people share the same life experiences and no communication process is free

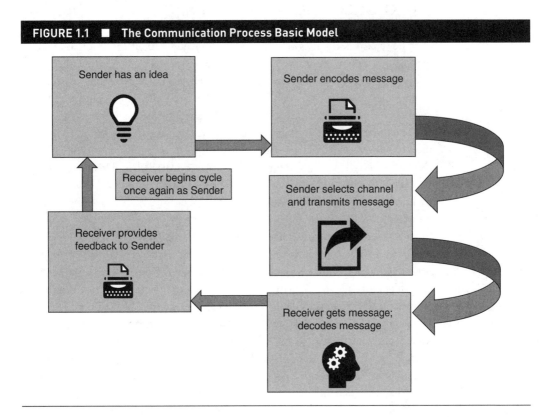

FIGURE 1.1 ■ The Communication Process Basic Model

from barriers—physical, cultural, and semantic—decoding a message to derive the meaning intended by the sender is very difficult.

The response a receiver makes to the message communicated by the sender is called feedback. In an optimum communication situation, the receiver will provide the sender with comments that let the sender know the message was received and processed as it was intended. The sender and receiver can engage in questioning or paraphrasing techniques to ensure a clear understanding of the ensuing messages. In any event, feedback is the final step in the initial communication process. Once the receiver provides feedback to the sender, communication may continue in a to-and-fro rotation between the parties, again encompassing the communication process.

COMMUNICATION STYLES[6]

In most instances, interpersonal communication means being able to talk with our friends, family, business acquaintances, colleagues, and others. In the criminal justice profession, however, optimal communication can mean the difference between life and death, success and failure, or guilty and not guilty. Merely knowing how to speak is not sufficient in these situations; law enforcement officials must be able to overcome many barriers to the communication process as well.

Effective communication occurs between a law enforcement officer and a citizen if—and only if—each person involved in the process assumes the appropriate communication style for the occasion. Traditionally, the style among law enforcement personnel has been authoritative, as in, *I'm the police officer here, and I will act in your best interests.*

The typical police officer really did not solicit any input or information about making a decision concerning the enforcement of law. This concept worked in its infancy because of the time frame and society's expectations concerning law enforcement. However, as the song says, "the times they are a-changing," and law enforcement officers have been mandated to change the way they relate to the public.

The turbulence of the 1960s and 1970s made police officers reevaluate not only their training regimen but also how they dealt with the public. The 1968 Chicago Democratic National Convention in which Mayor Daley advised his police officers that public order would be maintained is a prime example of a clash between the old traditional concept of communication and the change to a more adaptive communication style.

In 1996, the Pittsburgh Police Department became embroiled in an investigation conducted by the U.S. Department of Justice as the result of a lawsuit filed by the American Civil Liberties Union concerning the accusation of an institutionalized pattern of brutality over the last decade against minority citizens. The Department of Justice (DOJ) recommendations were not readily accepted by the mayor and chief of police in Pittsburgh. Rather than accept them in a constructive manner, Mayor Murphy, in a press conference that followed on the heels of the DOJ's announcement concerning its investigation, made the statement that "If they [think they] understand what it means to run a police department in a city today, then my son knows more than they do. And he is 6 years old."[7] This defensive posture is typical of the position taken by traditional law enforcement, and this stance further exemplifies the difficulty in transition from the traditional policing approach to the popular concept of **community policing**.

This defensive posture was typical of the position taken by traditional law enforcement at the time, and this stance further exemplified the difficulty in transitioning from the traditional policing approach to the popular concept of community policing.

As late as 2015, the United States attorney general launched an investigation into the Chicago Police Department and the city's Independent Police Review Authority (IPRA) as the result of a pattern of behavior by police officers involving use of force; racial, ethnic, and other disparities in the use of force; and the department's own systems of accountability.

On January 13, 2017, the Department of Justice announced its findings, saying, "The Justice Department . . . has found reasonable cause to believe that the Chicago Police Department (CPD) engages in a pattern or practice of using force, including deadly force, in violation of the Fourth Amendment of the Constitution." The report went on to say that CPD officers' practices were the result of systemic deficiencies in both training and accountability. Further, it stated that CPD officers were not properly training in de-escalation of situations and that the Chicago Police Department itself had failed to conduct proper investigations into cases involving uses of force.

In contrast to Pittsburgh's response to the Department of Justice report in 1996, the City of Chicago willingly entered into an **agreement in principle** with the United States Department of Justice in January 2017 to show its commitment to working with the DOJ to ensure that the Chicago Police Department acted in accordance with citizens' rights to afford them the services they deserve, to increase the trust between officers and communities, and to promote public and officer safety.[8]

As you can see from these examples, communication styles come in various forms. Researchers are unable to reach a consensus on the exact number of styles; however, most are willing to concede that they cluster around four dimensions: **blaming, directing, persuading**, and **problem solving**. The old style in law enforcement would be most comfortable with the blaming and directing dimensions; but with the advent of community policing, persuading and problem solving are rising to the forefront.

An officer who uses the blaming style basically attempts to find fault or to ascribe blame for a problem. For instance, "If these people would stay in school, stop having babies, and get a job, I wouldn't have to be here at 3 a.m. babysitting them." Clearly, this is an example of a frustrated officer. The use of the negative tone in this communication style evokes hostile feelings in the receiver, which could lead to the escalation of hostilities in an already tense situation. Since officers may find themselves in situations that are hostile by their very nature (domestic disturbances, neighborhood disorders, and assaults), one of the parties present may already be in a combative state or in an emotionally charged state. This style of communication should be avoided unless and until all other avenues of communication have been pursued and all of the facts of the case are absolutely clear.

The directing style of communication is just another name for the authoritative style of management. "It's my way or the highway!" No feedback is solicited; communication flows unidirectionally (from the top) and often creates an insurmountable barrier for communication. In limited situations, however, the directing style may be essential (SWAT teams or special operations) to ensure the safety of an individual or the successful conclusion of an operation, such as, "Halt! Put the gun down, or I will fire." Another example would be, "Put your hands on your head, and drop to your knees, crossing your ankles." Clearly, these examples of unidirectional communication are confrontational by definition and designed for prompt compliance, leaving no room for discussion. Due to the very nature of the aforementioned strategic teams, the directing style of communication is required so as to reduce or eliminate any ambiguities or confusion. The members of a special operations team are not only familiar with but also comfortable with this style of communication because it provides them with a sense of security and operational effectiveness.

The persuading style of communication involves information-sharing and acceptance techniques. Interviewing and interrogating suspects requires criminal justice personnel to utilize this method of communicating. When a police officer is attempting to persuade someone to reveal information that may be against his or her best interests in a court of law or an institutional hearing, he or she must use tact. Professionals realize that a great deal of psychological comfort may be attained by a suspect when the barrier of concealment is finally broken. Therefore, the officer will work to lower this barrier by being as persuasive as possible.

Crisis negotiation is another example where the persuading style would be effective and essential. The ultimate goal in this situation is to have the suspect surrender and neither the suspect nor the hostage(s) to be injured or killed. An officer utilizing a truly persuasive communication style will be able to have the suspect realize that resolving this standoff as peacefully as possible is in his or her best interest. To engender a peaceful resolution, however, mutual concessions are necessary. Utilizing a blaming or directing communication style in these types of situations may only serve to inflame the situation or to make the suspect more resolute in his or her efforts to carry out the original plan of action.

One problem with the persuasive style of communication is that it is not always productive. While an individual may be able to persuade others to follow his or her course of action, merely accepting or following does not ensure an identification or resolution of the original problem. If the problem can be identified and resolved, no need exists to revisit persuasion.

In discussing the four dimensions of communication styles, the evidence presented demonstrates that no single style is perfect for every occasion. The ability to select the appropriate style and to adapt your inherent communication style to fit that situation is the key to successful interaction with other individuals through verbal communication.

Types of Communication

Communication exists on two levels: verbal and nonverbal. To better understand communication, you must first understand the differences between the verbal and nonverbal processes of communicating. Whether a person acts in the capacity of police officer, district attorney, or judge, he or she must recognize the subtle differences conveyed through nonverbal communication to secure arrest, conviction, and punishment for the offender. The old adage, "It's not what you say but how you say it," is as true today as ever.

The person who believes that nonverbal communication is an unimportant component in this process is ill-informed. Nonverbal communication makes up 93%[9] of the information that is exchanged in a face-to-face situation. The old adage, "It's not what you say but how you say it," is particularly relevant because of its reference to the use of paralanguage as a nonverbal communication technique. Therefore, law enforcement officials, like all other people, must make sure that their spoken words and their nonverbal cues complement each other.

Verbal Components

Verbal communication includes the spoken word and the written word as well. Reports, memoranda, e-mail, and directives are all vital to the transmittal of information within a law enforcement agency. They provide the network by which individuals convey information and messages essential to the efficient operation of the department or agency. Chapter 6 will deal with these components in more detail.

The oral aspect of verbal communication is more spontaneous in nature and generally considered easier by most people. The reason for this belief is because we learn to speak long before we learn to write, and we spend a majority of our adult life engaged in conversation. While a great deal of difference exists between the casual conversation and a public presentation, they also share some commonalities.

Generally, three purposes are associated with either casual conversation or public speaking: to inform, to persuade, or to entertain. While law enforcement officials frequently are seen in the role of informing the public or persuading individuals to comply with various legal requirements, seldom are they placed in a position to entertain. Even though many officers have been placed in a particularly entertaining situation, this was not intentional on the part of the law enforcement officer. Chapters 2 and 3 will discuss further aspects of public presentations in greater depth.

KISS/Verbal Obfuscation

Early in my career, I had occasion to hear a radio transmission which advised all units to be on the lookout for a suspect in a particularly nasty malicious wounding described as a "corpulent, Caucasian female with a recently deviated septum." Of the 30 units which received this transmission, only 2 were able to decipher the encrypted message: "Fat, white woman with a broken nose." [Actual example from Dr. Grubb's police officer career]

KISS is an extremely effective acronym. "Keep It Short and Simple" is not an indicator of a lack of intelligence or professionalism but rather an efficient way to communicate. Some police officers, through a sense of misplaced importance, feel compelled to use language that is inappropriate for the situation—inappropriate in the sense that it does not fit well in the context of the conversation or in the message that the officer is attempting to convey.

To try to create or enhance an already established air of authority, officers may talk "above the heads" of suspects, witnesses, and the general public. Given that most local newspapers are written on a sixth-grade reading level, these language skills could serve as barriers to the communication process. The ability to utilize speaking skills on a continuum, ranging from the most basic elementary levels to a more sophisticated professional status, distinguishes the stereotypical police officer from the truly effective law enforcement officer.

Jargon or slang. Another common error is the use of **jargon or slang** in an attempt to ingratiate or include the police officer in the closed or cloistered community. Young police officers frequently endeavor to master the local jargon in an effort to solicit information or develop informants at the local level. While in some instances, this may be effective, the police officer's personality must still mesh well with the local language pattern. A Caucasian police officer with military bearing or persona would experience a great deal of difficulty in being accepted by a minority community. Even mastering the lingo would prove fruitless in this situation. For example, this officer might state, "I followed the dude to his crib, and homey tried to rabbit out the back." Rather than being accepted as a peer or ingratiating himself or herself to the community, this type of officer would be viewed as offensive if he or she did not possess the concomitant demeanor. In fact, the minority community might be insulted at his or her attempt to fit in because they would see it as a form of mockery, and this would serve to further alienate the community and the officer.

Legalese. **Legalese**—the incorporation of legal phrases or legal terms in general conversation with the community, witnesses, or suspects—may be ill-advised. Occasions arise where officers must be in compliance with local, state, or federal codes, and a specific phrase or warning/advisement may be necessary. However, these legalistic terms generally serve to confuse or cloud the individual's understanding of the officer's message. An illustration of this caveat may be clarified by the following example:

> **Police Officer (to suspect)**: "You are under arrest for robbery, and I want you to listen carefully as I read you your rights."

as opposed to

> **Police Officer (to suspect)**: "You are under arrest for violation of Section 18.2–3 COV, and I am going to advise you of your Constitutional rights under the *Miranda* decision."

As evidenced in this example, the use of legal terms serves only to add to the confusion of the arrest situation. Generally, the suspect is already either feigning or actually experiencing confusion or embarrassment at this point, and this use of legal terminology only enhances the confusion—making matters worse.

Nonverbal Components

Police academies teach young men and women to look, act, and behave like police officers. A variety of means are utilized to achieve this transformation, but one of the more important aspects of this socialization is the mastering of the command presence concept. In essence, recruits are instructed in how to establish and maintain control of a situation by their mere presence, and nonverbal communication plays a major role in establishing this command presence. **Nonverbal communication** comprises body language, voice, proxemics, gender, gestures, and touch.[10]

Body language. Body language is formally identified as **kinesics**. The use of the eyes, the head, posture, and stance convey meanings that sometimes might prove to be the antithesis of the verbal message. Federal law enforcement and corrections agencies instruct their investigators and correctional officers to use eye movement as one indicator of possible deception. For instance, suspects who look down and to the left may be deceptive in their description of an incident. The importance of body language in interviewing and interrogation situations has been well documented.

However, the interpretation of body language is bidirectional. (The suspect may be scrutinizing the officer's body language during the interview as well.)

Voice. Vocal characteristics are a type of nonverbal communication called **paralanguage**. The speed with which an individual speaks is sometimes perceived as an indicator of truthfulness or intelligence. Individuals who speak quickly are often thought of as having something to hide. Stereotypically, individuals who speak more slowly, particularly those individuals from the Deep South, are considered to be less intelligent because of their dialect.

Pitch is another voice characteristic which may be revealing. Individuals who speak in a high, shrill voice may be experiencing fear while those who speak in a deep, booming voice exude confidence and control.

Proxemics. The use of objects, clothing, and personal space in communication is known as **proxemics**. Police officers already present a strong nonverbal image—one that may be construed as contradictory in nature. The color blue is associated with trust. The blue uniforms and the squad cars of police officers are supposed to engender trust and integrity in the community. On the other hand, police officers are armed with guns, pepper spray, batons, and badges, which are all recognized symbols of authority and aggression. Basically, the community receives a mixed message regarding the police officer's role as protector or warrior in the neighborhood.

Law enforcement officials in cities with gang populations need to be aware of the nonverbal cues used by individuals to identify or signify membership in a particular group (flashing gang signs, wearing gang colors, and graffiti). The use of these cues frequently denotes the targeting of certain individuals for acts of violence or retaliation, as well as marking certain areas as gang turf. Officers also need to be knowledgeable concerning nonverbal communication with these groups to avoid misunderstandings and to make the communication process as effective as possible.

Gender. Men and women do not speak the same language. While they may use the same vocabulary, their interpretations may be radically different. Typically, female officers do not evoke or promote the "defensive response" from a male suspect. No posturing occurs with respect to establishing a sense of dominance, and therefore, hostility is not met with hostility. Rather than a combative atmosphere, a neutral atmosphere exists that frequently dissipates the suspect's anger, particularly in domestic disputes.

Female victims in domestic disputes may be more disposed to an open dialogue with a female officer than with a male officer. This is not always the case, but female officers may be perceived as more empathetic in these situations. Some female victims may find the presence of a male officer to be more comforting because it provides them with a sense of paternalistic protection and security. On the other hand, male suspects may prefer female officers to speak with them because they perceive these officers to be less judgmental and critical in certain situations. The understanding of the role of **gender** in communication is important in determining which officer may need to take the lead role in interviewing a witness, a suspect, or a victim. More information on this topic will be provided in a later chapter in this text.

Gestures and touch. The significance of **gestures** and touch in nonverbal communication should not be overlooked. The grip and duration of a handshake may be nonverbal signals that communicate a sense of being open and friendly or clandestine and antagonistic.

Many individuals feel that a violation of their intimate personal space that occurs with any type of touching automatically creates a fight-or-flight response. Not only does the definition of personal space vary from individual to individual, but the level of comfort also varies from culture to culture. Therefore, while a pat on the back may be an attempt on the part of the officer to provide comfort and assurance, this act may be perceived by the recipient as a threatening gesture.

Flow of Communication

Communication in organizations, whether public or private, tends to follow two succinct channels: **formal communication** or **informal communication**.[11] Formal communication follows the chain of command in an organization. Information concerning policies and procedures is most often communicated from the top of the organizational structure to the bottom (**downward**) through this formal channel. Formal communication flow, however, is not limited to downward but may also be upward or horizontal. **Upward** communication in organizations may take the form of employee feedback through memoranda, reports, departmental meetings, suggestion systems, and exit interviews. **Horizontal** communication occurs when workers at the same level share information. Horizontal communication may take place through e-mail, personal contact, memoranda, or meetings.

Informal communication takes place in organizations through the unofficial communication channel called the "grapevine." A recent study indicated that as much as two-thirds of an employee's information comes from the grapevine.[12] While social situations lend themselves to discussions of organizational problems and

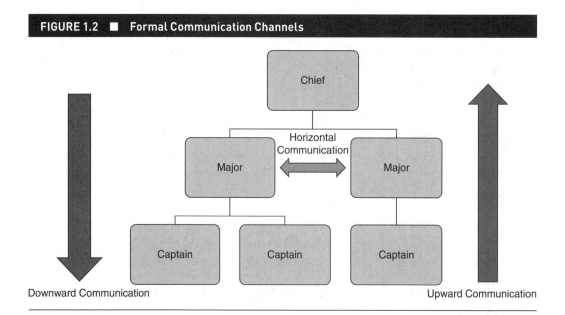

FIGURE 1.2 ■ Formal Communication Channels

Downward Communication   Upward Communication

processes, heavy reliance on the grapevine to disseminate detail suggests that insufficient information is being released through formal channels.

Barriers to Communication

As in any act of communicating, incidences of misunderstanding are likely to occur in criminal justice. No matter how attentive, empathetic, or effective an individual is during communication, certain barriers will arise that impede the flow of or the correct interpretation of information. These barriers or distractions to effective communication may be reduced or eliminated if the officer is aware of their existence. Having the knowledge to recognize and compensate for these differences may also allow agency personnel to acquire information that may have eluded them previously.

Bypassing[13]

Because individuals are different, they attach different meanings to the same words. Most people attempt to understand messages based on the context in which they are delivered. They decide what the words mean by the way in which they are used in conversation or in written documentation. Unfortunately, the meanings attached by the receiver are not always the ones intended by the sender. For example, an examination of the English language produces an overwhelming number of meanings ascribed to the word *fast*. As shown, *fast* has as many as eight different meanings. To avoid bypassing, the sender and receiver must attach the same meanings to words.

When faced with the task of creating understanding, law enforcement officials must assist the public in applying the appropriate meaning to statements delivered to the community. One way to avoid semantic bypassing is to define any terms that could be misunderstood. Another method for creating a common understanding is to use words properly in sentences. Most of the meaning behind our language comes from the way we arrange our sentences and paragraphs. We derive an understanding of what is said from the surrounding descriptions and concomitant arrangement of words.

The Meanings of Fast[14]

- A man is *fast* when he can run rapidly.

- But he is also *fast* when he is tied down and cannot run at all.

- And colors are *fast* when they do not run.

- One is *fast* when she or he moves in suspect company.

- But this is not quite the same thing as playing *fast* and loose.

- A racetrack is *fast* when it is in good running condition.

- A friend is *fast* when she or he is loyal.

- A watch is *fast* when it is ahead of time.

- To be *fast* asleep is to be deep in sleep.

- To be *fast* by is to be near.

- To *fast* is to refrain from eating.

- A *fast* may be a period of noneating—or a ship's mooring line.

- Photographic film is *fast* when it is sensitive to light.

- But bacteria are *fast* when they are insensitive to antiseptics.

Listening

Most individuals can process the spoken word at a rate of 400 words per minute.[15] Unfortunately, the average speaker has a rate of only 125 to 185 words per minute. This creates a critical gap during which the receiver may be distracted by a variety of sources. Daydreaming, forming a response or an answer, forming a question or rebuttal, noise, and time factors or constraints all serve to cloud or block effective listening. This cloud not only obscures the complete receipt of information but also obscures the interpretation of information.

Listening is an active process that requires an individual to be alert to both verbal and nonverbal cues. An active listener will note an increase in blood pressure, an increase in pulse rate, and a tendency to perspire. This physiologic response is indicative of a situation where an individual is observing nonverbal behaviors and processing verbal information, such as one would see in a therapist's office. By its very nature, law enforcement requires officers to be active listeners, not only in seeking the truth but also in providing them a means of protection.

Cultural/Language

Most law enforcement agencies actively seek recruits who possess a fluency in a second language, as it enables them to be more effective in communicating with a specific minority community. However, fluency in a language is not necessarily sufficient, in and of itself, to overcome cultural barriers. This knowledge of the language must be accompanied by an understanding and appreciation of the associated culture. The significance here is that the officer does not send or receive mixed messages but effectively communicates with citizens in the community.

Psychological (Defensiveness)

Traditionally, police officers have been wary of change, as it creates a new environment in which they must operate. Law enforcement officers feel a certain level of comfort and security with measures that have withstood the test of time. When officers are forced to change, they experience a great deal of anxiety because the environment is unfamiliar and may present new obstacles or dangers. Typically, fear and anxiety evoke a defensive response. This defensive response may be transmitted to the community.

A prime example of this type of reaction would involve community policing and the use of citizen police academies. Police officers who do not believe that involving the community in the prevention or detection of crime will be resistant to acceptance of these types of associations. Purely philosophical differences may be at the crux of the issue; however, in most situations, the law enforcement officers view community involvement as a loss of control for departments and officers. This loss of control results in the adoption of a defensive stance, thus creating a barrier to communication surrounding this issue.

Physical

The environment (light, heat, cold, wind, rain, noise, etc.) frequently competes with an individual trying to convey a message. The officer's attention may be distracted by any number of elements. Large groups of people milling about and talking, cars passing, and dogs barking serve as impediments to the communication process.

Experiential

When most individuals converse, they do so from a platform or base of experience. Unfortunately, not all individuals share the same experiences or view the same experience in the same manner; therefore, bias is built into the communication process. These differences or biases in experience serve to hinder effective communication and understanding; they are **experiential barriers to communication**. For instance, officers frequently experience difficulty in communicating with each other because of the wide gap created by varying levels of rank, seniority, income, education, previous military experience, and social class. Resentment may occur among senior officers due to perceived opportunities or privileges afforded younger officers prior to their entering the law enforcement profession. This resentment may also be transferred to citizens within the community.

Officers may also find communicating with citizens whose prior experiences are not synchronous with those of the officer to be difficult. The ability to empathize with and understand others decreases when shared experiences are not present. Since most law enforcement personnel view life through the window of their individual experience, adapting that perspective to the background of suspects, victims, or witnesses is difficult. Nevertheless, protecting the public and upholding the law is the responsibility of any officer, and part of that obligation encompasses the communication process.

Overcoming Communication Barriers

In addressing the barriers to the communication process, we must also identify methods for overcoming those barriers. As you plan your communication, ask yourself the following questions to ensure that you have anticipated communication obstacles.

1. Have you anticipated problems in communication? People are different, and in these differences, communication problems thrive. Be proactive in planning communication so that you address the needs of the receiver. Just knowing that things can and do go wrong will help you to prepare appropriate communication strategies to reduce any misunderstanding caused by bypassing.

2. Have you focused on the receiver and his or her frame of reference? Experiential barriers occur because people engaged in the communication process are inherently different, coming from different backgrounds, and having varied outlooks on life. Question what the receiver knows about your subject matter. Ask questions like these: "What does the receiver know about my message?" "Does he or she know as much as I do about the subject?" "How is the receiver likely to respond to my message—will he or she be happy, angry, frustrated, etc.?" The more often you put yourself in the receiver's place and attempt to anticipate questions he or she might have, the better you will be at successful communication. Remember to put yourself in the shoes of the receiver and to look at the subject matter from his or her perspective, and you will achieve effective communication.

3. Have you planned to listen? Unfortunately, most people are not taught to listen. If anything, families and schools teach us that we get more response

if we talk. We learn at an early age that if we ask someone to repeat what was said—whether it was an assignment for homework or a name or telephone number—he or she will repeat the requested information. This positive reinforcement of a bad behavior, poor listening, carries us into adulthood with little ability to hear and process information. In law enforcement, listening is often the key to a successful conclusion to a case. Often, witnesses or suspects do not verbalize every detail of a case in straightforward terms. The police officer must rely on his or her ability to hear what the suspect or witness is not saying. The only way to "hear between the lines" is to actively listen. Active listening requires you to focus on the speaker and to hear what is being said, as well as to process the nonverbal cues of the speaker. Overcoming the listening barrier to communication is not easy, but you can learn some techniques that will help you to be a more productive listener.

4. Have you created a psychologically appealing environment? When you are communicating with people, try to ensure that any defensiveness is eradicated as soon as possible. When people assume a defensive posture, they may fail to adequately listen or to communicate with you. As a law enforcement officer, you should try, wherever possible, to create a climate of acceptance and concern. If a suspect or witness is anxious or defensive, you will be unlikely to garner any cooperation from him or her. Try questioning witnesses in their own environment, in particular their homes. People are more willing to speak with an officer on their own turf. Merely having to go to the police station can cause witnesses to assume a defensive stance, which you will find difficult or impossible to overcome.

5. Have you eliminated physical barriers? Physical barriers, such as loud competing sounds or background noise, heat, cold, wind, rain, and so forth, cause communication mishaps. People will often get distracted by loud noises or inclement weather conditions. When possible, law enforcement personnel should move into an area to question witnesses or suspects where no physical barriers to the communication process exist. Something as simple as having a witness sit in the patrol car during questioning may be enough to eliminate noise distractions. Another example of a physical barrier to communication is distance. If a witness is not located in the same area as the police officer who is investigating a case, the officer should do whatever is possible to reduce the distance when speaking with the witness. This distance problem may mean that the officer must travel to speak with or to interview the witness. Eliminating the distance means that the officer also eliminates a physical barrier to the communication process.

Checklist for Improving Listening[16]

☐ Stop talking. Accept the role of listener by concentrating on the speaker's words, not on what your response will be.

☐ Work hard at listening. Become actively involved; expect to learn something.

☐ Block out competing thoughts. Concentrate on the message. Don't allow yourself to daydream during lag time.

☐ Control the listening environment. Turn off the TV, close the windows, and move to a quiet location. Tell the speaker when you cannot hear.

☐ Maintain an open mind. Know your biases, and try to correct for them. Be tolerant of less abled and different-looking speakers.

☐ Provide verbal and nonverbal feedback. Encourage the speaker with comments like "Yes," "I see," "Okay," and "Uh-huh," and ask polite questions. Look alert by leaning forward.

☐ Paraphrase the speaker's ideas. Silently repeat the message in your own words, sort out the main points, and identify supporting details. In conversation, sum up the main points to confirm what was said.

☐ Take selective notes. If you are hearing instructions or important data, record the major points; then, verify your notes with the speaker.

☐ Listen between the lines. Observe nonverbal cues, and interpret the feelings of the speaker. What is really being said?

☐ Capitalize on lag time. Use spare moments to organize, review, anticipate, challenge, and weigh the evidence.

COMMUNICATION ACROSS GENERATIONS

For the first time, more than two generations of people are living, working, and interacting together. Baby Boomers, Generation X, and Millennials compose the working public, with Millennials currently being the largest generation in the United States labor force.[17] These generations differ significantly in what they support or follow, in how they view their work, and, most importantly, in the way they communicate with others.

Definitions and Characteristics of Generations

The defining parameters of the generations vary by demographer, researcher, and/or author, each being identified by a specific range of birth years. However, each generation has a distinct set of descriptors that need to be understood to effectively build and maintain relationships. For purposes of its research studies, the Pew Research Center defined the generations as follows: the **Greatest Generation**, born before 1928; the **Silent Generation**, 1928–1945; **Baby Boomers**, 1946–1964; **Generation X**, 1965–1980; and the **Millennial Generation**, 1981–1997.[18]

The Greatest Generation members and most of the Silent Generation members have retired from the workplace; at the time this book is being published, their ages range from 73 to 100. However, in some workplaces, people 70-plus are still productive employees and continue to contribute to the organizational culture. So the Silent Generation needs to be included in this discussion. As this book is being published, the youngest Baby Boomer is 54 years of age and the oldest is 72. Members of this generation are still active participants in the U.S. labor force, and this group is included in the discussion. For now, Generation X and the Millennials make up the largest portion of the workforce, surpassing Baby Boomers.

The next generation to follow the Millennials has been absent from workplace-related research as members of this group have yet to enter full-time employment or have been employed for a period of time considered too brief to be of any consequence at this point. Members of this group have been labeled **Generation Z** (also called iGen, Founders, and Centennials).[19] Defining the parameters of generational divides is more of an art than a science, and marketers and demographers often disagree on the birth years of a specific generation.[20] However, most agree that members of Generation Z were born in 1996 and after.[21]

Generation Z is larger than the Millennials, outnumbering them by 1 million members. They are already impacting technology and will soon become the fastest growing group of consumers and employees.

The Silent Generation (1928–1945)

In its 2015 report, the Pew Research Center revealed that the Silent Generation accounted for 2% (3.7 million) of the United States labor force, down from 18% a decade earlier.[22] The Silent Generation grew up in the shadow of the Great Depression and World War II; members either fought in the war or were children during this time. Husbands usually worked and wives stayed home to raise the children. The Silent Generation has been labeled the wealthiest generation.[23] Characteristics of the Silent Generation include the following:

- Believe in the motto "Waste not, want not"
- Want to feel needed
- Strive for financial security
- Conservative
- Appreciate/desire simplicity and conformity

- Demand quality
- Patriotic
- Team players
- Patient
- Believe in the nobility of sacrifice for the common good[24]

As employees, Silent Generation members demonstrated numerous qualities of value to employers:

- Loyalty to employers—and expected the same from employers
- Measured work ethic on timeliness and productivity—and not drawing any untoward attention

- Raises, promotions, and recognition based on job tenure
- Enjoyed flexible job arrangements to work on their own schedule
- Possessed superb interpersonal skills[25]

The Baby Boomers (1946–1964)

In the first quarter of 2015, Baby Boomers accounted for 29% of the United States labor force, after seeing a decline in numbers during the previous year.[26] In 2014, the number of Baby Boomers in the workforce decreased due to retirements, and the number of Millennials (the fastest growing segment of the workforce) reached a record high. Baby Boomers grew up during the civil rights movement and the cold war. As such, they are very social cause oriented.

The Baby Boomer Generation earned its name because of the spike in the number of children born after World War II. The Baby Boomers were the largest generation and the single largest economic group. They are now often referred to as *empty nesters*. Characteristics of the Baby Boomers include the following:

- Free spirited
- Social cause oriented
- Individualistic
- Less optimistic
- Cynical
- Distrust government

- Experimental
- Believe rules should be obeyed—unless they run contrary to something they desire; then they are to be broken
- Want visual signs of their success (e.g., products and services)[27]

As employees, Baby Boomers created the term *workaholic* due to their belief that one's work ethic is measured in number of hours worked. Other elements of their work characteristics include their belief that teamwork is essential to success; relationship building is important; productivity is not as important as other facets of work; and people with whom they work should be loyal.[28]

Generation X (1965–1980)

Generation X has been referred to as America's neglected middle child, sandwiched between the Baby Boomers and the Millennials.[29] Even the name, Generation X, is a *redo*. In 1953, Robert Capa, a World War II photographer, coined the term *Generation X* as the name for a picture project focusing on the futures of young people born during World War II. The name was revived almost 30 years later when Douglas Coupland published his coming-of-age novel set in Southern California, *Generation X: Tales for an Accelerated Culture*.[30] In terms of demographics, Generation X bridges the gap between the predominantly white Baby Boomer generation and the diverse Millennials. However, Generation X spans only a 16-year time frame while other generations encompass approximately 20 years each.[31]

Generation X was also called the *Latchkey* Generation because as children, they were the first group to come home after school to an empty house and to be alone until a parent returned at the end of the workday.[32] Generation X members experienced the Space Shuttle *Challenger* explosion, the rise of the AIDS epidemic, the fall of the Berlin Wall, Watergate, and the Vietnam War. Generation X members have been called slackers, but they were the first generation to develop comfort and expertise with technology. Additional characteristics associated with Generation X include the following:

- Independent
- Very self-reliant
- Entrepreneurial
- Multitaskers
- Seek emotional security
- Expect immediate and continual feedback

- Reject rules
- Mistrust institutions
- Suspicious of Baby Boomer values
- Believe friends are not family
- Value family time[33]

From a labor force perspective, Generation X is interested in opportunities to "work smarter, not harder." They want a casual, friendly organizational culture with flexibility and freedom. Generation X members are more interested in finding a person in whom they can invest their loyalty rather than a company. Additionally, Generation X desires the following:

- Involvement
- A place to learn

- Open communication (regardless of title or position or tenure)
- Control of their time[34]

Generation Y/Millennials (1981–1997)

Millennials grew up with computers, smartphones, and the Internet—with technology. The Millennial Generation has been called the Entitlement Generation and digital natives,[35] and members were raised by Boomer and late Generation X parents who constantly worked to build Millennials' self-esteem. Thus, one of the characteristics ascribed to this generation is that they want instant gratification and have the mind-set that "everybody wins!"

The Millennials are the second-largest generation to enter the workforce since the Baby Boomers, but they are often saddled with high levels of student loan debt. They want to be like their peers but not totally; they want to put their own spin on it. The Millennials are often seen as ambitious but clueless, individualistic yet group oriented, and distrustful of "the man." Other characteristics of the Millennials include the following:

- Optimistic
- Patriotic
- Impatient
- Entrepreneurial
- Busy
- Very informal

- Short attention span
- Achievement oriented
- Financially savvy
- Accepting of change
- More culturally and racially tolerant[36]

Millennials in the workforce possess a different set of characteristics than those seen in previous generations. For example, they need constant communication and reassurance from their bosses. Millennials approach work from the perspective of working to live, not living to work. They search for individuals in the workplace who can serve as assets in their quest to achieve their goals. Millennials search for jobs that offer them personal fulfillment and opportunities to learn. They want to be close to their peers, but they also want—and expect—leadership from bosses, supervisors, and managers.[37]

Generation Z (Born After 1996)

Members of Generation Z are also known as Post-Millennials, the iGeneration (iGen), Founders, the Homeland Generation, and Plurals.[38] In 2016, Generation Z composed one-quarter of the United States population. With their numbers continuing to increase, Gen Z will account for one-third of the population by 2020.[39] This group of individuals is the most diverse of any generation, and that diversity encompasses gender, race, and sexual orientation. Members of Generation Z are entrepreneurial, with approximately 70% of teens in this generation being self-employed. Only 12% hold a traditional job.[40]

Generation Z members are constantly on their phones or devices, and 40% of them are self-identified technology addicts.[41] They have always known Amazon for online shopping—not as the river in South America.

Social media has always been a part of the lives of Generation Z, and members of this generation see social media as directly impacting how they feel about themselves. In fact, 37% believe social media affects their happiness. This generation has moved away from Facebook to embrace other platforms: Vine (54%), Instagram (52%), Twitter (34%), Pinterest (15%), and Periscope (11%). The choice of these top-five social media platforms clearly shows a movement away from social media sites favored by earlier generations. However, one cause for this divergence could be the timeframe when these social media platforms were introduced.[42]

Additional characteristics of Generation Z include the following:

- Independent and self-reliant

- Short attention span

- Use smartphones for entertainment rather than television

- More diverse family backgrounds (single-parent, same-sex families)

- Less likely to subscribe to traditional gender roles

- Bargain shoppers, prudent (savers, not spenders)

- Believe cell phone use is acceptable in any social setting (e.g., during a religious service, eating dinner with family, interviewing for a job, riding a bike, or during your own wedding)

- *More* concerned about online privacy than other generations in area of debit or credit card payments and online dating[43]

As Generation Z members enter the labor force, employers need to be aware of the items on their wish list:

- Want jobs with social impact

- Desire to make (or to feel they are making) a difference in the world

- Want to work collaboratively and remotely

- Desire constant innovation, instant communication

- Expect *dream job*[44]

Generation Z presents to the workplace with high expectations of their employers. They want to work from anywhere with the device of their choosing. Generation Z members also want to contribute ideas and new ways of thinking because they believe they can help the business where they work to move forward, a situation likely to cause friction with older workers and management.[45]

Internal Communication Across Generations

After reviewing the characteristics of each generation, you can easily see how communication problems might arise. However, every person—regardless of generation or age—wants to feel valued on the job. They want the opportunity to be recognized and appreciated for their contributions, some of the recognition and reward coming via compensation that is representative of the current marketplace.

Even though people of all generations may want the same things from the workplace, you will still find conflict and disharmony among employees. Some of the issues may arise because of stereotyping and the culture of the organization, still others through the way members of varying generations process information and how they define terms (semantics) such as *loyalty* and *hardworking*.

Barriers to Successful Communication Between and Among Generations

As discussed earlier in this chapter, communication is only successful when the individual receiving the message interprets and understands it in the way the sender of the message intended. Obviously, you have the commonplace problems of bypassing, perception, listening deficits, and other psychological and physical barriers previously addressed that create obstacles to effective communication. However, when you throw the generational aspect into the mix, you find the same barriers that you ordinarily see when people from different countries are attempting to communicate.

Stereotyping

You hear news stories, read factsheets, observe people, and draw conclusions about those individuals. Based on a limited amount of information, you determine that all people in the same age group, ethnic group, gender, or race are the same. You stereotype. One example of **stereotyping** among generations occurs when you hear a Millennial say that he or she does not wish to work with a certain Boomer employee because that person is old and does not understand technology or that person is old and refuses to change. And this impression is rendered by the Millennial without the benefit of ever working with the specific Baby Boomer—and totally based on stereotyping. After all, Baby Boomers are known to be afraid of change, anxious about technology, slow, and resistant to working with younger people. Really? Says who?

The reverse can also be said about a Baby Boomer being asked to work with a Millennial. The Boomer can balk and complain, saying that the Millennial has no respect for the job, is too flighty, needs too much attention, will not listen, wants to do the job his or her way, has no work ethic—and so on. Again, the Boomer does not know the Millennial employee but is sure that the partnership will fail to produce any type of valid work product based on perceptions of the Millennial stereotype.

Workplace Culture

Workplace culture is also called corporate culture. Workplace culture encompasses the shared attitudes and values, social norms and mores, and beliefs of the people in an organization. Workplace culture stems from the organization's goals, strategies, and structure, as well as its approach to managing employees, customers, and the community as a whole. A healthy culture leads to increased employee commitment and productivity, but an unhealthy culture can inhibit growth or lead to a collapse of the business. Culture flows from the top down, so changes to it can be difficult to accomplish and will require an intense time commitment and strong leadership.[46]

When people work in an environment that is accepting and encouraging, they are more likely to feel comfortable with change and will more readily embrace opportunities to work with others. If they feel undervalued and anonymous with little understanding of how they fit into the "big picture" of the organization, they will have little trust and be fearful of change. In this type of environment, older workers (Baby Boomers) fear losing their jobs to the more tech-savvy Millennials or Generation Z employees and will be unwilling to share information with them.

Addressing the Barriers and Meeting Generational Communication Needs

Instead of relying on tried-and-true methods of communicating or the adage "We've always done it this way," criminal justice agencies need to employ training to ensure that their officers, administrators, and employees effectively communicate across generations and across hierarchical lines within the organizations. Criminal justice agencies need to build bridges across generations so that they can recruit, develop, and retain the most qualified and high-quality staff. Also, agencies benefit from multigenerational work teams because they can meet the needs of a diverse public (that they serve) and relate more effectively to their communities.

The following section discusses each generation in the law enforcement field specifically—and in criminal justice in general—and how each generation's communication strategies can affect understanding and cooperation between and among these groups.

Baby Boomers in Law Enforcement and Criminal Justice

The Baby Boomers are today's senior members of the law enforcement community. Many have been working for decades and are part of the "command-and-control" culture that began in the 1950s and continued into the 1970s.[47] Also, Boomers occupy most of the leadership positions in law enforcement and think of themselves as stewards of their agencies—those who look after the culture of those agencies. Boomers passionately fought for change and believe in putting the job first.

Boomers believe that Generation X, Millennials, and Generation Z must "pay their dues" just as the Boomers did when beginning their careers in law enforcement. Many Boomers are still supportive of the "command-and-control" culture, especially where leadership is concerned. In addition, most Boomers are highly competitive and do not like (nor want) to share power. They are still very entrenched in the traditions of law enforcement and corrections, especially the "rites of passage" required to get ahead (promoted).[48]

Baby Boomers born after 1954, termed "second-half" Boomers, brought a different set of leadership skills to criminal justice agencies.[49] These Boomers are more progressive and believe that employees have internal motivation to succeed, and they merely need to be encouraged, not controlled. These Boomer leaders brought community policing into law enforcement in the 1970s as a way of empowering their officers. This participatory style of shared leadership has been shown to improve departmental effectiveness, both inside and outside.[50]

Because of community policing, Boomer leaders in law enforcement realized that the unidirectional flow of information should not be the norm. Instead, law enforcement agencies must change and move away from the Industrial Age to the Information Age, away from hierarchical controls of information flow and away from the detachments between and among levels of the organization. Generation X and the Millennials have moved to the Information Age, and thus, the Baby Boomer leaders in criminal justice agencies must embrace communication technologies to gain a more efficient means of communicating or transferring information to officers and supervisors. In-person communication that is favored by the Baby Boomer Generation must give way to the advancements in technology that provide alternative channels for disseminating information.

Generation Xers in Law Enforcement and Criminal Justice

Generation X grew up in fear during the 1970s and 1980s. The members of this generation were raised during the time of layoffs that replaced lifetime employment, AIDS, the *Challenger* disaster, the Three Mile Island disaster, the "Black Monday" stock market crash in 1987, inflation, gas lines, and many others. They learned to distrust everyone and everything. Because many of Generation Xers' parents lost their jobs as the result of downsizing of organizations in the 1970s and 1980s, they have no institutional loyalty.

Generation Xers are comfortable with computers; however, members of this generation use technology to avoid face-to-face contacts. Because they come from two-income families, Generation Xers grew up as latchkey kids, feeling unwanted and neglected by parents who had little time to devote to their children. Thus, they have a comfort with being alone, are self-centered, and are fiercely independent. While these characteristics may appear to be positive, they can also be disadvantages in the interpersonal communication area. Generation Xers are often labeled loners who lack the people skills needed to be successful in law enforcement.

The Millennial Generation in Law Enforcement and Criminal Justice

The Millennial Generation grew up sheltered by parents who were very supportive and protective. They were affected by the "build their self-esteem" movement that left them believing they were special and capable, that they do not need others, and that they should always put themselves first. Therefore, the Millennials were never taught how to connect with others, how to care what others think, how to balance putting themselves first over others, and how to seek support from others—also called relational skills.[51]

While Generation Xers' workplace communication characteristics may include direct and immediate, Millennials favor e-mail and voice mail. They demand immediate feedback and see work as a means to an end. This generation does not measure success in the same way as previous generations nor does it believe in working 50-plus hours per week. Millennials view technology as a mechanism to connect to others, such as in chat rooms or via interactive gaming.

Millennials are usually on the receiving end of comments refuting their ability to work well with others and to function in situations requiring them to follow rules and to adapt. However, qualities associated with gaming can be harnessed to be of benefit to criminal justice agencies because gamers "think differently, are global, are tough, and are self-educating."[52] In other words, Millennials are not afraid of trial and error and believe that constant change is a natural part of life. Because of their involvement with gaming, this generation is familiar with cultures and cultural differences. Millennials have also learned that if they wish to be successful, they must keep trying. If they do not win this round or level of the game, then they just need to try again. Of course, gaming also allows Millennials to be the expert or the superstar, something they relish because of their "me-centered" approach to life. On the bright side, though, gamers believe that anything is possible. So Millennials embrace opportunities to learn because they believe an answer is always available somewhere.

Leaders in Law Enforcement and Criminal Justice

Since one of the issues discussed previously focused on how the culture of an organization can dictate the actions of its employees, we must address ways in which leaders in law enforcement/criminal justice can ensure that their agencies are highly successful in managing the multigenerational workforce. Principles for successfully managing generations may include the following:

- Initiate conversations within your department about generations. These discussions can help reduce the occurrences of stereotyping as you are asking people to bring those thoughts and beliefs out into the open. When these issues are brought out, they become less personalized, so they are easier to talk about. You also help department members develop respect for other generations through these conversations.

- Offer generational and diversity training to boost understanding and respect and to prompt discussion among the ranks. Similar to what can happen in the conversations you might initiate within your department, training sessions give participants the opportunity to discuss issues in a nonthreatening environment.

- Commit to age diversity in your agency by including representatives from all generations to serve on hiring boards and/or committees. Choose members with varying backgrounds and perspectives.

- Know what motivates members of each generation so you can keep them engaged. Ask your people about their needs. Most often, people project their own needs and preferences onto others. If you really want to know what someone's needs and preferences are, you should ask.

- Gear benefits and/or options toward the needs of different generations. Generation X and the Millennials favor work–life balance, but the majority of workers ages 45 and older also prefer flexibility in the workplace. Also, when possible, offer benefits that match an employee's stage of life.

- Establish rewards and recognitions to reflect each group's preferences and priorities.

- Include officers from different generations on policy development, strategic planning, and other organizational committees.

- Establish and offer two-way mentoring programs: (1) younger employees help older ones adapt to new technologies, social media, and other areas of interest; (2) senior employees teach younger employees about the mission of the department.

- Personalize your style. Be flexible. Learn about the preferences of members of your department, and attempt to creatively meet those expectations.

- Build on strengths. Encourage members of mixed-generation teams to build on their own strengths, to be who they are and not try to blend in with the rest of the team.[53]

Once you have established a culture of acceptance and intergenerational opportunity, you still must plan for the future needs of your department and/or agency. You need to be forward-looking and recognize that change is always on the horizon. You should answer four strategic questions for your department:

1. What current departmental human resource practices support generational differences?

2. What will your department's generational composition be in 5 years?

3. How are the generations represented in your community or the community you serve?

4. What will your community or the community you serve look like in 5 years?[54]

Answers to these questions will ensure that your department or agency will continue to effectively manage generational differences for today and into the future.

Suggestions for Bridging the Communication Generation Gap With External Groups

Much of what has been presented in the preceding text has focused on identifying and defining the generations, including the characteristics associated with those generations. In addition, suggestions were presented to help criminal justice professionals address barriers to communication between and among generations and for leaders of law enforcement and criminal justice to build a supportive culture for intergenerational communication. This portion of the chapter presents tips for bridging the communication generation gap, both internally and externally. Communicating across generations should include the following actions:

- Match formality to the culture
- Understand value difference
- Use multiple communication channels
- Be aware of motivating factors
- Individualize your approach
- Ask—do not assume

- Be willing to learn
- Be willing to teach
- Acknowledge the differences
- Do not take it personally[55]

Criminal justice and law enforcement training stresses effective communication, and knowing your audience (the generation of the individual or individuals as well) will help in that process. Law enforcement officers know that they must create a trust relationship with the general public. To do so, they must overcome their own biases and those of their community by working to learn about their community members and to acknowledge that differences exist.

For some generations of law enforcement officers (Millennials, in particular), interpersonal communication skills—active listening, problem solving, critical thinking, persuasion, and conflict management—are not fully developed. These skills, together with technical training, form the two prongs of all police work. Therefore, criminal justice agencies and law enforcement leaders need to ensure that the officers are fully vetted before being released into the community. Poor communication skills can lead to an increase in and ongoing poor community relations despite the technical skills available to that department and the officers.[56]

With available technology, law enforcement officers now have multiple ways to reach their community members and the general public—everything from departmental webpages to Twitter, Facebook, Instagram, and Snapchat. Knowing the generational makeup of your community can help you decide which of these communication channels would be most effective in building and maintaining relationships. Many departments and agencies now use Facebook as a means for pushing information out to the general public, as well as a mechanism for community members to share complaints or information about suspects and to gather evidence to help solve cold cases or hate crimes. In any event, the use of social media sites is a way of connecting with members of your community and the general public to involve them in creating safe and crime-free communities.

Law enforcement officers are also aware of the importance of listening—active listening (covered in more detail in Chapter 2). This aspect of communication is often overlooked in favor of speaking, as talking is the most expedient way to question suspects, witnesses, or victims. However, the general public or the law enforcement officer's specific community can benefit from an officer who actually listens to what people say and how they say it. Chapter 3 in this book will delve into nonverbal communication and help you see how important your body language and your vocalics are in a face-to-face conversation or meeting and how nonverbal communication plays a major role in active listening.

Regardless of whether you are communicating with colleagues, the general public, or a witness, suspect, or victim of a crime, you have the responsibility of providing those individuals with your undivided attention and speaking with them from their own perspective—not yours, that of a law enforcement officer. Whether you have generational differences, cultural differences, or perceptual differences, you must practice empathy in all of your communications with others.

The remainder of this book will apply the principles from Chapter 1 to situations that might occur in the criminal justice profession. A sound knowledge base in relation to the concepts presented here will allow students, trainees, and law enforcement officials to become better communicators and, thus, better criminal justice professionals.

SUMMARY

In this chapter, we examined the process and cycle of communication. Communication is a process that involves at least two people, the sender and the receiver, who exchange information through a system of shared symbols or language. The sender encodes the message and sends it through an appropriate channel or medium to the receiver, who then decodes the message and provides feedback to the sender. This process continues until the sender and receiver have completed their communication. Barriers to communication exist in such areas as bypassing, listening, cultural differences, experiences, physical differences, and psychological problems.

Individuals have different styles of communication: blaming, directing, persuading, and problem solving. The old style in law enforcement would be most comfortable with the blaming and directing dimensions, but with the advent of community policing, persuading and problem solving are rising to the forefront.

Communication is either verbal or nonverbal. The verbal components of communication were identified as both the oral and written word. Verbal obfuscation and the use of jargon/slang or legalese were identified as problem areas in verbal communication. Nonverbal communication comprises a variety of aspects: the body (kinesics), the voice (paralanguage), objects (proxemics), gender, and gestures and touch (**haptics**).

Communication also flows through formal or informal channels. Formal communication follows the chain of command in an organization and may flow upward, downward, or horizontally. Informal communication in organizations takes place through the unofficial communication channel called the "grapevine."

Barriers to communication are either experiential, listening, bypassing, cultural, psychological, or physical. Understanding that these obstacles are present in the communication process is important, but developing methods for removing these barriers is paramount to the success of any communication. Experiential, cultural, and bypassing barriers can be removed or reduced if you attempt to practice empathy in your communication process. Looking at the situation from another's perspective will allow you to provide answers to questions that might arise and to address the particular needs of the other party. Practicing active listening skills will help you to be able to hear and process more information. Active listening is a difficult task that requires practice. Learn to paraphrase what has been said, to link new information to existing information, and to question the speaker so that you can be sure you have received the correct communication.

Generational differences play major roles both in the workplace and within the general public. Interactions with people must be handled with diplomacy, and understanding the perspective of others is vital to ensuring that communication is effective. Whether you are a member of the Baby Boomer Generation, Generation X, the Millennials, or Generation Z, your goal is to make sure that whomever you communicate with understands your message the way it was intended.

Members of different generations choose to communicate in various ways. The Baby Boomer Generation prefers face to face, but Millennials prefer e-mail or text messages. Leaders in the criminal justice and law enforcement communities must create opportunities within their departments and agencies for training and meetings to discuss generational differences. The success of a department or agency rests solely on the members of that department or agency and their ability to interact with one another and with the public. Interpersonal communication skills are one requirement for success in law enforcement. Without these skills, law enforcement officers are at a disadvantage that technical skills alone cannot overcome.

KEY TERMS

Agreement in principle 7
Baby Boomers 17
Blaming 7
Bypassing 4
Communication 3
Communication channel 4
Community policing 6
Decoding 4
Directing 7
Downward 12
Encoding 4
Experiential barriers
    to communication 15
Feedback 4

Formal communication 12
Gender 11
Generation X 17
Generation Z 18
Gestures 12
Greatest Generation 17
Haptics 28
Horizontal 12
Informal communication 12
Jargon or slang 9
Kinesics 10
KISS 9
Legalese 10
Message 4

Millennial Generation 17
Noise 5
Nonverbal communication 10
Paralanguage 11
Persuading 7
Problem solving 7
Proxemics 11
Receiver 4
Sender 4
Silent Generation 17
Stereotyping 22
Upward 12
Verbal communication 9

FOR FURTHER REFLECTION AND DISCUSSION

1. What role does communication play in the criminal justice process?

2. Describe the process and cycle of communication.

3. Why is it important for criminal justice professionals to be aware of the various communication styles?

4. Why are the formal and informal channels of communication so important to the criminal justice professional? Give examples of the formal and informal communication channels in a criminal justice agency.

5. List and discuss barriers to communication.

6. Observe a police officer directing traffic at an intersection. Where applicable, discuss the nonverbal components you observe occurring between the officer and the motorists.

7. Using the same scenario, discuss the officer's reaction to inattentive motorists or defiant motorists who ignore his or her direction.

8. Discuss the appropriateness of an officer using neighborhood slang or jargon in a conversation with the public.

ETHICAL ISSUE EXERCISES

1. Should criminal justice professionals be allowed to express their personal feelings even if they conflict with their professional position?

2. Should personal bias be reflected in the way in which a criminal justice professional addresses other individuals?

3. Should criminal justice professionals be permitted to join or hold membership in organizations that have an expressed or implied racial or sexist creed?

4. Should police officers be allowed to express their displeasure or disgust through (a) the use of nonverbal signals or (b) the use of profanity? Explain.

5. Should criminal justice professionals use their knowledge of nonverbal behaviors to determine if their colleagues are being deceptive?

6. Should criminal justice professionals with advanced education use words or phrases that are unclear or confusing in their discussions with their colleagues or subordinates?

SELF-ASSESSMENT OF COMMUNICATION STYLE[57]

Indicate the degree to which you do the following:		Very Little	Little	Some	Great	Very Great
1.	Make judgments early in the conversation.					
2.	Share my feelings with others.					
3.	Talk about the issues.					
4.	Have analyzed others' motives.					
5.	Talk about the person.					
6.	Use clear and precise language.					
7.	Decide on the action before the conversation.					
8.	Encourage the other person to discuss feelings.					
9.	Am open for new information.					
10.	Ask questions that seek agreement with me.					
11.	Talk the majority of the time.					
12.	Ask questions that get others to describe events.					
13.	Talk half the time or less.					
14.	Allow others to defend their position to me.					

SCORING SHEET

Item No.	SCORE	
1.	_____	
2.		_____
3.		_____
4.	_____	
5.	_____	
6.		_____
7.	_____	
8.		_____
9.		_____
10.	_____	
11.	_____	
12.		_____
13.		_____
14.	_____	
TOTALS	_____	_____

Total Column 1   _____

Total Column 2   _____

Interpretation of Scores:

Very Little =	1 point
Little =	2 points
Some =	3 points
Great =	4 points
Very Great =	5 points

Source: From O'Connell, S. W. *The Manager as Communicator.* 1986, Rowman & Littlefield, originally published in 1979 by Harper & Row Publishers, Inc. Reprinted with permission.

2 THINK BEFORE YOU SPEAK
The Verbal Component

LEARNING OBJECTIVES

After students have completed this chapter, they will be able to do the following:

1. Identify the two components of verbal communication

2. Explain the importance of listening in oral communication

3. Differentiate between hearing and listening

4. Describe the different types of listening behavior

5. Compare letters, memoranda, and e-mail and identify appropriate uses for each

6. Handle/manage media relations

The drunk says something about teaching you a lesson for all those times you treated him bad. You realize he's only 15 feet away; well within the 21-foot limit set by Tueller and court decisions. Without really thinking about it you draw your weapon and start screaming at him as the gun comes up into your line of sight, the weapon's sights lining up on the drunk jerk's chest.

Here's the million-dollar question: What are you screaming?

We like to think that we scream coherent orders to drop weapons; get on the ground; stop or I'll shoot! Most of us have seen the training video where one police officer says, "I'll shoot your ass!" eight or nine times without pulling the trigger in a lethal force situation. . . . WHAT he said and WHAT you find yourself screaming can make all the difference in the world [as to what] the witnesses say.[1]

—Frank Borelli, "Think Before You Speak"*

Even though its name implies speech, verbal communication consists of all oral *and* written communications. The life and work of a criminal justice professional involves both aspects of oral and written communication. Preparing reports that are grammatically sound while providing all essential information is an imperative. By the same token, the oral component of verbal communication requires careful planning and thoughtful preparation prior to speaking. This chapter introduces you to the concepts involved in both speaking and writing. Chapter 3 will further address

---

*Reprinted with permission of Frank Borelli. For more information about this author, please visit www.frankborelli.com.

issues related to presentations and public speaking, including the use of visual aids in presentations. Also, Chapter 4 explores the role nonverbal communication plays in oral communication's authenticity and acceptance.

VERBAL COMMUNICATION: THE ORAL COMPONENT

Consider how limited we would be as a society if we could not ask questions or give instructions. Oral communication is the only way we have of receiving immediate answers to questions or of providing feedback to others. How would you know if you had performed a job well or if you required further information if you and others around you could not speak? Another facet of oral communication involves listening skills. Speaking and listening are reciprocal parts of the communication process.

Three Myths of Listening[2]	Three Truths of Listening
Listening cannot be learned; it is a natural occurrence.	Listening is not a natural activity; it is learned.
Hearing and listening are the same.	Telling someone something is not the same thing as communicating.
When you speak, everyone listens.	You speak to one person at a time—even in an audience situation.

LISTENING

Just as important to the oral component of communication as the spoken word is our ability to listen. Listening skills are vital in any profession, but in matters of law enforcement, listening effectively is a top priority. Consider that, on average, we can listen to 450 words per minute.[3] Although we might be able to hear that many words per minute, our brain cannot process them at the same rate. Add our less-than-perfect listening ability, and most of us remember approximately 17% to 25% of what we hear in any conversation.[4] If we remember only one-fourth of the information, then three-fourths of the content of that conversation is lost.

Listening and speaking are part of a natural process that should occur together. Most of the time we both converse and listen; rarely are we required to do only one or the other. Five concepts of listening underscore the reciprocity involved in speaking and listening: **attending**, **understanding**, **remembering**, **analyzing critically**, and **responding empathically**.[5]

The attending concept of listening refers to the process of selecting or focusing on specific stimuli from among the countless number of stimuli we receive. To effectively listen, the attending process gives us parameters to follow.

1. Prepare yourself, both physically and mentally, to listen. Compel yourself to focus on what is being said.

2. Give the speaker the appropriate time to complete his or her statement(s) before you react. In other words, do not rehearse what you are planning to say

in response to something the speaker said—LISTEN to what is being said until the speaker's intent is complete.

3. Adjust your listening to the goal of the situation. Determine the goal of your communication. Do you need to understand, to evaluate, to respond, or to comfort? Depending on your goal in the communication situation, your listening will range from pleasure listening (i.e., listening without much intensity) to critical analysis.

A second aspect of listening is understanding. When we decode (or translate) a message accurately by assigning an appropriate meaning to it, we can understand the message. To fully understand what another individual says requires **active listening**. When we engage in active listening, we use specific techniques of empathizing, asking questions, and paraphrasing. More discussion on active listening will follow later in this chapter.

Remembering, the third concept of listening, is being able to process information and store it for later retrieval (or recall). Unfortunately, our ability to remember is very limited. Often, we cannot remember the name of the person to whom we have been introduced merely moments earlier. Several techniques are available that can assist us in remembering information: repetition, mnemonics, and taking notes.

1. **Repetition** helps listeners store information in long-term memory. Repetition refers to saying something two, three, or even four times to reinforce the information. If we do not engage in repetition, whatever we hear will be held in short-term memory for approximately 20 seconds and then discarded.

2. Constructing **mnemonics** is another technique we can use to help us remember information. "Mnemonics (pronounced "ne-moń-ics") assist the memory, using a system of rhymes, rules, phrases, diagrams, or acronyms. These devices help to remember, memorize, and recall information such as names, dates, facts, or figures. They do that by turning original information into an easy, more appealing rhyme or sentence. This can be stored in your brain as an easy reference for larger 'meaningful' chunks of data. When you need to recall the original facts you can, by translating the mnemonic memory."[6] When attempting to remember items in a sequence, you can try to form a sentence using the words themselves, or you can take the first letter of a list of items you are trying to remember and form a word. Examples such as the keys in music for treble clef lines, **E**very **G**ood **B**oy **D**oes **F**ine, or colors of the light spectrum, **ROY G BIV**, serve as excellent memory devices.

3. **Note taking** provides an additional venue for retaining information. While you would not want to take notes during a casual interpersonal encounter, telephone conversations, interviews, interrogations, and so forth would benefit from this powerful tool for increasing your recall of information.

Critical analysis, the fourth concept of listening, is the process you engage in when attempting to determine whether information you hear is truthful, authentic, or believable. Critical analysis requires you to be able to distinguish between facts and inferences. You also must be able to evaluate the quality of inferences.

Factual statements can be verified or proven. **Inferences**, on the other hand, are assertions or claims that are based on observation or fact but that are not necessarily true. As an effective listener, you must be able to distinguish between statements that can be accepted at face value as truths and statements that require proof (inferences).

The final concept of listening involves responding empathically. When we respond empathically to give comfort, we are indicating that we have understood a person's meaning but also affirming that the person has a right to his or her own feelings. Offering support to others shows that we care about them and what happens to them. As an effective listener, you will want to offer supporting statements to demonstrate that you empathize with the person's feelings, regardless of intensity or direction.

The Listening Process

We are taught as young children that listening is a passive activity that requires no effort on our part. Our educational institutions, families, and friends condition us to believe that we do not need to work at listening. Remember when you were in elementary school and the teacher gave you an assignment? That assignment would most likely be repeated several times, or in frustration, the teacher would simply write it on the board to avoid the need to repeat it. Your parents would often have to call you several times for dinner or remind you repeatedly to take out the garbage or to clean your room. When confronted about your behavior, you might even have said, "I didn't hear you."

Listening and Hearing

Can you determine any difference between **hearing** and **listening**? Hearing involves the perception of sound—a physiological process whereby sound waves strike the eardrum and cause vibrations that travel to the brain.[7] Listening means we attach a meaning to the sounds that have been transmitted to our brain. When we listen, we go beyond the sound itself. We discern various sounds and ideas and comprehend and attach meanings to them. Listening, therefore, is an active skill.

Much like speaking, reading, or writing, listening requires us to be engaged both physically and psychologically. Physical responses to listening involve an increased pulse rate, higher blood pressure, and a slight elevation in body temperature. When counselors and negotiators proclaim that they are exhausted at the end of a day's work, they are merely stating a fact. Their responses to the listening process have effectively rendered them physically drained—much as if they had been performing a type of manual labor.

Psychological responses to listening are much harder to identify. Since we each have our own beliefs or perceptions of the world, we find it difficult (sometimes impossible) to truly listen to others. If listening to another means that we would have to change, most of us would prefer to maintain the status quo and to avoid a variation in our beliefs. After all, change is frightening, so listening could involve considerable risk that we would have to examine what we think or feel and perhaps how we act.

Forms of Listening

Three general types of listening have been consistently noted in research. However, the level or intensity of listening activity in which you engage varies with the conversation topic, the relevancy of the subject matter to your needs, and the people involved in the conversation. The types of listening are **casual or marginal listening**, **attentive listening**, and active listening.[8]

Casual or marginal listening occurs when listening is secondary in importance to some other activity in which you are engaged. The listener in this situation is not required to learn, comprehend, or remember any materials for later recall and action. An example might be someone who reads or studies with the television on or listens to music in the background. Another example would be Millennials who monitor their cell phones while performing some work-related task or engaging in some recreational activity. Even some off-duty law enforcement officers monitor police activity by having a police scanner operating at home. The officer is not actively listening to what is being said on the scanner when he or she is engaged in watching television or interacting with his or her family; he or she simply has the scanner on in the background. A similar scenario would occur when an individual is driving to work with the radio on in the car. The major focus would be on driving and watching for other vehicles, not on listening to what is being said on the radio.

Attentive listening occurs when a need exists to obtain some information that might be required for a future action. To follow through with the example of the off-duty police officer and his scanner, if he is watching television and suddenly hears an emergency come through, such as "officer needs assistance" or "officer down," then he would suddenly be compelled to listen attentively to the scanner to determine the location of the officer in trouble. The scenario where the individual is driving to work and listening to the radio could become one requiring attentive listening if an emergency broadcast were suddenly to be issued. The driver would then be motivated to hear, understand, and remember what was being said in the broadcast.

The final type of listening is active listening. This type of listening occurs most frequently in counseling, interviewing, and interrogating situations. In these situations, you are required to listen for more than just the words or the content of the message. You need to pay attention to the nonverbal language and emotions of the speaker. Active listening is most difficult because it requires you to put aside personal preferences and to physically and psychologically listen.

Active listening also requires you to demonstrate four types of behavior: **acceptance**, **congruence**, **empathy**, and **concreteness**. Acceptance says to the speaker that the listener will not pass judgment or will not criticize the speaker. An important first step in getting a speaker to trust you is to demonstrate acceptance. Once the speaker trusts you, he or she will feel free to share feelings or thoughts.

Congruence is defined as agreeing or harmonizing. In active listening, congruence refers to the agreement or harmony between the speaker's experience, the way he or she feels about the experience, and what the speaker then conveys to others about that experience. In law enforcement, a sergeant is required to take the lieutenant's examination to be placed in line for promotion. For example, Sergeant Mary Smith takes the exam and achieves a score of 93. She is ranked number one in the line for promotion to lieutenant. When the next available lieutenant's slot opens, the sergeant is promoted. She has worked very hard for this promotion and feels very good about it. Thus, Sergeant Smith tells her friends and coworkers about the promotion and how excited she is. At this point, total harmony exists between her experience, her feelings, and her communication to others. As an active listener, you need to be aware of the congruence or absence of congruence in a speaker. When congruence is not present—when no harmony exists between the speaker's experience and feelings—communication will not take place.

In active listening, congruence becomes problematic when an individual is lacking harmony or agreement in his or her experience, feelings, and communication. To use the foregoing example, if Sergeant Smith were to be passed over for the promotion and the person who was ranked second were to be promoted in her place, she would find it very difficult to assist the new lieutenant with his or her duties. Sergeant Smith would be angry that her belief in hard work was ill founded. She would then find it difficult to listen to the new lieutenant when he or she discussed loyalty and duty among the department.

Empathy refers to putting yourself in another's position. To be empathetic toward another, you must attempt to vicariously experience his or her feelings, thoughts, and emotions. When a listener is successful in practicing empathy, he or she is better able to respond appropriately to the concerns or needs of the speaker. Empathy is particularly important in situations of cultural diversity. We must learn to subordinate our opinions and emotions and to approach situations with an open mind. This task is especially difficult given our tendency as humans to judge people. However, the only way to be successful in communication is to listen with empathy.

The final critical behavior for active listening is concreteness. Concreteness refers to the speaker's need to concentrate on actions over which he or she has control. We have all heard statements such as this: "I don't know what to do about Mary. She used to be such a good worker." Nothing the speaker says here has any specific meaning. An active listener would encourage the speaker to give definitive statements about the problem with Mary's work. In this way, a plan of action can be formulated to help Mary work through whatever issues are involved in the situation.

Types of Ineffective Listeners[9]

Through research, we have come to recognize several types of listeners: **the faker, the continual talker, the rapid-writing note taker, the critic, the "I'm in a hurry" listener, the "hand on the doorknob" listener, the "make sure it is correct" listener, the "finish the sentence for you" listener, and the "I've done one better" listener.** Each of these listeners has characteristics you will recognize from your own or others' actions.

Barriers to Listening

Mental and Emotional Distractions

One of the greatest deterrents to listening involves mental distractions. We can comprehend information at a rate 3 times that at which most people speak. Because we have a "gap" between the time the words are spoken and the time we hear and process them, we tend to let our thoughts drift. We take a mental vacation, perhaps picturing ourselves lying on the beach in the warm sunshine, composing a list of items we need to accomplish today, or even preparing for our next meeting or activity. While we wander away from the speaker, we often lose track of what is being said and have trouble returning our concentration to the matter at hand. Consequently, we find that our efficiency as listeners is very low. In fact, we forget as much as

TABLE 2.1 ■ Types of Listeners	
Type of Listener	**Characteristics**
The Critic	• Listens merely for points of fact which he or she can take issue with. • Waits only to hear something that he or she finds emotionally charged and then proceeds to formulate a mental argument, neglecting to continue listening to the speaker.
The Faker	• Appears, for all intents and purposes, to be paying close attention to what is being said. • Nods his or her head at all the right places, makes appropriate eye contact, and appears to be following the conversation closely. • In reality, this type of listener is merely faking—doing what is necessary to convince another that he or she is listening intently.
The Continual Talker	• Finds it very difficult to listen to anyone since he or she never stops talking! • Always has something to say, interrupts conversations to talk, and rarely allows anyone else to contribute to the conversation.
The "I'm in a Hurry" Listener	• Too busy to stop whatever he or she is doing and look at the speaker. • This listener is usually performing some other task while "listening" to others—shuffling papers on a desk, searching for a lost object, etc.
The "Make Sure It Is Correct" Listener	• The person who listens for facts and who will be the first to point out mistakes or errors. • Seems to thrive on pointing out the mistakes of others. • Will interrupt in order to make a point and cause the speaker to look bad.
The "I've Done One Better" Listener	• Listens only for the points of action in a story and then proceeds to intrude with statements of his or her own. • Always climbed a higher mountain, captured a more violent criminal, drove faster in a high-speed chase, etc. than the speaker. • Doesn't really process what the speaker has said since he or she believes that the speaker's story is not nearly as dangerous or adventurous as his or her own.
The "Hand on the Doorknob" Listener	• Always in a hurry and has little time to waste listening. • He or she will signal when the conversation is at an end by reaching for the doorknob or placing his or her materials away, regardless of whether the speaker has actually completed the conversation. • Once the listener has indicated that he or she has finished listening, to continue speaking would be futile—nothing is penetrating the "hand on the doorknob" listener's brain.
The "Finish the Sentence for You" Listener	• Will intrude on a speaker to complete the sentence if the speaker pauses. • Impatient. • Sure that he or she knows what the speaker was going to say next.
The Rapid-Writing Note Taker	• Attempts to write everything down on paper that is being said. • Unfortunately, in attempting to write verbatim what the speaker has said, this individual misses the entire point of the conversation. In the legal field, court reporters are charged with creating verbatim transcripts of depositions, testimony at trials and hearings, and sworn statements. However, other than this profession, few exist that require individuals to write down everything that is being said. • In attempting to write down everything in a presentation or conversation, this listener is missing the main points because he or she is so busy writing that he or she does not have the mental capacity to process the information.

80% of what we hear within the first 24 hours of hearing it. As an example, try to recall yesterday evening's top stories or what you heard on the radio yesterday . . . difficult, right?

Emotional distractions are like mental distractions. However, emotional distractions refer more to our overreaction to the words or message that the speaker is delivering. Each of us has a *buzzword* capable of diverting our attention away from the message. We then concentrate on the word or phrase and become so preoccupied that we neglect the speaker. A police officer who detests being called a "pig" would become incensed by a perpetrator's use of the term in an interrogation. The question-and-answer session would be hindered by the officer's emotional response to the use of the word "pig."

Common Frame of Reference

Another barrier to effective listening stems from the absence of a common frame of reference. The speaker and the listener must have a level of shared knowledge. In other words, they must have a common vocabulary. A probation and parole officer, if using legal terminology, would find it difficult to speak with an individual unfamiliar with the court system. Terms such as presentence investigation (PSI) or presentence report (PSR) may prove challenging for someone not familiar with the language shorthand or vernacular. For that reason, the officer would have to use words or phrases common to the individual.

Physical Distractions

We have all been in situations where the room was too warm, the noise in the hall outside the door was too loud, or our stomach was growling from hunger. These are physical distractions that impede our ability to listen actively. Even though it may be difficult to return to listening following one of these physical disruptions, we should try to consciously move back to the speaker as quickly as possible.

Evaluation/Judgment

Unfortunately, we as human beings tend to judge others by their appearance, opinions, or knowledge. Even though we know that you "can't judge a book by its cover," we still make assumptions about others without knowing all of the facts. When we make a rush to judge someone, we cease to listen to anything that person has to say. In effect, we shut down and close our minds.

Miscellaneous

Several conditions also exist that might affect our ability to listen. Examples of these conditions are

- our interest in the topic or activity;

- our attitude toward the presenter and subject;

- any distractions we face, either emotional, mental, or physical;

- the nonverbal behavior of the speaker; and

- the time of day for the activity or presentation.

Guidelines for Effective Listening

Instruction in listening skills has been neglected in our educational institutions. As mentioned earlier, if we are taught anything about listening, we are taught that we *really don't have to listen*. Educational facilities need to incorporate programs of instruction in listening. However, we may still acquire good listening skills on our own. Some steps for improving your listening ability are as follows:

- **Stop talking!** Remember, you cannot listen if you are speaking.

- **Pay attention!** Give your full attention to the speaker. You cannot communicate if both parties are not actively involved in the process.

- **Read nonverbal cues.** Along with hearing and processing the words of the speaker, you should pay careful attention to the nonverbal language being communicated. Watch for eye contact, facial expressions, gestures, posture changes, and any physical responses (i.e., fidgeting).

- **Ask questions.** A good way to ensure that you have accurately understood the message is to ask questions.

- **Resist distractions.** Stop doodling! Do not shuffle papers, draw, or doodle when you are listening.

- **Don't interrupt!** Even though you may get angry or upset by something the speaker says, do not interrupt. Let the speaker finish and resist the temptation to focus on your emotional response to the speaker's words.

- **Open your mind.** Try to look at the situation from the speaker's point of view and not just your own. Be flexible.

- **Paraphrase.** Use your own words to mirror what you have heard. Restating information in your own words helps you to remember what you have heard.

CRIMINAL JUSTICE PROFESSIONALS AND VERBAL COMMUNICATION

Criminal justice professionals are involved in five primary areas of verbal communication: responding, reporting, interviewing, interrogating, and testifying. Each area has both a formal and an informal aspect. In the same vein, each component may be delegated to a different level of supervision within the agency. For instance, only in the most extreme cases or in very small agencies would the chief of police be involved in a suspect interview and/or interrogation. By the same token, rarely do patrol officers make presentations to the city council or mayor. However, every member of a law enforcement agency should be able to speak publicly and to present the agency in the best light possible. Interviewing and interrogating will be discussed further in Chapter 7.

Responding

Two methods are employed for responding to complaints or inquiries from the general public: formal and informal. These responses are also ascribed a certain priority depending on the nature of the complaint and, unfortunately, the status of the complainant.

The most common type of citizen inquiry or complaint is one made to the chief of police concerning either a local problem (e.g., parking on the street in neighborhoods or barking dogs) or a complaint about an officer's conduct or behavior. Generally, these issues necessitate a formal written response from the chief or corresponding head of the local law enforcement agency. The chief or other agency head will usually delegate this matter to a first-line supervisor (sergeant) for investigation. However, if the complaint or inquiry is of an extremely sensitive nature, it may be delegated to a midlevel manager or shift commander (lieutenant).

The investigation then follows an established procedure whereby the investigating officer will frequently travel to the area to observe firsthand the nature of the complaint, if possible. This visit may include a personal contact with the complainant, as well as interviews with witnesses or neighbors affected by the complaint. The officer will review the local ordinance and/or law specific to the complaint, if such exists, and offer an opinion based upon the officer's interpretation of the statute. At this point, the investigating officer will prepare a formal written report to the chief detailing the findings and analysis of the problem. The officer may make a recommendation based upon a careful examination of the issue. The report is then forwarded to the chief, who will review the provided information, formulate an opinion, and prepare a written response to the complainant's inquiry or complaint. The chief is the only person who will issue an official response to the complaint or inquiry.

Informal complaints are generally handled via the telephone or by personal contact with a local or district patrol officer. These issues may be just as significant to the complainant; however, they do not carry the same sense of importance since they are not in written form. Some of the informal issues police officers are asked to resolve involve alien abductions and other sometimes amusing requests, as well as public service questions concerning directions to certain locations and the requirements for becoming a police officer. Frequently, the officer will make a spontaneous decision concerning the nature of the problem and the best way to resolve the issue. If the complainant initiates no further contact, the officer considers the problem to have been solved.

Verbal Communication: The Written Component

As explained earlier in this chapter, verbal communication comprises two parts: oral and written. Writing is more difficult than speaking because you do not have access to immediate feedback. In other words, you must be able to communicate your message without the benefit of being able to see the person with whom you are communicating. Written communication may take the form of letters, memoranda, e-mail, text messages, or reports. Each of these types of messages has an appropriate use and a corresponding purpose.

- **Letters**. Letters are used to communicate outside the agency. Typically, a criminal justice agency will have an existing letterhead (stationery) on which all letters must be typed.

- **Memoranda**. A **memorandum** is a written message used to communicate within the agency. Traditionally, a memorandum includes the headings

"To," "From," "Date," and "Subject." These memoranda may be interdepartmental (within governmental departments) or intradepartmental (within the department only).

- **E-mail** (electronic mail). E-mail is a message transmitted electronically via the use of a computer network. E-mail may be sent either within the agency or outside the agency. E-mail's appearance is like that of a memorandum, with the same headings, "To," "From," "Date," and "Subject." E-mail should be given the same considerations as other forms of communication. The rules of grammar, punctuation, and spelling also apply to e-mail.

The subject line in an e-mail message is of paramount importance—to both the writer and the reader. The subject should be the purpose of the message. You should ask yourself, "Why am I writing this message?" Your answer to that question is your subject line for the e-mail you are about to the write. For example, if your supervisor asked for an update on a particular inmate's condition, your subject line would read something like "Subject: Update on Inmate X's Medical Condition." Avoid using vague or missing subject lines. And remember to change your subject line in back-and-forth messages when the subject of that e-mail has changed. If you begin your e-mail message about inmate X's condition with that as your subject, but your supervisor, in his response to your initial message, asks about something other than inmate X's condition, your response should contain a different subject line (if your supervisor did not change it when he responded to your first e-mail and introduced a new element into the communication process). Subject lines are what tell your readers why you are writing. Most people make decisions on the importance of e-mail messages by their subject lines. If you use vague subjects or leave the subject area blank, your e-mail message is likely to get relegated to the bottom of the pile. So avoid the use of *report*, *question*, *information*, *request*, or other vague terms as your subject. Be specific.

- **Text message.** Text messages are usually a limited form of communication. You should follow these guidelines[10] when contemplating a text message as a written communication:

  o Pay careful attention to what you are typing on your phone, as the autocorrect feature (depending on the manufacturer of your phone) will sometimes change words to what it "thinks" you meant to say.

  o Do not use ALL CAPITAL LETTERS in text messages as you are showing high emotions, such as anger, panic, or excitement.

  o NEVER use a text message to share bad news. You certainly may use text messages to remind people of meetings or of business transactions but should not rely on them as your only form of communication.

  o Avoid excessive length in your text message since this form of communication is designed for rapid access to relevant or significant information. Information that cannot be relayed succinctly or that requires a more detailed account should use another avenue for transmittal.

- **Reports**. **Reports** are the most frequently used form of written communication. Reports are documents written in an organized manner

used to communicate findings or developments, to provide updates
for projects, and more.

While the oral component of verbal communication is important in obtaining
and maintaining interest, the written document serves as a permanent record for others to review in the future. In the criminal justice profession, written documentation
is vital to the success of any agency.

Writing Techniques: Choosing the Right Words

Our choice of words in written documentation is very important to the effective transfer of information. Improper or inappropriate word choice can hinder even
the best attempt at communication. The following principles of word choice should
guide you in developing your written documentation.

- **Write clearly.** You must write in a complete, accurate manner. Give the
  reader a message he or she can understand and act on.

  o *Accuracy.* As a writer, you must use your integrity to make sure your
    communications are ethical. Your credibility is the most important facet
    in communication with others, and if you damage or destroy the trust of
    your reader through misleading information, you may never be able to
    repair the damage.

  o *Completeness.* Your message must contain all necessary information for the
    reader to make an informed decision. A good place for you as the writer to
    start is to develop the five W's: who, what, when, where, and why.

  o *Jargon and word familiarity.* Every field has its own special vocabulary.
    When communicating with others in your area, the use of jargon is
    appropriate. However, you should remember that the use of jargon is
    inappropriate when you are writing for a reader outside your agency. You
    should strive as a writer to use terms that are familiar both to you and to
    your reader.

- **Use simple words**. Using long words in communication is not necessary
  to achieve your purpose. Short, simple words are a better choice. Your
  reader is less likely to become confused when you opt for words that convey
  the precise meaning you desire. You want your readers to focus on the
  information you are presenting, not on the words themselves.

- **Use concrete language**. Concrete words give the reader a mental picture of
  what you mean in your writing. Try to avoid using words such as *several, a
  number of, a few, a lot of,* and *substantial*. Give definite numbers or specific
  information.

- **Avoid the use of clichés and slang**. A **cliché** is an expression that has
  been overused in our language. Examples might consist of "according to
  our records," "if you have any further questions," "if I may be of further
  assistance," or "please find enclosed." **Slang** is informal word usage usually
  identified with a specific group of people. For this reason, you should avoid

the use of slang in your writing. Words or phrases such as *perp, person of interest* (POI), and *privately owned vehicle* (POV) may be confusing or misconstrued by the reader.

- **Avoid wordiness**. Because people are exceedingly busy, you should strive to be concise in your writing. When one or two words will suffice, why would you use four or more to say, in effect, the same thing? Examples of excessive wordiness would be "enclosed herewith," "enclosed you will find," "a long period of time," "continuous and uninterrupted," and others.

- **Use positive language**. You are more likely to build goodwill with your reader if you write using positive, as opposed to negative, language. You should attempt to avoid the use of negative or negative-sounding words in your writing. For example, eliminate or minimize the use of words like *cannot, will not, failure, refuse, deny*, and *mistake*.

Developing and Writing Effective Sentences and Paragraphs

In addition to selecting appropriate words, using a variety of sentences in your writing is important to the complete development of logical paragraphs. When we vary our sentence types between simple, compound, and complex, we keep our writing interesting and our reader interested.

- A **simple sentence** is one in which you present a single idea. Example: The room is dark.

- A **compound sentence** contains two or more independent clauses, each of which presents a complete idea. Example: The room is dark, and I need a flashlight.

- A **complex sentence** contains one independent clause and at least one dependent clause. Typically, the dependent clauses present additional information that is not as important as that contained in the independent clause. Example: The room is dark because two light bulbs need to be replaced.

A **paragraph** is defined as a group of sentences that focus on one main idea or topic. Paragraphs must be unified and give information that is directly related to the topic. This information must be organized in a logical manner and contain all relevant details. Paragraphs also must be cohesive. That is, they must integrate the words together in such a way as to create a relationship between the sentences. Transitional words should be used to join sentences for a step-by-step movement. These "road signs" tell your reader where your message is heading.

Transitional Expressions

also	too	so
besides	as a result	therefore
furthermore	because	thus
in addition	consequently	likewise
moreover	hence	although

- nevertheless
- still
- for example
- in other words

- at last
- finally
- in conclusion
- meanwhile

- since
- next

You should attempt to control the length of your paragraphs so that they provide enough information to support your main idea or topic but are not so long that your important information or ideas get buried in the middle of a long block of unbroken text. Effective paragraphs typically fall somewhere within the 60- to 80-word range.

Law Enforcement Professionals and Verbal Communication Reporting

The situation or scenario of reporting in a paramilitary organization can be one of the most delicate and politically sensitive actions taken by an agency member. No matter what position you occupy in the chain of command, reporting can always be filled with hazards. The individual department member needs to be aware of the nature of the reporting situation and whether it is formal or informal.

Generally, when making a report, the recipient is a "higher" authority in the chain of command. Therefore, the presenter is put at a psychological disadvantage in this reporting situation. For that reason, the presenter must be prepared and rehearsed, when possible. The agency member should be aware of the topic for discussion prior to the actual formal meeting and should attempt to control the environment in which the reporting occurs. In addition to giving the advantage to the presenter, this allows time to properly prepare the report and to rehearse the presentation. The presenter should pay attention to any areas that may be sensitive or offensive to the recipient. While certain comments may seem innocuous to the presenter, they may produce or provoke an inadvertent response. An example might occur when an officer must report to the shift commander regarding matters of impropriety with respect to gender or ethnic issues. In this scenario, the officer must be cognizant of the lieutenant's biases in these areas. Occasions have arisen in which inadvertent remarks later impacted an officer's opportunities for promotion or transfer. Every opportunity should be taken to eliminate biased or sexist language from the vocabulary.

Testifying

In the courtroom, credibility is the benchmark by which all witnesses are evaluated. In January 2017, Kellyanne Conway coined the term *alternative facts*. The term arose over a discrepancy concerning the size of the crowd attending President Trump's inauguration. Chuck Todd of NBC News questioned her about the issue, and she used the term *alternative facts*. Todd stated, "Alternative facts aren't facts; they are falsehoods." Thus, Conway has been under a cloud of suspicion concerning her versions or interpretations of the new president's policies, and her public appearances have been severely curtailed.

Testifying is a recitation of facts or information, under oath, gained during an investigation. Testifying usually involves only those facts of which the officer has direct knowledge. However, in some instances and under specific guidelines, officers can proffer an opinion. Law enforcement officials may be called upon to testify in courtroom proceedings, in depositions, and in sworn statements. Furthermore, in certain select instances, criminal justice professionals may be called upon to testify before governmental bodies.

The Officer Speaks in the Courtroom

When an officer testifies in court, he or she is in a confrontational setting. Obviously, the defendant's attorney, to seek the best defense possible for his or her client, is going to question the officer's recollection of the facts, gathering of the evidence, procedural propriety, or professional integrity. Frequently, the officer is at a distinct disadvantage in the courtroom setting from an educational standpoint. The major participants in the courtroom all have law degrees or three years' postgraduate education while the typical police officer has a high school diploma or, at most, an associate's degree from a local community college.

Any discrepancy noted in the officer's written reports or testimony will be thoroughly examined. When testifying in a court action, an officer must carefully review all materials prior to taking the stand. Oftentimes, the officer will be prepared by the prosecuting attorney for the types of questions he or she can expect to be asked both by the prosecution and by the defense. The officer can cast himself or herself in the best light possible at this point by being prepared.

The Officer Gives a Deposition

The courtroom is the legal arena for fact-finding and the determination of guilt or innocence. A deposition, however, is an opportunity for discovery, or a "fishing" expedition. The latitude in a sworn deposition regarding questioning is much broader in scope. Queries made of the officer need not be limited to the parameters of the case at hand. Therefore, an officer's performance in previous cases, matters of professional or career development (regarding previous disciplinary actions due to poor performance or inappropriate behavior), and matters involving an officer's personal life are all open for examination in a deposition. Delving into the officer's life in this way is an attempt to discover any biases or prejudices that would alter or affect his or her testimony or perception of facts as they relate to the case.

Depositions are stress inducing and frequently confrontational in nature. Even the most patient officer may find that a deposition tests the limits of that patience.

The Officer Makes a Sworn Statement

Sworn statements are typically written documents that serve in lieu of an officer's personal appearance in a legal proceeding. More information on sworn statements will be discussed in Chapter 8.

VERBAL COMMUNICATION: THE VIDEO COMPONENT

Up to this point, the discussion has focused on face-to-face verbal communication. Face-to-face communication is indicative of the adage "You can't unring a bell." Once a statement has been made in a one-on-one situation, the information can never be retrieved nor the statement recanted. However, in videotaped communications, the opportunity exists for misstatements or faux pas to be retaped prior to distribution.

While law enforcement officials predominantly rely on face-to-face communication, certain instances exist in which videotaped presentations are more efficient and more cost-effective. This is particularly true regarding training tapes. With the increase in costs associated with training and given that training is essential due to the high incidence of litigation against law enforcement agencies, training tapes are vital to insulating a department against excessive civil judgments.

Training tapes are routinely prepared or created by officers who have a certain area of expertise. Training tapes are also generated quite by accident through the recording of officer–citizen interaction on the street. The use of these tapes allows training officers to continue with their normal duties rather than having to interrupt a busy schedule to instruct in the academy. Furthermore, if travel is involved, these tapes eliminate the costs associated with transportation, room, and board for the sponsoring department.

Media Relations and Law Enforcement: The History

In the early decades of the 20th century, law enforcement enjoyed unparalleled support and popularity. With the creation of the FBI and under J. Edgar Hoover's tutelage, high-profile arrests were frequently documented in newspapers across the country. Violent gangsters were arrested by well-dressed and well-educated "G-men" personally selected by the Hoover machine. The media was seldom critical of federal law enforcement. This support may have been the result of good personal relationships between government agents and local newspaper reporters or the result of some government control exercised by local field offices to ensure the agency was always portrayed in a positive manner.

Local law enforcement was not as fortunate, however, since scandals involving police officers and deputy sheriffs were frequently reported, and wire services would publish these improprieties nationwide. While Hoover had the wisdom, foresight, and personnel to orchestrate public relations opportunities, local law enforcement was left to its own devices. The chief or sheriff either failed to recognize the public relations value of the local department success or would not fully capitalize upon the success, preferring instead to opt for humility and to let the "deed speak for itself." While noble in its sentiment, this humility only garnered brief coverage, which was at best covered by the local newspaper.

During the 1940s and 1950s, law enforcement began to lose some of the respectability and credibility associated with federal agencies, and scandals continued to plague cities such as New York, Chicago, and Los Angeles. The media became more sophisticated technologically and procedurally. Local events of note were no longer relegated to just local or regional coverage. Radio and television could produce remote broadcasts and taped delays bringing good and bad news to the consumer's living room. Reporters, while still dependent upon police sources, were becoming more dependent upon research. Journalism schools were turning out increasingly better educated and more sophisticated graduates (interviewers). These interviewers could glean significant amounts of information from witnesses and bystanders and, in some cases, became more proficient in gathering information than their law enforcement counterparts.

The civil strife and social unrest of the 1960s and 1970s set the stage for some of law enforcement's most publicized disasters. Videotapes of Bull Connor in Birmingham, Alabama, allowing police dogs to attack peaceful protestors, Governor George Wallace surrounded by Alabama State Police making his infamous "segregation now . . . segregation forever" remarks, and Chicago police officers clubbing protestors at the 1968 Democratic National Convention all served to embarrass and degrade law enforcement. These agencies "circled the wagons" and attempted to shift the blame to the populace and the situation rather than to attempt damage control by accepting responsibility and promoting new training programs for handling civil disobedience.

In a 1973 *Police Chief* editorial, Don R. Derning, International Association of Chiefs of Police president, stated, "The foundation of police/public relations is built on public trust. It cannot be demanded or bought. It must be earned with efficient police service. Communication with the public is a never-ending process and should be viewed as the lifeline between the police and the communities they serve."[11] Furthermore, he advised administrators that only through open and productive lines of communication will support for law enforcement be established. Yet less than 5 years later, the New York City Police Department, failing to heed Derning's advice, was attempting to minimize the damage of a massive corruption scandal. Frank Serpico, an honest cop and typical of New York's Finest, was on the front page of every New York newspaper in an effort to divert attention from the real issue, the depth and breadth of departmental corruption. Perhaps admitting that the department had serious corruption problems and instituting enforceable sanctions would have been more advantageous to the reputation of the organization, which underwent another massive corruption scandal a decade later.

In October 1978, Mike Brake, a police reporter for the *Oklahoma Journal*, outlined five essential responsibilities for the public information officer (PIO) as follows:

1. Media accessibility to answer inquiries on matters of public interest.

2. Assistance to the media in developing feature and documentary items.

3. Monitoring media contacts with other agency personnel and moderately controlling information disseminated by such contacts.

4. Advice to the command staff in formulating press policies.

5. Service to the agency in matters requiring journalistic skill, such as the publication of an internal newsletter or the publication of public service materials.[12]

Having created this list, Brake admonished law enforcement executives not to confuse the roles of the PIO and the community relations officer, as they are both unique and need to be separate. The PIO needs to maintain continuity of identity as a media liaison to sustain efficiency and integrity. Brake believed that the PIO must have the full support of the administration and receive cooperation from all levels of the agency.

To staff such a position, officers must possess certain characteristics that promote a rapport with people and establish an aura of credibility. Brake suggested that perhaps civilian personnel would be an excellent choice to fill this position since they may possess certain journalistic skills not found in the rank and file of most police agencies and would be intimately familiar with the inner workings of the media. Furthermore, the media may be less likely to view civilian personnel as people with an extraordinary stake in the image of the agency and, therefore, more credible.

Brake concluded that the positive characteristics of a PIO should include the following:

- A commitment to the free press philosophy and an aversion to the unfair suppression of information concerning the agency.

- The ability to work with minimal supervision and control and a willingness to use initiative and imagination in dealing with the media.

- A strong respect for facts, to avoid the slipshod dissemination of erroneous information.

- A command of written and spoken English, to ensure that press releases, interviews, and other materials distributed to the media and to the public are clear, readable, and not open to misinterpretation.

- Patience and tactfulness, valuable tools in dealing with an often-demanding press.

- An overview of the agency's structure, policies, operating techniques, and personnel, and a thorough knowledge of the criminal justice system.

- Loyalty to the agency first, then the administrator, to avoid an image as a press agent for the executive.

- Personal integrity.

Brake's article provided sage advice since nearly 20 years later, in 1995, Ray Surette examined the use of civilian versus sworn personnel in the role of public information officer. His article in the *Journal of Criminal Justice* explored the backgrounds of PIOs and discovered that most civilian PIOs tend to be female with education backgrounds and have prior media-related experience while their sworn counterparts were male with criminal justice degrees who had little or no media-related experience. Furthermore, the civilian PIOs were more satisfied with their role.

According to Surette, it was not until the 1980s that agencies began to establish formal media relations units.[13] In April 1997, Tim McBride, commanding officer of community affairs at the Los Angeles Police Department, announced the hiring of a public relations practitioner, stating, "We're cops. We're not PR people."[14] In the wake of the Rodney King beating, the O. J. Simpson trial, and Willie Williams's public dispute with the L.A. Police Commission over the nonrenewal of his contract and his threat to sue, the LAPD could use professional public relations assistance.

In 2002, Don Kelly stated, "The luxury of deliberation and reflection is disappearing, as the traditional news cycle erodes into a continuous blur. We find ourselves inundated with broad requests, even demands, for information from varied sources, all conditioned to expect immediate answers."[15] With this tremendous demand for information and an omnipresent news media, more and more agencies have come to rely on full-time professional PIOs. Every agency should consider this position a funding priority since the support of the public is essential to the law enforcement mission. An informed and content public will be much more likely to increase funding for local agencies through increased taxes or funding referendums.

No police or sheriff's department is without blemishes or problems, but the way they handle these negative events will determine how they are accepted or rejected by their local community. A vital goal and essential quality of law enforcement agencies should be that they are viewed as a community partner, not an occupying force.

Law Enforcement Professionals: Responding to the Media

Aside from training tapes, recorded prepared statements to the news media are often used to inform the public of ongoing investigations or critical incidents. The advantage of using recorded statements is that the officer is given the opportunity to review a list of questions that the media will ask, to prepare appropriate responses, and to rehearse those responses. The officer must confine his or her responses to only those questions that have been previously submitted. He or she should not attempt to or be lured into responding to questions outside the scope of the current issue. Spontaneity at this point could be extremely detrimental to the integrity of the investigation or the reputation of the department.

On occasion, officers are confronted by news media at the scene of a crime or critical incident. At this point, no opportunity for advance preparation is present. Therefore, the officer must be extremely guarded in his or her response to questions from the media. Officers should inform the media that the investigation is in the preliminary stages and specific details at this time are not available or may serve as a barrier to a successful investigation. The officer should attempt to be candid in his or her statements but should not allow the media to force a hasty or inappropriate response. Officers need to be wary of the "60-second sound bite." Some reporters or news agencies will attempt to create or capture a headline to make the early evening or late news.

Regardless of whether the interview situation is spontaneous or planned, the responding officer should maintain proper decorum and adhere to the fundamentals of proper speech. A short film clip provides the opportunity for an officer to greatly enhance or to rapidly destroy the image of the department due to the tremendous number of viewers. More damage can occur in that 30-second sound bite than the department could incur in 30 years of service to the public. Unfortunately, the adage that may be most appropriate is "Often an ounce of perception is worth more than a pound of performance."

Following the guidelines for effective oral presentations affords opportunities for the law enforcement community to enhance its image. As important as good oral communication skills are, communication is a bifold process, involving both verbal and nonverbal skills. If what the officer says is contradicted by inappropriate nonverbal cues, then the officer's credibility is questioned. Chapter 3 introduces the concepts of nonverbal communication and explains how these skills supplement or complement the spoken word of the officer, and Chapter 5 addresses the visual component of presentations.

SUMMARY

Verbal communication involves both the oral and written facets of communication. Oral communication is a reciprocal process that involves both listening and speaking. Listening is a vitally important skill because we get the information we need to cope with our environment through listening. However, hearing and listening are not synonymous terms. Hearing involves the physiological response to sound while listening is both the physical and psychological processing of sound. Many barriers exist to listening, but we should try to overcome our tendency to close our minds to new information.

The written aspect of verbal communication typically involves the preparation of letters, memoranda, e-mail, and reports. In our writing,

we should remember to chose our words carefully, trying to maintain clarity and conciseness in our selections. The reader must be able to understand our message, and he or she will not be able to do so if we use jargon or slang inappropriately.

Sentences and paragraphs are important to the logical transfer of information. Simply choosing the appropriate word will not suffice when preparing written communication. Our sentences must vary in length between simple, compound, and complex styles, and our paragraphs should logically develop our main idea or topic while holding to a 60- to 80-word maximum. We should remember to use transitional words in paragraph development so that our sentences flow in a progressive and understandable manner.

KEY TERMS

Acceptance 36

Active listening 34

Analyzing critically 33

Attending 33

Attentive listening 36

Casual or marginal listening 36

Cliché 43

Complex sentence 44

Compound sentence 44

Concreteness 36

Congruence 36

Continual talker 37

Critic 37

Critical analysis 34

Empathy 36

Factual statements 35

Faker 37

"Finish the sentence for you" listener 37

"Hand on the doorknob" listener 37

Hearing 35

"I'm in a hurry" listener 37

Inferences 35

"I've done one better" listener 37

Listening 35

"Make sure it is correct" listener 37

Memorandum 41

Mnemonics 34

Note taking 34

Paragraph 44

Rapid-writing note taker 37

Remembering 33

Repetition 34

Reports 42

Responding empathically 33

Simple sentence 44

Slang 43

Understanding 33

FOR FURTHER REFLECTION AND DISCUSSION

1. Differentiate between listening and hearing.

2. Describe in detail the types of listening. As a criminal justice professional, which type of listening behavior should you engage in, and why?

3. Identify the most important factors that influence our ability to listen.

4. Identify a word or words that might elicit an emotional response from you and cause you to

"tune out" a speaker. Why do you believe this word(s) can affect you in this way?

5. As a criminal justice professional, you are often called upon to produce written communication in the form of incident reports, memoranda, and so forth. Give an example of one way you will attempt to avoid negative language in this written communication.

6. As a police chief, you oversee preparing a press release announcing the establishment of a Citizens Police Academy in your city. This press release will appear in the local newspaper and will be recorded for delivery by radio stations in the area. Think about how you can use words, sentences, and paragraphs to explain this addition to your police department.

   a. What do you want to accomplish with this press release?

   b. What should you know about your audience(s) before you start to write?

   c. What jargon or technical terms should you define in this press release? Why?

   d. Will you use any negative language in this press release? Why, or why not?

   e. Write a concise headline for this press release.

ETHICAL ISSUE EXERCISES

1. Should an officer knowingly withhold information in a statement to the press that could later affect the prosecution of a suspect?

2. Should an officer attempt to correct a mistake in his notes when giving a deposition?

3. When giving a deposition, is it improper for an officer to knowingly withhold information if not specifically asked for that information?

4. Should an officer ignore a mistake in previous testimony when the mistake is not specifically brought to the attention of the defense or the court?

5. Since a good public relations program is built upon trust, would it be appropriate for the public relations officer (PRO) to deliberately mislead the press if the information offered would aid in the capture of a suspect or aid in the prosecution of a suspect?

6. Would it be improper for the PIO to release information to one reporter prior to releasing the same information to other reporters, allowing the first to "scoop" the others on a local newscast?

7. Good public information officers know how to "set the stage" for interviews or press releases. Is this sound professional work or manipulating the press?

3

ACTIONS SPEAK LOUDER THAN WORDS

Nonverbal Communication

[O. J.] Simpson always denied any role in the 1994 slaying of his ex-wife, Nicole Brown Simpson, and her friend Ron Goldman. And after an exhaustive search, police and prosecutors could never present the jury in his murder trial with the knife they claim he used to kill them.

What the prosecution did have was blood-soaked gloves.

During the trial, Simpson tried on one of the gloves. He held up his hands in front of the jury box to let everyone see the leather bunched up around his broad palms; it didn't fit. That demonstration became a powerful symbol for the defense, summed up by Cochran: "If it doesn't fit, you must acquit."[1]

—Richard Winton, *Los Angeles Times*

LEARNING OBJECTIVES

After students have completed this chapter, they will be able to do the following:

1. Identify the functions of nonverbal communication

2. Explain the different types of nonverbal communication

3. Classify the categories of body language

4. Interpret nonverbal behaviors in criminal justice settings

5. Identify limitations and exceptions to nonverbal communications

As briefly discussed in Chapter 1, nonverbal communication involves more than merely body language. Nonverbal communication includes the individual's use of personal space, gestures, touch, voice, and objects. In addition, nonverbal communication within criminal justice agencies creates the culture or subculture of those organizations. For example, in law enforcement, nonverbal signs indicate when a junior officer should pay respect to senior officers in the form of a salute. Also, certain norms and expectations are communicated nonverbally, especially rules of engagement in law enforcement.

While being able to interpret nonverbal communication can be important to the average individual, the criminal justice professional should learn to decode body signals as a means of protection, self-preservation, and deception. Nonverbal communication can uncover trustworthiness, honesty, fear, and anger in suspects, victims, and witnesses. Therefore, the ability to interpret nonverbal messages ensures criminal justice professionals' safety when working with the public or in suspect/criminal situations.

THE FUNCTIONS OF NONVERBAL COMMUNICATION[2]

Nonverbal communication's functions are both wide and varied—contradicting, complementing, substituting, accenting, or regulating verbal messages. **Contradicting** nonverbal communication occurs when a person's words and actions do not express the same or similar meanings. An example would be a potential witness to a crime who says he or she saw nothing when questioned by an officer but who refuses to look the officer in the eye when making this denial. Contradicting verbal messages with body language, vocalics, and gestures creates the potential for misunderstandings between the officer and the public. Distrust arises when people see that an officer's actions do not support the spoken message. In these situations, the nonverbal message becomes more reliable.

Complementing and **accenting** nonverbal communication are similar in nature. Complementing behaviors occur when the actions expressed complete the picture created by the verbal message. Normally, the complementing behaviors are widely accepted ones, such as a hug when telling a parent you love him or her. The nonverbal hug complements or completes the verbal message of the expression of love.

Accenting nonverbal communication is the result of actions that stress the underlying meaning of the verbal message. Using an upraised hand to signal a driver to stop is one example of an accenting behavior. Also, following an anger-producing scene, if an officer slams the door on the cruiser when loading a prisoner, he or she is expressing the rage or frustration caused by the arrest. The slamming of the door is an accenting behavior that emphasizes the officer's feelings of anger.

Substituting nonverbal communication involves the use of symbols to replace the verbal message. Law enforcement officials utilize substituting nonverbal communication through uniforms, badges, handguns, batons, and blue lights. No words have to be spoken for a police officer to be identified if he or she is wearing a uniform or driving a marked vehicle. Substituting nonverbal communication also occurs in the use of certain street signs (pedestrian crossing, merging traffic, or right lane/left lane ends). The universal symbol for "No" is also a substituting nonverbal communication tool.

Regulating nonverbal communication serves as a governor in verbal communication. To fully understand this concept, picture a law enforcement officer interacting with a suspect. The officer may regulate that individual's behavior or communication by touching his or her arm to signal that the officer wishes to speak or to interrupt the suspect's conversation. Therefore, nonverbal cues serve as the regulator in the conversation. A pause in the conversation, a raised hand, or a quizzical look—any of these behaviors may signal a desire by one of the parties to speak.

Regardless of its function, nonverbal communication comprises a variety of aspects: the body (kinesics), the voice (paralanguage), objects (proxemics), and touch (**haptics**). Each component is a distinct facet of any communication process.

Kinesics: The Science of Body Language

Rarely do we convey our messages verbally. Instead, we use gestures involving the body to indicate disbelief, puzzlement, protection, indifference, intimacy, impatience, or forgetfulness. Most of our gestures are conscious—we realize we are raising our eyebrow in disbelief, tapping our fingers for impatience, and shrugging our shoulders for indifference. While these acts are predominantly deliberate, some gestures are mostly unconscious. We do not always realize that we rub our nose when we are puzzled or that we clasp our arms to protect ourselves from a perceived verbal or physical threat. Nonetheless, these signals can be vitally important in the interpretation of messages between two individuals.

Kinesics, the study of body movements in communication, has been classified into nine categories: emblems, illustrators, affect displays, regulators, adaptors, body size and shape, posture and gestures, the face and head, and eye movement.

- **Emblems** approximate sign language and are intentional gestures that have a universal meaning. Examples of an emblem would be the raised hand of a police officer facing a driver's vehicle when the officer is attempting to control traffic. The driver interprets the raised hand signal to mean stop the vehicle.

- **Illustrators** help to support or underscore the verbal message we are attempting to deliver. For example, a witness describing the size or shape of an object used by a suspect when committing a crime might use his or her hands to form the shape or dimensions of the object. Also, a crime scene sketch or map used to show positions of objects can help in providing greater clarity to the verbal explanation.

- **Affect displays** typically involve the face and are movements which show the emotional condition of the person speaking. Affect displays are impossible to intentionally control because they involve our facial expressions. Since affect displays are truthful reports of what we are feeling, they often contradict our verbal message. Wide eyes and pursed lips in a witness convey that he or she is frightened or anxious. An astute criminal justice professional would recognize these affect displays and attempt to reduce the witness's fear and/or anxiety.

  Criminal justice professionals must pay close attention to a suspect's face. Frowns, partial smiles, or complete smiles convey what the suspect is thinking. For example, if the suspect smiles with wide eyes, he or she is conveying confidence and happiness. If the suspect frowns and has narrowed eyebrows and flared nostrils, he or she is communicating anger or sadness.

- **Regulators** involve head and eye movements and vocalizations that are used to regulate a conversation. Rapid head nodding coupled with an upheld palm signal to the speaker to pause so that the listener can comment. On the other hand, slow, periodic nods from the listener indicate that he or she is listening and understands the message and, further, that the speaker should continue talking.

- **Adaptors** are unconscious motions, tics, or gestures we use as a means of dealing with stress or anxiety or to adjust to an unusual situation. Examples of adaptors that might be seen when interviewing a witness, suspect, or victim would be drumming fingers, tapping feet, shaking a leg, cracking knuckles, stroking the chin or the beard, smoothing or twisting the hair, and tugging at the ears.

- Body size and shape have long been associated with certain stereotypical characteristics or traits. Three body types identified through previous research are **endomorphs**, **ectomorphs**, and **mesomorphs**. Each of these body types has distinctive behavioral attributes affiliated with it. In the same vein as body size and shape are other body features that convey nonverbal cues. These features include skin color, gender, physical impairments, blemishes, hair color, and body odor.

Body Type	Characteristics	
Endomorphs **Description**: short, fat, round	• sympathetic • warm • sociable	• soft-hearted • content • affable
Ectomorphs **Description**: tall, thin	• shy • tense • cautious	• serious • self-conscious
Mesomorphs **Description**: muscular, well-proportioned	• active • cheerful • energetic	• courageous • hot-tempered • dominant

- Posture and gestures are learned responses that we acquire throughout our early socialization. This category of body language tends to be bound to the culture in which we are raised. In other words, we tend to lean forward toward a speaker when we like and are interested in the speaker. If we lean backward, away from the speaker, however, we are expressing dislike or disinterest. Posture also is a status indicator. Persons of high status in criminal justice agencies typically assume a more open and relaxed posture when in the presence of lower status individuals. Also, an officer who leans back from a suspect, witness, or victim when that individual is speaking shows disbelief or skepticism.

- The face and head are probably the most expressive nonverbal communicators. Since we tend to have the remainder of our bodies clothed, the face and head are the most exposed body parts, thereby drawing the most attention. The face tends to communicate the most information because emotions tend to be intensified through facial expression. The position of the head also conveys many nonverbal signals. For example, cocking the head back slowly indicates disbelief or doubt. A bowed head reveals a shy, withdrawn individual; whereas an upright head indicates confidence and interest. If an officer inclines his or her head toward the suspect, victim, or witness, then he or she is expressing sympathy and indicating that he or she is listening attentively.

- Eye movement is one of the most important facets of nonverbal communication. The eyes can provide many cues in conversation. They can be used to read the response of a listener, to regulate or control the speaker, and to express interest or involvement. Two patterns of eye contact associated with doubt or suspicion are the **eye dart** and the **slow blink**. The eye dart occurs when an individual is unable to maintain eye contact for a reasonable amount of time (between 10 seconds and 1 minute or more). Their eyes are constantly darting from place to place, usually conveying disinterest or dishonesty. The slow blink occurs when a person closes his or her eyes for 2 to 4 seconds and then slowly opens them. If a person is condescending or impatient, the slow blink conveys disinterest or superiority.

Paralinguistics: The Voice

When you speak, you add a dimension to your words. The way you speak can often change the meaning of the words you spoke—even contradicting their actual meaning. **Paralinguistics** deals with the voice—how something is said rather than what is said. Essentially, we are looking at the characteristics of the voice. Paralinguistics typically consists of four categories: voice qualities, vocal characterizers, vocal qualifiers, and vocal segregates.

- **Voice qualities** include things associated with the voice, such as pitch, rhythm, tempo, and volume. Voice qualities can make a tremendous difference in the perception of the spoken word. For example, a high-pitched voice indicates anger, but moderate rate, pitch, and volume indicate boredom.

- **Vocal characterizers** include things such as grunting, clearing the throat, yawning, and coughing. Characterizers should be avoided when speaking because they are very annoying.

- **Vocal qualifiers** refer to changes in tone or volume of speech. A good method for illustrating how vocal qualifiers can change the nonverbal meaning of a sentence can be obtained by repeating the statement "I didn't say he stole your car" seven times; each time place the emphasis on a different word in the sentence.

- **Vocal segregates** are nonfluencies, or periods of silence between words. Nonfluencies are identified as the ahs and ums that you utter in speaking.

Proxemics: Space and Objects[3]

People communicate much about themselves and their feelings or relationships with others by the amount of space they maintain between them. Our approach to personal space is tied to our culture. As long as we and others maintain what we consider to be the appropriate amount of personal space, we do not feel threatened. However, if these zones are violated, we become nervous and uncomfortable, causing communication to be inhibited. Most Americans observe the following space zones relative to the concomitant situation:

- **Intimate:**   0 to 18 inches
- **Personal**:   1.5 to 4 feet
- **Social:**   4 to 12 feet
- **Public:**   more than 12 feet

The distance between an officer and a suspect, witness, or victim is important. The closer the officer stands to a suspect, for example, the more intimate the encounter. The officer's discretion determines if a distance is too close or too far in these situations. For example, if a victim begins to back away from the officer, the officer should take that as a nonverbal message to step back as well. If a victim or suspect moves toward the officer, then the officer should remain stationary until the victim or suspect ceases his or her movement to indicate a comfortable space has been reached.

In addition to space, **proxemics** refers to the use of objects in communication, one of which may be our personal attire. As humans, we have three basic reasons why we clothe ourselves:

1. To protect ourselves from the elements

2. To obey the laws of civility and modesty

3. To look good to others

Our clothing reflects many characteristics, such as image, power, wealth, authority, and mood. The way we dress communicates to others *who we are*, *what we are*, and *how important we are to the world*.

Haptics: Touch

Shaking hands has become a universal greeting. Giving someone a "high five" or a pat on the back communicates "job well done" or "good work." Perhaps no other form of nonverbal communication causes as much physical reaction as touch. We judge others based on the strength or weakness of a handshake. However, we reserve hugs for those persons closest to us (i.e., family, friends, and significant others), and if we receive a hug from someone outside our inner circle, our response is vastly different.

The following table presents a list of the most common nonverbal cues and their "perceived meanings."

Nonverbal Behavior	Perceived Meaning	
Bouncing your leg	• Impatience	• Lack of interest
	• Urgency	
Nodding your head	• Approval	• Understanding
	• Encouragement	
Raising an eyebrow	• Disbelief	• Surprise
	• Questioning	
Remaining silent	• Concentration	• Respect
	• Interest	
Slouching shoulders	• Tired	• Discouraged
	• Unenthusiastic	
Looking away	• Impatience	• Lack of interest
	• Distraction	

INTERPRETING NONVERBAL BODY LANGUAGE IN CRIMINAL JUSTICE PROFESSIONS

The eyes have often been called "the windows to the soul." When you consider the fact that so many of our personal feelings are unconsciously mirrored in our eyes, you can understand that statement much better. The key for a criminal justice professional is to learn to "read" those visual clues so that information is not overlooked.

Much research has been conducted to understand nonverbal communication, and most studies have produced similar findings. From this information, conclusions have been drawn regarding certain nonverbal cues and their concomitant meanings. In particular, the FBI has identified types of behaviors that occur spontaneously during interviews under stressful conditions. Body movements, personal distance, facial color, facial expressions, and paralanguage offer insight into a subject's truthfulness. Learning to interpret this nonverbal behavior correctly could result in a successful resolution of an ongoing investigation, whether through additional leads or clarification of a verbal statement.

Body Movements

Movement of various body parts is the least controllable nonverbal characteristic. You have probably met or know someone who finds it necessary to "speak" with his or her hands. In fact, if you were to tie that individual's hands to his or her sides, no communication would be possible. Just as these natural gestures occur unconsciously, so too do those movements that are deceptive in nature. A suspect or parolee who has a calm, emotionless face but who constantly shifts his hands, arms, legs, and feet is conveying a message of deception. A witness, suspect, or parolee who does not lean forward and who moves his or her legs and feet during an interview is not being entirely truthful.

Hands and arms also provide critical insight into an individual. Arms folded tightly across the chest signify refusal or defiance. Arms loosely folded convey relaxation. If this gesture is difficult to interpret merely from the arms, the hands provide additional information. If the hands are closed in a fist or tightly grasping the biceps, this supports the refusal or defiance state; open and relaxed means the individual is relaxed.

In addition, drumming or tapping fingers is indicative of nervousness and often associated with deceit. While a person who makes hand-to-chest gestures is generally considered honest, one who makes a hand-to-mouth gesture is communicating self-doubt and is believed to be lying. As a matter of fact, truthful individuals most often gesture away from their body while liars tend to gesture toward themselves.

Leg and knee movements also provide nonverbal signals. When an interviewer asks particularly probing, critical questions, he or she may notice an increase in movement in the suspect's legs, indicating nervousness. Individuals may also use their legs as barriers by crossing them. When their legs are crossed, suspects are erecting a barrier to the interrogator and his or her questions. A suspect feels much more comfortable in this protected environment he or she has created. Leg crossing behaviors are also used by the suspect to stall. The suspect may listen to the question, but before responding, he or she will break eye contact, cross or uncross the legs, and then, after he or she is completely settled, respond to the question.

In addition, movement of the knees can be a means for handling a stressful environment. A suspect may wobble his or her knees back and forth to diffuse a tense situation. The more stress the person is under, the faster the knee movements.

As a final caveat concerning body movements, criminal justice professionals should keep in mind that deceitful people are often aware of delaying tactics involving nonverbal communication. Any grooming gestures or clothing adjustments that allow the suspect or witness to busy his or her hands and allow a delay in responding to any questions also provide the individual with an opportunity to release his or her anxiety before answering.

Proxemics: Space and Objects

As indicated earlier in the chapter, Americans have a zone of protective space with which we surround ourselves. This personal space varies from as far away as 4 feet to as close as 6 inches, depending on the relationship the individuals share. Criminal justice professionals can make use of the personal space zone in interrogation and interviewing settings. A good interviewer creates high levels of anxiety by beginning an interrogation session at a comfortable distance from the suspect or witness and by asking for general information. As the questions begin to center more on the subject at hand, the interviewer moves closer to the suspect or witness and backs off during desired responses. In this manner, the interviewer is programming the witness or suspect to provide the desired information in a cooperative manner. A psychologically normal person experiences a high level of anxiety when his or her personal space is invaded in this manner. Moreover, an individual finds it increasingly difficult to lie in this type of situation.

In law enforcement, objects such as tables, chairs, books, and other items that may be found in an interrogation or interviewing room may unfortunately aid the suspect or witness. Any kind of obstacle of this nature may give the suspect or witness a certain amount of confidence and relief. These obstacles prohibit invasion of the individual's personal space zone, thereby preventing the officer from achieving the goals of an interview or interrogation.

Facial Color

When an individual lies, the body responds through physiological changes. Perspiring, flushing or paleness of the skin, an increased pulse rate, and the appearance of veins in the head, neck, and throat are all signs that the individual is not being truthful. Also, if the person stutters, appears to have a dry tongue or mouth, exhibits changes in breathing, licks his or her lips, and has thickening speech, the officer should view these as indicators of deception.

Dramatic changes in facial color signal that our bodies are under stress. In an interview, criminal justice professionals may notice that a suspect's face and the sides of his neck turn chalky white. In a fight-or-flight situation, the body's response is to cause the cutaneous capillaries on the surface of the skin to constrict in order to provide more blood flow to the deep muscles and the core of the body. Since the blood in the cutaneous capillaries is what contributes to our skin tone, the removal of this pigment will make the skin appear lighter.

Conversely, in a situation where the interrogator is asking "hot" questions, he or she may notice that the suspect's neck and face begin to redden. The suspect's blood pressure has become elevated, and the same cutaneous capillaries are now dilated. The interrogator may notice the reddening crawl up the suspect's neck and face. The whites of the eyes may even become red, as may the insides of the ears.

Facial Expressions

Facial asymmetry is a noticeable fact. The two halves of an individual's face are not identical—one nostril may be larger, or one eye may sag more. When a person smiles or makes another facial expression, one side of the mouth may droop more than the other, or one nostril may flare more. Spontaneous facial expressions tend to produce muscle movements that are about the same on both sides of the face. When a subject is attempting to be deceitful, the muscles on the left side of the face move more than those on the right.[4] Using these facial cues, an astute law enforcement officer may be able to detect whether a person is being sincere.

What accounts for this difference in facial muscular movement? When a person exhibits a spontaneous facial movement, such as a smile, it bypasses the brain's cognitive centers. When you attempt to regulate a facial movement, the signals to move the required muscles pass through the cortex of the brain, the center of conscious decisions. Because the portion of the cortex involved in this process has close ties to the left side of the body, the greater movement of facial muscles occurs on the left.[5]

Aside from the asymmetrical facial cues an officer may receive in an interview or interrogation, the eyes are also particularly helpful in ascertaining deceit and truthfulness. When an individual is being intentionally deceitful, "Liars blink less frequently than normal during the lie, and then speed up to around eight times faster than usual afterwards."[6] Internal stress will also cause a suspect's eyes to open wider than usual. Of course, the usual avoidance of direct eye contact, or looking away when responding to questions, provides additional clues to a suspect's deceit. Remember that a certain amount of eye movement is normal, but you may spot a trend when you probe into specific areas.

Eyebrows are another facial feature that communicates nonverbally. The eyebrows enhance the expressions of the eyes and the rest of the face. When the subject is responding in anger, the eyebrows form a "V" shape with the tips of the eyebrows pointing downward toward the nose. When the subject experiences shock or surprise, you will notice the eyebrows raise high on the brow. The interviewer may have caught the suspect off guard by the particular inquiry being pursued. The interviewer should then vigorously continue along this line of questioning since there appears to be some unresolved issue surrounding this specific area.

Another part of facial expression involves the nose. In fact, the nose is the most stress-sensitive part of the body. During the same fight-or-flight response as we have discussed previously, the nose also undergoes several physiological changes. The tissue in the nose will become engorged with blood when an increase in blood pressure occurs, and this same tissue will constrict as blood pressure drops. Since an interrogation involves constant changes in heart rate and blood pressure, the resulting response is a stimulation of the nasal membranes. The only way a suspect can deal with this stimulation is by touching, scratching, pinching, or massaging.

Paralanguage (The Voice)

Everyone, at one time or another, has heard the expression "It wasn't what he said; it was *how* he said it." **Paralanguage** refers to the way an individual speaks and all of the characteristics of the voice. The focus is not on the words themselves but rather on the manner in which the words are spoken. Pitch, loudness, rate of speech, voice quality, vocal segregates, and nonfluencies are characteristics of paralanguage that can aid in the identification of deception.

Suspects who attempt deception will be less fluent and stutter more often. Also, these individuals will provide answers that are less believable and longer, and they will use more nonfluencies and repeated phrases throughout their responses. In addition, as these suspects become more nervous, they often respond in a high-pitched voice with heightened quivering or other breakers, they have a slower rate of speech with a longer hesitation prior to answering, and they offer less volunteered information.

LIMITATIONS AND EXCEPTIONS TO NONVERBAL COMMUNICATION

Accurate interpretation of nonverbal communication comes with experience and practice. Since nonverbal communication is as individualized as a person's speaking style, the longer you know an individual, the more adept you become at correctly interpreting his or her nonverbal signals. However, nonverbal communication is not the same for all cultures. In addition, nonverbal behaviors of individuals with cognitive disabilities also vary. In Chapters 11 and 12 of this text, we will offer a full discussion on communication issues (including nonverbal) between criminal justice professionals and special populations such as people with cognitive, physiological, psychological, and emotional disabilities, the elderly, youth, and those from different cultural and ethnic backgrounds.

No dictionary of nonverbal cues exists from which you might learn all you need to know about this issue. Observing an experienced, successful interviewer is a good place to start your learning process, though. Nonetheless, an important note to remember is that nonverbal communication has limitations and exceptions just as any other form of communication. Keep the following in mind when interviewing or interrogating suspects and witnesses:

- **The intelligence of the suspect.** The higher the intelligence of the suspect, the more reliable the behavior exhibited. Low-intelligence individuals may not completely understand the questions, and their behaviors are less reliable.

- **Emotional stability of the suspect.** When the suspect has serious emotional or psychological problems, you cannot place reliability on the individual's behaviors.

- **Children and juveniles.** These individuals may not have a developed sense of social responsibility, and the lack of fear of the consequences of their actions leads to the lack of reliable behavior.

- **Drugs and alcohol.** The use of drugs and alcohol modifies the behavior of suspects. If possible, the investigating officer should wait until such time as the individual is free from the influence of these agents before questioning him or her.

- **Cultural differences.** In revealing findings from his research, Fast stated that "the average man, unschooled in cultural nuances of body language, often misinterprets what he sees."[7] The best advice to the investigating officer is to know the culture with which you are dealing.

As a criminal justice professional, increasing your awareness and understanding of the impact of nonverbal communication can ensure continued success in the area of interviewing and interrogation. Again, you should avoid the belief that nonverbal behaviors mean the same across all cultures, and you should refrain from stereotyping individuals based on nonverbal qualities. Practice in recognizing the importance of nonverbal behavior in communication will promote success in all areas of criminal justice. The first step in identifying and understanding nonverbal communication comes through recognizing your own behaviors. The checklist that follows provides you with some tips for improving your nonverbal communication.

CHECKLIST FOR IMPROVING YOUR NONVERBAL COMMUNICATION

- ☐ **Establish and maintain eye contact.** Appropriate eye contact indicates interest and credibility.

- ☐ **Use posture to indicate interest.** Lean forward, sit or stand erect, and look alert so that you show interest in the subject.

- ☐ **Reduce or eliminate physical barriers.** Where possible, remove desks, chairs, and any other barriers. Step out from behind the desk unless you are engaged in an interrogation where the desk is serving an environmental purpose.

- ☐ **Improve your decoding skills.** Watch facial and body language to process and comprehend the entire message.

- ☐ **Probe for more information.** If nonverbal cues contradict the spoken message, you should politely seek more information.

- ☐ **Avoid assigning nonverbal meanings out of context.** Understand a situation or culture before you make nonverbal assessments.

SUMMARY

Nonverbal communication is not an exact science. No dictionary exists in which we can search for the meaning of a gesture or touch. We predominantly rely on the socialization we have received as children to teach us the meanings of nonverbal communication. As such, our nonverbal behaviors vary from culture to culture. Americans have a great need for personal space and feel threatened when that space is invaded by "outsiders." We also place a great deal of emphasis on eye contact, believing that deception is conveyed by those who fail to meet and maintain eye contact with us.

In the criminal justice profession, nonverbal communication plays a vital role in determining the truth or falsehood of suspect and witness statements. A novice investigator may experience great difficulty in recognizing the nonverbal behaviors of suspects or witnesses. The only way to improve your skill and enhance your ability to reach the truth is to work with others who are more experienced in the interpretation of nonverbal behaviors.

KEY TERMS

Accenting 54

Adaptors 55

Affect displays 55

Complementing 54

Contradicting 54

Ectomorphs 56

Emblems 55

Endomorphs 56

Eye dart 57

Haptics 54

Illustrators 55

Kinesics 55

Mesomorphs 56

Paralanguage 61

Paralinguistics 57

Proxemics 58

Regulating 54

Regulators 55

Slow blink 57

Substituting 54

Vocal characterizers 57

Vocal qualifiers 57

Vocal segregates 57

Voice qualities 57

FOR FURTHER REFLECTION AND DISCUSSION

1. Compare and contrast verbal and nonverbal communication.

2. List the specific functions of nonverbal communication, and give an example of each.

3. Discuss the limitations of nonverbal communication. Give a criminal justice example of how misinterpretation of a message can be traced to one or more of these limitations.

4. A suspect has volunteered to take a lie detector test to prove his innocence concerning a recent homicide. What role will nonverbal communication play in this lie detector test? Can the nonverbal behavior of the suspect have an impact on the outcome of the lie detector test? Why, or why not?

5. Each courtroom has pre-established boundaries and barriers, a part of nonverbal communication called proxemics. List and explain each object and its corresponding nonverbal purpose. *Example: The judge's robe—communicates professionalism, power, and authority.*

6. How might nonverbal communication assist a probation and parole officer when he or she is assigned a new parolee? What behaviors would the officer need to look for?

7. List as many nonverbal behaviors as possible. Create "definitions" for these behaviors. In other words, list the nonverbal action and describe what you believe the action indicates.

8. **Your Opinion:** Do you believe nonverbal communication is more important, as important, or less important in the criminal justice professions than it is in everyday life. Why, or why not?

ETHICAL ISSUE EXERCISES

1. When a uniformed officer approaches a vehicle or a citizen, what distinguishes confidence from arrogance?

2. Should officers be allowed to use psychological ploys to secure information from reluctant or hesitant suspects?

3. Should nonverbal cues, without verbal confirmation, be allowed as sufficient probable cause for an arrest? Can you identify situations where this might occur?

PART
II

PREPARING FOR EFFECTIVE COMMUNICATION

4 GRAMMAR
A Lesson in the Basics

Incident reports are one type of written communication investigating officers are required to prepare. Just as details of the incident must be accurate, so too must the words used to describe the situation. Consider the following example of a robbery incident report:

"I, Officer Jackson, arrived at the location of West 47th and 17th Streets at 05:30. And apon my arrivel I spoke to the victim a Mr. Mike Parks. I asked Mr. Parks what had happened and Mr. Parks stated that he was walking home from work, when he crossed the alley way between Little's Bookstore and Dr. Greens florist a noise startiled Mr. Parks so he turned to see what the noise was and at that moment Mr. Parks states that a man with a gun pulled Mr. Parks into the alley way and tolled Mr. Parks to give him all of his money and watch. The man then pistol wiped Mr. Parks. After taking his statement I called in the detectives and waited for their arrival. I cleared the scene upon their arrival."

After reading this excerpt from an actual incident report, do you know what took place? Between the misspelled words and the run-on sentences, this incident report makes virtually no sense. Imagine the impression your department would create if this document were to be introduced as evidence into a court of law. Imagine if you were Officer Jackson; how would you feel if your superior officer asked you to explain your report since he or she could not understand it?

A review of grammar and the role that it plays in written and spoken communication is essential to this text. Criminal justice professionals must be able to write clearly and coherently. Excerpts from reports are often introduced into court proceedings, and superiors review them as part of the investigative process. While entire books have been devoted to the subject of grammar, this chapter will merely review some of the most important aspects of grammar, as well as introduce some commonly mis-used words in the English language. Criminal justice professionals frequently prepare reports, e-mail, memoranda, and other intra- and interdepartmental documentation. These documents may be reviewed by judges, attorneys, the mayor, and other city officials, who form their impressions of you and your organization or department from this writing sample. Therefore, you must make the best impression possible by ensur-ing that your writing sample is grammatically sound and free from error.

PARTS OF SPEECH

The eight traditional parts of speech are nouns, adjectives, adverbs, pronouns, conjunctions, prepositions, verbs, and interjections.

Nouns

A **noun** is typically referred to as a person, place, thing, or idea. Most nouns are **common nouns**. They name any one of a class or kind of people, places, or things. A **proper noun** is the official name of a particular person, place, or thing and should always begin with a capital letter. Proper nouns include personal names, names of nationalities and religions, geographic names, names of holidays, and names of time units (i.e., months and days of the week).

Proper Nouns	Common Nouns
We'll go to the mall **Saturday**.	What **day** would you like to go?
I was born in **March**.	This **city** is beautiful!
My horse is in **Mexico**.	What is your **religion**?

Nouns are also categorized as concrete or abstract. If the things they name are physical, tangible, and visible, they are **concrete nouns**. On the other hand, **abstract nouns** name a mental quality or concept, something that exists only in our minds. A review of the following list reveals that many criminal justice concepts fall into the category of abstract nouns.

Concrete Nouns	Abstract Nouns
Book	Truth
Plant	Justice
Court	Mankind
Sentence	Idea
Magazine	Love

Up to this point, we have examined nouns in their singular forms. Another example is a noun used to describe a group of people or things that is considered a single unit. This unit is referred to as a **collective noun**. Some examples of collective nouns follow:

orchestra	family	band
herd	flock	chorus
gang	Congress	audience
team	majority	bunch
group	personnel	crowd

The difficulty with collective nouns is in deciding what form of the verb to use with them in a sentence. Is the collective noun singular, or is it plural? The answer depends on the meaning of the sentence and where the emphasis is placed. For example, if you are referring to individual members of the group, the plural verb is required. If you are focusing on the group in its entirety, the singular verb is used.

- **Singular:**   The chorus meets at noon every day.
- **Plural:**   The chorus are unable to work together.

Collective nouns also can be used in the plural form—for example, orchestras, teams, audiences—when you are referring to more than one group.

In fact, most nouns can be either singular or plural. The majority of them will form their plural by adding an "-s" to the end of the word.

Singular	Plural
Desk	Desks
Boy	Boys
Letter	Letters
Report	Reports
Book	Books

However, much like many other rules in life, exceptions to this rule exist—in fact, four of them.

1. If the word ends in "-y" and is preceded by a consonant, change the "y" to "i," and add "-es."

Forty	Forties
Country	Countries
Lady	Ladies
Category	Categories
Baby	Babies

2. If the last sound in the word is "s," "z," "ch," "sh," or "x," then "-es" is added to form the plural so that the word is easier to pronounce.

Class	Classes
Fish	Fishes
Kiss	Kisses
Match	Matches

3. If the "ch" ending to a word is pronounced "k," only "-s" is added.

Stomach	Stomachs
Monarch	Monarchs

4. If a one-syllable word ends in "f" or "fe," then form the plural by changing the "f" or "fe" to "-ves."

Half	Halves
Wife	Wives
Life	Lives
Leaf	Leaves

Of course, exceptions to even this exception to the rule exist. In this case, *chief* and *roof* form their plurals by simply adding "-s" to the end.

Pronouns

Pronouns are used to refer to people, places, or things that have already been mentioned in the sentence. They usually replace some noun. The noun for which the pronoun stands (or replaces) is called an **antecedent**. The antecedent usually comes before the pronoun in the sentence or paragraph. The pronoun and its antecedent must agree in number, gender, and person. That means if you have a plural noun (antecedent), then your pronoun should also be plural. Further, if you have a feminine noun, your pronoun must also be feminine in gender.

- I heard **one dog** barking **its** loudest.

- I heard **three dogs** barking **their** loudest.

- The **man** raised **his** hand to ask a question.

- The **men** raised **their** hands to ask questions.

- The **woman** read **her** magazine.

- The **women** read **their** magazines.

The English language has approximately 50 pronouns. In fact, of the 25 most frequently used words, 10 of them are pronouns. Pronouns are traditionally divided into six groups or categories: **personal pronouns, relative pronouns, interrogative pronouns, demonstrative pronouns, indefinite pronouns,** and **reflexive pronouns**. In addition to its name, each category has its own definition and special function.

Personal Pronouns

The group of pronouns most frequently used are the personal pronouns. Because of their many forms, however, this group can be troublesome.

Relative Pronouns

Relative pronouns often assume the role of the subject of a sentence. More often, though, they refer to nouns that have preceded them. Relative pronouns are **who (for persons), whom (for persons), whose (for persons), that (for persons and things),** and **which (for things)**.

PRONOUNS

Number	Person	Subject	Object	Possessive	Possessive Adjective
Singular	First	I	me	mine	my
	Second	you	you	yours	your
	Third (masculine)	he	him	his	his
	Third (feminine)	she	her	hers	her
	Third (neutral)	it	it		its*
Plural	First	we	us	ours	our
	Second	you	you	yours	your
	Third	they	them	theirs	their

*Its: Often confused with it's (it is)

- Mr. Smith, **whom** I know well, came by my office yesterday.
- The boy **who** lived down the street was injured in an accident today.
- The car, **which** was red, was his favorite.

Interrogative and Demonstrative Pronouns

Interrogative and demonstrative pronouns are easy to recognize. Interrogative pronouns are **who**, **what**, **which**, **whom**, **whose**, **whoever**, **whichever**, and **whatever**.

- **Who** is on the phone?
- **What** do you need me to bring to dinner?
- **Which** kind of soft drink do you prefer?
- **Whom** did you stay with last night?
- **Whatever** you mean by "star-crossed lovers," I don't know.

Demonstrative pronouns are used to point to something or someone clearly expressed or implied: **this**, **that**, **these**, and **those**.

- **That** is the car I want.
- **These** are the shoes I've been looking for.
- Give **this** to my sister for me, please.

Indefinite Pronouns

Indefinite pronouns acquired their name because the noun for which they are standing in is indefinite: **everybody**, **somebody**, **anybody**, **nobody**, **everyone**, **someone**, **anyone**, and **no one**.

- **Everybody** joined in the race.

- **No one** took more time than he did.

- Is **anyone** home?

Reflexive Pronouns

Reflexive pronouns are those pronouns which end in "self" or "selves": **myself, yourself, yourselves, himself, herself, itself, ourselves,** and **themselves**. The main purpose of reflexive pronouns is to reflect back on the subject of a sentence.

- She cut **herself** with the knife. (*herself refers to "she"*)

- I bought **myself** a new car this week. (*myself refers to "I"*)

- You are just not **yourself** today, are you? (*yourself refers to "you"*)

- Reflexive pronouns may also serve to provide emphasis in a sentence. When they serve this purpose, they appear at the end of the sentence.

- I will go to the store **myself**.

- I suppose I will have to write the paper **myself**.

Errors to Avoid With Reflexive Pronouns. You should avoid using reflexive pronouns when your sentence calls for a personal pronoun, such as "I," "me," or "you." Remember that a reflexive pronoun should "reflect back" on the subject of the sentence.

NO: Both Officer Smith and **myself** plan to go.

YES: Both Officer Smith and **I** plan to go.

NO: Either Captain Jones or **yourself** will prepare the report.

YES: Either Captain Jones or **you** will prepare the report.

Verbs

Every sentence *must have* a **verb**. Verbs express action or a state of being. Verbs can be either singular or plural, depending on the subject of the sentence. Verbs and subjects are like the black and white keys on a piano keyboard; they complement or support each other in the harmony of the sentence. Verbs change tense (time) to tell us when the action is occurring or when the action has occurred as well as what action is occurring. The two main forms of any verb are the present and past tense. The past tense is usually formed by adding "-ed" to the end of the basic verb.

PRESENT	PAST	PRESENT	PAST
achieve	achieved	assess	assessed
administer	administered	assist	assisted
analyze	analyzed	brandish	brandished
apply	applied	chair	chaired
approve	approved	complete	completed
arrange	arranged	conduct	conducted

PRESENT	PAST	PRESENT	PAST
consult	consulted	operate	operated
control	controlled	organize	organized
coordinate	coordinated	plan	planned
decide	decided	produce	produced
design	designed	provide	provided
develop	developed	punch	punched
enter	entered	research	researched
establish	established	schedule	scheduled
evaluate	evaluated	select	selected
examine	examined	serve	served
guide	guided	shout	shouted
help	helped	slap	slapped
hire	hired	solve	solved
identify	identified	stab	stabbed
inspect	inspected	supervise	supervised
investigate	investigated	talk	talked
manage	managed	train	trained
monitor	monitored		

As with almost everything in grammar, exceptions always follow rules. While most verbs, called **regular verbs**, follow the foregoing pattern of present and past tense, about 100 commonly used verbs *do not*. Verbs that do not form their past tense by adding "-ed" are called **irregular verbs.**

PRESENT	PAST	PRESENT	PAST
am	was	leave	left
cut	cut	get	got
shot	shot	blow	blew
flee	fled	go	went
run	ran	draw	drew
drive	drove	read	read
drink	drank	lie (to rest)	lay
fight	fought	lay (to place)	laid
break	broke	swear	swore
hit	hit	write	wrote
spit	spat	build	built
dive	dove	teach	taught
lead	led		
know	knew		

Errors to Avoid With Verbs

1. Learn the irregular verbs. Do not add "-ed" to irregular verbs.

   NO: He **hitted** the car with his fist.

   YES: He **hit** the car with his fist.

| NO: | I **sweared** to tell the truth. |
| YES: | I **swore** to tell the truth. |

2. Do not use the present tense of the verb for the past tense.

NO:	Yesterday, he **sees** her twice.
YES:	Yesterday, he **saw** her twice.
NO:	Tuesday, I **says** to my friend, "Let's go to the store."
YES:	Tuesday, I **said** to my friend, "Let's go to the store."

3. Do not shift tenses in the same phrase, sentence, or paragraph.

NO:	He **runs** into the room and **pointed** the gun.
YES:	He **runs** into the room and **points** the gun.
NO:	The officer **forgot** the evidence and **runs** back for it.
YES:	The officer **forgot** the evidence and **ran** back for it.

4. Make sure that the subject and verb of the sentence agree in number (i.e., either both are singular or both are plural).

NO:	All of the officers, including Captain Shields, **hopes** the criminal is arrested.
YES:	All of the officers, including Captain Shields, **hope** the criminal is arrested.
NO:	Every one of you **know** your *Miranda* warning.
YES:	Every one of you **knows** your *Miranda* warning.

Notable Exception: The verb "plead" has long been considered an irregular verb that formed its past tense as "pled." However, updated style guides now consider pled to be a colloquial past-tense form of the verb plead but not the accepted form. As further proof of the change from pled to pleaded, a senior litigation associate at Alston & Bird, Brian Boone, conducted a Westlaw search revealing the United States Supreme Court used "pleaded" in more than 3,000 opinions and "pled" in only 26. As further evidence of the change, in some of those 26 opinions where the U.S. Supreme Court used "pled," it was merely quoting others.[1]

Adjectives and Adverbs

Adjectives and adverbs are modifiers. They always appear in relation to some other word. An **adjective** modifies or describes a noun, pronoun, or any other word or group of words playing the part of a noun. Adjectives tell what kind of, which, or how many.

- Living **well** is **the best** revenge.

- The **opposing** team played an **aggressive, sophisticated** game.

Adverbs modify verbs, adjectives, or other adverbs. They tell how, when, and where.

- **Slowly** he turned and saw her waiting **patiently there.**

- The book is **more easily** understood if you read **quickly** through the **least** difficult chapters **first.**

Most adverbs end in "-ly" but not all do. To add confusion to the situation, some adjectives end in "-ly" also.

ADJECTIVES	ADVERBS
truthful	truthfully
intentional	intentionally
theoretical	theoretically
cowardly	cowardly
hourly	hourly
lovely	now
lively	quite
homely	soon
orderly	very
friendly	often
kindly	then
timely	when
lonely	down
jolly	yet
still	
here	
too	
around	
almost	

Rather than the way the word ends, the difference between adjectives and adverbs actually depends on the way the word functions in the sentence. If the word modifies or describes a noun, it is an adjective. If it modifies an adjective, adverb, or verb, the word is an adverb.

Prepositions

Prepositions are connecting words that connect the word or words that follow them to the other part of the sentence. The preposition and the word or group of words that follow it are called a **prepositional phrase.**

The following table contains a list of the most commonly used prepositions:

Aboard	About	Above	Across
After	Against	Along	Among
Around	As	At	Before
Behind	Below	Beneath	Beside
Besides	Between	Beyond	But

By	Concerning	Despite	Down
During	Except	For	From
In	Inside	Into	Like
Near	Of	Off	On
Onto	Opposite	Out	Outside
Over	Past	Since	Through
Throughout	Till	To	Toward
Under	Underneath	Until	Up
Upon	With	Within	Without

The next table provides examples of **compound prepositions**:

According to	Ahead of	As of	Aside from
Because of	In addition to	In back of	In front of
In spite of	Instead of	In view of	Next to
On account of	Out of	Prior to	

Errors to Avoid With Prepositions

Do not overuse or omit necessary prepositions in formal writing. Remember that by the nature of their definitions, the words we "tack" prepositions to in overuse situations already mean what we are attempting to say. An example of overuse that occurs quite frequently involves "stand up." The word "stand" means to bring your body to an upright position; therefore, to add the word "up" to this phrase is not necessary and redundant.

In the other extreme, the omission of necessary prepositions makes your writing nonparallel. Parallelism is an important quality in clear and coherent writing. When you omit prepositions, you allow your reader to interpret the writing, and his or her interpretations may not agree with your original meaning.

Overuse

NO: Let's divide **up** the paperwork.

YES: Let's divide the paperwork.

NO: When did they finally get **down** to the problem?

YES: When did they finally get to the problem?

Omission

NO: She was concerned **about** George and his many cats.

YES: She was concerned **about** George and **about** his many cats.

NO: **At** his office and home, he tried to be the same person.

YES: **At** his office and **at** home, he tried to be the same person.

Conjunctions

Conjunctions are also connecting words, much like prepositions. They connect words, phrases, and clauses. Four kinds of conjunctions exist: **coordinating conjunctions, conjunctive adverbs, correlative conjunctions,** and **subordinating conjunctions**.

Coordinating Conjunctions

Coordinating conjunctions connect parts of a sentence that are equal. The following are commonly used coordinating conjunctions: **and, but, yet, for, or, nor,** and **so.** Coordinating conjunctions may join a word to another word: Mom **and** Dad, Jill **or** Mary, firm **yet** kind, slowly **but** surely. They may also join a phrase to another phrase: out of sight **and** out of mind, running down the street **or** meandering through the traffic.

Conjunctive Adverbs

Conjunctive adverbs are used to connect independent clauses and to illustrate the relationship between these clauses. Clauses joined by a conjunctive adverb must be punctuated by either a semicolon or a period. Conjunctive adverbs often serve as transitional words connecting one paragraph to another. Examples of conjunctive adverbs are **therefore, however, consequently, accordingly, for this reason, for example, on the other hand, furthermore, besides, moreover, still, likewise, in addition, nevertheless, indeed, thus, on the contrary,** and **hence**.

- He won the choral competition; **consequently**, he went on to have a successful career.

- I would like to visit my parents; **however**, I am extremely busy at work and have no time.

- His testimony provided many fine insights. **Moreover**, it was eloquently spoken.

Correlative Conjunctions

Correlative conjunctions always come in pairs: both–and, either–or, neither–nor, if–then, not only–but also, since–therefore. The parts of the sentence they join *must* be parallel.

- **Either** the captain **or** chief must preside.

- **Since** you were late, **therefore** I cannot seat you.

- **Neither** your crying **nor** your protesting will change my opinion.

Since the sentence elements you join with correlative conjunctions must be equivalent, avoid the following mistakes:

NO: Her main interests were **that she succeed and running**.

YES: Her main interests were **success and running**.

NO: She loved him dearly **but not his dog**.

YES: She loved him dearly, **but she did not love his dog**.

Subordinating Conjunctions

Unlike coordinating conjunctions which connect parts of the sentence that are equal, subordinating conjunctions are used to connect parts of a sentence that are unequal. Some examples of subordinating conjunctions are **as**, **since**, **provided that**, **in order that**, **until**, **how**, **where**, **because**, **although**, **after**, **when**, **if**, **so that**, **as though**, **though**, **before**, **while**, **unless**, and **that**. Typically, subordinating conjunctions introduce descriptive clauses and connect to the main clause.

- I'll go with you **provided that** you allow me to drive.

- **Because** she did not run quickly, she arrived late.

- He will call home **after** his meeting.

- **If** you dislike the noise of the city, move to the country.

Having reviewed the parts of speech, we will now examine their placement in the sentence structure.

PARTS OF THE SENTENCE

What is a **sentence**? A sentence may be as simple as two words: **He ran.** A sentence may also be a group or collection of words that may be complex. In either instance, a sentence is designed to convey a complete thought. It is the basis for communication. Every sentence has two parts: a **subject** and a **predicate**. The subject is the noun—the person, place, thing, or idea. The predicate is the verb—the action taking place. In order to form a complete sentence, you must have a subject and a verb. In some sentences, however, no apparent subject (noun) is present. In these instances, most often commands, the subject is understood to be "you."

- **[You]** Run as fast as you can!

- **[You]** Drop the gun!

- **[You]** Stop the car!

A sentence should have a certain order or design. This order may follow this sequence: SUBJECT-VERB-DIRECT OBJECT.

- James smokes cigars.

- Bill drives cabs.

A more complex design may follow this sequence: SUBJECT-VERB-INDIRECT OBJECT-DIRECT OBJECT.

- Bill gave me some flares.

- The captain promised me the promotion.

Sentence Errors

Two of the most common and confusing structural problems are dangling participles and misplaced modifiers. These errors create confusion because the sentence is unclear. The reader is forced to try to determine the writer's intent. This lack of clarity is particularly troublesome in police reports that rely on facts and accuracy. The investigator may not interpret the report in the same manner as it was written by the initial responding officer. Furthermore, this ambiguity may present a clever defense attorney with an avenue of attack in the officer's court presentation.

NO:	I saw two stores and a movie theater walking down the street.
YES:	Walking down the street, I saw two stores and a movie theater.
NO:	He found a black Labrador driving his truck through town.
YES:	Driving his truck through town, he found a black Labrador.
NO:	The officer saw the airplane pulling into his space.
YES:	Pulling into his space, the officer saw the airplane.
NO:	He climbed the ladder with a bad leg.
YES:	He climbed the ladder even though he had a bad leg.
NO:	I saw two boys running down the street with a television.
YES:	While I was watching, two boys ran down the street carrying a television.
NO:	He was shot in the driveway.
YES:	He was standing in his driveway when he was shot.
NO:	He went missing.
YES:	He is missing, or he cannot be located. He disappeared or vanished.

Sentence Fragments, Run-On Sentences, and Parallel Structure

Sentence fragments, run-on sentences, and a lack of parallel structure are three other common errors. **Sentence fragments** are incomplete thoughts that occur because either a verb or a noun is missing. Sentence fragments frequently occur because police officers write like they speak in a conversation. Sentence fragments in conversation are acceptable since both parties are present and understand the context of the discussion. However, when only one party is privileged to the communication, sentence fragments damage the integrity of the writer.

NO:	And danced for joy at the news.
YES:	She danced for joy at the news.
NO:	A tree as old as your father.
YES:	The tree is as old as your father.

NO:	No one. Not even the chief.
YES:	No one, not even the chief, could do it.

Run-on sentences occur because of a lack of punctuation or an inability of the writer to organize thoughts appropriately. Run-on sentences are often a result of officers attempting to hurriedly write reports due to an increase in calls for service. Occasionally, when officers save the report-writing task for the end of the shift, run-on sentences become a natural result of this hurried attempt to complete the job and go home.

NO:	You run too fast your side will hurt.
YES:	You run too fast, and your side will hurt. OR You run too fast; your side will hurt.
NO:	It was a beautiful day the sun was shining.
YES:	It was a beautiful day because the sun was shining.
NO:	The suspect said the gun was fired once I think it was fired more.
YES:	The suspect said the gun was fired once, but I think it was fired more.

To eliminate run-on sentences or to correct them, many writers will simply insert a comma between the clauses. However, they are just creating another error—the **comma splice**.

NO:	Speak softly, someone is listening.
YES:	Speak softly; someone is listening. OR Speak softly, because someone is listening.
NO:	If you know, you must tell us, we will handle the investigation.
YES:	If you know, you must tell us. Then, we will handle the investigation.

Like ideas should be expressed in a like manner. **Parallel structure** in sentence writing means that like elements of a sentence are written in similar form.

NO:	The suspect shot into the roof, wall, and floor.
YES:	The suspect shot into **the roof, the wall, and the floor**.
NO:	The drunk driver failed to properly perform the heel-to-toe walk, balance test, and the finger-to-nose test.
YES:	The drunk driver failed to properly perform **the heel-to-toe walk, balance test, and finger-to-nose test**.

As mentioned earlier, punctuation is a way to organize thoughts and express those thoughts clearly to others. Punctuation serves as the ties that bind sentences together. Sentences form the foundation of paragraphs, and paragraphs act as columns that support the crest or theme of the story the writer is attempting to relate or convey.

PUNCTUATION

For purposes of this chapter, four basic components of punctuation will be discussed. These components are the end-of-sentence punctuation (i.e., the period, the question mark, and the exclamation point), the comma, the semicolon, and the colon.

Period, Question Mark, and Exclamation Point

The **period** is the most powerful form of punctuation. It denotes the end of a complete thought. A **question mark** and an **exclamation point** are also used to end sentences. Question marks follow direct questions; exclamation points end emphatic statements.

- Go get my newspaper.

- Where will we go next?

- Would you prepare that report for me?

- Let go of me!

- Help!

Comma

The **comma** is the most versatile form of punctuation. Commas are used to separate words in a series, in dates, and to set off direct quotations. However, one of the most important uses of the comma may be to separate two independent clauses (sentences) with two main ideas (compound sentences). One of the ways to correct run-on sentences is to use the comma. A compound sentence has two subjects and two verbs that are typically joined by a conjunction (and, but, or, yet, for, nor, so). A comma should precede the conjunction in a compound sentence.

- He is supposed to be released from prison tomorrow, **but** who knows if his parole will be approved.

- She said she was separated from her husband, yet she allowed him to enter her apartment.

Semicolon

The **semicolon**, much like the comma, may be used to connect two main ideas in a sentence; however, unlike the comma, it requires no conjunction. A semicolon may also be used to separate items in a series when commas previously have been used in the same sentence. The use of the semicolon in this situation makes the meaning of the sentence clearer.

- It was a dark and stormy night; a shot rang out.

- Violent crimes rose in October, 15%; dropped in November, 10%; and dropped 5% in December. These data indicate no significant increase in violent crimes during the last quarter.

Colon

The **colon** is the least frequently utilized mark of punctuation. Colons most often are used to introduce a series or a list.

- Only a few of the officers were at roll call: Sgt. Smith, Officer Jones, Officer Jackson, and Officer Johnson.

- Please order the following supplies: 50 index cards, 20 envelopes, and 15 pens.

Colons are also used in place of a comma in the introductory salutation of a business letter.

- Dear Sgt. Smith:

- Dear Mayor Jones:

Proper punctuation is as crucial to the construction of a sentence as the use of the appropriate words. Unfortunately, mistakes are made not only in the choice of punctuation but also in the proper selection of words.

FREQUENTLY CONFUSED WORDS

Mark Twain once said, "The difference between the almost right word & the right word is really a large matter—it's the difference between the lightning bug and the lightning."[2] As evidenced by this quote, selecting the inappropriate word changes the entire meaning of a sentence. In today's litigious society, the importance of word selection can be the difference between a dismissal and a judgment. Prior to the sophistication of the 21st century, the 1960s sitcom *All in the Family* supplied a wide list of spoonerisms or malapropisms. Archie Bunker's verbal gaffes served as a platform from which to launch a variety of humorous commentaries concerning race, religion, and ethnicity. Today, these culturally insensitive phrases would serve to alienate audiences. In this same light, criminal justice professionals need to be very conscious of the words or phrases they select in their spoken or written communication.

Most Frequently Confused Words

flee	flea
led	lead
its	it's
there	their/they're
passed	past
were	where
are	our
compliment	complement
ensure	insure
capital	capitol
counsel	council
except	accept

affect	effect
know	now
no	know
knew	new
quiet	quite/quit
than	then
to	too/two
who's	whose
your	you're
personnel	personal
principal	principle

In addition to the most frequently confused words in the foregoing list, you may also want to include the following words to ensure you have an understanding of the correct spelling and usage for them:

All right (two words)	NOT alright
A lot (two words)	NOT alot
Among	NOT amongst
Regardless	NOT irregardless

ABBREVIATIONS VERSUS FULL WORDS

Many abbreviations in writing are standard. We have used them so frequently that they have become second nature, and the full form of the words almost never appears. In other instances, however, abbreviations should be used in only certain circumstances.

Titles and Ranks

Mr., Mrs., and *Ms.* should be used when they appear before names.

- Mr. John Doe

- Mrs. Jane Doe

- Ms. Jackie Doe

Jr. and *Sr.* should be used when they appear as part of a name.

- Robert E. Grubb Jr.

Dr. should be used when the title appears before a name.

- *Dr. Grubb*

Civil and Military Titles. You may abbreviate civil and military titles when they appear before a full name. However, you should not abbreviate them when they appear before a last name ONLY.

- CORRECT:
    - Cmdr. Jim Terry
    - Capt. Mark Rhodes
    - Sgt. Angie Howell
    - Lt. Dickie Parker
- CORRECT:
    - Commander Terry
    - Captain Rhodes
    - Sergeant Howell
    - Lieutenant Parker
- INCORRECT:
    - Cmdr. Terry
    - Capt. Rhodes
    - Sgt. Howell
    - Lt. Parker

You may abbreviate **Reverend** and **Honorable** when they precede a full name and do not follow *the*. You may not, however, abbreviate these titles when they appear before a last name alone or when they follow *the*.

- CORRECT:
    - Rev. Phillip R. Hemby
    - Hon. Margaret Phipps-Brown
- CORRECT:
    - Reverend Hemby
    - the Honorable Margaret Phipps-Brown
- INCORRECT:
    - Rev. Hemby
    - the Hon. Phipps-Brown

Degrees and Certifications

Scholarly degrees (BA, BS, MS, MEd, PhD) can be abbreviated. An important point to remember is that no other title should precede a name when a degree follows it.

CORRECT: K. Virginia Hemby, PhD

INCORRECT: Dr. K. Virginia Hemby, PhD

Time, Days, and Months

Time designations such as a.m., p.m., EST, or CDT are not frequently utilized in law enforcement reports. Most agencies prefer to use the military designation of time (e.g., 0800, 1300, etc.).

CORRECT:	The crime was reported at 8:32 p.m.
CORRECT:	The crime was reported at 2032 hours.
INCORRECT:	The crime was reported at 8:32 PM.
INCORRECT:	The crime was reported at 2032 p.m.

Names of the days of the week and months of the year should be written in full in formal reports and correspondence. However, in officers' field notes or on field interrogation cards, abbreviations for the days of the week and months of the year are acceptable. An important note here, though—not ALL months of the year have abbreviations (March, April, May, June, July).

Days of the Week

Monday	**Mon.**
Tuesday	**Tues.**
Wednesday	**Wed.**
Thursday	**Thurs.**
Friday	**Fri.**
Saturday	**Sat.**
Sunday	**Sun.**

Months of the Year

January	**Jan.**
February	**Feb.**
March	**March**
April	**April**
May	**May**
June	**June**
July	**July**
August	**Aug.**
September	**Sept.**

October	**Oct.**
November	**Nov.**
December	**Dec.**

Acronyms and Familiar Initials

The full forms of initials are often pronounced as words (or acronyms). The full words are almost never written out: *snafu, tarfu, fubar, WYSIWYG, and FOMO.* The full forms of familiar initials in the law enforcement field are also rarely spelled out: FBI, DEA, ATF, ID, DUI/DWI, CCW, DL/OL, VIN, and PI.

Address Abbreviations

In law enforcement, geographical locations are frequently cited. For example, *street, avenue, boulevard, road, building,* and *highway* are often used in both written and oral reports.

Street	**St.**
Avenue	**Ave.**
Boulevard	**Blvd.**
Road	**Rd.**
Building	**Bldg.**
Highway	**Hwy.**

In addition, compass directions are also a major component in offense reports and radio communications. In written form, when a compass direction precedes a street name, it is part of the name and is not abbreviated: *95 Southeast Hickory Street.* When a compass direction follows a street name, however, it indicates a city's section and is abbreviated: *95 Hickory Street, SE.*

Because the use of periods in abbreviations changes from time to time, always check current practice in an up-to-date dictionary. You will find that some abbreviations contain periods, some have optional periods, and some have none.

State Abbreviations

The United States Postal Service has designated two-letter codes for abbreviating the names of states. In all but the most formal writing, you have the option of using these abbreviations.

Alabama	AL	Connecticut	CT
Alaska	AK	Delaware	DE
Arizona	AZ	District of Columbia	DC
Arkansas	AR	Florida	FL
California	CA	Georgia	GA
Colorado	CO	Hawaii	HI

Idaho	ID	New York	NY
Illinois	IL	North Carolina	NC
Indiana	IN	North Dakota	ND
Iowa	IA	Ohio	OH
Kansas	KS	Oklahoma	OK
Kentucky	KY	Oregon	OR
Louisiana	LA	Pennsylvania	PA
Maine	ME	Rhode Island	RI
Maryland	MD	South Carolina	SC
Massachusetts	MA	South Dakota	SD
Michigan	MI	Tennessee	TN
Minnesota	MN	Texas	TX
Mississippi	MS	Utah	UT
Missouri	MO	Vermont	VT
Montana	MT	Virginia	VA
Nebraska	NE	Washington	WA
Nevada	NV	West Virginia	WV
New Hampshire	NH	Wisconsin	WI
New Jersey	NJ	Wyoming	WY
New Mexico	NM		

Capitalization

Everyone understands that the first letter of the first word in a sentence is capitalized. Additionally, we are aware that rules govern capitalization of proper names and titles. However, the rules for capitalizing proper names and titles are complex. Authorities disagree, and conventions change. Add to the mix the fact that a word may be capitalized in one instance but not in another. What you need to know is the solution to capitalization problems can be found in standard up-to-date dictionaries or handbooks. "When in doubt, check it out!"

Capitalization of First Words

As mentioned in the previous paragraph, you should capitalize the first letter of the first word in a complete sentence.

CORRECT: Students broke the security of the computer system.

You should also capitalize the first letter of the first word in a quotation that begins a new sentence within a sentence.

CORRECT: Sergeant Jones asks, "Will all the witnesses be present in court?"

If the quotation does not begin a new sentence, however, the first letter of the first word in the quote is not capitalized.

CORRECT: Mussolini believed that only war put "the stamp of nobility upon the peoples who have the courage to face it."

Capitalization of Proper Names and Proper Adjectives

Proper nouns are the specific names of persons, places, or things. You should capitalize these nouns and any adjectives that are derived from them. The following are categories that illustrate the kinds of words considered proper nouns and adjectives.

Names of People and Animals (Real and Fictional)

- Roy Rogers, James Bond, King Kong

Place Names (Natural and Artificial)

- Australia, Delaware River, Washington Monument, Statue of Liberty, Mars

Organizations (Government, Business, and Social)

- Fraternal Order of Police, Department of State

Historical Names

- Tonkin Resolution, Monroe Doctrine, Custer's Last Stand

Religious Terms

- God, He, His, Him (referring to God in a religious context), Palm Sunday

Names in Education

- University of Southern Mississippi, Department of Business and Interpersonal Communication, Graduate Record Examination

Awards, Medals, and Prizes

- Medal of Honor, Distinguished Service Cross, Silver Star, Bronze Star, Purple Heart

Calendar Terms (Days, Months, and Holidays)

- Friday, July, Memorial Day, Christmas

Product Names—Trade Names and Specific Names

- Nissan Pathfinder, Volkswagen Jetta, Apple iPhone, Maytag washer (The common term of a product's name is usually not capitalized.)

Ethnic Terms—Nationalities, Races, and Languages

- English, Chinese, Sioux, African American

Scientific Terms—Classifications (Except Species) and Chemical Abbreviations

- O (oxygen), Au (gold)

You also capitalize nicknames or substitutes for proper names.

Official Name	Nickname
Mississippi	Magnolia State
New York City	The Big Apple
Mayor Jones	Mayor

Capitalization of Titles of Honor or Rank

You should always capitalize titles of honor or rank when they precede names—whether those titles are governmental, military, ecclesiastical, royal, or professional. In instances where these titles do not precede names, usually you do not capitalize them.

CAPITAL:	In Tennessee, Governor Bill Haslam served two consecutive terms.
NO CAPITAL:	Bill Haslam of Tennessee served as governor of Tennessee and helped its citizens to secure a college education.
CAPITAL:	In 1863, General William S. Rosecrans fought at Chickamauga.
NO CAPITAL:	William S. Rosecrans, a general with the Union army, fought at Chickamauga.
CAPITAL:	After a serious accident, Professor Hemby resigned from teaching.
NO CAPITAL:	After a serious accident, Dr. Hemby, a professor of business and interpersonal communication, resigned from teaching.

Capitalization of Academic and Professional Degrees

Academic and professional degrees should be capitalized only when they appear immediately after a name or when they are abbreviated.

CAPITALS:	John Henry, Doctor of Laws, died yesterday.
CAPITALS:	John Henry, LLD, died yesterday.
NO CAPITALS:	Skip Grubb earned his doctor of laws degree in 2002.
CAPITALS:	Matt Jackson completed his BS degree in 2006.
NO CAPITALS:	Matt Jackson completed his bachelor of science degree in 2006.
CAPITALS:	Mark Smith, CPA, handled the bookkeeping for the organization.
NO CAPITALS:	An independent certified public accountant handled the bookkeeping responsibilities for the organization.

Inappropriate Capitals

The following should not be capitalized:

- Common nouns, even when they appear in phrases that contain capitals

    o American history

    o Dell computer

    o Heinz ketchup

- Words referring to areas of study, unless they are titles of specific courses

  - **CAPITALS:**   Economics 121

  - **NO CAPITALS:**   economics

  - **CAPITALS:**   Algebra II

  - **NO CAPITALS:**   algebra

  - **CAPITALS:**   Microbased Computer Literacy

  - **NO CAPITALS:**   computer literacy

- Words expressing family relationships—mother, father, aunt, uncle, grandmother, and grandfather—unless they precede or substitute for names

  - **CAPITAL:**   I learned to ride my bike by watching Uncle Ruben.

  - **NO CAPITAL:**   I learned to ride my bike by watching my uncle.

  - **CAPITAL:**   When he was 52, Grandfather had a heart attack.

  - **NO CAPITAL:**   When he was 52, my grandfather had a heart attack.

- The words north, south, southwest, and so on when they refer to compass directions. These words should be capitalized when referring to regions.

  - **CAPITAL:**   The South is changing its image.

  - **NO CAPITAL:**   Drive south.

  - **CAPITAL:**   The first trip I took to the Southwest was very exciting.

  - **NO CAPITAL:**   My house lies southwest of town.

SPELLING ERRORS

Spelling errors are a common problem in written communication. As law enforcement professionals, you must read any documentation closely and slowly so that your eyes fall on each individual word. We tend to "read into" our written documents. We know what we intended to say, and when we breeze through our writing quickly with a minimal scan, we are very sure that our words are correct and are spelled correctly. When others read our written documents, however, they note misspelled words, improper word usage, poor grammar, and incorrect punctuation. A good rule of thumb to incorporate into your writing practice is to read each word of your document in reverse order—starting at the end and working backwards; thus, you are reading isolated words and not "ideas" or "what you intended to say."

Another method for detecting misspelled words requires you to be alert to those words that have frequently caused you problems. Some of these words may be *received, occurred,* and *commitment.* If you pay attention to those problem words, you can then take special care in spelling them correctly.

One electronic means of detecting misspelled words is found on your computer in your word processing program. Microsoft Word offers you an opportunity to check your spelling as you write and once you have completed your writing process.

These built-in spell-checkers will check the spelling of words in an entire document or of just a single word. The computer can check hundreds of words in a short amount of time. Unfortunately, even the best of word processing program spell-checkers can neither catch nor correct problems such as confusing words—*affect* for *effect, their* for *there, its* for *it's, manger* for *manager*—since the words are spelled correctly. The form of the word you chose is incorrect.

Checklist for Improving Your Use of a Computer Spell-Checker

☐ Keep a dictionary available to use in checking the definition of terms. Do not rely on the spell-checker to tell you the correct spelling of a word. Oftentimes, the alternative spellings are not useful.

☐ Create a personal dictionary within your word processing program. Proper names, technical terms you use frequently, and other words that may not be included in the computer dictionary can be added. Make sure the words you add, though, are spelled correctly!

☐ Most spell-checkers will not find words that are used in the wrong context. If the words are spelled correctly, the computer spell-checker will ignore them. *I told them the dog was over* **their** *and* **Its** *my belief that time heals all wounds.*

Fifty Most Commonly Misspelled Words[3]

The following list includes the 50 most commonly misspelled words. The spellings given are the American spellings. Variants listed in your dictionary should *not* be used. Remember, just because a particular word or word spelling is included in the dictionary does not mean you should use it. (For example, *ain't* is listed in the dictionary, but that does not mean that using the word is acceptable—or correct.)

1. Anoint	15. Desperate	29. Dissipate
2. Coolly	16. Liquefy	30. Weird
3. Supersede	17. Seize	31. A lot
4. Irresistible	18. Cemetery	32. Accommodate
5. Development	19. Subpoena	33. Embarrassment
6. All right	20. Definitely	34. Ecstasy
7. Separate	21. Occasion	35. Repetition
8. Tyranny	22. Consensus	36. Battalion
9. Harass	23. Inadvertent	37. Despair
10. Desiccate	24. Minuscule	38. Irritable
11. Indispensable	25. Judgment	39. Accidentally
12. Receive	26. Inoculate	40. Liaison
13. Pursue	27. Drunkenness	41. Memento
14. Recommend	28. Occurrence	42. Broccoli

43. Millennium   46. Independent   49. Exceed

44. Yield   47. Sacrilegious   50. Privilege

45. Existence   48. Insistent

Learning to properly spell these commonly misspelled words will aid you in your writing. You may not use them all in your day-to-day work activities; however, when you do find yourself using one of these words, you will know how to spell it correctly.

SUMMARY

In summary, while most criminal justice professionals (police officers, deputy sheriffs, parole officers, bailiffs, etc.) are not particularly interested in nor overly concerned about grammar and sentence structure, these items are just as vital in the preparation and prosecution of their cases as physical evidence or the confession. Inappropriate grammar or sentence structure may jeopardize the credibility or competence of the officer's investigation or testimony. Judges and attorneys have had the benefit of and experience associated with writing courses in law school. Therefore, they may be particularly sensitive to or aware of errors in grammar and sentence structure. If the same amount of care and concern that went into an investigation is given to the spoken word and written report, the credibility of the officer and the organization will be enhanced immensely.

KEY TERMS

Abstract noun 67
Adjective 73
Adverb 73
Antecedent 69
Collective noun 68
Colon 81
Comma 80
Comma splice 79
Common noun 67
Compound preposition 75
Concrete noun 67
Conjunctions 76
Conjunctive adverb 76
Coordinating conjunction 76
Correlative conjunction 76
Demonstrative pronoun 69
Exclamation point 80
Indefinite pronoun 69
Interrogative pronoun 69
Irregular verbs 72
Noun 67
Parallel structure 79
Period 80
Personal pronoun 69
Predicate 77
Preposition 74
Prepositional phrase 74
Pronoun 69
Proper noun 67
Question mark 80
Reflexive pronoun 69
Regular verbs 72
Relative pronoun 69
Run-on sentence 79
Semicolon 80
Sentence 77
Sentence fragment 78
Subject 77
Subordinating conjunction 76
Verb 71

QUESTIONS FOR REVIEW

1. Underline all *nouns* in the following sentences, and identify whether or not they are common, proper, concrete, or abstract.

   a. Jonathon celebrated Memorial Day in Washington, DC, this year.

   b. Spring vacation begins next Friday.

   c. The jury found the defendant not guilty by reason of insanity.

   d. In Plato's dialogue *The Crito*, the concept of justice is discussed.

2. Change the following words to the plural form.

   a. Motto

   b. Stomach

   c. Basis

   d. Idea

   e. Fly

   f. Crisis

   g. Deer

   h. Sheriff

   i. Lady

   j. Appendix

3. In the following sentences, choose the correct form of the pronouns given in parentheses:

   a. Both Mary and (I, me) went to the mall on Saturday.

   b. They missed the bus because of (he, him).

   c. (We, Us) officers must be ready for combat at all times.

   d. You and (I, me) do not understand each other.

   e. Neither Sam nor (they, them) will be going to the FBI Training Academy.

4. Fill in the correct form of the verb in parentheses.

   a. I _____ sad to leave. (to be)

   b. They _____ to walk the dog occasionally. (to forget)

   c. We _____ in the concert. (to sing)

   d. I _____ 20 pages in my book this afternoon. (to read)

5. In the following sentences, underline the *subject* once and the *verb* twice.

   a. John, along with the rest of his battalion, is attending the memorial.

   b. Every officer has a trip planned for vacation.

   c. There go the prisoners on their work detail.

6. In the following sentences, identify and label the adjectives and adverbs.

   a. Her commander is a jolly middle-aged man.

   b. Are they late?

   c. She almost passed the driving examination.

   d. Which gun did you buy?

   e. He answered the lawyer's questions honestly.

7. In the following sentences, underline the prepositional phrase.

   a. They wouldn't think of going without you.

   b. He sat in front of me in training academy class.

   c. They went into the house to get a cup of coffee.

   d. According to the report, crime has gone down.

8. Make any necessary corrections in the use of abbreviations.

   a. The oldest house in town is at 242 E. Orange Street.

   b. My uncle used to tell stories about his friend from the police department, Sgt. Smith.

   c. Miss Jones was the nicest crossing guard in our hometown.

   d. The council elected Robert Grubb, Junior, as its representative.

   e. The officer's case was heard by the Hon. James Cash Jackson.

f. The first lecture will be delivered by Dr. K. Virginia Hemby, Ph.D.

9. In the following sentences, correct any incorrect capitalization.

    a. A Federal indictment was issued by U.S. attorney Benson S. Jackson.

    b. A majority of democrats joined the republicans in support of a resolution sponsored by a senator from West Virginia.

    c. Husbands and Wives may file a Tax Return jointly.

    d. This Summer, the Brookhaven police department announced that three Personal Computers would be given away in a raffle drawing.

    e. During the raid, DEA Agents Armstrong and Jackson seized 248.5 Lbs. of marijuana.

5 PREPARING TO SPEAK
Presentations and Visual Aids

In court, explain how you felt, the fear, the intensity, the emotion of a sudden confrontation, a terrifying moment when a drunk driver skids by only a few inches from you, causing an utterance that would make a sailor blush.

If you are a supervisor, explain to your people that even if you can't explain an expletive enough to justify it, lying about it will be far worse. This is just one of those times when you have to simply take your medicine.

. . . We have some powerful words that let us express ourselves at the deepest emotional level . . . we just need to do it carefully.[1]

—Dave Smith, *Police: The Law Enforcement Magazine*

As children, we all learn that speaking gains us attention. Speaking is how we communicate information about our environment, how we provide feedback to others, and what we do to interact socially with others. We control our own and others' behaviors through speaking.

Considering that each of us speaks every day to friends, colleagues, and superiors, you might be prone to wonder why the idea of making a formal presentation is met with such hesitation, angst, and fear. In an examination of anxiety-inducing situations where participants were asked to rank a list of items based on personal fear, public speaking came out as the number-one response—even surpassing the fear of death.[2] Despite the shortcomings of speech making, though, researchers and the public alike agree that a charismatic speaker can captivate an audience, communicating logically, clearly, and confidently.

Can good speakers be created, or are they born with some innate ability to control an audience? First, we must examine the components of formal speech and everyday communication. Everyday speech and formal presentation share several similarities. When we communicate with friends and family, we organize our speech pattern in an orderly fashion. We would never place words in a random order. When we describe our new job, we would not say "officer police to hired start week in a was as I one." Just as we discussed in Chapter 1, for communication to be effective, the sender and receiver must agree on the meaning of the communication. Therefore, our thoughts must be organized in a logical way so that we can communicate with others. Then, we must construct our conversation using a common language. Even if our thoughts and words are organized logically, to communicate with another, we must share a system of language.

We speak to tell a story, building from the least important fact to the most important fact. Consider how you tell a funny story or joke to your friends. Do you start with the punch line? No, you begin with the main points of the story or joke and build the momentum of your conversation so that when the punch line is delivered, your audience is hanging on your every word to get the full value of the story or joke.

Everyday Speech Versus Formal Presentations	
Similarities	1. Orderly
	2. Builds from least important to most important
	3. Common language
Differences	1. Time constraints
	2. Formal language
	3. Location
	4. Topic
	5. Posture

Just as similarities exist between everyday conversation and formal presentation, so too do differences. In a formal presentation or speech, you are usually required to adhere to certain guidelines concerning the location of the presentation, the amount of time available for you to speak, and the topic about which you must speak. For example, a corrections officer asked to speak at one of the weekly meetings of the local Rotary Club will be told the date and place of the meeting, as well as the amount of time he or she will be given to speak and a selection of topics in which the membership has expressed interest. The officer will then be required to put the information into a formal speech, allowing for time and audience constraints.

While everyday speech is often filled with "colorful metaphors," a formal presentation is much more restrictive. Profanity and "off-color jokes" are inappropriate in this setting. Also, in everyday communication, we tend to be very relaxed in our posture and often lean on desks, chairs, and any available object. In formal situations, however, you should remember to stand up straight and not to rely on any "crutch" when delivering your speech.[3]

PURPOSES OF SPEECHES

The first step in preparing a speech is to determine the purpose—what do you want to accomplish with your speech. Speeches predominantly have six purposes: *to inform, to instruct, to persuade, to inspire or motivate, to activate or stimulate,* or *to entertain.*[4] In each situation, however, the subject matter, the situation, and the persons involved vary.

After deciding the purpose of your speech, the second step in your preparation involves analyzing the audience. You will need to know whether you will have a large, medium, or small audience and what the age, gender, educational levels, experience, and attitudes of the audience are, particularly as they relate to your topic.[5]

To accommodate the varying levels of involvement, four basic types of speech delivery exist: the **impromptu style,** the **extemporaneous style,** the **manuscript style,** and the **memorized style.**[6]

Impromptu Style

An impromptu speech is one that involves no advanced preparation or practice. This delivery style is spontaneous and occurs commonly in small groups and one-on-one situations. Rarely are we asked to give an impromptu speech in a large group or public gathering. When we are asked to deliver an impromptu speech in a large group, the situation often dictates that we be asked to say a few words or to offer a comment.

Impromptu speeches present a challenge to the speaker—to be able to think on your feet. Since you have no preparation time, you must be able to adjust your comments and material for the audience, time, and place. The best rule of thumb is to keep your comments brief and to the point.

Extemporaneous Style

Speeches delivered extemporaneously are both spontaneous and planned. They are planned because you know ahead of time that you are going to be asked to speak on a certain topic. They are spontaneous, however, from the standpoint of your delivery style. You do not memorize your speech, nor do you read it; you deliver the speech and make needed adjustments in your remarks for your audience and the situation. For example, the speaker might prepare a brief outline on his or her topic using index cards. The speaker then proceeds to speak from the outline, filling in the information as he or she moves along.

This delivery style allows the speaker to have a great deal of interaction with the audience and to concentrate more on sharing ideas with the audience rather than on delivering the message. And since it involves a conversational and interactive manner that is generally very effective with listeners, the extemporaneous style of speech delivery is the most popular of all the presentational styles.

Manuscript Style

Many people are afraid of trying to speak spontaneously. They are also afraid of memorizing a speech because they tend to sound wooden and to create the impression in the audience that the speech is memorized. Therefore, they choose what they consider to be the next best thing to memorization—reading the speech in its entirety.

Adults dislike nothing more than having an entire speech *read* to them.[7] When a speaker engages in this type of speaking, he or she is implying that the audience is too unsophisticated to be able to properly read and comprehend the speech themselves. Or perhaps the speaker is indicating that the audience is incompetent or incapable of reading at all! If you plan to read your speech to the audience, just hand out copies and forget about the presentation. Let the audience read the speech for themselves.

In addition to the problems already mentioned, a speaker who chooses the manuscript delivery style loses the ability to interact with the audience. In fact, no eye contact can occur between the speaker and the audience when the speaker's eyes are focused solely on the material being read. If, by chance, the speaker does attempt to make some eye contact during the speech delivery, he risks the possibility of losing his place and becoming embarrassed as he searches to regain it.

The old expression, *never say never*, is true about the speech that is read, however. If I were to advise you to *never* read a speech, you would be receiving some faulty advice! If you must present very technical data that cannot be properly committed to memory or that cannot be spoken about spontaneously, you should read that portion of your speech containing the technical facts. In addition, if you are required to address a controversial topic where the need for precision is vitally important, you should write and then read your comments. A good example in police work involves the media questioning a department representative concerning a crime. The officer's best response is to plan ahead. Write down as many details of the crime as can be legally and ethically released and then read the statement to the reporters. In this way, the officer ensures the proper release of information in a precise manner without fear of being caught off guard or ill prepared.

Memorized Style

A memorized speech really needs no definition since it is exactly what its name implies—a speech that you, the speaker, memorized prior to its delivery. A memorized speech has many disadvantages, the most important one being that a speaker who uses this method of delivery loses the ability to change or modify the speech to accommodate the audience. Also, if for some reason the speaker needed to deviate from the memorized speech, he or she would have difficulty returning to the original point—possibly even forgetting everything and being unable to continue. The major weakness with the memorized speech is that the speaker is so obsessed with simply getting the words to the speech out, that he or she cannot pay attention to details such as listener nonverbal feedback (i.e., questioning expressions and blank expressions).

GUIDELINES FOR AN EFFECTIVE ORAL PRESENTATION

Many things affect the preparation and delivery of an effective speech or presentation. The purpose of the speech, the audience, the location, your choice of vocabulary, your voice control, and your body movements and gestures all play a role in the process. The most important things to remember in any presentation, however, are your purpose and your audience. To whom are you speaking, and why are you speaking to them?

Your Purpose

You cannot prepare for a presentation without first knowing what you want to accomplish in that presentation. Do you want to persuade the members of your community to increase the number of police officers in your district? Do you want to inform your subordinates of important ways to prepare written communication within the department? Regardless of the goal of your presentation, you must have a plan of direction for your speech. A good rule of thumb is to ask yourself, "At the conclusion of my presentation, what do I want my audience (listeners) to remember or to do?"

Your Audience or Listeners

Since the audience is one of the first priorities in the development of the presentation, you must have as much background information as possible in that regard. Language skills, biases, educational backgrounds, and other demographics play a major role in the acceptance and/or rejection of your ideas, concepts, or findings. Also, you must be aware of the existing knowledge of your audience, as well as how vocal the audience is likely to be concerning your topic of presentation. Some specific questions to consider concerning your audience are as follows:

- How will this topic appeal to this audience?

- How can I relate this information to audience members' needs?

- How can I earn respect so that they accept my message?

- Which of the following would be most effective in making my point? Statistics? Graphic illustrations? Demonstrations? Case histories? Analogies? Cost figures?

- What measures must I take to ensure that this audience remembers my main points?[8]

Knowing something about the general characteristics of your listeners may suggest what type of evidence and which authorities will be most effective with them. For example, citing statistics may bore many listeners; but if you are speaking with a group of criminal justice professionals interested in the United States' increasing crime rate, you will find them to be interested in your topic. While demographic information does not offer precise insight into any one individual, this analysis can offer you some general information about groups of people.[9]

ORGANIZING YOUR PRESENTATION

Once the purpose of your speech and the characteristics of your audience have been identified, steps toward the preparation of your oral presentation may be initiated. Your presentation must be clear, concise, and complete. However, in some situations—to protect the integrity of an ongoing investigation or because of the sensitive nature of certain personnel matters—the presentation of some facts may need to be selectively screened or omitted. The selective screening or omission of information is not intended to deceive but merely to ensure the preservation of these matters.

The Perception of the Speaker

The audience in any presentation looks to the speaker for information. That information must be given in a manner that is easily understood by the audience. In that regard, speakers must be aware of several aspects of speech development: language, biases, and delivery. Language patterns should be appropriate for the average educational background and knowledge levels of the audience. Jargon and slang may be appropriate in certain agency presentations but may be inappropriate or offensive to general audiences. Also, grammar and pronunciation skills are vitally important to the audience's perception of the speaker. If an officer responds with an air of confidence, *"Nobody done nothing wrong,"* certain audiences would likely disregard the statement believing the officer to be ill-educated or undereducated and, therefore, ill-informed or even deceptive. In other words, the officer's veracity is in question. However, the officer who boldly states, *"At this time, proper procedure appears to have been followed,"* not only enhances individual credibility but departmental integrity as well. This officer is perceived by most audiences to be competent and truthful.

The Speaker's Voice

The quality of the speaker's voice and the way a speaker moves during a presentation are elements of the delivery. To deliver a successful presentation, loudness, pitch, rate, pauses, articulation, and pronunciation must be considered.

Loudness refers to the volume of the speaker's voice. An audience must be able to hear the speaker, but the speaker must be able to project his or her voice without shouting. However, the speaker must remember to regulate the loudness of his or her voice based on the size of the room and the acoustics.

Pitch defines how high or low the speaker's voice sounds. Appropriate modulation of the pitch enhances certain elements of a presentation. A monotone voice does not denote severity or the gravity of a situation. Frequently, law enforcement officers, while attempting to project a serious image, utilize a monotone. The use of a monotone voice only serves to guarantee that the listener will be easily distracted and that the content of the message will be weakened or lost.

Rate deals with the speed with which the speaker talks. Speakers who speak too rapidly give the impression that they are deceptive or attempting to *gloss over* certain facts. On the other hand, speakers who talk too slowly give the impression of being dimwitted or poorly prepared. Varying the rate of speech is particularly appropriate and effective when the speaker is attempting to emphasize a certain point or to recount familiar material.

Pauses can add emphasis, power, and effective timing to the delivery of presentations. Pauses may add dramatic effect to specific points in a story and may influence the impact of a joke or a series of rhetorical questions, a quotation, or a visual aid. These pauses should be planned for maximum impact in your presentation. Unplanned vocal pauses (umms, ers, you know, ahs), however, detract from the presentation and reduce the speaker's credibility.

Articulation and **pronunciation** refer to the way the speaker vocalizes words in the presentation. While certain variations in pronunciation exist due to international or regional dialects, mispronunciation may hinder an otherwise effective speaker. Southerners tend to drop the "-g" from the endings of words. This speech pattern, though, is not representative of mispronunciation but is part of the colloquialism pattern associated with the Southern dialect. However, if a person used the term *dashhound* instead of *Dachshund* to refer to a specific breed of dog, this would be indicative of a mispronunciation.

The Parts of an Oral Presentation or Speech

Speeches and oral presentations have many things in common with written reports and other documentation. First, they all have a beginning, a middle, and an ending. As such, the parts of an oral presentation or speech include an introduction, the body of the speech, and a conclusion. Therefore, you should introduce the topic and tell your audience what you plan to say; you should effectively say what you intended to say; and then you should conclude with a review of what you just said.

You should also remember to include **verbal signposts** in your speech. Since your audience or listeners cannot flip back through the pages of your speech to review the main points, many of them get lost along the way. A good way to ensure that your audience can identify the main points of your presentation is to include verbal signposts. These *notices of information to come* help your listeners follow the presentation. The following verbal signposts are some examples of previews, summaries, and transitions:

- To preview

  o The next portion of my presentation discusses five reasons . . .

  o Let's now examine the problems associated with . . .

- To summarize

  o Let's review the major issues I've just addressed . . .

  o As you can see, the most significant contributions are . . .

- To switch directions

  o Thus far we've discussed . . . ; now, let's examine . . .

  o I have argued my position that . . . , but an alternate view is . . .

The use of transitional words or phrases also helps to improve your oral presentation. Words and phrases like *therefore, moreover, however, on the other hand, in conclusion, first, second,* and *next* emphasize your points and lead your audience or listeners in the direction you are headed.

The Introduction

The introduction to a speech or oral presentation should account for no more than 10% of the entire presentation. In the first 60 to 90 seconds of the presentation, the audience decides whether the speech has any merit and whether to pay attention to the speaker. The opening of your presentation should strive to accomplish three specific goals:

- "Capture listeners' attention and get them involved.

- Identify yourself and establish your credibility.

- Preview your main points."[10]

Some techniques for effectively introducing your subject are as follows:

- Ask a question. As a speaker, asking a rhetorical question encourages the audience to think of responses without actually answering your question aloud. Generally, a speaker proposes rhetorical questions to an audience because he or she plans to answer them during the presentation.

- Tell a funny story or joke. Using humor is one of the most effective ways of capturing the attention of an audience. Humor establishes an immediate connection between the audience and the speaker.

- Use an anecdote. Recount a short, entertaining account of some event.

- Make a startling statement. Say something unexpected. Remember, however, a difference exists between the effective startling statement and the offensive shock tactic. Using profanity or telling offensive jokes reduces credibility.

- Quote someone. Quoting a well-known authority on your subject matter adds credibility to your speech or presentation.

- Demonstrate something. Bring in prototypes or samples to demonstrate a process or product. Demonstrations are attention-grabbers.

The Body

The body is the heart of your speech or presentation and should receive the most attention and should account for the most speaking time. Support your main points through evidence, statistics, brief or extended examples, testimony, quotations, or analogies. An important point to remember is that listeners have a limited ability to absorb information. As a rule, limit your presentation to between two and five main points. Support each of those points with a minimal amount of explanation and detail. Remember to keep the information simple and to the point. Unlike a book, a speech offers the audience no material or pages to review. One caveat to remember: Always prepare more material than you think you will need. Experienced presenters know that having something in reserve is important just in case they finish quicker than anticipated.

The Conclusion

The conclusion of a speech or oral presentation serves four important functions: to summarize your message, to place your message in a broad context, to personalize your message, and to call for specific future action. The conclusion should, like the introduction, take about 10% of the presentation time. The speaker may use the same techniques in the conclusion as in the introduction—anecdotes, rhetorical questions, quotes, demonstrations, startling statements, and humor.

You should never end a presentation with a statement such as "*I guess that's all I have.*" Remember that the conclusion is your last chance to ensure that your audience gets your main points. Use this opportunity to review your major points and focus on the goal of your speech. You should specifically concentrate on what you want your audience to remember, to do, or to think. Use some of the remaining time to ask for questions. If the audience is hesitant, you could offer to take individual questions following the completion of the presentation.

USING VISUALS IN YOUR PRESENTATION

The impact of a visual aid should never be underestimated. Visual aids can be an exciting and dramatic addition to any speaker's presentation. If properly prepared, the visual aid may increase the speaker's ability to establish a point and may enhance retention by the audience members.

Visual aids serve two basic purposes: (1) to enhance a presentation by reinforcing the important points covered in the presentation and (2) to provide the speaker with an alternate delivery method or system. The use of visuals in a presentation gives the speaker an opportunity to redirect the audience's attention away from him or her so that any anxiety (stage fright) can be minimized. Visuals may be utilized in the form of an introduction or segue or as a conclusion to a presentation.

Types of Visual Aids

The choice of visual aid for a presentation may vary widely, anything from models and objects to photographs and slides are possible. In selecting visual aids, the speaker must adhere to certain guidelines regarding the purpose of the speech, the size of the audience, the environment or location of the presentation, and the speaker's skill and expertise in utilizing the selected medium. Remember that visual aids complement a presentation, not stand in the place of the presentation.

Objects and Models

To use **objects and models** as visuals in a presentation, the environment or location must be small in scope. Attempting to pass an object or model around a room of several hundred people would be ill advised. Attention would be focused away from the speaker and onto the object or model and its position in the audience. However, in intimate group settings, the utilization of models or objects is entirely appropriate when the presentation would be enhanced by their use.

Flip Charts, Marker Boards, and Posters

Flip charts, marker boards, and posters are most useful when presenting information to small interactive groups. They provide an excellent opportunity for problem-solving or idea-generating discussions. These media enhance speaker–audience interaction by allowing the speaker to ask questions and then to record key ideas as they are contributed.

Handouts

Speakers often use handouts as reference materials for the audience. However, timing of the distribution of handouts is important to the success of the presentation. Many speakers distribute printed materials as they speak so that the audience may refer to them. If the material is particularly complex, then the distribution of the handouts at the beginning of the presentation might be beneficial. When the handout is merely to reinforce the important points covered in the presentation, however, delaying the distribution until the conclusion of the presentation would be the better option.

Computer-Generated Presentations

Programs such as Microsoft PowerPoint and alternative programs such as Prezi, Slidebean, and Keynote have allowed speakers to create computer-generated slides. These programs offer speakers options such as embedding sounds, animation, and video clips to enhance the quality of their presentation. A drawback, however, to the use of these types of media is that speakers must be well trained in their use so that appropriate design guidelines are followed and the visual operates smoothly and seamlessly during the presentation. Table 5.1 compares the features of some of the visual aids that we have examined in this section.

Designing Visual Aids

In today's technological society, some speakers become dependent on the use of visuals in a presentation. However, the excessive use of visual aids detracts from the

TABLE 5.1 ■ Some Examples of Visual Aids Used in Presentations			
Type of Visual	**Audience/ Environment**	**Advantages**	**Disadvantages**
Flipcharts and whiteboards	Small Informal	1. Aids in organization 2. Helps to summarize 3. Low human error 4. Informal 5. Flexible	1. Not very dramatic 2. No "bells and whistles"
Document camera	Medium to large Formal or informal	1. Portable 2. Flexible 3. Easily tailored to different groups 4. Easy to use	1. Limited visual impact 2. Can be distracting
Multimedia slides	Medium to large Formal or informal	1. High impact 2. Easily tailored to different groups 3. Flexible 4. Very persuasive 5. Able to show motion or animation and to use sound bites	1. Expense 2. Requires technical skills 3. May overshadow the speaker or the topic being presented 4. May provide more flash than substance 5. Not easily transportable 6. Requires equipment
Handouts	Any size (Unlimited) Formal or informal	1. Easy 2. Portable 3. Relatively inexpensive 4. Aids in organization 5. Serves as reminder of presentation	1. Not flexible 2. Can be bulky 3. When to distribute? 4. Generate minimal impact

effectiveness of the message. A caveat to keep in mind is that visuals should supplement your presentation and should reinforce important points. Also, be aware of your description of the visual. Do not repeat everything contained on the visual when it is displayed. Allow the audience to scan the information projected on the visual by pausing after the initial main point. Speaking on top of the visual only forces the audience to choose between what you are saying and what the visual is projecting. In other words, you are competing with your own visual for the audience's attention.

The following guidelines are useful in the development and design of effective visual aids:

Simplicity

In the design of visual aids, particularly computer-generated slides, the speaker should remember to adhere to the 6 × 6 rule or the rule of 7. These rules limit the number of words per line and lines per slide such that you have either six lines of text with six words per line or seven lines of text with seven words per line for each slide. These lines of text should not be full sentences or paragraphs but merely phrases or words—much like you would use when drafting an outline for a report, paper, or presentation.[11]

For most individuals, processing more than seven points of information at any given time may be too complex or even impossible. To ensure the speaker's message is communicated in a simple and direct manner, visuals should be limited to a series of related concepts.

Size

The total size of the audience is equal to the total size of the visual plus the total size of the print or font used in the visual. The larger the audience, the greater the overall size of the visual and the greater the size of the print or font within the visual. In this manner, all audience members are afforded an opportunity to clearly see and to process the information contained in the visual.

Color

Color can enhance the effectiveness of a visual when used correctly, making the visual easier to read and more attractive. However, when used incorrectly, color has the opposite effect on the visual, making it more difficult to read. Research has indicated that blue backgrounds for computer-generated presentations are the most effective. Using a yellow or white type on the blue background produces the best results among all audiences. Since more males than females are color-blind, the use of colors like red and green or red and blue as contrasting background and print selections may render those visuals useless to a significant portion of the audience.[12] Remember to use the same color palette for every visual and to maintain the same print type or style throughout.

Appendix A is an example of ineffective PowerPoint slides.

Appendix B is an example of effective PowerPoint slides.

You can find these appendices online at **http://study.sagepub.com/grubb**

Points to Remember in Using Visual Aids Effectively

Visual aids are an enhancement to any presentation and should be used whenever possible. However, a few rules apply that will make your presentation run more smoothly.

Avoid Overdoing It

Some people believe that if a few visuals are good, then a lot of them must be better. You should refrain from adopting this attitude. Visual aids should be used only for major points or for information requiring clarification. Too many visuals will impact their effectiveness. If your audience would find a visual helpful in understanding a specific point in your speech or in remembering important ideas, then a visual aid at that point in the presentation would be appropriate. However, if the use of a visual (regardless of how exciting it would be) does not contribute to your overall presentation in terms of the audience's understanding, then do not use the visual.

Refrain From Cramming Too Much Information on Each Visual

Remember the 6 × 6 rule and/or the rule of 7: Use only six or seven lines of text per slide and include only six or seven words per line of text. Each visual should headline one major point.

Use Appropriate Text or Type Styles

Remember that everyone in the room needs to be able to see and read your visuals. Be sure you use the correct size type (font) so that your visual can be seen from any point in the room.

Allow Appropriate Time for the Audience to Read and Digest Information on the Visual

Put the visual up so the audience can see it. Give them time to read and digest the information contained in the visual before you begin explaining it to them. You should paraphrase what the visual says and not read it word for word. And you should *never* turn your back to the audience when displaying a visual and/or explaining a visual.

Practice, Practice, Practice

When you rehearse your presentation, include the use of visuals in your preparation. Make sure you know how to use the equipment properly and that you allow sufficient time for the audience to read the visual. **Remember**: Always speak to your audience—not to your visual.

Prepare for Problems

The best intentions of every speaker in the use of visuals are often sidetracked by failures in technology, air carriers who lose or misdirect luggage, mail and/or package services who "fail to deliver," and any number of incidents or accidents outside the realm of the speaker's control. The best plan of defense for these types of problems is an adequate offense: *Have a backup plan!*

When you choose to use a PowerPoint presentation as the visual in your speech, you should remember that in the event of computer failure, cloud password failure (you forgot it!), USB problems, or server or Wi-Fi issues, you can always rely on handouts. Therefore, as the speaker, you should always prepare enough sets of handouts of your presentation to give to each attendee at your speech. In addition, you should print one full copy of each slide using a color printer so that, in the event your venue has a document camera and projection unit, you would be able to project each slide. Your audience would get the full effect of the color presentation they would have gotten through PowerPoint, but the power of point-and-click technology of the computer and PowerPoint interaction would be eliminated.

A good point to reinforce here is that you should always store or save your visual in a safe location. If you are using cloud storage (via Google, Dropbox, Microsoft, or Apple), you should make sure you remember your password to access your cloud storage. In addition, you should send yourself a copy of your visual file to your e-mail. In this way, you have access to your presentation file in two locations—and you can make it three if you desire to save your presentation file to a USB flash drive and to physically carry the flash drive to your speech location.

If you are traveling by plane to the venue where you will deliver your presentation, and you have handouts, objects, photographs, or other visuals (not requiring a computer), you will want to carry those items in your carry-on luggage. This small acquiescence to discomfort at being unable to check your briefcase or laptop case will ensure that your visual arrives at your destination at the same time you arrive. Thus, you eliminate the possibility of the "lost" or "misdirected" luggage problem. Additionally, if you carry your own visual with you to your speech destination, you also eliminate the need for a mail or package carrier service. Again, you are planning ahead by handling your own visual needs and not relying on others to ensure its or their arrival.

Another means of ensuring your speech will occur without a problem is to get an adequate estimate of the number of attendees at your presentation. By having an accurate count of those individuals who will be present at your speech, you will have a sufficient number of handouts to distribute at your presentation so that each person gets his or her own copy. Always err on the side of too many handouts rather than too few. If you are given an estimate of 30 attendees, make 40 copies of your handouts to take with you. Again, you will be better prepared with too many copies than too few. Also, if you are speaking at a meeting or conference where speeches or presentations overlap, individuals who are unable to attend your presentation will greatly appreciate receiving a handout from your speech. Extra copies of handouts rarely go to waste in these settings.

Overcoming Barriers to Effective Presentations

Stage fright is a natural occurrence. Nearly every person suffers from some form of stage fright. Being afraid results from physiological responses or changes in our bodies that occur when we are faced with threatening situations. The fight-or-flight syndrome provides your body with increased energy to deal with those situations. The dry mouth, sweaty hands, increased heartbeat, and butterflies in your stomach are all responses to your body's perceived threat.

Ask any speaker if he or she suffers from stage fright, and you will find that the honest ones all admit they do. Consequently, all effective presenters know that successful presentations do not just happen; they require practice. Thoroughly preparing and rehearsing presentations can lessen stage fright. Realize that fear is not an either/or matter but more a matter of degree. Most of us fall between the two extremes of no nervousness at all and total fear.[13] In fact, research conducted by Gerald Phillips, a speech scholar, reveals that nervousness helps us to do our best job.[14] If we are unconcerned about a presentation, we will probably not put forth our best effort; thus, we will not do our best job. Keep in mind these reassuring facts about stage fright:

- Very few people are unable to make it through a speech, despite their nervousness. You may not enjoy your experience, but you can still deliver an effective speech.

- Members of an audience are not as likely to recognize your stage fright as you might think.

- When you are well prepared, your nervousness will be lessened. You show more nervousness when you are not well prepared or when you believe you are not well prepared.

- Speak as often as you can. Volunteer to make speeches or presentations whenever possible. Experience is the best teacher and offers you an opportunity to gain confidence in your ability.[15]

CHECKLIST FOR PREPARING AND ORGANIZING ORAL PRESENTATIONS[16]

Getting Ready to Speak

☐ **Identify your purpose**. Decide what you want your audience to believe, to remember, or to do when you finish. Aim your speech toward this purpose.

☐ **Analyze the audience**. Examine the demographic makeup of your audience, and adapt your message toward their knowledge and needs.

Organizing the Introduction

☐ **Get the audience involved**. Begin your speech with an attention-getting opener. You can ask a question, tell a story, give a startling fact, use a quote, make a promise, or tell a self-effacing joke.

☐ **Establish yourself**. You need to identify yourself and your position, expertise, knowledge, and qualifications so that you establish your credibility.

☐ **Preview your main points**. Introduce your topic, and give a summary of the principal parts of your presentation.

Organizing the Body

☐ **Develop two to four main points**. Focus on two to four major issues so that you can streamline your overall topic.

☐ **Arrange the points logically**. Sequence your points either chronologically, from most important to least important, by comparison and contrast, or by some other strategy.

☐ **Prepare transitions**. Use bridge statements between each major point so that you connect each item to the next item. Use transitional words or expressions as verbal signposts (to tell your audience where you are going to take them next). Examples of transitions include *first, second, then, however, consequently, on the contrary,* and so on.

☐ **Have extra material ready**. Always be prepared for the unknown. Be prepared with more information and/or visuals in case you have additional time to fill.

Organizing the Conclusion

☐ **Review your main points**. Emphasize your main ideas in the conclusion so that your audience will remember them.

☐ **Provide a final focus**. Close by telling your audience how they can use the information you have provided, why you have spoken, or what you want them to do.

Designing Visual Aids

☐ **Select your medium carefully**. Consider the size of your audience, the degree of desired formality in this presentation, the cost and ease of preparation of visuals, and potential effectiveness.

☐ **Highlight main ideas**. Use visual aids to illustrate major points only. Keep them brief and simple.

☐ **Use aids skillfully**. Talk to the audience—not the visuals. Paraphrase the content of the visuals; do not read their content to the audience.

Developing Electronic Presentations

☐ **Learn to use your software program**. Know the basics of using the software, such as template and slide layout designs and how you can adapt them to your needs.

☐ **Select a pleasing color palette**. Work with five or fewer colors for your entire presentation.

☐ **Use bulleted points for major headings**. Make sure your points are all parallel and follow the 6 × 6 rule or the rule of 7.

Prior to Your Presentation

Prepare!

Thorough preparation is one of the most effective ways to reduce stage fright. When you know your subject matter, you feel more confident. People who try to "wing it" are the ones who suffer the worst butterflies—and the ones who make the worst presentations.[17]

Rehearse

Rehearsing involves practicing your entire presentation. You can use note cards on which to place your topic sentences. Use your cards as you practice, and remember to include visual aids in your practice sessions as well.

A good way to check your presentation savvy is to video record your practice sessions. Make your practice session and environment as close to the speech one as possible. When you view your video practice session, concentrate on your message and delivery style. Pay attention to the following:

- **Your speed.** Are you speaking too fast? Too slowly?

- **Your volume.** Are you speaking too softly? Can everyone in the room hear you?

- **Your nonverbal message.** Are you engaging in any annoying habits, such as jingling the coins or keys in your pants pocket, tugging on your clothes, swaying, pulling on your hair (or ears), or stroking your beard or mustache?

- **Your enthusiasm.** Are you excited and animated during your presentation? Are you speaking in a monotone and boring the audience?

Time Your Presentation

When you are given the opportunity to deliver a speech or presentation and are not provided any parameters for time, you want to limit your presentation to no more than 20 minutes since most audiences tend to lose interest if you go longer than that. However, the length of your presentation will depend on its purpose. Are you trying to inform, persuade, or entertain your audience? What is the message you want your audience to remember from your presentation?

When your goal has been decided for your speech, all preparation has been concluded, and you are ready to begin practice, you should use a timer to practice your presentation. Begin speaking and continue speaking until your presentation is complete in its entirety, even if the timer sounds. You need to know exactly how much time your speech takes so that you can modify areas where you can eliminate excess material to keep your presentation within the allotted time.

Check Your Location

You have spent a great deal of time and effort in the preparation for your presentation. You have researched your topic and your audience, planned and drafted your speech outline, and practiced your delivery. Now comes the next step—visiting the location of your presentation.

You need to know what to expect in the room where you plan to speak. As soon as possible, you should either visit the site of your presentation or contact the person who arranged for you to speak and ask for details. You need to know how large the room is so you can plan most adequately for the appropriate visuals. You also need to know what type of audiovisual equipment is available in the room and whether you will need to wear a microphone or to stand behind a podium or lectern. On the day of your presentation, you should plan to arrive at least 1 hour before your speech to double-check the room, to correct any problems, and to mentally prepare yourself.

Breathe!

While waiting to begin your presentation, use deep breathing techniques to help you relax. Take in deep breaths, and let them out slowly. Count to 10 as you inhale and exhale. Realize that you are prepared for this speech. Feel confident of your ability.

The Presentation

The moment has arrived for you to deliver your speech. The following list of guidelines will help you make the best out of your speaking opportunity.

- Calmly walk to the podium, the lectern, or the front of the room. Take a moment to gather your thoughts and to take a deep breath. *Relax!*

- Begin your presentation with direct eye contact. You can establish a rapport with your audience when you establish eye contact and maintain it. You also appear confident and knowledgeable. Try to maintain eye contact through your entire presentation. Remember not to pick out one or two people in the room on which to focus. You will make these individuals very uncomfortable if you look only at them, and others may feel uncomfortable from the message you are conveying. Try to establish eye contact with several members of your audience around the room. Try to hold eye contact with your audience members for a few seconds and then move on to others.

- Moderate your speed and vocalics. Sometimes speakers tend to rush or to talk rapidly because they are nervous. Another noticeable sign of unease is fillers like *um, ah, er, like,* and *you know.* You can just remain silent while thinking of your next idea since silence is preferable to a speech punctuated by ah, um, and er.

  - If you happen to stumble in your presentation, just move on. Do not apologize or confess to being nervous. The audience might not have noticed your faux pas anyway; and if they did, they tend to quickly forget mistakes.

- If you plan to move around during your presentation, do so naturally and casually. Just remember not to pace—otherwise, you will resemble one of the shooting games at the fair, and **you** will be the target people are trying to hit! Pacing is not a natural or casual movement!

- Remember to use your visual aids and to follow the outline for your speech. Summarize your presentation and conclude when you say, "In conclusion." The audience does not appreciate your talking for 5 or 10 more minutes after you have announced your intent to conclude.

- When you have finished your presentation, ask for questions—when the situation allows. Try to repeat a question when it is asked so you can be sure everyone in the room heard it. Repeating the question also gives you time to formulate your response.

- If you have prepared handouts for the audience, you should wait until the conclusion of your presentation before distributing them. If you offer handouts to the audience in advance of or at the beginning of your presentation, you risk losing a high percentage of your audience. The distraction of pages turning and audience members reading ahead and ignoring the speaker are not conducive to an effective presentation.

- At the conclusion of your presentation, remember to express appreciation to your audience for allowing you the opportunity to speak with them.

Televised or Recorded Presentations (News Reports, Presentations, and Updates)

Rod Bernsen began his career as a radio reporter, becoming a Los Angeles police officer and serving in that role for 17 years before returning to the news media as a reporter for Fox 11 News in Los Angeles. Because of his life experience, Bernsen has a different perspective on the relationship between the media and law enforcement. He understands the difficulties inherent in police work and in explaining that work to citizens who understand only what they see on television—the inaccurate portrayal of the most critical moments of policing.[18]

One of the most important suggestions Bernsen makes is for police departments to become proactive in reporting news or incidents. Many criminal justice agencies sit idly and wait for someone else to report on the occurrences within the community. The problem inherent with this wait-and-see attitude is the distortion of information that proliferates on the airwaves and the Internet because of negative or biased reporting.

Technological innovations have assuredly led to an increase in demand for up-to-date news coverage, and the public has not been shy about finding ways to report their own brand of news through smartphone cameras and Internet applications. Many 24/7 news channels have sprung up with eager reporters attempting to be first on the scene of any breaking news story. Therefore, criminal justice agencies and law enforcement departments have employed their own brand of news reporter, the public information officer.

Many criminal justice agencies and law enforcement departments have a public information officer (PIO) or a chief public information officer (CPIO). This individual directs media and public relations for the agency or department that he or she serves. The PIO manages the writing, editing, and production of materials related to the media and for use by the agency and/or department, other law enforcement agencies, and the public.

The PIO responds to media inquiries about the agency's or department's activities and conducts press conferences and other public meetings, so this individual frequently appears on news and radio programs. The PIO facilitates photographic and audiovisual content of agency and department materials; prepares reports, speeches, copy, scripts, and other written communications; and oversees all social media aspects of the agency and/or department.[19]

PIOs embrace the technology tools available to them, often creating their own online news feeds that push official messages out to the public. By employing Real Simple Syndication (RSS), Twitter, Facebook, and YouTube feeds, PIOs control information and communicate it fairly to all news outlets in their community.[20] Additional information about the use of these technological advances and tools is covered in Chapter 9 of this text.

Criminal justice agencies and law enforcement departments should have experts on standby, ready to speak with reporters and to answer questions to counter the negative messages with fact and thoughtful discourse. The best approach to ensure a skeptical public is convinced of the truthfulness of the information is to have individual officers or members of the agency—not merely PIOs or chiefs and commanders—speak to the media whenever possible. However, few officers and agency members are prepared to deliver off-the-cuff remarks or to answer questions regarding an ongoing investigation or a breaking news incident. They typically were not trained to do so during their academy and/or other agency preparation.

Nonetheless, agencies and departments can select an officer or staff person to handle a communication situation; but before doing so, they must consider the following questions:

- What is the purpose of the meeting? Community update? Question-and-answer session? Issues?

- Who is the best person for the job? The officer on duty? The supervisor? The CIO? Which person can best serve the purpose?

- What message does the agency or department wish to convey—besides addressing the purpose of the meeting itself?

- Are your officers or staff in a position to answer the questions? Would they be comfortable in saying they do not know the answer if they needed to do so?

These questions can be equally effective in preparing the novice officer or staff person, as well as the chief or command-level personnel.[21]

If an agency or department desires further training for its personnel, the Federal Bureau of Investigation offers a Media and Public Relations course to all sworn and professional law enforcement staff. An interesting note here at this section of the text is that the first day of this training is spent discussing image, branding, and perception.[22] Perception is a major part of nonverbal communication, particularly on the part of the audience or listener.

Nonverbal Messages

So what do criminal justice agency members, law enforcement officers, PIOs, chiefs, and commanders need to know to be successful in their interactions with the media? They need to have a basic understanding of the communication process and the role that nonverbal communication plays in the message they are attempting to convey. Chapter 4 delves into nonverbal communication in greater detail. However, for recorded presentations, televised sessions, news reports, and other video updates, the details are as important as the information to be shared in the report or session because the details also tell part of the story.

Appearance (Clothing, Hair, and Makeup)

Most law enforcement officers and agency officials have a specific dress code or uniform. As part of that uniform, regulations set forth the way tools of the trade are displayed or managed. However, appearance goes beyond the clothing and into hair and makeup (for female officers), as well as how tattoos and piercings are handled and whether chewing gum is appropriate during an interview or press conference.

Chief information officers may not wear a uniform. In that case, they would most likely wear a suit with shirt and tie for men or a suit with a blouse for women. When appearing on television or being recorded for televised or online display, you should be cautious about the pattern of the suit jacket you wear. Some types of patterns cause a distortion when viewed on television or camera. Some colors also make your skin tone appear washed out or pale. The best choice is a solid color suit—navy blue is always the first choice since dark blue is associated with trust, dignity, intelligence, and authority.[23] Shirt and blouse colors should also be solid white or light blue. In the case of a tie, more subdued colors with small patterns are also the best choices. You want your words to be the focal point, not any faux pas in your physical presentation.

Grooming standards that mandate the appearance of hair and any facial hair are also established by criminal justice agencies and departments. In the event of a televised or recorded session, officers and staff should be sure that their eyes are clearly visible—no bangs encroaching on the eye area. Hair should be away from the face in its entirety. Facial hair should be trimmed and create no problem for visibility of facial features and not serve as a distraction. You want people to look at you to pick up nonverbal cues to complement the words you are speaking and not to try to figure out what is going on with your hair or your mustache.

In any situation where an officer or staff person is speaking to the media for either real-time or recorded viewing, that individual should ensure that he or she is not chewing gum or eating any type of mint or hard candy. People often think they can hide the gum while they are speaking and no one will see it, and they certainly do not intend to chew it. But as we all know, accidents happen. If people think you are eating something or chewing gum, they fixate on the chewing—or trying to see if you are chewing—and do not hear the words you are speaking.

Gestures and Posture

Because the session is being broadcast live or recorded for later viewing, you need to manage your gestures and posture to stay within the viewing area. You cannot pace, stand with your hands in your pockets, use broad and expansive gestures (e.g., arm and hand movements), or stare at your notes (or read from them).

Stand up straight, and manage your space at the podium or in the area where you are asked to stand. Use your gestures to reinforce your words and not detract from them. Make your gestures natural, not forced. If you must point, use your entire hand and not your index finger. Pointing with the index finger alone is an attempt to display dominance.[24] If you are using a podium or lectern, do not lean on it. Also, do not clutch or hold onto the podium.

Location or Environment

Be aware of your surroundings—something that is part of a law enforcement officer's training. When preparing to speak to the media, you must be aware of the location of lighting, cameras, audience members, and others who may be part of the platform (e.g., other speakers, officers, and community members). You must treat the camera as if it were a member of the audience, to look at it as if it were a person into whose eyes you look during your presentation or speech. You do not need to stare at the camera alone and ignore other audience members, but you do need to be aware that the camera is present and part of the audience.

If you do not have an audience aside from the newscaster and the camera, you treat the camera as your audience. For many people, staring at a camera makes them uncomfortable and they will look around the room and at other locations. Practice makes this process easier. Even using a webcam on your computer to record a podcast or to connect with someone via Skype helps you to learn how to treat the camera as your audience.

Paralanguage or Vocalics

The voice is a major player in the nonverbal communication game. The expression "It's not what you said; it's how you said it" is often used to help others understand how miscommunication occurred. You should sound interested in what you are saying. Focus on your pace. Do not speak too quickly. Do not speak in a monotone voice. Vary the pitch and tone of your voice to keep your audience interested in your information.

Talking Points: Keep the Message Concise but Complete

Determine your talking points for your speech or presentation. Keep your comments concise but complete. Do not provide too much information. Try to avoid going off on a tangent as you will find returning to the subject at hand to be difficult. Provide complete information—and correct information—but not excessive details.

Vocalics: Avoiding the "Ah" and "Um" Curse

Nothing turns an audience off faster than a speaker who uses "ah" and "um" repeatedly. Other fillers (or nonfluencies), such as "like" and "you know," can also create the same angst and frustration among your audience members. You should evaluate your presentation and speech skills by doing the following:

- record your speech or presentation, and listen to it so you can identify areas where you need improvement, and/or

- ask a colleague or coworker to observe you and provide feedback as to your use of filler words and words you overuse.

Once you have identified your speech issues, you can then attempt to rectify them by employing specific techniques, such as pausing and chunking.

The pausing and chunking process allows the speaker to package information for the audience or listeners that helps them to follow the meaning of the speech or presentation. When you chunk, you divide your speech into chunks of information—words, phrases, or groups of words—to communicate a thought or idea. When speaking, you say the chunk of information and then pause to let your audience absorb it.

Sample 1[25]	Sample 2
Chunking your copy also makes it easier to consume in today's hectic environment. When reading a dense document online, it's easy to lose your place if you're interrupted. But when reading a piece chunked into bite-size pieces, you can pick up right where you left off.	Chunking your copy / also makes it easier to consume / in today's hectic environment. / When reading a dense document online, / it's easy to lose your place / if you're interrupted. // But when reading a piece chunked / into bite-size pieces, / you can pick up / right where you left off. //

Read the examples that follow out loud. Speech chunks and pauses are indicated with a slash (/), or longer pauses are indicated with a double slash (//). Which would you understand better?

Using the pause-and-chunk model encourages speakers to slow down and avoid those fillers that distract. Silence (from the pause) is a great method to gain the attention of your audience. People always stop whatever they are doing when a speaker pauses in his or her speech. So, in addition to helping eliminate the use of fillers and nonfluencies, you are also employing a mechanism to keep the attention focused on the speaker's words.

The nonverbal component of communication in a face-to-face setting is especially important. However, in a televised or recorded session, the nonverbal message takes high priority because of the ability of the nonverbal to overshadow the actual content of the verbal message. Learning to manage your nonverbal message is vital to the success of your agency and/or departmental communication.

SUMMARY

Everyday speech and formal presentations share many similarities in that they are orderly, build from least important to most important information, and require common language. They also have differences, such as length of time or time constraints, use of formal language, location, topic, and posture of the individual delivering the formal presentation.

Speeches have various purposes: to inform, instruct, persuade, inspire or motivate, activate or stimulate, or entertain. Also, speeches are delivered in one of four ways: impromptu, extemporaneous, manuscript, or memorized. The most popular delivery method is the extemporaneous style since the speaker is able to have a great deal of interaction with the audience and to concentrate more on the nonverbal feedback from audience members rather than on the message. This style is very popular with listeners as the speaker employs a conversational and interactive manner that is generally more effective.

Speakers must carefully plan their presentations by identifying the purpose of the speech or presentation and who will compose the audience or listeners. Once that part of the work is complete, the next step is to organize your presentation and plan and create any visuals that will be used to complement the information being presented.

The use of visuals to support your presentation is important to its overall effectiveness. Your visuals must be used properly—and created in such a way as to complement and support your presentation, not detract from it or replace the message.

Televised and recorded presentations (e.g., news reports and recorded presentations and updates) are also important to criminal justice agencies. While these types of formal presentations require some of the same planning and delivery styles, they also require additional focus on appearance, particularly in the areas of clothing, hair, and makeup. The voice is a major player in the televised and recorded presentations area. You want to be perceived as professional and knowledgeable when speaking to the television camera. Pausing and chunking of information allows the speaker to package information for the audience and listeners to help them follow the meaning of the presentation or speech.

Planning and delivering formal presentations is an important facet of your work life, regardless of your position. Police and corrections officers are often asked to appear at civic organizations' meetings to discuss a topic of concern to the membership. The media expects interviews to discuss criminal occurrences in the community. Officers must testify at depositions and in court. Understanding how to handle these situations can make your presentations run more smoothly and can produce a better rapport with your peers, subordinates, and superiors.

KEY TERMS

Articulation 99

Extemporaneous style 96

Flip charts 102

Impromptu style 96

Loudness 99

Manuscript style 96

Memorized style 96

Objects and models 102

Pitch 99

Pronunciation 99

Rate 99

Stage fright 106

Verbal signposts 100

FOR FURTHER REFLECTION AND DISCUSSION

1. As a juvenile detention officer, you have been asked to make a presentation at the local Rotary Club luncheon. You have been told that your time frame will be between 20 and 30 minutes. The meeting will be held at the local Holiday Inn in Meeting Room C. The membership of the organization would like to hear about the new juvenile detention facility that is being constructed in the county. What steps should you take in developing your presentation?

2. Two criminals escaped from the maximum-security prison located in your community. As the warden of the prison, you have been contacted by the media for a statement. Your investigation has revealed a possible location for the escapees, but you are not sure of their whereabouts. Prepare a statement for the media, taking into consideration the information you have available and being careful not to divulge too much in case the escapees are listening to the transmission.

3. As a city police officer, you have been invited to the elementary school (Grades K–5) to talk to the students about crime and how to protect themselves. Several recent occurrences where a strange man attempted to entice children into his van after school have led the school board to request that you specifically talk to the children about these types of situations. How would you develop your presentation? Prepare an outline of the speech you would give to the students. Would you use visuals? Why, or why not?

ETHICAL ISSUE EXERCISES

1. As the chief or sheriff of your department, you have been invited by a civic group to make a speech on the community's declining crime rate to a very affluent body of corporate leaders. Realizing that your officers need bullet-resistant vests, would it be inappropriate for you to attempt to solicit funds during your speech to this group of individuals for the purchase of these vests?

2. As the shift commander, you have been asked by the chief to make a few remarks at the retirement dinner of one of your officers. You have had conflicts with this officer's style of policing. You have had to discipline this officer on three recent occasions. How should you approach your assignment? What should be the content of your speech?

EFFECTIVE COMMUNICATION IN YOUR PROFESSIONAL SPHERE

WRITTEN COMMUNICATION
An Agency's Lifeline

Many times, reports are written without providing essential background information and filled with useless or non-relevant information that is both useless and harmful to the report's purpose and intent. Fact remains that poor reports don't add value to an incident and only require more follow up work to be done to get the right information to begin with thus a loss of precious productivity and time regarding the outcome of such investigations or reviews. Many reports are recycled or rewritten several times before they are both legible and understandable to the reader and for the purpose it serves at the time. This is happening because many fail to proofread their own or other's [sic] writings before submitting the report.[1]

—Carl Toers-Bijns, "Report Writing for Correctional Officers"

LEARNING OBJECTIVES

After students have completed this chapter, they will be able to do the following:

1. Identify and explain the types of reports used in criminal justice agencies

2. Demonstrate effective writing principles for report development

3. Explain the importance of proper note taking

4. List elements common to incident reports

5. Explain techniques involved in writing effective reports

6. Describe the records life cycle and why it is important to criminal justice agencies and their records

Communication occurs on many levels in criminal justice agencies. This chapter presents the most basic types of written documentation you may encounter in your criminal justice career. The most important fact to keep in mind when preparing written communication is to identify who will ultimately read the document. Your reader is the most important consideration in preparing your written communication. If your reader cannot understand your communication, the process has not been successful and you must begin anew, thus requiring additional time and effort.

WRITING PRINCIPLES FOR REPORT DEVELOPMENT

Writing begins with word selection—appropriate word selection. Words are the building blocks of **sentences** and paragraphs and, ultimately, of reports. We can view the writing process as a stair; step one is where we begin at the bottom level with the category *words*. At this point, we begin with clear and concise writing, choosing short, simple words. The next step involves generating sentences. Your sentences should vary in type among simple, compound, and complex ones. You should also use passive and active voice appropriately. The final step in the writing process is paragraph development. You need to keep your paragraphs unified and coherent and to control their length.

Words

Word choice is vital to achieving the appropriate response to your writing. In planning and developing your writing, you always want to keep in mind that the "reader" is the most important element in this process. While each of us knows what we desire to express, our reader does not always have the benefit of questioning us if our writing is unclear. Also, if the reader fails to comprehend our message, our writing will not achieve its desired purpose.

Software packages allow us, with the click of a button, to select a synonym for any word of our choice. Unfortunately, the word selections available do not always serve your writing well. The following suggestions cover some basic concepts concerning the writing process and your choice of words:

Use Familiar Words

For your message to be understood, you must use words that are familiar to both you and your reader. If you are in doubt as to whether your reader will define a word the way you do, then you should make sure to thoroughly explain your meaning by providing either a definition or an appropriate synonym. In the example that follows, a brief definition has been included in parentheses to ensure the reader's understanding will match your intended meaning.

- My watch always seems to be running *fast* (ahead of time).

Avoid Unnecessary Jargon

While the criminal justice professions have their own technical jargon or specialized words, you should be wary of using jargon in writing that will be read by persons outside the field. For example, a jury composed of ordinary people with no experience in criminal justice may have problems understanding a report containing numerous jargon references.

Use Concrete, Specific Language

If you use concrete words in your writing, you will be selecting terms that bring a mental image to your reader's mind. Be sure that your words give the reader as much information as necessary so that he or she can react appropriately.

Write Concisely

You should avoid redundancy and wordy expressions in your writing. A **redundancy** is the unnecessary repetition of a previously expressed idea.

NO: Combine the ingredients together.

YES: Combine the ingredients.

Wordy expressions are not necessarily writing errors, but they should be avoided since they tend to slow the communication process. The following examples of wordy expressions should be avoided in your writing, with the preferred one-word substitutes in parentheses:

- Due to the fact (because)
- For the purpose of (for *or* to)
- In the event that (if)

- With regard to (about)
- Came to an agreement (agreed)
- Gave an explanation (explained)

Use Positive Language

Positive language helps to build goodwill between you—the writer—and the reader. You also are much more likely to achieve your purpose if you use positive words. In addition to avoiding words such as *cannot* or *will not*, you should avoid negative-sounding words, such as *mistake, damage, failure,* or *refuse*. However, in most situations in the criminal justice professions, you may have no alternative but to use negative wording. Since negative language is strong and emphatic, sometimes you will want to use it.

Choose a Precise Conjunction or Preposition to Indicate Cause and Effect[2]

In many instances, criminal justice professionals write reports that must demonstrate a cause-and-effect relationship between two actions. Writers (and speakers) often use certain words interchangeably when attempting to explain a cause-and-effect scenario, usually conjunctions or conjunctive and prepositional phrases: because, since, as, for, after, due to, now that, given that, and inasmuch as. These words have varying meanings and are often used specifically in advertising and public relations as these words are ambiguous in nature. The word that best expresses a causal relationship is *because*.

Example: Skip bought two new business suits because he was transferred from uniform patrol to the detective division.

You may use a few other words—thanks to, owing to, as a result of, on account of, and courtesy of—to indicate a causal relationship when you need to avoid excessive repetition of the word *because* in your writing. However, you must be certain to select only these terms to avoid ambiguity in your writing so that it is not subject to possible misinterpretation.

Sentences

Chapter 4 discussed the basics of grammar, placing particular emphasis on sentence fragments and run-on sentences and the appropriate means for eliminating these problem areas. In this chapter, we examine sentence development and its importance in creating documents such as reports, proposals, and agency documentations.

Some sentences are very simple, having only a subject and a predicate. Still others are longer and contain more details. Regardless of its length, a sentence is meant to convey a complete thought. The sentence is the basic unit of communication, and sentences are the building blocks for paragraphs.

When you read something that was written using short, choppy sentences, you find yourself unable to mentally picture the scene. Writing in this manner usually indicates that the writer simply wrote each thought as it occurred to him or her. Although no grammatical problems exist with short, simple sentences, they often separate ideas that need to be brought together. Varying sentence length creates well-balanced writing that flows. The reader gets the feeling that the writer really knows the subject well. In the following quote, Gary Provost explains how varying sentence length can create music for a reader:

> This sentence has five words. Here are five more words. Five-word sentences are fine. But several together become monotonous. Listen to what is happening. The writing is getting boring. The sound of it drones. It's like a stuck record. The ear demands some variety. Now listen. I vary the sentence length, and I create music. Music. The writing sings. It has a pleasant rhythm, a lilt, a harmony. I use short sentences. And I use sentences of medium length. And sometimes, when I am certain the reader is rested, I will engage him with a sentence of considerable length, a sentence that burns with energy and builds with all the impetus of a crescendo, the roll of the drums, the crash of the cymbals—sounds that say listen to this, it is important.[3]

Two problem areas exist in sentence development: wordiness and rambling. **Wordiness** refers to the cluttering of sentences with unnecessary words. As mentioned in the foregoing section on *words*, you should always attempt to write concisely. However, if a word serves a purpose, it should remain in your sentence. Notice the difference in the following pairs of sentences:

Wordy: The psychological examination that he gave me was entirely complete.

Concise: The psychological examination he gave me was complete.

Wordy: It will be our aim to ensure the safety of each and every one of the citizens in the State of Mississippi.

Concise: Our aim will be to ensure the safety of all Mississippians.

In his text, Richard Lanham created a process he titled "the Paramedic Method" for writers to use in achieving user-centered, concise work, especially when employing passive voice in their writing.[4] His method included the following steps:

- Look at individual sentences, one at a time—and examine every word to determine whether that word is providing something important and/or unique to the meaning of the sentence.

- Circle the prepositions in the sentence (about, after, among, behind, beyond, of, for, into, at, with, until, over).

- Draw a box around "is" verb forms (is, are).

- Ask yourself a question: Where is the "action"?

- If you can identify action that is taking place in the sentence, change your "is" verb to a simple action verb.

FIGURE 6.1 ■ The Paramedic Method

Example: The point I wish to make [is] that the corrections officers working (at) Soggy Bottom Prison are (in) need (of) a much better security system (for) their protection (from) the inmates.|

Revision: Corrections Officers at Soggy Bottom Prison need better security.

- Make sure that the subject (the "doer" of the action) is placed properly in the sentence.

- Eliminate any unnecessary words (indefinite expressions or filler words such as there is, there are, it is, this is, and empty words and phrases such as in my opinion, I think that, for all intents and purposes, until such time as, with the possible exception of, at this point in time, in the neighborhood of).

- Eliminate any redundancies (each separate incident, many different ways, as to whether, dash quickly, advance notice, completely finished).

A **rambling sentence** seems to have no end. Consider the following examples illustrating how rambling sentences can be improved:

NO: The night was foggy, but the road was clear; the moon was shining, and we all had the spirit of adventure in our heart and a song of the open road on our lips, so we took the turn that took our car up the winding mountain road.

YES: The night was foggy, but the road was clear. The moon was shining. All of us had the spirit of adventure in our heart and a song of the open road on our lips. So we took our car up that winding mountain road.

NO: Everyone knows someone like that, a person who has no concern for others, who will pretend to be a friend, but only because she profits from the relationship, and she never really gives of herself, she just takes, and one cannot call her a friend in any sense of the word.

YES: Everyone knows someone like that, a person who has no concern for others. She will pretend to be a friend but only because she profits from the relationship. She never really gives of herself; she just takes, and one cannot call her a friend in any sense of the word.

Although rambling sentences typically are grammatically correct, they present a problem to the reader. They interfere with the reader's comprehension. A good rule of thumb to follow in writing sentences is if a sentence runs for more than two typewritten lines, you probably want to rewrite it. You could be "rambling."

Another important aspect in writing sentences centers on **voice**. Voice is the feature of the verb that indicates whether the subject of the sentence acts or is acted on. Two types of voice are used in writing: **active voice** and **passive voice**. In active voice, the subject does the action expressed by the verb, whereas in passive voice, the subject receives the action of the verb. Active voice is preferable in writing because it is emphatic and direct. However, passive voice is essential when the action of the verb is more important than the person doing the action, when the person doing the action is unknown, or when the writer wants to emphasize the receiver of the action and not the doer. The following are examples of passive and active voice:

PASSIVE: The garbage can was hit by the Nissan Pathfinder.

ACTIVE: The Nissan Pathfinder hit the garbage can.

PASSIVE: The witnesses were questioned by the investigator.

ACTIVE: The investigator questioned the witnesses.

Using appropriate word choices, a variety of sentence types, and active or passive voice can help make your sentences more effective. By learning these basic writing premises, you are now ready to combine them into logical paragraphs.

PARAGRAPHS

The sentence and the paragraph are the two most fundamental units of communication. Merriam-Webster defines a paragraph as "a subdivision of a written composition that consists of one or more sentences, deals with one point or gives the words of one speaker, and begins on a new usually indented line."[5] Paragraphs also have several common characteristics that help them to focus on and to develop their subjects more fully. No rule of thumb exists regarding the length of paragraphs. However, the suggestion for the maximum length of a paragraph seems to be between 100 and 200 words, with the caveat that a paragraph should draw your reader in, not lose the reader's attention because it is too long.[6] Even single-sentence paragraphs are acceptable. Use paragraph breaks to signal a change in ideas—to a new idea—to emphasize a point, to indicate a shift in time or place, or to simply break up text so that you do not lose the reader's attention.

Topic Sentences

The sentence that tells the reader what the paragraph is about is called the **topic sentence**. Topic sentence placement is usually as the first sentence in the paragraph. However, not all topic sentences come first. Often, they are found at the end or near the middle of the paragraph. As a writer, you should decide where you want your topic sentence to be placed. If you write it at the beginning of the paragraph, the topic sentence can capture the readers' attention or interest and tell them what to expect next. Most magazine and newspaper articles use this placement of the topic sentence for the very purpose of getting attention. If you place the topic sentence at the end of the paragraph, though, you can reinforce or emphasize details that were discussed in the paragraph.

A topic sentence guides and influences readers. Nonetheless, the writer should find it equally important as well. The topic sentence gives you, the writer, a focus. By referring to the topic sentence, you should be able to keep your work organized and consistent. Remember that your writing should be coherent and composed of thoughts logically arranged.

Expanding your topic sentence into a paragraph involves the use of detailed information. Remember that your topic sentence is a statement that the remainder of your sentences must clearly and completely support. The following methods can be used to develop a topic sentence:

- **Facts.** Used to substantiate historical and scientific writing.

- **Examples.** Help to clarify a statement by offering the reader evidence.

- **Argument.** Used in editorials, philosophical writing, and literary criticism to support a theory.

- **Anecdote.** Often found in narrative writing. Used to entertain the reader while clarifying a point. (An **anecdote** is a short account of an incident, usually personal.)

- **Definition**. Gives the writer an explanation through definition of a concept or term.

- **Comparison and contrast**. Essential qualities of two people or theories can be highlighted through this mechanism.

- **Analogy.** Can be used to bring out the essential qualities of a subject. (An **analogy** is explaining something by comparing it point by point with something else.)

- **Cause and effect**. Usually involves the use of data or general observation to explain a theory or subject.

Transitions

Arranging sentences logically will not ensure a coherent paragraph. Using linking expressions or phrases is crucial for smooth **transitions** between ideas and subjects. As discussed in Chapter 4, *conjunctive adverbs* are useful for transitioning from paragraph to paragraph. Pronouns are also helpful for referring to a previous sentence without repetition. The following examples demonstrate various methods for linking or connecting your text:

1. To elaborate on an idea already discussed

again	furthermore	moreover
also	in addition	similarly
too	for example	and

   Examples:

   a. I intend to vote for Mayor Bryant in the upcoming election. He is a diligent worker with a good personality. *Moreover*, he has experience.

   b. We feel it would be best to change the date of the dance. Many members said they could not attend. *Also*, we have a reunion scheduled for that night.

2. To qualify, limit, or contradict a statement

but	yet	although
however	on the other hand	nevertheless

Examples:

a. After I located the suspect, I thought I could get him to confess. I had to simply ask the right questions. *However*, I didn't anticipate his speech difficulty, and a speech pathologist had to be called to assist me.

b. Officer Smith thought she had secured the crime scene. All the necessary precautions had been taken. *Yet*, for some unknown reason, the evidence became tainted.

3. To show a time or place arrangement of an idea

at the present time	second	meanwhile
at the same time	finally	eventually
at this point	first	further

Examples:

a. After going over the testimony several times, I decided to ask my supervisor for help. After we had discussed it fully, I reviewed the testimony one more time. *Finally*, I began to see the cracks I was searching for.

b. The day was hectic. First, I was late for work. Then, a car pulled into traffic in front of me, and I was forced to go into the ditch to avoid it. When I finally reached home, it began to rain. *At this point*, I was about to cry.

4. To conclude a paragraph effectively

as a result	for these reasons
as can be seen	hence
consequently	therefore

Examples:

a. We were cautioned not to move if we heard voices. Suddenly, something fell. *As a result*, no one moved an inch.

b. The weatherman has forecast a blizzard for tomorrow. He expects the accumulation to be heavy. *Therefore*, I decided to stock up on food items at the grocery store today.

You may also use pronouns as transitional words, as well as a repetition of key words or ideas appearing in the preceding paragraph or line. Remember that the aim in your writing should be to enable the reader to connect paragraphs and ideas in his or her mind. Deciding to use a transition is a matter of common sense. The more you write, the easier it will become.

Consistency

In writing, consistency is equally as important as unity. If you change point of view or tone abruptly, you will confuse your reader. **Point of view** is the way in which something is viewed or considered; it is the writer's standpoint or the attitude the writer has toward the subject. **Tone** is the manner of speaking that indicates a certain attitude. Tone can be informal, formal, or dramatic, as determined by the writer's word choice and phrasing.

Example (Point of View):

NO: From his vantage point, Sgt. Jones could see the men enter the house. They broke the lock on the front door and went in that way. After that, he lost sight of them. *His partner saw everything from the top of the stairs.*

YES: From his vantage point, Sgt. Jones could see the men enter the house. They broke the lock on the front door and went in that way. *Although Sgt. Jones lost sight of them at this point, his partner was inside and saw everything.*

Example (Tone):

NO: At a special press conference at the White House today, the president offered reporters details of his new economic policy. Hoping to lower Medicaid funding, he proposed a series of tax cuts that will be made over the next 3 years. Many economists believe *it's about time the president did something.*

YES: At a special press conference at the White House today, the president offered reporters details of his new economic policy. Hoping to lower Medicaid funding, he proposed a series of tax cuts that will be made over the next 3 years. Many economists believe *the time is right for the president to implement his new plan.*

REPORT WRITING IN CRIMINAL JUSTICE

Criminal justice professionals write countless reports as part of their day-to-day job responsibilities. Well-written reports document actions, provide information or data, facilitate investigations, and showcase the professionalism of the writer. By contrast, a poorly written report creates an inaccurate portrayal of the competence level of the writer. Report formats vary from agency to agency, depending on the mission of the agency and what types of incidents and investigations that agency is charged with conducting. However, the layout for these reports typically includes a standard set of questions that must be answered: the who, what, when, where, why, and how regarding an incident. Because reports are the lifeblood of the criminal justice profession—whether law enforcement, corrections, or private security—the next part of this chapter covers the report writing process for each of these agencies.

Reports in Law Enforcement

The most common types of law enforcement reports include the following:

- Offense or incident report
- Arrest report
- Supplemental reports

Offense or Incident Report

The most frequently created report in law enforcement is the **offense or incident report**. Virtually every department has its own unique or personalized form for reporting an offense or incident. Yet, while the form design may be unique to that organization, the information required to complete it is essentially the same. This preliminary report is completed by the investigating officer and is used to document all crimes and investigations and includes the basic information relevant to the incident or investigation (e.g., dates, times, location of incident or offense, type of crime, and a file or case number). In addition to the basic information, these reports also identify the victim(s), witnesses, suspects, informants or reporters, and any assisting officers and provide addresses and contact information for these individuals. The form has fill-in-the-blank and/or open sections for reporting the required information, again depending on the agency's design preferences. The use of the fill-in-the-blank or open portions for the offense or incident report to collect needed demographic and statistical data allows the investigating officer to focus on details in the narrative section.

The most critical part of any offense or incident report is the narrative. It is an integral component of any sound offense or incident report and should be clear, concise, complete, and correct while addressing a detailed account of the incident. The investigating officers should construct a narrative that tells a story, including all the main players and their actions during the investigation and their

> See the study site for this book for examples of incident reports: ***http://study.sagepub.com/grubb***

testimony regarding their observations, as well as a detailed description of the crime scene and any evidence collected. The information contained in the narrative should be in chronological form and should allow the reader to envision the scene and follow the investigation through the facts as presented. The narrative should end with a logical conclusion or finding that does not leave the reader questioning its outcome. (See examples at the end of the chapter.)

Arrest Report

Arrest reports share many commonalities with offense or incident reports, with fill-in-the-blank or open sections focused on the date, time, and location of the arrest, along with specific demographic information regarding the person or persons arrested. However, the information in these reports is used to support probable cause for an arrest and must be complete in documenting facts and

> See the study site for this book for examples of arrest reports: ***http://study.sagepub.com/grubb***

evidence. Law enforcement officers involved in an arrest must know the accurate code, charge, and/or statute number to include on arrest reports because an incorrect one can jeopardize the case.

An arrest report should be clear, concise, complete, and correct. Law enforcement officers must ensure that the needed facts to support an arrest are included. Unlike most offense or incident reports, arrest reports will be reviewed by prosecutors and judges to ensure that probable cause was present to warrant the arrest. Officers can put themselves and their agencies at risk for a civil lawsuit if the arrest report is questionable and does not fully address the investigation process. Arrest reports can appear in newspapers and in courtrooms. Therefore, you want to ensure that you provide all relevant information and that your report is well written so that you do not find that the arrest is invalidated because of missing details. You want to be viewed as a competent professional. If your reports are poorly written, your reputation will suffer—as will your agency's reputation. (See examples at the end of the chapter.)

Supplemental Reports

Supplemental reports are necessary because of the number of officers and investigators involved in criminal investigations or incidents. Each officer or investigator must create his or her own report of observations and actions, and these individual reports eventually become part of the official record of the case. In addition, as each case progresses, you will need to update information related to that case. Supplemental reports are used at each stage to allow for additional information to be added to the offense or incident report after it has been filed.

Supplemental reports contain the same fill-in-the-blank or open sections as offense or incident reports and arrest reports. The largest section on a supplemental report is for the narrative. You must follow the same guidelines for writing the narrative on the supplemental report as on any other report—use clear, concise, complete, and correct information.

Every offense or incident report, arrest report, or supplemental report begins with field notes taken by the officer or investigator. These notes are vital to the completion of reports as they contain pertinent information to answer the questions of who, what, when, where, why, and how—and they provide the details that an officer encounters that further corroborate the arrest of a suspect or the testimony of a witness to the offense or incident in question. Later in the chapter, we will discuss the importance of field notes and ways that you can ensure your notes are detailed and complete. (See examples at the end of the chapter.)

Reports in Corrections

Corrections officers, like law enforcement officers, are required to write various reports as part of their jobs. Reports serve as permanent records for important facts; therefore, all reports written by corrections officers are subject to discovery in court. Reports written by corrections officers have varying intended audiences, such as supervisors, attorneys, judges, counselors, the media, defendants, members of local government, and family members. These reports also serve numerous purposes for the department, including data collection to identify crime trends and the elimination of some liability in cases when departments have documentation readily accessible.

See the study site for this book for an example of a corrections daily log: **http://study.sagepub.com/grubb**

Reports are used by departments to evaluate a corrections officer's performance or to serve as training materials for demonstrating good and bad reports. In addition, corrections officers themselves use their reports when testifying in court to refresh their memories. Reports are used to identify crime trends, to collect classified information, and to assess a department's needs. They can provide documentation prior to the start of a legal action or offer information obtained through testimony when a legal action has begun.

The three major types of reports used in corrections are as follows:

1. Incident reports   3. Supplemental reports

2. Disciplinary reports

Incident Reports

Much as in law enforcement, the most common report in the correctional setting is the incident report. As a corrections officer, you write incident reports to document the facts surrounding the event and to provide a permanent record of the actions you take in response to the incident. Also, you will want to record your observations of the events and offenses that occurred. Your report should address the following:

- Who (identification of the person[s] involved)
- What (violation or offense)
- When (time and date)
- Where (location of incident)
- Why (motive)
- How (method of operation)
- Action taken (end result, outcome, or response)[7]

As you begin the writing process, you want to consider the intended audience for your report. Who will be reading it? Put yourself in the reader's shoes. Since you are attempting to convey information, you want to avoid using any slang, technical, or unfamiliar terms that your reader would not understand. While you work in the correctional setting and know what is meant by "one hitter," "shank," or "lock in a sock," not everyone does, especially those who have never worked in a prison.

INEFFECTIVE: I found a lock in a sock in his pocket. Inmate is in violation of having dangerous contraband.

EFFECTIVE: During a targeted pat search, due to the inmate's suspicious behavior, I did discover a lock tied inside of a sock, which is commonly used as an impact weapon.[8]

The effective statement makes sense to someone who has no prior experience in the correctional setting. Anyone can understand that the item is dangerous from that description. In addition, the effective statement demonstrates professionalism. The author of that statement is perceived as a corrections professional, not merely a prison guard.

In writing your reports, unless your department specifies otherwise, you have the choice between a chronological and a structured approach to your report content. Each of these approaches has advantages and disadvantages, but one may work better for you based on whether you have a need for consistent structure or prefer more free-form writing. Each approach is discussed in the following section.

Using the chronological approach for organizing your report. Your report should begin with a paragraph giving the date and time of the incident and the type of incident and describing how you became involved. Your second paragraph should discuss what you were told by the victim(s) and any witnesses (if applicable), using a separate paragraph for each individual involved in the incident. The third paragraph should explain what you did based on the information you received. And the final paragraph should explain the disposition of the case. The advantages to following the chronological approach are that you can use a storytelling model to discuss the incident in the way it happened, the reader can easily comprehend the information put forth in this approach, and you use a systematic sequence of events to report the incident. Disadvantages to this approach, however, can be exacerbated by the time encumbered by the investigation. As the investigation continues, keeping details in order can become almost impossible to achieve. In addition, you run the risk of leaving out details.

See the study site for this book for examples of report narratives: **http://study .sagepub.com/grubb**

Using the structured approach for organizing your report. Your report should have topical headings: Involved Persons (Victim[s], Witness[es], and Suspect[s]); Narrative (The Story); Property; Evidence; and any other headings that you feel are necessary to support the narrative. The advantages to using the structured approach are that you have a simple format to follow, you have uniformity in your reports (i.e., they all look the same), and you have a lesser chance of missing important details because of the use of the topical headings. Using the structured approach, however, does not allow your writing to flow like a story; and your information appears to be or reads as if it were fragmented. These disadvantages may not be important to your department or to you because the structured approach helps to curb omissions of detail or important information in your incident report.

One of the most important actions you can take after you have written your incident report is to proofread it to ensure that you have provided clear, complete, concise, and correct information. Ask yourself the following questions as you review your incident report:

- Is the description of the incident accurate? Does it give specific details that are both factual and correct?

- Are all elements of the incident properly identified and explained? Did you provide explicit and concise information? Did you include all essential information?

- Is your report well organized? Did you organize the information chronologically?

- Did you include all necessary information to answer the questions who, what, when, where, why, how, and what action was taken?

- Are your conclusions supported? Did you include a full description of the actions on which you based your conclusion?

- Is your report relatively free of errors? Did you use the proper department form or format?

Once you have completed your review and responded affirmatively to these six sets of questions, you can assume your report is ready for submission. However, a good rule of thumb is to ask a fellow officer or associate to read your report draft and provide feedback on its effectiveness. If he or she fails to fully understand what happened during the incident or seeks to ask numerous clarifying questions, you can assume you need to revise your report to address these issues.

Disciplinary Reports

Disciplinary reports are written when an inmate violates a rule. Most correctional facilities have a form with both fill-in-the-blank and open sections that officers complete. These reports are used to justify administrative segregation and to identify cause of action for disciplinary hearings. The Department of Corrections in each state has specific classifications for offenses or violations.

Supplemental Reports

In the corrections setting, supplemental reports may involve record keeping. Major types of record keeping required in a correctional facility include safety records, housing logs, restraint device checks, and suicide watch. The format for some of these supplemental reports may include observation logs. However, you must remember that written documentation is crucial, as it shows what was done, when, by whom, and for what purpose, so do not fail to put complete information into your reports or record-keeping logs. Do not speculate. State facts and pertinent details.

Corrections officers have a responsibility to write appropriate reports that are accurate and not filled with grammatical, spelling, or punctuation errors. These reports, regardless of type, should convey clear, concise, complete, and correct information to readers. Reports are the backbone of the judicial process. Just as they are used in law enforcement to support arrests and convictions, reports are also used in the corrections field to support decisions, actions, and processes. Professional, well-written reports can be the difference between a favorable outcome in an investigation and a corrections officer losing a civil suit filed by an inmate.

Reports in Private Security

Private security and private police are terms that are used interchangeably to describe individuals who work as in-house security or contract security for various business enterprises.[9] People who work in private security have not always been accepted as part of the criminal justice field. In the early part of the 20th century, private security agencies supplied contract security guards to serve as strikebreakers, and that action tarnished the reputation of private police among the law enforcement community.[10]

See the study site for this book for an example of a daily security log: **http://study.sagepub.com/grubb**

Moving forward to the present day, however, private security agencies contract with businesses, organizations, and corporations to provide security services designed to meet the needs of the specific company. Grocery stores, shopping malls, restaurants and bars, nightclubs, and sports venues have private security officers who patrol their grounds and facilities to ensure the safety and security of their patrons. In May 2016, the United States Bureau of Labor reported the number of individuals employed as private security guards at more than 1.1 million.[11] Most of these individuals work in the investigation and security services industry, and many are retired police officers or active police officers who moonlight with security companies for extra income.

Private security officers generally do not have the authority of public law enforcement. Nonetheless, they can perform the same tasks as any United States citizen: arrest, investigate, carry weapons, defend themselves, and defend their property or property entrusted to their care. A security officer can lose his or her private person status, though, if the state in which he or she is working requires a licensing process for private security officers.[12] The private security officer is then governed by the regulations and laws set forth as part of the licensure.

Private security officers are required to capture a substantial amount of information in their day-to-day work activities. This information becomes part of the reports that the officer writes. The most common types of reports in private security are as follows:

1. Daily activity reports

2. Incident reports

3. Progress or supplemental reports

Depending on the company or organization where the private security officer is employed, the types of reports may also include maintenance requests, equipment logs, pass-on logs, and truck and visitor logs.

Daily Activity Reports

Daily activity reports are the most common type of reports in the private security field. Each security officer must complete one of these reports for every shift. These reports are important to the organizations for whom the security officer works, so the information should be relevant and follow the same guidelines as those previously covered for both the law enforcement and corrections communities. The information in these reports should be concise, clear, complete, and correct.

Some private security organizations may employ daily activity report software to assist officers in the completion of this important task. Regardless of whether private security officers are using a program or still using handwritten reports, the following steps are important to ensuring all needed information is included:

1. Make sure reports are time stamped, and make sure the location to which the report pertains is included as well. Include notes from the start of the shift. The security officer should (a) record any notes or instructions he or she receives from the client or supervisor; (b) record an inventory of the items he or she receives and the condition of these items; and (c) record the shift that he or she is working.

2. Make the information easy to locate. Readers should be able to quickly locate any information they are seeking in your report. For example, you may include an "Observations" section in your report where you log information about any additional officers on duty, any general notes, or if you found any issues when signing on (e.g., the lights were left on in the main office but should have been turned off, as instructed by the property manager). If you are asked to perform an activity that is not part of your usual responsibilities, you want to include a separate note (e.g., you are asked to do an "employee escort," so that activity needs to be separate and distinct in your report because that duty is not one you perform each shift).

3. Show consistent activity. Any time that you engage in any activity or make any observation, that information—along with a time stamp—should be included in your report. You want to show that you are active during the entirety of your shift. In addition, your daily activity report may be subpoenaed or submitted for review to determine its potential legal significance in a lawsuit or arrest, so the more detailed your notes are with observations and time stamps, the better.

4. Be descriptive. In this section, security officers are encouraged to adhere to the who, what, when, where, why, and how format for observations. Answers to the following questions can be very helpful as well:

   a. How long did it take you to complete a patrol?

   b. What people did you see or talk to?

   c. What did you observe when looking out of the window?

   d. What did you hear during your patrol?

5. Keep it simple. Stick to the facts in your report, and keep your opinions to yourself. Do not embellish. Follow the guidelines to make your report clear, concise, correct, and complete. Be as descriptive as you can, but do not speculate.

6. Use common language. Unless you are instructed to do so, you should avoid including any codes, unfamiliar abbreviations or acronyms, or any words that would prohibit a civilian from understanding the report.

7. Include images (where possible). If you are using daily activity report software, you may be asked to include images and photos as needed in your report.

8. Follow up. If you receive additional information after your daily activity report has been submitted, you should time stamp the information and log it into the daily activity report program or on the back of the handwritten report, depending on which process you are using.

The goal for following these steps in preparing your daily activity reports is to ensure that your report is professional. These reports may be reviewed by customers, lawyers, or law enforcement officers, so you need to ensure that they are high quality and convey the right amount of information in the proper form.[13]

Incident Reports

As with law enforcement and corrections officers, private security officers often prepare incident or accident reports. The purpose of these reports is to document details of an incident or accident and to provide a factual account of these unusual occurrences. When encountering an incident or accident, you must make notes of the details surrounding it—observations you make, actions you take, person(s) involved, witness(es), and suspect(s).[14] Private security guards should be aware of the protocol and/or procedures established by their employer to guide them in reporting an incident or accident. Some companies have their own incident report forms, and others require private security guards to write incident reports by hand. Regardless of form, you should follow these steps when writing your incident or accident report:

1. **Use everyday language**. Avoid using jargon, police terms, acronyms, or unusual terms so that the people who read your report (supervisors, law enforcement, or jurors) will be able to understand its content.

2. **Answer the who, what, when, where, why, and how questions**.

   - *Who*: Who was involved (people)? Who witnessed the incident or accident? What is their contact information?

   - *What*: What actions and events happened? Tell the story from the beginning, and go point by point or event by event. Include as much detail as possible.

   - *When*: What was the date and time of the incident or accident? If appropriate, you may want to describe the weather, the lighting, or other conditions at the time of the incident.

   - *Where*: Where did the incident or accident occur? Include the address and details about nearby objects or buildings. Be as precise as possible about the location.

   - *Why*: You may not be able to answer this question. You should not speculate or guess as to the reason for the incident or accident. Stick to the facts of the situation only.

   - *How*: Describe how the incident or accident occurred. You may have included some of this information under the "what" question, but you need to explain how the incident or accident occurred. What precipitated it? (e.g., Was water or ice on the floor?)

3. **Stick to the facts**. Do not offer your own opinion or make inferences or conjectures about the cause of the incident or accident. Report only the facts—the things you saw with your own eyes and heard with your own ears.

4. **Take photos and videos on your smartphone**. Most companies have video surveillance; however, you should use your smartphone to record video and to take photos because they will provide additional objective information.

5. **Be professional**. Use correct grammar, punctuation, and spelling. If you write your report by hand, you should take time to make sure your writing is legible. Avoid the use of slang or rude language. Choose your words carefully, and do not judge anyone in your report. Refer to people that you have identified in the report with a courtesy title and last name (i.e., Mr. and Ms.).[15]

Incident or accident reports should be written within 24 hours of the event. Most security officers complete their incident or accident reports prior to the end of their shift, and some company or agency policies may require that these reports be submitted prior to the security officer's departure at the end of his or her shift.[16] If you wait longer than 24 hours to complete your report, memories begin to fade; so you will be less likely to remember specific facts and circumstances surrounding the incident or accident—even with the notes you took at the time of the incident or accident.

Law enforcement, corrections, and private security officers are all charged with the preparation of various types of reports. The previous section described these reports in detail and provided suggestions for professional preparation of those reports. From this information, you can easily see that report writing across criminal justice agencies is a time-consuming activity. Numerous technologies, ranging from automated report writing systems to dictation and word processing software programs, are available to assist criminal justice professionals in the preparation of their reports. Chapter 9 of this text discusses the technology tools employed by criminal justice agencies in the completion of their work. The technologies in use for report writing will be addressed as part of that chapter.

Field Notes and Note Taking

Criminal justice professionals on every level have been instructed to take notes about any offense, incident, accident, or event they investigate. The starting point for every effective report is the field notes you took from the point you arrived on the scene until the assignment was completed.

Good field notes are vital to the preparation of a thorough and inclusive report. So you should be prepared to take notes. Of course, we live in a technology era, and you may have a laptop in your patrol car or a computer in your office, at the correctional facility, or at your house, but this equipment does little to help you in an emergency. So you need to have some type of notebook on your person, along with a couple of pens, to use in taking your field notes. Notebooks should be reserved for information that relates directly to your investigations. Personal information or materials should never be included in your field notebook since this notebook may be subpoenaed as evidence in a case or possibly examined by a defense attorney on the witness stand.

Research has shown that field notes are more reliable than your memory. (Ninety-eight percent of information contained in police investigators' notes is accurate.)[17] In fact, the longer time between the incident or offense and the time you write your report, the less information you remember. Your field notes help you combat this potential loss of important details. In addition, having detailed notes may reduce the need for you to contact parties involved in the incident. Most victims and witnesses resent an intrusion into their lives by someone who failed to get the pertinent facts at the time of the accident or incident. They can get very annoyed or angry and do not care that you simply need additional information to complete your report.

See the study site for this book for examples of victim/witness supplemental reports: **http://study.sagepub.com/grubb**

The content of the notes should serve as an outline or brief synopsis of the event. These notes should contain personal observations, statements made by the victim, witness(es), and suspect(s). Descriptions of important persons, places, or things and any other relevant information should also be included. Information that may be construed as opinion rather than fact should be omitted.

The importance of field notes cannot be stressed enough. Memories fade, but written notes do not. If you maintain good field notes, you will be able to use those notes during courtroom testimony to refresh your recollection of the events of the incident. Without sufficient field notes, you will struggle to complete incident or offense reports and to testify in court. Also, your field notes can defend the integrity of your incident or offense report.

Guidelines for the Note-Taking Process

In addition to having your proper equipment (spiral-bound notebook in the size and type that best suit your needs, along with an ink pen or two), you should think about the basic and primary questions you need to ask and/or answer: *who, what, when, where, why,* and *how.*

- Who?
  - Who is the victim(s)?
  - Who is the suspect(s)?
  - Who are the witnesses?
  - Who is the informant(s)?
  - Who are the other officers on scene (if applicable)?
  - Are any emergency medical personnel on scene? If so, who are they?

- What?
  - What type of offense has occurred?
  - What type of action has occurred or is occurring (in the case of a domestic disorder or neighbor dispute, etc.)?
  - What behaviors are you observing?
  - What weapons do you see?
  - What damage has occurred (if any)?
  - What was the victim's routine (if applicable)?
  - What property is missing (if applicable)?

- When?
  - When did this offense take place, or when was the crime discovered or reported?
  - When did you (the officer) arrive and depart?
  - When did the suspect flee the scene or leave the area (if known)?

- Where?
  - Where was the offense committed (specific address)?
  - Where are the victims, witnesses, and suspect(s) now?
  - Where are the hiding places of suspect(s)?
  - Where is the suspect's residence?

- Why?
  - Why was the offense committed? (CAUTION: You may not have and/or may not be able to discern a motive at this point in time.)

- o Why were the victim and suspect(s) in this location?

- • How?

  - o How was the crime or offense committed?

  - o How did the suspect flee the area (on foot, in a vehicle [description or license plate

  - o Why did the suspect choose this victim and this time to commit this offense?

  - number], and direction of travel)?

  - o How many victims, witnesses, and suspects were involved in the crime or offense?

You should also train yourself to observe and remember. Use your senses of smell, sight, and hearing. When you first arrive on the scene of the incident, look for injuries, blood, broken furniture, glass, and weapons. Listen for sounds and voices. See if you can identify any smells, such as alcohol or other substances.

Record the information you obtain as promptly and thoroughly as possible. The details in this information will prevent problems from arising later. Again, do not rely on your memory. Write a complete set of notes. You do not wish to have an inaccurate or incomplete report because you could not remember or did not record all the details surrounding the incident.

Once you have handled this portion of the investigation, you must next interview the witnesses, suspects, and victims—where possible. You will have to deal with the emotions of these individuals before you can begin your interviews. People need to be reassured that they are safe or that you have the situation in hand. Maintain a professional demeanor; be calm. Your actions have a greater impact on the individual with whom you are speaking than the words you say. Try to provide as much privacy as possible because witnesses may be more forthcoming with information if they are not being observed by others, particularly the suspect or suspects. Record what the witnesses relay about the incident; use quotation marks in your notes if you write exactly what a witness stated. Do not correct slang or foul language. Just write exactly what the witness said.

Make sure your notes are complete. Secure contact information from anyone you believe may be able to provide information regarding the incident. Ask for backup telephone numbers for friends or family members if you suspect you may have difficulty contacting these people. The more work you accomplish during the initial gathering of evidence, interviews, and observations, the easier the report writing process will be.

MAINTENANCE OF RECORDS: FIELD NOTES, REPORTS, INTERVIEWS, AND EVIDENCE

Criminal justice agencies are extremely protective of their records. They prefer having security surrounding the information they gather in order to protect and preserve the confidentiality of their records. Initially, agencies are concerned about compromising ongoing investigations. Secondarily, agencies are concerned about compromising undercover investigations and jeopardizing undercover officers. A third concern is that some investigations may not lead to criminal prosecution, and individuals who might be the target of these investigations would have their reputations damaged if this information were to be made public.

Citizens do have a right to certain information gathered by criminal justice agencies under the Freedom of Information Act. However, agencies retain the right to censor sensitive material and to restrict access in some instances to those individuals directly involved or mentioned in their records. For example, individuals involved in a traffic accident are entitled to receive a copy of the accident report for their insurance companies or attorneys. Defendants are entitled to certain information involving their defense, but this information is generally released by the commonwealth attorney or state attorney rather than the law enforcement agency.

The most frequent inquiry concerning law enforcement agency records comes from the media, particularly in high-profile cases. Television reporters and newspaper reporters are relentless in their pursuit of information. To boost ratings or beat deadlines or the competition, these individuals will go to great lengths to secure confidential information. A major concern of all law enforcement agencies is that in reporters' zeal to report the news, an investigation will be compromised and a suspect will evade prosecution or fail to receive appropriate punishment due to premature influencing of the community.

Records Management Systems

A records management system is a valuable source of relevant information essential to the investigative, arrest, and judicial processes. The failure to manage the records function can result in liability or a loss of public confidence. Most criminal justice agencies have a set of standardized guidelines for the management of records, including practices for the receipt, storage, and disposition of records maintained by the agency. These policies and procedures are designed to ensure the integrity of the records process.

Life Cycle of Records

The life cycle of records refers to the different stages records go through as part of their lifespan: creation, maintenance, and final disposition.[18] When an incident, accident, or event occurs, the first step is to investigate it. During the investigation process, the criminal justice professional (whether law enforcement, corrections, or private security officer) writes field notes (as discussed in an earlier section of this chapter). Those notes become the initial documents used to create a record.

Most criminal justice agencies located in metropolitan and urban areas use an electronic records management system to store and maintain their records. Smaller or rural agencies rely on paper copies and filing systems using cabinets or some form of manual storage to house their records. Whatever process is used for the maintenance of records, the goal is to ensure the records are readily accessible and continually updated as information changes or is presented. The maintenance stage of the life cycle is the most work intensive, especially depending upon how long your records are in existence.

The final stage of the life cycle, disposition, is the point where the record is determined to be of no further need or where the record must be archived due to federal or state laws or agency requirements for retention of the information. Table 6.1 shows an example of a records retention schedule established by the State of Connecticut, Division of Criminal Justice.[19] This schedule was established based on the records' administrative, fiscal, legal, and historical values, in addition to any statutory or regulatory requirements also in existence. The retention period listed is considered the minimum requirement. Other states and agencies have created their own records retention schedule that also works in accordance with federal statutory and regulatory requirements for records maintenance.

TABLE 6.1 ■ State of Connecticut, Records Retention Schedule, Division of Criminal Justice		
Records Series Title	**Description**	**Retention**
Closed Grand Jury Investigations—No Arrests	Documents grand jury investigations that do not lead to an arrest	5 years
Civil Litigation Case Files	Documents civil litigation proceedings	5 years after expiration of appeal period
Felony Dispositions—Capital	Documents criminal litigation proceedings for capital felonies	Permanent
Felony Dispositions—Class A and B	Documents criminal litigations for Class A and B felonies	20 years after expiration of appeal period
Felony Dispositions—Class C, D, and E	Documents criminal litigations for Class C, D, and E felonies	10 years after expiration of appeal period
Felony Dispositions—Unclassified	Documents criminal litigation proceedings for unclassified felonies	10 years after expiration of appeal term
Juvenile Dispositions	Documents juvenile litigation proceedings for Family with Service Needs and Youth in Crisis	1 year after case closed
Misdemeanor Dispositions	Documents criminal litigation proceedings for Class A, B, C, D, and unclassified misdemeanors	2 years after expiration of appeal period
Motor Vehicle Stop Reports	Consists of traffic stop data recorded pursuant to CGS §54-1/(Alvin W. Penn Racial Profiling Prohibition Act). Data should be submitted to the African-American Affairs Commission.	30 days from date information entered into system
Uncorroborated Criminal Allegations	Consists of records that document case investigations of alleged criminal activity that have not been supported by additional and confirming facts or evidence	15 months after creation
Violations and Infractions Dispositions	Documents criminal litigation proceedings for violations and infractions	1 year after expiration of appeal period
Regulatory Referrals	Documents regulatory action information that is associated with an identifiable health care entity	2 years after receipt

Once a record is no longer needed and can be destroyed, agencies must follow the protocol set forth to do so. The same is true for archiving records.

Records management is an important part of the criminal justice system that we do not always consider. Writing field notes; completing reports; and interviewing witnesses, suspects, and victims—these are the duties we most often ascribe to criminal justice professionals. However, the creation and maintenance of those records are what details the story. Without records, you have no support or corroboration for your work.

SUMMARY

Written communication serves as the backbone for criminal justice agencies. Thousands of pieces of information are processed daily through the course of normal operations. This information is important to establishing the chain of custody for evidence and to the ultimate resolution of cases.

No discussion of written communication within criminal justice agencies would be complete without addressing the issues of reports. Writing reports involves more than merely placing words on a page. Knowing how to select the appropriate words and how to compose sentences and paragraphs is vital to the success of the communication.

The sentence and the paragraph are the two most fundamental units of written communication. Paragraphs must be fully developed using a topic sentence to guide and influence readers. Transitional words or phrases must also be utilized in developing a coherent paragraph.

The most frequent type of report in criminal justice is the offense or incident report. Supplemental reports are the second most utilized form in law enforcement and corrections fields. Every offense or incident report or supplemental report begins with field notes taken by the officer or investigator. Good field notes are vital to the preparation of a thorough and inclusive report.

The content of field notes should serve as an outline or brief synopsis of the incident. These notes should contain personal observations and statements made by the victim, witness(es), and suspect(s). Descriptions of important persons, places, or things, as well as any other relevant information, should also be included.

The offense or incident report should be clear, concise, and complete. The questions of who, what, when, where, why, and how should be answered. The first paragraph should set the tone for the report. Every effort should be made to ensure that reports are readable—in terms of both legibility and grammar.

Supplemental reports may be utilized to record suspect statements with the intent to impeach the suspect's credibility or to compromise the suspect's integrity. These reports also provide supervisors with the pending status of a case and allow them to manage case logs. Supplemental offense reports are also used to denote the gathering, processing, and disposition of physical evidence.

The preservation of records is of utmost importance to criminal justice agencies. Without the records obtained through the proper processes and procedures, these agencies would have nothing on which to build a case. Criminal justice agencies establish procedures for the storage of records, including their location and the official time frame for retention, as well as the processes for disposition of those records once a case has been resolved or concluded. Protecting their work and retaining it in a secure facility or location is a priority for all agencies, so most have security procedures established to ensure that evidence does not become displaced or disappear entirely during the process of resolving a case or claim.

Investigating an incident, accident, or event requires more than physically surveying the site. Criminal justice professionals have the responsibility of collecting evidence, witness statements, suspect information, and all possible information impacting the investigation. Writing reports to present this information is a vital part of this process. Therefore, criminal justice professionals must follow proper procedures for writing, including using correct grammar, spelling, punctuation, and word choice. Also, they must ensure that their information is correct, complete, clear, and concise so that the average person could understand what is written in the way in which it is intended.

KEY TERMS

Active voice 122

Analogy 124

Anecdote 124

Offense or incident report 127

Passive voice 122

Point of view 125

Rambling sentence 122

Redundancy 119

Sentence 118

Supplemental report 128

Tone 126

Topic sentence 123

Transition 124

Voice 122

Wordiness 121

FOR FURTHER REFLECTION AND DISCUSSION

1. The following topics can be developed into paragraphs. Choose two, and write a topic sentence for each. From these two, expand one of your topic sentences into a well-developed paragraph.

    a. A hero

    b. The quality of your training

    c. Your most memorable day on the job

    d. Your favorite supervisor

    e. Your most embarrassing moment

2. In the following sentences, change the voice when necessary. Also, explain the reason for the change.

    a. The brakes were not completely fixed by the garage repairman.

    b. The car crashed into the large oak tree during the rainstorm.

    c. The driver was absolutely lost.

    d. The recruits are learning the necessity of basic writing skills.

3. Analyze the effect word selection has on the development of solid sentences and paragraphs, and explain your findings.

4. Analyze the following statement, and decide whether you support the statement. If you support the statement, state your reasons for doing so. If you disagree with the statement, explain your position.

    "I have been a police officer for 17 years. I have never read a report after I completed it. I don't need to. I know what I said, and that's enough for me. I can always explain it later if I have to."

5. Create an incident report involving a purse snatching. The victim's name is Mary Leaves. Develop your own details, and prepare this report in the appropriate format. Be sure to answer the questions who, what, when, where, why, and how.

ETHICAL ISSUE EXERCISES

1. Could the manner in which a report is written affect the course of an investigation?

2. Should a report be written in such a manner that it could help a friend collect insurance money? Why, or why not? Explain your answer.

3. Should you write a report to aid the prosecutor's case? Why, or why not? Explain your answer.

4. Should you write a report in such a way as to aid an abused spouse? Why, or why not? Explain your answer.

5. Should you write a report in such a way that it will help clear an officer of misconduct charges? Why, or why not? Explain your answer.

See the study site for this book for examples of various criminal justice reports, forms, logs, and narratives: **http://study.sagepub.com/ grubb**

7

INTERVIEWING AND INTERROGATING

Witnesses and Suspects

A private-sector investigator employed as a security officer has scheduled a meeting with an employee of the company to discuss her involvement in the theft of thousands of dollars in petty cash. The investigator might begin the conversation with: "... My name is Joe and I work for the company too, mostly with the audit group from accounting. I want to talk with you about some small inconsistencies in our petty-cash expense reporting and what we can do to correct this problem going forward."

Each of these sentences is in some way a deception. . . . Deceptions are powerful tools available to the investigator. Using them incorrectly will result in confessions that the courts consider coercive. For example, an investigator is permitted to use props such as impressive-looking files or videotapes. . . . Remember that just because an investigative technique is legal does not mean that its use is ethical.[1]

—Christopher D. Hoffman, CPO,
"Investigative Interviewing: Strategies
and Techniques"*

At the very core of effective law enforcement is the ability to initiate and to sustain a conversation with people. Whether the intent is to gather information or to elicit a confession, good communication skills are essential.

Criminal justice professionals, by their very nature, are outgoing, gregarious individuals—in other words, people who like to talk. Speak with a police officer for 5 minutes and then realize how much information has been gathered by the officer in this brief time span. This process is a natural occurrence, not intrusive or offensive. Were you comfortable? Did you feel at ease with the officer? Congratulations! You have just been the unwitting subject of a police interview.

THE INTERVIEW PROCESS

Before you begin your study of interviewing and interrogation, you need to understand the difference between these two processes. An **interview** is conducted when a person who is not a suspect is questioned to determine whether the person possesses information that is of value to the investigator's cause. The definition for **interrogation** is essentially the same as that of an interview, *except* that the person being interviewed is a suspect in the case.

Interviewing

Interviewing may best be described as a conversation with a purpose. In a situation such as this, a speaker or interviewer is attempting to solicit information that may or may not be detrimental to the individual being questioned. Interviewing is more than a list of questions; it is an opportunity to establish a rapport.

Three basic purposes exist for an interview:

1. **Securing information**. The success of this type of interview is based on the interviewer's ability to solicit information with proper questions and to listen effectively.

2. **Giving information**. In this type of interview, the interviewer is the one providing information. Success here is determined by the interviewer's ability to choose and articulate the right information.

3. **Influencing behavior**. In these situations, the interviewer is attempting to persuade the interviewee to change behavior or to make a decision. The success of this type of interview is dependent upon the interviewer's ability to engender trust and credibility and to use persuasive tactics.

Successful interviewers develop a plan. This plan entails putting the interviewee at ease and allowing that individual to talk. This conversation frequently occurs in a relatively private setting. Good interviewers minimize distractions and select questions carefully. They know how to ask questions and when to ask questions. Good interviewers take brief notes and maintain control of the interview at all times. They do not overwhelm their subjects. Above everything else, good interviewers are good listeners. They try to conclude an interview on a positive note to maintain a connection with the interviewee.

Becoming a good interviewer takes practice, but you also can follow several suggestions to help you develop and perfect your technique.

- **Carefully prepare**. The key to a successful interview involves preparation.

- **Maintain control**. A good interviewer maintains control of both himself or herself and the direction that the interview is taking. No matter how upsetting a crime is, you must be able to act sympathetic and nonjudgmental.

- **Listen**. An effective interviewer must also be a good listener. You need to be able to read both the verbal and nonverbal messages that your witness is delivering to know the appropriate direction for your attack.

- **Be alert and patient**. An effective interviewer is not pushy but is flexible in his or her attack. Maintain mental alertness and be patient.

- **Be a good actor**. An effective interviewer is a good listener, but he or she is also a good actor. You should be self-confident and maintain a professional image.

Scenario: A market owner observes a purse snatching incident through the window of his store. He is reluctant to become involved. An officer arrives at the scene to take a report from the victim and, in the process, interviews any persons he believes may have witnessed the incident. After taking the victim's statement, he goes into the market to interview the owner.

Officer:	Good morning, sir, how are you today?
Owner:	I'm fine. How are you, officer?
Officer:	Fine, thanks. My name is Officer Jackson. I'm here investigating a purse snatching, which occurred approximately 10 minutes ago. I was wondering if you heard or saw anything.
Owner:	I'm not sure. Where did it occur?
Officer:	It occurred across the street from your store.
Owner:	What happened?
Officer:	According to the victim, she was walking down the street across from the front of your store when someone ran up behind her, grabbed her purse, and fled.
Owner:	What did the purse snatcher look like?
Officer:	She described him as a young white male, approximately 15 to 18 years old, with blond hair, and wearing a black leather jacket.
Owner:	No, I'm sorry. I didn't see anyone like that around here this morning.
Officer:	Have you seen anyone that looks like this person hanging around your store before today?
Owner:	No, not around my store.
Officer:	Have you seen anyone hanging around the area that looks like this person?
Owner:	Yeah, now that you mention it. I've seen a blond kid in this area early in the morning over by the produce lot. There's a bunch of guys that hang around over there hoping to get a day job from the produce shippers.
Officer:	Would you happen to know which produce shipper he might have worked for?

Owner: Try Johnson's Apples; they're always looking for extra help to load and unload the trucks. As a matter of fact, I think I saw a blond kid over there last week. Had a gold cross earring in his right ear.

Officer: Thank you. I really appreciate your help. I'm sorry, I don't think I got your name when I introduced myself.

Owner: Oh, I'm sorry. My name is David Hedgepeth.

Officer: Mr. Hedgepeth, if you see the young man you described in the area again or if you remember anything else, would you please call me? Here is my name and department telephone number. I really appreciate your taking the time to speak with me. Also, if there's anything I can do for you, be sure to give me a call. Thanks again.

As evidenced by the foregoing scenario, interviewing is a process of acquiring information through carefully worded questions. Good interviewers have a keen intuitive sense. They elicit information and expand upon prior information by being sensitive to the needs of the interviewee. They have a high emotional quotient; they are empathetic to the interviewee, placing themselves in the interviewee's position and understanding that people are often reluctant to provide information or to get involved because they are afraid of the consequences that may follow.

Interviewers should try to conclude an interview by offering an opportunity for future assistance, thus establishing a **quid pro quo** (one hand washes the other) relationship. The interviewee then feels as if he is assisting the officer in the investigation and developing a friend at the police department—an invaluable contact for future reference.

In some instances, officers will conduct interrogations rather than interviews, specifically where a suspect is involved. Interviews and interrogations differ in the approach an officer takes. The next section specifically discusses interrogation and the ways you should prepare for it.

Interrogating

Interrogating is confrontational by nature. While interviewing attempts to solicit information through congenial or persuasive means, interrogating is a process by which the suspect is carefully maneuvered into a position of no retreat. The goal of interrogation is to solicit or acquire information that is generally not in the legal best interests of the individual being interviewed.

Interrogating involves a variety of psychological manipulations to facilitate a confession from a suspect. Most interrogations begin with an interview. As the focus becomes narrow or more specific, though, the interview transitions from a pleasant conversation to an accusation. Once the officer has initiated the interrogation process, however, no opportunity exists for a return to the pleasantness of the interview technique. Interrogations are structured, exacting, and lengthy, usually commanding a minimum of 4 hours and perhaps longer, depending on the skill of the interrogator and the resistance of the suspect. The interrogation may then follow a process that might include several steps, some of which are direct confrontation; theme development; eliminating denials; overcoming objections; gaining the suspect's attention; and, finally, the confession.

- **Direct confrontation**. The interviewee (suspect) is told that he is suspected of being involved in a crime. The officer presents the suspect with a synopsis of what occurred and then presents some evidence to support the scenario (evidence that may or may not be factual). The officer then observes the suspect.

- **Theme development**. The interviewee (suspect) is provided with some justification or excuse for having committed the crime. An example would be a shooting incident involving the suspect and a friend who had slept with the suspect's wife. The officer might say, "If he had slept with my wife, I might have shot him myself." This type of statement gives the suspect an opportunity for an explanation for the crime and serves as a transition from the previous confrontation.

- **Eliminating denials**. The interviewer (officer) is attempting to eliminate or narrow the opportunity for evasion. The officer uses facts of the case to support the involvement of the suspect in the crime.

- **Overcoming objections**. The interviewer (officer) proposes a reason why the suspect did not commit the crime. In this regard, the officer is attempting to allow the suspect to realize that no other explanation exists that fits the facts of the case. The suspect begins to realize that the evidence cannot be explained away.

- **Gaining the suspect's attention**. The interviewer (officer) attempts to project a sincere attitude to gain the suspect's trust. In this way, the suspect may feel compelled to confess to the crime to absolve himself or herself of the psychological burden of guilt. The success of this technique is measured by the suspect's silence and acceptance of comfort.

- **Confession**. In this instance, the suspect finally surrenders to the officer and admits involvement in the crime. At this point, the officer must provide the suspect with comfort through a variety of physical and emotional techniques. Officers encourage the suspect to put his or her story in writing as a means of alleviating feelings of guilt. Officers should be particularly supportive to convey a sense of absolution of guilt and to ensure compliance on the part of the suspect.[2]

Officers involved in interrogations should seek to calm a suspect prior to the conclusion of an interrogation segment. This debriefing is performed to reduce the propensity of the suspect for personal harm in the wake of a confession.

By developing proper interrogation techniques, officers facilitate the resolution of crimes and provide guilty suspects an opportunity for psychological relief or forgiveness. An element to be considered in this psychological manipulation, however, is the appropriateness of the setting.

Preparing for an Interview or Interrogation

When preparing for an interview, you must gather information or data from three areas: case information, background information, and personal information. You also must address the setting and the questions you will pose. The following information addresses each of these areas, beginning with the gathering of data or information.

Case Information

To be successful as an interviewer, you must have the answers to several questions that you will ask. In this manner, you are prepared to recognize deception on the part of the interviewee early on, and you can confront him or her and attempt to have him or her believe you have all the answers.

Obtain case information by doing the following:

- Review a copy of the incident report and make note of the date and time of occurrence

- Review all photographs of the scene

- Review the information obtained from other interviews

- Identify key information that is known about the case that can be used to verify the suspect's truthfulness

Background Information

Obtain background information for this incident by reviewing the following:

- Prior arrests. You should know what the suspect's prior involvement has been. Specifically, you should pay close attention to notes of past techniques used by the suspect and/or his or her associates. People tend to maintain the same habits. Therefore, this knowledge could be used against them.

- Arresting officers. If possible, you should interview officers who arrested the suspect on prior occasions. They could possess useful information.

- Prior interviews. Obtain copies of any previous interviews conducted with the suspect. Examine video or audio tapes for mannerisms and defenses that the suspect used.

Personal Information

Obtaining information of a personal nature about the suspect may give you some insight into which techniques will be most effective in questioning him or her. Specifically, you will need to

- Know age, date of birth, where the suspect was born, where he or she has lived, and the conditions under which he or she has lived.

- Identify the suspect's likes and dislikes. Use this information in your interview.

- Identify the suspect's marital status; the number of children he or she has; the children's names, if possible; and the suspect's parental information.

The Setting

The appropriate setting for an interview and interrogation may vary with the intent of the investigator. However, privacy is an essential element regardless of the setting. Prior to the initiation of any formal investigation, the officer will develop a plan or theme for acquiring information. In the development process of this theme is the issue of the appropriate setting. The appropriate setting may be divided into two broad categories: informal and formal.

Interviewing in the Informal Setting

Interviews of this nature may run the gamut from the casual conversation to the point at which the officer initiates an accusatory phase, also referred to as a "narrowing of the focus." When a police officer narrows the focus of an interview to one suspect or begins to accuse one individual of a crime, a transition to the interrogation aspect occurs. However, prior to this transition, plenty of settings exist in which to gather information. The simplest and most effective technique may be the "street corner" conversation. With the renewed interest in "beat police officers," or community policing, the art of conversation is more important than ever. This simple technique allows police officers to network or become friendly with the citizens in their assigned areas of patrol.

Street corner conversations are designed primarily to build a rapport with the citizens and to become more familiar with the individuals and their respective positions in the community. Officers begin to develop a schematic or diagram of informal and formal social relationships among individuals and their families, as well as individuals and their associates. The significance of this background work is that it places officers in a position to gather information more easily. People tend to be more open and more candid with their friends than with a formal symbol of authority. Furthermore, these same people are more willing to take a stand or speak out against deviant or criminal elements in their neighborhoods if they have confidence in "their" police officers.

While not a formal setting, when an individual is asked to have a seat in a police cruiser, the tone or complexion of the conversation changes. This setting provides the officer with a little more control of the situation and tends to reduce outside distractions. Officers may be more focused in the intent of their interview. In fact, this type of interview may be more goal directed in attempting to elicit specific information concerning a crime. By merely inviting the individual into the police cruiser, the officer has subtly increased the amount of psychological pressure.

By the same token, when an officer enters an individual's residence to interview a witness, the psychological pressure becomes less because the officer is in the domain of the individual. Officers frequently interview citizens in their home so they can attempt to establish rapport; to gather information; or, in some instances, to initiate the previously mentioned "narrowing of the focus." Since most individuals are comfortable in their homes, if the interview becomes too specific or borders on accusation, these individuals are provided with a variety of distractions that can ease the psychological pressure.

Another informal interview setting is the place of employment or business. Most individuals are relatively comfortable in their place of employment since they are generally surrounded with acquaintances, friends, or familiar objects. This location provides them with a sense of psychological comfort. However, the arrival of a police officer may disrupt this comfort. Police officers frequently enter businesses to converse with the owners or managers about a broad array of topics. Yet when the officer arrives to speak with a specific individual or with a specific intent, the workplace may become anxiety filled. The mere presence of the officer will certainly arouse curiosity and generate gossip among the workers. The individual being questioned loses his or her anonymity among colleagues and becomes the center of attention. This unwanted attention frequently induces a defensive response that may serve as a barrier to the communication process. However, the officer may overcome this barrier by merely asking a few questions and establishing a later date and time to continue the line of inquiry. This date for further interviewing or questioning may be scheduled in a more formal setting, which is usually associated with the individual coming to the police department to speak with the officer.

Interviewing in the Formal Setting

The officer who conducts interviews at the police department enjoys almost complete control of the situation. He is familiar with the physical surroundings and the official operations of the organization. The individual who comes to the police department, however, is usually ill at ease or anxious. The symbols of authority associated with law enforcement adorn the walls of the facility, tremendous numbers of uniformed and nonuniformed police officers are milling about, and the omnipresent police radio can be heard in the background. These symbols set the stage for the officer and the individual's exchange.

In a formal setting, the officer attempts to isolate the individual being interviewed and to remove all distractions or to minimize the number of distractions. This process usually occurs by placing the individual in an interview room that is generally sparsely furnished and usually devoid of items that will serve to draw the focus away from the officer. Often, the casual tone of questioning is abandoned in favor of a more direct or pointed line of inquiry—in other words, specific answers to specific questions.

This type of interviewing is not to be confused with interrogation since the officer has not crossed the line from conversation to confrontation. Pointed questions or direct questions need not be confrontational yet may remain specific in nature. At some point, the officer may be compelled to change the focus of the interview to an interrogation. If the mood or tone of the interview changes from the interview to interrogation or if the officer's questions are structured in a such a manner as to narrow the focus of the investigation to this specific individual as a suspect, then legal issues concerning individual rights (***Miranda v. Arizona*** decision) arise.

While interviews may be conducted in a variety of settings, most of which lend themselves to the informal, interrogations are mostly formal by nature. The interrogation does not lend itself to an informal setting as interrogations, by definition, are confrontational. They imply an accusation, and the individual being accused is the one who is present before the officer.

Interview and Interrogation Questions

A question is a request, either direct or implied, for an interviewee to think about a specific subject. Interview questions should be kept simple so that you encourage the interviewee to answer. Remember that interview questions are the key to obtaining the interviewee's knowledge, feelings, or information about a specific incident. If you keep the interview as conversational in tone as possible, you will ensure that the interviewee provides responses to your questions. After all, holding a conversation requires a certain amount of give and take during the interview. An important point to remember is to ask questions—not to make statements. Statements do not require answers, and the interviewee will not provide you with information.

Types of Questions

Two main types of questions are generally asked during investigative interviews: **closed questions** and **open questions**. Closed questions typically require a simple "yes" or "no" response or some undeniable fact, such as the interviewee's address, telephone number, or place of employment. This type of question is usually asked in the beginning stage of an interview to put the interviewee at ease. Closed questions are useful when you want to maintain maximum control over the interview or when you want to save time because they limit the interviewee's response. You may also use this type of questioning with reluctant witnesses or interviewees who are not expected to give detailed explanations. Closed questions limit the ability to establish a rapport between the interviewer and the interviewee.

Open questions cannot be answered with "yes" or "no." These questions require the interviewee to think clearly and to reveal the greatest amount of information and cause the most distress in the interviewee. Open questions can help you

- Discover the interviewee's needs, attitudes, values, priorities, and aspirations.

- Build rapport.

- Encourage the interviewee to express feelings in a nonthreatening environment.

- Determine the interviewee's frame of reference.

Open questions come in a variety of types, each with its own characteristics and purpose. The types of open questions are reflective, directive, pointed, indirect, self-appraisal, diversion, and leading.

- **Reflective questions**. These types of questions use the interviewee's comments as a means of handling objections the interviewee has to responding to an initial question. "Let me see if I've got this straight . . ." or "What I'm hearing you say is that you do not want to comment because you don't want our conversation to get back to . . . ; is that correct?" You can then assure the interviewee that your conversation is confidential, that any statements he or she makes will not get back to whomever, and then repeat the question that triggered the objection by the interviewee.

- **Directive questions**. Directive questions help the interviewee understand the advantages of cooperation. These questions are designed to help the interviewee see the common ground he or she shares with the investigator. "You do want to get to the bottom of this, don't you?" "I know you would like your side of the story to be written in my report, right?"

- **Pointed questions**. Pointed questions are specific in nature. They are complex, detailed, and persuasive. The interviewer asks exactly what is desired so that the interviewee understands that you believe he or she is ready, willing, and able to answer your questions. Pointed questions must be thoughtfully developed and not necessarily accusatory or offensive in nature.

- **Indirect questions**. Indirect questions are often used at the beginning of an interview or at some point where you require a change of pace in your discussion. This type of question helps interviewees express opinions, suggestions, or feelings. With indirect questions, interviewers can grow to understand the interviewee's thoughts or needs.

- **Self-appraisal questions**. This type of question is used to stimulate conversation between the interviewer and the interviewee. The interviewer uses this type of question to identify with the interviewee. An investigator can develop hypotheses about an incident through self-appraisal questions. Usually deceptive or evasive interviewees find it almost impossible to be consistent in answering self-appraisal questions.

- **Diversion questions**. Diversion questions have two purposes: (1) to distract the interviewee's thoughts from the issue and (2) to build rapport between the investigator and the interviewee. Diversion questions are particularly useful when attempting to distract highly emotional interviewees. For example, if you are interviewing a witness to a homicide, you might notice that the witness is extremely agitated and shaken by his or her experience. The witness requires time to realize that the danger is over. You might use diversion questions unrelated to the homicide to reassure her or him that all is well. You could ask, "What type of work do you do?" or "Have you lived in this area for very long?" As the witness begins to calm down, he or she will be able to focus on what was seen or heard during the homicide.

- **Leading questions**. Leading questions can be used to build rapport and to communicate understanding and acceptance to the interviewee. When using leading questions containing implicit messages, an interviewer can maintain moderate emotional tension in the interview. When poorly used, however, leading questions can elicit unreliable, invalid responses. Nonetheless, leading questions used to build rapport can stimulate dialogue and encourage cooperation.[3]

Principles of Effective Question Development

The following guidelines will help you to develop effective questioning strategies:

- Use open questions when appropriate.
- Use closed questions when appropriate.
- Keep questions simple.
- Avoid third-degree-type questions.
- Ask leading questions where appropriate (i.e., assisting the interviewee in saving face).
- Ask tough questions.
- Ask self-appraisal questions.

In developing your questions, consider that people often do things that we would consider "dumb," "stupid," "dangerous," or "foolish." Once you acknowledge that people do, in fact, commit crimes we cannot possibly begin to understand, then you can see how important the process of questioning witnesses, suspects, and victims really is. You must be brave enough to ask questions that would be considered rude or intrusive in polite society. You should also pursue unanswered questions by repeating those questions the interviewee has failed to answer. You should not demand an answer to your question or point out to the interviewee that he or she failed to answer your question, but try rewording the question. Many interviewees try to provoke an interrogator, even if they are not suspects but merely witnesses or victims.

After thoughtfully considering the questions you wish to pose to a suspect, victim, or witness, you must also address any potential legal issues that might arise during your investigation and questioning or interviewing. The next section of the chapter discusses legal issues relevant to gathering acceptable information.

Legal Issues

Generally, the laws surrounding admissions or confessions do not apply in the interview situation since interviews are generally construed to be a conversation. The tone of the conversation may vary depending on the type of information the officer is attempting to gather, but unless and until the investigator narrows the focus of the investigation to one individual, ***Escobedo v. Illinois*** (378 U.S. 478, 1964), *Miranda*, and subsequent court cases do not come into play.

In the mid-1960s, the Supreme Court set the tone for the use of confessions and admissions by introducing *Escobedo* and *Miranda*[4] into police parlance. In 1960, Danny Escobedo was arrested for murder. He was interrogated by investigators who stated that they had an "airtight" case, and he should confess. Escobedo requested an attorney and was advised that he could not simply walk out. Meanwhile, his attorney, who was present at the police station, was advised that his client was being interrogated and could not be disturbed. Eventually confessing, Escobedo was convicted and appealed his case to the United States Supreme Court. The Court stated that suspects are entitled to counsel during police interrogations to protect their rights, and counsel should be provided when requested.

Miranda went a step further in 1966 when the Court stated that defendants must be advised of their rights prior to questioning by police because of the inherent coercive nature involved in police interrogations. Ernesto Miranda was arrested for kidnapping and rape in Phoenix, Arizona. He subsequently signed a confession after a lengthy police interrogation. Miranda appealed this conviction, and the United States Supreme Court set forth the guidelines for the issuance of the infamous Miranda warning and waiver of rights.

While these cases did not serve as a barrier to acquiring confessions, they did serve to provide some structure in which police conducted interrogations. To acquire statements of guilt, police officers became more sophisticated in their questioning techniques. The introduction of deception, trickery, and psychological manipulation allowed investigators to resolve their cases.

Attorneys responding to this new approach to obtaining confessions began to question the tactics of police officers regarding their interrogation. Voluntariness of the confession was no longer the focal point of the confession but whether police officers should be allowed to use trickery, deceit, and psychological manipulation in interrogating their clients.

Trickery, deception, and psychological manipulation do not necessarily render a voluntary confession inadmissible. However, in ***Lynumn v. Illinois***,[5] the Court ruled that a suspect's free choice was impaired by going beyond the evidence connecting her to a crime and introducing a completely extrinsic consideration in the form of an empty but plausible threat. In ***Spano v. New York***,[6] another extrinsic factor was examined when coercion was used to lead the suspect to believe that failure to confess would result in adverse consequences for others.

On an individual basis, these factors may become confusing and burdensome for the court to resolve. Therefore, to establish clarity and a reasonable alternative, in ***Arizona v. Fulminante***,[7] the Supreme Court used a totality of circumstances test to determine that a confession made to an informant in exchange for the promise of protection from other prison inmates was involuntary because it was coerced by a credible threat of physical violence.

Some courts will not accept confessions induced by either direct or implied promises. The United States Supreme Court and courts of local jurisdiction will allow police officers some gamesmanship when it comes to interrogating suspects. Nevertheless, no court will allow an admission of guilt if it is coerced by a government official. Latitude in this area will be determined by the local court of jurisdiction. Therefore, the officer must become acquainted with the practices of the local judges and their rulings concerning the admissibility of evidence concerning confessions. However, the issuing of a Miranda warning need not serve as an impediment or a major hurdle in the process of acquiring a confession. The Miranda warning may be issued in such a way that the suspect is not deterred from speaking with the criminal justice professional.

Sample Interrogation Scenario: At 1:50 a.m., district officers were advised of a robbery that occurred at the local 7-11. The suspect was described as a white male in a dark jacket who had brandished a knife at the clerk and taken the cash from the register. The suspect had fled from the store on foot and was stopped by responding units two blocks from the 7-11 at 2:00 a.m. The officers conducted a pat-down search of the suspect and found a knife. The clerk was brought to the location of the suspect and made a positive identification. The suspect was arrested and booked. The next day, prior to an arraignment hearing, the suspect was questioned by investigators concerning this incident.

Investigator:	Good morning, Mr. Jackson.
Suspect:	Mornin'.
Investigator:	How are you feeling this morning?
Suspect:	Okay. How 'bout you?
Investigator:	Fine, thanks. Can I get you some coffee?
Suspect:	Yeah, black is good.
Investigator:	I'm glad you could come down to the department this morning. I just want to clear up a few things since the last time we spoke. Is that okay with you?

Suspect:	Yeah, okay.
Investigator:	Now, before we get started, I need to inform you of your Miranda rights. This is just a formality, so we can clear up those few things. Okay?
Suspect:	Okay.
Investigator:	You have the right to remain silent. Anything you say can and will be used against you in a court of law. You have the right to talk to an attorney and to have an attorney present while you are being questioned. If you desire an attorney and cannot afford one, an attorney will be appointed for you before any questioning begins. If you answer questions now without an attorney present, you still have the right to stop answering questions at any time. Do you understand these rights as I have explained them to you? If so, please place your initials by the "yes" box.[8]
Suspect:	Yeah. Okay.
Investigator:	Good. Please put your initials here.
	(Suspect places initial where indicated.)
Investigator:	Do you wish to waive these rights? (In other words, do you want to talk to me?) If so, please sign on the line, and place the date and time.
	(Suspect places initials where indicated.)
Suspect:	Yeah. Okay.
Investigator:	Good. Now that we have that out of the way, let's talk. Mr. Jackson, I need to just clear up a few things. According to my notes, the last time we spoke, you stated you were on your way back from the 7-11 when the police stopped you. And you told the officer that you had gone to the 7-11 to buy a pack of cigarettes. Is that correct?
Suspect:	Yeah, that's right.
Investigator:	Well, Mr. Jackson, you didn't have any cigarettes at home? So you came out in the rain in order to get a pack of cigarettes?
Suspect:	Yeah, that's right. Do you smoke?
Investigator:	No, I don't.
Suspect:	When you need a cigarette, you need a cigarette. I didn't have any butts or anything in the ashtray.
Investigator:	I guess I understand. Now, according to what you told the officers, you didn't see anyone at all run past you?
Suspect:	No, I didn't see nobody.

Investigator:	Well, Mr. Jackson, how is it then when the officer searched you, you had a knife in your jacket pocket?
Suspect:	It's a dangerous neighborhood, and I carry the knife for protection.
Investigator:	After you were arrested and taken to booking, why did you ask the officer for a cigarette? And why were there no cigarettes listed on the booking property intake slip?
Suspect:	I must have lost them.
Investigator:	Mr. Jackson, can I call you Bob?
Suspect:	(Nods in the affirmative.)
Investigator:	Bob, isn't it true that you went to the 7-11 with the idea of robbing the place?
Suspect:	No. I just went for some cigarettes.
Investigator:	Bob, what happened to the cigarettes between the time you left the 7-11 and the two blocks in which the officer stopped you?
Suspect:	I don't know.
Investigator:	Bob, let's look at this from my position. Suppose you were me. What would you think about what you just told me?
Suspect:	I don't know. I'd guess you would think I was lying.
Investigator:	Bob, I'm not trying to say that you're lying. I just want us to get to the truth here together. I know you're under a lot of pressure. Why don't we take a break, and you can have a cigarette, okay?
Suspect:	No, I quit about two years ago. I'll just have another cup of coffee.

While this scenario is certainly a brief and simple example of the interrogation process, the elements essential to acquiring an inculpatory statement are present. The investigator has endeavored to establish a rapport and level of trust with the suspect to find the truth. The Miranda warning was presented in a lawful manner but in such a way that it did not present a major obstacle or hurdle to the interrogative process. While some deception or trickery may have been utilized, the suspect was not placed in an environment that could be construed as coercive when viewed through the Supreme Court's edict—totality of the circumstances.

Avoiding False Confessions

False confessions occur for a number of reasons, on the part of law enforcement, as well as the suspect. Law enforcement officers engage in misclassification, coercion, and contamination behaviors that can result in a false confession. Likewise, suspects make one of three distinct types of confessions: voluntary, compliant, or persuaded. A false confession is an admission of guilt on the part of the suspect (including a written narrative or detailed description of the crime and "how" and "why" it occurred) of a crime, even though the individual did not commit the crime.[9]

False confessions occur for a multitude of reasons, with no one cause being totally responsible. For example, individual suspects who have particular personality traits or dispositions are more likely to be pressured into giving a false confession than others subjected to the same questioning process. Law enforcement officers do, however, engage in certain behaviors that begin the process of false confession.

Misclassification error. The first mistake takes place when law enforcement personnel decide a suspect is guilty, even when that individual is innocent. Once the suspect is targeted, each step in the process that follows is built on the presumption of guilt. The most consequential error that law enforcement officers can make is that of misclassification of an individual from innocent person to guilty suspect.

Misclassification errors sometimes occur because police officers' training has provided them with erroneous information regarding their ability to be human lie detectors. Because of their training, many officers believe certain behaviors to be indicative of deception when those behaviors are not. The accuracy rate for police detectives and other professionals in identifying deception is only 45% to 60%.[10]

Another reason for an innocent person being misclassified as a suspect might have to do with the individual's appearance. Perhaps the innocent person is the most readily noticed who fits the general description of the suspect given by witnesses. The individual could be reported to police by someone who saw a police sketch of the suspect, could be falsely identified in a lineup or from a mug shot, or could simply fit the official profile of the perpetrator.

Individuals may also be misclassified as suspects because of widespread crime-related themes. For example, family members may be led to falsely confess to a murder of a wife, children, or parents because police assume that most such murders are committed by family and will proceed to rule out family before considering other potential suspects.

Coercion error. Once an innocent person has been misclassified as a guilty suspect, that individual is subjected to interrogation. Law enforcement personnel want to establish guilt. So they use psychologically coercive methods, such as implicit or explicit promises of leniency and threats of harsher treatment. Another method simply relates to the interrogation methods as a whole. The individual is in a custodial environment designed to isolate and disempower. The longer interrogation lasts, the more stressful and unpleasant it becomes. Once the suspect becomes worn down or fatigued or sees no other way to escape the situation, he or she may believe a false confession to be the only way out. Others will comply when they are led to believe they can avoid a feared outcome by confessing. However, when a suspect believes his or her only choice is to comply, his or her confession is involuntary and the product of a **coercion error**.[11]

Contamination error. Once an individual has "confessed" to a crime, the police detectives then assist him or her in writing the postconfession narrative. At this stage, the suspect is subjected to "suggestions" from the police as to the reason for the crime. The detectives may use scenario-based inducements. (For example, in a rape case, the police pressured the suspect to admit to committing the rape because he had discovered his wife was having an affair. The police promised him counseling instead of prison if he would confess to that motive for the crime.) Police also will often provide vivid details and suggest facts of the crime to the suspect, thereby contaminating the suspect's narrative. Only interrogations captured entirely on video or audio can reveal how and when the interrogator (police detective) implied or suggested correct responses for the suspect to include in his or her narrative.

In most cases of false confession, no audio or video recording is available with which to prove **contamination error**.[12]

Reasons Some Individuals Confess

People who are highly suggestible, are compliant, have developmental disabilities, or have cognitive impairments; juveniles; and people with mental illnesses are most likely to falsely confess.

Highly suggestible people tend to have poor memories, high levels of anxiety, low self-esteem, low assertiveness, and personality factors that make them extremely susceptible to interrogation pressures. Compliant individuals avoid conflict and are acquiescent and eager to please others.

Because of subnormal intellectual abilities, low intelligence, short attention spans, poor memory, and poor conceptual and communication skills, people with developmental disabilities do not always understand statements made to them or the implications of their answers to specific questions. These individuals are not likely to grasp the complexity of situations or to understand that the police detective is really an adversary, not a friend. Individuals with developmental disabilities are also extremely eager to please. They will answer affirmatively when they feel that response is what the person asking the questions deems to be desirable.

Young children and adolescents are also characterized by many of the developmental traits that characterize people with developmental disabilities. These individuals are often immature, trusting of authority, and eager to please adult figures. Young children lack the cognitive capacity to understand the gravity of the situation or the long-term consequences for their responses to police questions.

People with mental illnesses are more likely to make false confessions because their psychiatric symptoms make them more likely to agree with, suggest, or "make up" false or misleading information. Individuals with mental illnesses may be more likely to make voluntary false confessions, but they are also easily coerced into making compliant ones.[13]

Despite the idea that false confessions are secured from individuals who are incapable of protecting themselves from making statements to that effect, the majority of false confessions are not elicited from them. On the contrary, most false confessions are obtained from people who have no disabling or limiting conditions.[14]

Types of False Confessions

The implication that the police detectives (or other officers) are solely to blame for false confessions disregards the potential for individuals to simply "confess" to a crime. Three distinct types of false confessions exist: **voluntary false confession**, **compliant false confession**, and **persuaded false confession**.

In the first, *voluntary false confession*, the suspect simply confesses to a crime—with no police interrogation involved. In some cases, the individual feels an internal compulsion or experiences an external pressure from someone other than the police to make a false confession. Individuals volunteer false confessions in the absence of police involvement for a variety of reasons:

- A desire for notoriety or fame

- The need to eliminate guilt over imagined or real acts

- An inability to distinguish between fantasy and reality

- A pathological need for acceptance or self-punishment

However, individuals do not need to have a psychological malady that leads them to falsely confess to a crime, as they can provide that confession for other reasons: to protect (or aid) the real criminal, to provide an alibi for a different crime, or to get revenge on someone. In most cases, the police discount voluntary false confessions.

Compliant false confessions are those given in response to coercion, stress, or pressure from police detectives. In most cases, the suspect knows that he or she is innocent of the crime and that what he or she is saying is false. The confession is usually recanted within a short time following the interrogation process. Compliant false confessions occur most frequently.

The last type of false confession is called *persuaded false confession*. When a suspect begins to doubt his or her own memory and becomes temporarily persuaded that he or she committed the crime (even if he or she has no memory of such a crime), the police interrogation tactics have succeeded in eliciting a persuaded false confession. In these interrogations, police detectives supply the suspect with a reason or reasons as to how he or she could have committed the crime and not remember it. In addition, they suggest a "repressed" memory (e.g., alcohol- or drug-induced blackout, PTSD, or that the crime was a traumatic experience for him or her and he or she repressed the memory of it). Once the suspect is convinced of the theory of amnesia, he or she will admit to committing the crime and begin to construct the postconfession narrative.

The narrative will contain numerous errors as the suspect must infer what happened during the commission of the crime—usually from what the police detectives told him or her rather than actual knowledge. Some suspects will use speculative and uncertain language (e.g., "I must have done it," "I probably did it," "I guess I did it," or "I could have done it") in their narratives.

Once the suspect is removed from the interrogation environment, he or she will often recant. These types of confessions usually occur in high-profile murder cases. They occur less frequently than the compliant false confessions, however.[15]

Ways to Prove a Confession Is False

You can prove that a confession is false by one of the following:

1. You can objectively establish that the suspect confessed to a crime that did not occur (e.g., the alleged victim of a murder is not dead).

2. You can objectively establish that the suspect could not have committed the crime due to physical impossibility (e.g., the suspect was in jail or prison at the exact time the crime occurred).

3. You can identify the true perpetrator of the crime and objectively establish his or her guilt.

4. You have scientific evidence (e.g., DNA) that conclusively establishes the suspect's innocence.

As a criminal justice professional, you must consider all possibilities when questioning suspects, witnesses, and victims. You cannot assume you have the perpetrator of a crime because an eyewitness identified that individual as being present at the time the crime was committed. You also cannot rely on your own interpretation of a suspect's body language or vocalics to accurately identify deception. Everyone wants to get a crime "off the books" as quickly as possible. However, speed does not equate to accuracy. It is better to take the time to properly conduct a thorough investigation than to incarcerate an individual based on a coerced and false confession.

Once you feel that you have effectively questioned the suspect, victim, or witness, you then must conclude the interview or interrogation. You want to use a structured approach to clearly bring an end to the session. The following section of the chapter offers suggestions for ending the interview or interrogation.

Terminating the Interview or Interrogation

Just because you seem to be at the end of the interview, you should not assume that no more information is forthcoming from the interviewee. On the contrary, you should continue to assume that more information is available, and you should ask questions such as "What else is there that you can tell me about what happened?" or "What else should I know about this incident?"

At some point, however, you will determine that the interview has reached its concluding or termination point. Then, you can end the interview in one of the following ways:

- Tell the interviewee you may contact him or her sometime in the future for a follow-up interview.

- Make an appointment with the interviewee for a second interview, and give yourself time to prepare further.

- Lead into a confrontation with the interviewee by announcing that you believe inconsistencies are present in his or her story and that these inconsistencies must be addressed.

- Attempt to gain a confession or admission of guilt.

The key to a successful interview or interrogation comes from a thoughtful approach to the process—holding the interview or interrogation in an appropriate location, asking the right types of questions, adhering to lawful interaction and questioning techniques, and closing the interview or interrogation properly. You want to maintain a relationship with the person you interviewed if you believe that he or she has more information to share, or you want to bring the matter to a close if the individual has revealed himself or herself to be the person committing the crime. You must determine the best way to conclude your meeting and follow through.

SUMMARY

Several keys are associated with becoming a good interviewer or a good interrogator. Chief among these is patience, patience, patience. The art of conversation takes time to learn and develop. The art and science of interrogation is no less demanding in its utilization of time. Good interviewers and interrogators are good listeners. They are empathetic and sometimes sympathetic to the people they are speaking with. However, any interview is a conversation with a purpose, and every interrogation is confrontational.

By developing good interview and interrogation techniques, criminal justice professionals facilitate the resolution of crimes and provide guilty suspects an opportunity for psychological relief or forgiveness. In addition to devising effective questioning methods, criminal justice professionals should prepare for interviews by obtaining case, background, and personal information. Reviewing copies of previous incident reports, speaking with prior arresting officers, and obtaining information of a personal nature concerning a witness are important in the development of a case. Remember to avoid false confessions by following appropriate steps to ensure that you do not coerce a suspect into admitting to the commission of a crime that he or she did not commit.

Interview questions are the key to obtaining the interviewee's knowledge, feelings, or information about a specific incident. If you keep the interview as conversational in tone as possible, you will ensure that the interviewee provides responses to your questions. Both closed and open questions should be a part of any interview setting.

At the end of an interview, remember that the interviewee probably has additional information to convey. You should continue to assume, therefore, that more information is available, and you should ask questions such as "What else is there that you can tell me about what happened?" or "What else should I know about this incident?"

You should attempt to end your interview by asking for a possible follow-up interview, scheduling a second interview to give yourself further preparation time, and/or leading into a confrontation with the witness to attempt to elicit a confession or admission of guilt.

KEY TERMS

Arizona v. Fulminante 154

Closed questions 151

Coercion error 157

Compliant false confession 158

Contamination error 158

Directive questions 151

Diversion questions 152

Escobedo v. Illinois 153

Indirect questions 152

Interrogation 144

Interview 144

Leading questions 152

Lynumn v. Illinois 154

Miranda v. Arizona 150

Misclassification error 157

Open questions 151

Persuaded false confession 158

Pointed questions 151

Quid pro quo 146

Reflective questions 151

Self-appraisal questions 152

Spano v. New York 154

Voluntary false confession 158

FOR FURTHER REFLECTION AND DISCUSSION

1. Compare and contrast settings that are appropriate for conducting an interview versus settings that are appropriate for an interrogation.

2. Are some settings more conducive to soliciting information than others?

3. Can the setting in which an interview or interrogation is conducted be manipulated to aid the investigator?

4. What are the legal guidelines concerning interrogations?

5. Does coercion, trickery, or deception nullify the admissibility of a confession? Why, or why not?

6. As a probation and parole officer, you routinely conduct interviews with your clients. During such an interview, a client inadvertently slips and admits to having information concerning a highly publicized ongoing homicide investigation. At this point, does the probation and parole officer have a legal obligation to stop the client from speaking any further concerning this matter? Why, or why not?

7. A corrections officer inadvertently overhears two inmates bragging about their past crimes. One of the inmates states that he committed a murder that was pinned on another individual. The other person not only was arrested but was convicted of the crime and is currently in another state penitentiary. Should the corrections officer make his or her presence known and stop the inmate from speaking any further about the crime? What should the corrections officer do with the information he or she has already obtained?

8. A security officer in a local department store was advised by the clerk that a shoplifter had removed a watch from the jewelry counter. The security officer detained the suspect and escorted him to the rear of the store where a small security office is located. At this point, the security officer asked the suspect, "Did you steal the watch?" What are the legal implications or restrictions placed on the security officer in this situation?

ETHICAL ISSUE EXERCISES

1. Should an officer be obligated to question a suspect when the physical evidence clearly points to the suspect's guilt? Why, or why not?

2. During the interrogation process, should an officer be allowed to lie to the suspect to elicit a response or open another avenue of questioning? Why, or why not?

3. Should an officer be concerned with trying to provide the suspect some psychological relief or support after a confession, particularly if the crime was heinous in nature? Why, or why not?

4. Should an officer be obligated to question a suspect in an effort to solicit incriminating responses when the physical evidence clearly points to the suspect's guilt? Why, or why not?

8 THE COURT SYSTEM

Preparing for and Testifying in Court

I was recently in a courtroom and witnessed two state correctional officer sergeants appear by subpoena from the defense attorney to testify on behalf of a state prisoner. As each officer took the stand the state attorney and I made eye contact—not saying a word, but knowing what each was thinking. The lead bailiff and I made eye contact—not speaking a word, only slightly shaking our heads. The judge's facial expression during testimony made it obvious we were not the only ones in the courtroom witnessing a poor representation of the corrections department. . . .

[The sergeants] were unprepared and caught off guard by the state attorney. Remember the defense called up the two sergeants in their behalf. . . .

I was embarrassed for not only the sergeants but for the agency.[1]

—Gary York, *CorrectionsOne*

LEARNING OBJECTIVES

After students have completed this chapter, they will be able to do the following:

1. Identify and explain the procedures involved in criminal and civil actions

2. Identify and explain the roles various personnel play in criminal and civil actions

3. Explain and demonstrate proper procedures for testifying in court and in discovery (depositions)

4. Explain pretrial preparation processes

5. Identify appropriate ways to demonstrate professionalism when testifying

As a member of a criminal justice agency involved in the investigation of an offense, incident, accident, or event, you may be required to testify in court. These cases may be either criminal or civil and can involve a jury or be designated as a bench trial (judge is the decision maker). Most cases, both civil and criminal, settle before trial. Criminal cases are often settled through a plea bargain; a guilty plea; or, occasionally, a dismissal of charges. Nonetheless, criminal justice professionals must understand the process of testifying and the preparation required to do so, as not all cases are subject to settlement. In this chapter, we will discuss the components of the trial process, suggest preparation methods for those officers facing the daunting task of testifying, and make recommendations for how to be the consummate professional when taking the witness stand.

THE COURTROOM SETTING

The success of any criminal investigation is ultimately related to the adjudication of the case in a court of law. The investigating officer, therefore, plays a major role in determining the outcome.

The quality and effectiveness of the officer's presentation is of paramount importance in the judicial process. Every officer, whether uniformed or otherwise, should become skilled at testifying on the witness stand. Several steps can be taken to help officers become proficient in the courtroom, beginning with the following:

- An officer should have a working knowledge of the **rules of evidence**. Possessing an understanding of these guidelines can help an officer to work more efficiently at gathering evidence in the field and help him or her to gain a grasp of courtroom procedures and the functions associated with the prosecution and the defense.

- An investigator should understand the **rules of admissibility** and the relevance of evidence collected. Only testimony that is relevant will be allowed into evidence. The judge or defense counsel may object to any testimony that fails to follow the rules of admissibility.

- An officer or investigator should understand his or her role in the courtroom, and he or she must understand the functions of all other parties in this process. Specifically, the officer or investigator should understand the functions of the judge and the jury in relationship to his or her role as witness.

THE PARTICIPANTS IN THE CRIMINAL COURTROOM DRAMA

Any criminal trial process primarily involves several parties or actors: the judge, the jury, the prosecutor, the defense attorney, the witnesses, and the defendant. Each of these individuals has a specific role in the courtroom setting.

Judge

The **judge** is routinely referred to as "the trier of law" (unless a jury trial is waived, at which time the judge becomes "the trier of fact"). He or she sits as an impartial party whose responsibility is to determine that the trial is conducted in an orderly and lawful manner. Issues that arise concerning the admissibility of evidence or testimony are solely the responsibility of the judge. The judge also resolves any disputes concerning points of law.

After all testimony has been completed, the judge performs a vital phase of the trial process by charging (instructing) the jury. The significance of this action cannot be overemphasized since many cases have been overturned on appeal because of disputes surrounding instructions to the jury.

Jury

The role of the **jury** is at the crux of the American criminal justice system. The jury is referred to as the "trier of fact." The jury was historically created with the intent to afford the accused a fair and unbiased trial by a jury of peers. Some question the role of the jury in modern times. However, no other element is more fundamental to the process of justice.

Most juries are selected through a process known as **voir dire.** Potential jury members are screened and selected predicated on their responses to a series of questions posed to them by both the prosecution and the defense attorneys. To form a favorable or at least balanced jury, the prosecution and defense are allowed a series of strikes (or removals) of potential jurors who are deemed to be unsuitable (unsympathetic or damaging to one side or the other).

Acting as a member of the jury is not an easy task. As human beings, we are influenced by details outside the written rules and regulations to which a jury is subjected. Therefore, a jury does not make its determination of guilt or innocence based solely on the presentation of evidence or the testimony delivered in a trial. Nonetheless, juries are charged with the responsibility of determining guilt or innocence, and in **bifurcated trials**, punishment that may include life imprisonment or death.

Attorneys

All attorneys have a responsibility or obligation to their clients. In the case of the **prosecutor**, this obligation or responsibility is to represent the citizens of the state or commonwealth. The **defense attorney** represents the interests of his or her client. These clients may be referred by the court (pro bono or indigent) or may seek the assistance of legal counsel on their own. In either case, defense attorneys have the responsibility for representing their clients to the fullest extent of their abilities or capabilities.

Prosecuting attorneys, also referred to as state attorneys or commonwealth attorneys, are charged with the responsibility of vigorously investigating and prosecuting those individuals accused of a crime. Mere suspicion and accusation are not sufficient for a criminal conviction. Therefore, prosecutors must prove that defendants are guilty of a crime beyond a reasonable doubt.

Defense attorneys, on the other hand, seek to create or reveal a reasonable doubt in the minds of the jurors or the judge as to the guilt of their clients. The issue of reasonable doubt may be examined or explored by defense attorneys through a variety of means. These means include but are not limited to the following:

- highlighting the absence of evidence either directly or indirectly linking their client to the crime,

- discrediting or minimizing the importance of physical evidence, or

- discrediting or impugning the testimony or integrity of prosecution witnesses.

Witness

The role of any **witness** in a courtroom setting is to present firsthand knowledge of facts to the jury for consideration. From this statement, you should be able to ascertain that "personal conclusions" are not relevant and may not be offered as part of the testimony. Only information that the witness has observed or gathered using the five senses (sight, smell, sound, taste, and touch) is admissible. Attempting to restate what someone else told you is inadmissible because it is **hearsay**. Some exceptions to the hearsay rule do exist; however, as a rule of thumb, hearsay testimony is almost always inadmissible in court.

Defendant

The **defendant** comes before the court accused of a crime. Defendants are presumed innocent until proven guilty and need not offer testimony in their defense. Furthermore, the fact that defendants fail to testify cannot be brought to the attention of the jurors to infer guilt by silence.

THE PARTICIPANTS IN THE CIVIL COURTROOM DRAMA

Much as in the criminal courtroom, civil actions involve several actors or players: the judge, the jury, the **plaintiff**, the defendant, their respective attorneys, and witnesses. In this setting, financial compensation, punitive sanctions, or a redress of grievances is the goal rather than incarceration. Therefore, the judge may grant a wider latitude to attorneys in their respective representation and defense of clients. However, the role of the judge in the civil courtroom is quite similar to his or her criminal counterpart, and little variation occurs in this setting.

Not all civil cases are presented before a jury. In many instances, a judge serves as the final authority. In those situations where a jury is requested or impaneled, the responsibility of the jurors is the same as that of the jury in a criminal trial.

Civil cases are initiated by individuals or a corporation that has suffered some injury or wrong. The initiators of a civil lawsuit are called plaintiffs. The persons or corporate entities that are being accused of the wrongdoing or injurious behavior are referred to in civil cases as defendants. The standard of proof in a civil case is much less than that required in a criminal prosecution. The plaintiff need merely prove guilt based on a **preponderance of the evidence**. In other words, the slightest hint of guilt or injury is adequate to sustain a finding for the plaintiff. The defendant must show a lack or absence of responsibility or guilt to avoid an award being given to the plaintiff. However, if the defendant can show that the plaintiff was in some small way responsible for the wrongdoing or injury, then this mitigates the responsibility of the defendant and may allow him or her to eliminate or minimize a finding of guilt.

Attorneys for the plaintiff and the defendant both attempt to gain a strategic advantage by gathering as much information as possible about the evidence to be presented and the testimony to be given by potential witnesses. This information may be gathered via two routes: depositions and discovery. Depositions are sworn testimony given by witnesses in pretrial preparation. Attorneys for each side are permitted to ask questions of potential witnesses to ascertain the relative strength or weakness of their respective clients' positions. The same care should be given to testimony related in depositions as to that given in trials since this information may be used later to discredit or impugn the witness.

Much like a courtroom setting, the deposition is an adversarial setting. The defendant (the accused), the defense attorney, the prosecutor or state attorney, and witnesses are present. However, no judge is present. A deposition is a process whereby witnesses are questioned to discern what information or facts they possess surrounding an occurrence. Witnesses are placed under oath to tell the truth regarding facts of the case just as they are in a courtroom setting, and penalties of perjury apply. **Perjury** is lying under oath and punishable by fine and imprisonment, depending on the finding of the judge. A court reporter (a neutral party) is hired to record the verbatim testimony of each witness, including questions of attorneys, responses of witnesses, and objections raised by either party. This written record (transcript) is first reviewed by the witness, who may clarify any statements that he or she feels the court reporter did not appropriately record. The witness is then required to sign the transcript under oath stating that the transcript is a true and correct statement of facts as he or she knows them. The transcript may then be examined by the prosecutor, the defense, and the judge for rulings on inappropriate questions or unresponsive witnesses.

Depositions are a means of gathering facts and information that may be used to compromise or discredit witnesses later at trial. The scope of the questions is not necessarily limited to the particular case at hand. However, most attorneys will attempt to limit the breadth of the questions so that they pertain specifically to the matter in question. Therefore, officers should not rely on notes or offense reports in depositions because they can become part of the record as attachments to the transcript and may be used later to hinder or damage prosecution.

Discovery is a term given to describe a pretrial procedure by which the plaintiff or defendant gains information held by the other. Discovery is usually conducted to probe the other party's position for possible weaknesses or areas that may be attacked to gain a legal advantage. Discovery may take the form of **interrogatories** propounded to either party, **motions** to suppress or produce key evidence or records, and meetings with investigators and expert witnesses.

THE GRAND JURY

In many jurisdictions, prior to a criminal trial, a **grand jury** is convened. Unlike the courtroom setting, the grand jury is not an adversarial proceeding. Composed of citizens from the community, the grand jury may, as a general rule, range in number from 6 to 12 individuals, depending on governmental statute. The setting is less formal than that of the courtroom, and this lack of formality allows testifying officers to use their notes without fear of having them examined by the defense.

In a grand jury setting, only members of the grand jury; the individual testifying; and, in some states, the prosecuting attorney are present. The officer may use his or her notes or the actual offense report itself. In the instance of a lengthy case, the case folder may be utilized, as well as hearsay evidence. The grand jury is impaneled merely to determine whether sufficient evidence exists to bring an accused to trial.

THE CRIMINAL TRIAL

Criminal trials and their civil counterparts follow the same procedural guidelines, with minor modifications previously identified. Seldom do police officers or investigators play a major role in civil cases; therefore, we will examine the criminal trial process and their role therein.

A criminal trial has several distinct parts. Initially, the court is called to order by a deputy, usually referred to as a **bailiff**. After following a series of procedural steps, the jury is sworn in, and the trial begins with the opening statements of the prosecution and the defense. In the opening remarks, the prosecutor will outline the manner in which he or she intends to prove the state's case. The prosecutor is not allowed to present evidence or question witnesses but merely to establish the means by which he or she intends to prove the guilt of the defendant. Defense attorneys may waive opening remarks or may choose to highlight the weaknesses in the state's case.

After opening remarks, the prosecution calls its first witness to the stand, and the trial is under way. When the prosecution questions witnesses called to testify on behalf of the state, this procedure is referred to as **direct examination**. Following questioning by the prosecutor, defense attorneys have an opportunity to ask further questions of prosecution witnesses or to clarify answers to their previous responses. This procedure is referred to as **cross-examination** since the witnesses were called on behalf of the prosecution. In the event the defense manages to raise an issue during cross-examination that may require further clarification, the prosecution has an opportunity to conduct a **redirect examination** after the defense attorney is finished. Likewise, the defense may conduct **recross-examination** following any redirect examination of the prosecution. The judge serves as a final arbitrator with respect to ending the questioning of a witness.

After both parties have presented all evidence and witnesses, each attorney may make a closing argument. The prosecution summarizes the evidence against the defendant to the jury and entreats them to weigh all aspects of the testimony presented and to return a finding of guilt. The defense, however, takes this opportunity to highlight all of the weaknesses in the prosecution's case by enumerating the lack of physical evidence or the confusion of witnesses. The defense attorneys request that the jury return a finding of not guilty since the prosecution has failed to prove its case beyond a reasonable doubt.

Following the closing arguments, the judge instructs the jury as to their responsibility and the points of law applicable to the case. Specifically, the jury is instructed to carefully weigh the testimony of witnesses and the evidence presented. Also, the judge details the aspects of the law that concern the degree of proof necessary to sustain a finding of guilt and the law concerning punishment for such a finding.

THE LAW ENFORCEMENT OFFICER'S ROLE IN THE TRIAL PROCESS

As soon as the investigator or police officer enters the courtroom, he or she is under scrutiny from all involved. The manner of dress, body language, voice, and vocabulary all play an integral part in establishing his or her credibility and professionalism. Seasoned officers establish a routine to ensure they are perceived as open and honest. This routine includes the following preparations.

- **Appropriate dress.** Whether in uniform or civilian attire, the witness should be neatly groomed. If not in uniform, the officer should wear dark, conservative clothing that gives the impression that he or she is a professional. Clothes should be clean and pressed, shoes shined, and hair neatly trimmed. Excessive jewelry, makeup, and perfume or cologne should be avoided.

- **Speech patterns.** Speak clearly and with sufficient volume, so you can be heard by the judge, jury, attorneys, and court reporter. Avoid the use of jargon or slang unless specifically directed by the prosecution to include those terms. Also, attempt to limit the number of fillers ("ah," "um," "er," "like," and "you know") you use in your testimony since they make you appear unsure.

- **Body language.** Nothing enhances credibility more than the appropriate body language. A posture that exudes confidence clearly indicates to the jury or the judge that the testifying officer is sure of the facts and/or details of the case. Fidgeting or crossing and uncrossing your legs are indications that you are unsure of your testimony or are uncomfortable with questions asked by either the prosecution or defense attorneys. Therefore, testifying officers should sit in an erect manner and face the jury and/or the judge to ensure proper eye contact. Hands should be kept in your lap or on the arms of your chair. One caveat to remember is that a witness should always be natural. Your credibility is always enhanced when you do not attempt to "act" or to use theatrics.

Preparing to Testify

While previous court testimony or experience is the best teacher, several tips may enhance your testimony in the interim:

- **Always review your field notes and reports prior to testifying in court.** This review should be thorough so that you refer to your notes as little as possible. In other words, testimony delivered from memory is generally deemed more credible by the jury or the judge. The officer or witness must rely on an accurate memory and an alert prosecutor. While cases often take weeks or months—or in some cases, even years—to go to trial, officers are expected to remember the most minute details of an investigation. To facilitate an officer's memory, notes or reports must be reviewed prior to the courtroom appearance. Officers who take their notebooks or copies of offense or incident reports to court subject these documents to seizure by the defense. Furthermore, they give the impression that they are not fully aware of the facts of the case and need a memory boost or prop to aid their recollection of the facts. This creates a doubt in the mind of the judge, jury, or defense attorney as to how accurately an officer recalls the events of that investigation.

- If an officer is unable to recount the events of an investigation without notes or an offense report, the officer must realize that the notebook or offense report may be examined by the defense attorney. Examination of the notebook by the defense attorney should be restricted or limited to those notes or accounts of the incident before the court. However, defense attorneys may try to examine other areas of the officer's notebook to discredit the officer's integrity or thoroughness by revealing errors or inappropriate remarks noted only for the officer's information involving other matters. If a defense attorney attempts to examine the officer's notebook beyond the scope of the case before the court, the prosecutor should strenuously object. Two ways to avoid this scrutiny are (1) to not take the notebook onto the witness stand or (2) to ensure that only that portion of the notebook pertaining to the case before the court is available for examination. Two ways to ensure that only the portion of the notebook pertaining to the case at hand is available for review by the defense attorney is to staple together the pages not associated with this case (as in the case of a spiral-bound notebook) or to remove those pages associated with this case from your notebook (as in the case of a loose-leaf notebook).

- **If possible, always try to meet with the prosecuting attorney prior to the case to clear up any areas that may be confusing.** Prior to testifying, an officer should review his or her notes and the offense or incident report in a meeting with the prosecutor to clear up any areas of confusion or ambiguity and to become acquainted with the questions the prosecutor intends to ask. Furthermore, you may find having the prosecutor play devil's advocate and anticipating what questions the defense attorney may ask on cross-examination to be helpful.

- **When you arrive in court, an important rule of thumb is to always _listen_ to the question before answering.** Never anticipate the question or assume that you know the direction in which the attorney is attempting to proceed. The testifying officer should wait for the question to be delivered in its entirety before framing a response. If you are asked multiple questions or questions that are combined, you should ask the attorney to rephrase the questions so that you may answer them individually.

- **Only answer those questions that are asked.** Do not attempt to embellish or add to your answer unless requested to do so. Also, do not guess or speculate.

- **If you do not know the answer to an attorney's question, do not be afraid to say, "_I do not know._"** Nothing damages a witness's credibility more than getting caught up in the speculation trap (or the guessing game). As a testifying officer, you are not a court-recognized expert witness, but oftentimes, attorneys will attempt to place you in that precarious position to undermine your credibility.

- **Do not argue with the attorneys or lose your temper.** When you do so, you are perceived as antagonistic or arrogant rather than a professional. Criminal justice professionals present the facts of the case in a detached, impartial manner. When you allow yourself to become angry or to argue with other courtroom officials, you lose your objectivity and damage your credibility.

Law enforcement officers are a pivotal part of most criminal cases, as they are the ones who investigated the incident or offense. The way you present yourself in court has a profound impact on the perception of the jury, judge, and other members of the court. Having properly written your incident or offense report and being fully aware of the information surrounding the investigation allows you to testify in a truthful and compelling manner. If your report has missing or incomplete information, that will be brought out into open court by the defendant's attorney. So your goal is to make sure you keep your investigative information updated in supplemental reports and to ensure that every piece of valid data is addressed in those documents. To be viewed as a professional, you must have well-written documentation that is clear, concise, complete, and correct. Being confident in what you have written will assist you in testifying as you will be sure that you have your story in order, with no need to defend your investigation.

In discussing preparation for trial, most people default to the law enforcement officer as witness. However, officers from the various criminal justice agencies may also be called to testify in either criminal or civil trials. Private security officers also investigate incidents and accidents, as do corrections officers, and their testimony can have a profound impact on cases.

THE CORRECTIONS OFFICER'S ROLE IN THE TRIAL PROCESS

The corrections officer usually has a tangential role in the trial process, except in cases where he or she is the charging officer or a witness to a crime committed in a detention facility. These officers may be called to testify in court regarding appeals, crimes, or infractions that occurred within their jail or prison setting, as they may be in the position of lead investigator. Corrections officers serving as lead investigators will be called to establish probable cause in state or federal court preliminary hearings and court of record proceedings, depending on the nature of the violation.

Appeals of sentences are automatically forwarded to a court of record for review after they have been screened for merit. In both state and federal courts, these appeals are normally handled as a review of the records, so testimony from corrections officers is rarely required. Crimes committed at state penal facilities may be investigated by either the state police or the local law enforcement authorities. Therefore, corrections officers are called as witnesses to aid the investigation. Additionally, violations of institutional rules by inmates are usually handled "in house." After a hearing by an inmate board or correctional staff, the punishment is determined and sanctioned by the chief administrator of the facility.

On the rarest of occasions, corrections officers may be requested to provide testimony to the parole board to establish an inmate's behavior while incarcerated or to clarify any confusing information contained in the record being reviewed by the board. This testimony would be sought if or when the board needed additional assistance to determine suitability for an inmate's release.

If you are called to testify—in any venue—you should adhere to the same principles set forth for both law enforcement and private security officers in this chapter: dress professionally (in either your uniform or a suit); have your reports in order, with all information written clearly, concisely, completely, and correctly; and be aware of your nonverbal communication (e.g., posture, gestures, eye contact, vocalics—tone, pitch of your voice, fillers [ah, um], and rate or speed of your speech—and affect displays—facial expressions such as eye rolling, smiling, or frowning). You should review your documentation prior to the court or board hearing and be prepared to speak without the necessity of reading from your notes. You will be more credible if you can speak from memory and not rely on notes.

Specific steps you can take to assist you when testifying include the following:[2]

- **Dress appropriately.** As you can see from the start-of-the-chapter scenario, the personal appearance of a corrections officer (also law enforcement and private security officers) is paramount to his or her success in the courtroom. Officers must present to court dressed in a freshly ironed uniform (or professional business suit) with shoes or boots cleaned and shined. Hair and facial grooming should be within agency guidelines and policies. If you convey professionalism through your personal appearance, you will be perceived as professional.

- **Remember why you are in court.** You may occasionally be called to testify because an inmate is claiming innocence in the commission of a crime and stating that you are lying or that you did not perform your job properly. Realize that the job of the defense attorney is to prove his or her client is being truthful, so be prepared.

- **Assume the jury is skeptical of you.** The jury selection process is not without fault. Trying to choose unbiased jurors is an arduous task and one that is not likely to produce the desired results. You should assume that you will have jurors who are biased against corrections officers. You should prepare to testify in the case knowing that the jury will be scrutinizing you intensely.

- **Be prepared.** Review your reports carefully, and do not merely skim them. Take the time to go over the details and any notes you have. As mentioned earlier, many cases have aged, and your memory of them has been affected. However, you cannot appear to be unprepared during your testimony. Your credibility will be seriously impacted, and you will feel more pressure and stress if you are unprepared.

- **Know your professional scope.** You must know how your prison or jail operations are conducted, the layout of your facility, and your agency's policies and procedures. Review your handbook, and know what your job duties and responsibilities are. Know any associated legislation for the case in which you are called to testify. In other words, have a working knowledge of your case.

- **Be concise, clear, complete, and correct.** State the facts only. Do not offer your opinions. Listen carefully to each question, and think about your response. Answer the question after careful deliberation, and be concise in your response. Defense attorneys will try to introduce tangents into the story and try to pull you in directions beyond the information to which you are privy. Do not respond to questions of that nature with responses containing unnecessary information.

- **Speak to the jury.** Remember that most of the members of the jury have no experience with your job, the field of corrections, or any jargon or language indigenous to criminal justice. Speak in plain language, and direct your comments toward the jury. Be both professional in your responses and kind when speaking to them. They are civilians. Do not allow your anger or frustration at the defense attorney's questions to cause you to lose control, as the jurors will be affected by your actions and responses.

- **Refresh your knowledge of presentation skills.** If you have had no reason to present in any public forum for a time, you should review the basic tenets of delivering presentations. That information will assist you in testifying. First impressions are hard to forget. You do not want your first impression in the courtroom to be one that calls into question your credibility and professionalism.

Corrections officers have standards of professionalism that must be adhered to when testifying in court. Those standards are consistent with law enforcement and private security. Regardless of the criminal justice agency where you are employed, you have the ultimate duty and responsibility to conduct yourself in a professional manner during the court process.

THE PRIVATE SECURITY OFFICER'S ROLE IN THE TRIAL PROCESS

Private security officers are often called to appear in court or before other official bodies. Therefore, you must be prepared when called on to testify. A major problem that occurs regarding the investigation of an incident or accident is the time lapse. Most often, you will be called to investigate an incident or accident, collect the information you deem important and necessary to the establishment of a case, write your incident or accident report and submit it, and then wait. At some point, you will be called to participate in the discovery portion of the case in a deposition. You will need to make sure your reports—the initial incident or accident report, as well as any supplemental reports—are complete. You also want to review the information to refresh your recollection of the incident.

Once in the deposition, you will be asked questions by both sides, the attorney for the plaintiff (the individual involved in the incident or accident or the state, depending on whether the case is filed in criminal or civil court) and the attorney for the defendant. You will be expected to divulge the facts of the case as you encountered them and wrote them in your reports. Following the conclusion of your deposition, you may find that you do not hear anything further about the case until months later, when you hear that you must appear in court for this case.

Many months have passed since the incident, and your memory is not as clear as it was at the time you gave your deposition or when the incident occurred. So what steps can you take to ensure that you are prepared to testify in court?

- **Be prepared.** Review your original incident report and all supplemental reports (if applicable). Your job is to tell the truth. Make sure that your testimony matches anything you said during your deposition. Attempts will be made to discredit you or to impeach your testimony during court, so you need to ensure that you are telling the truth and that your testimony is consistent with your reports and your deposition. You must "do your due diligence" before going to court by reviewing your reports and previous testimony. If you do not, you risk your credibility because you may make mistakes while testifying. If you make any conflicting statements, you open the door for the defense to discredit you and your testimony.

- **Look professional.** Dress appropriately—either in uniform or in a professional business suit. Your appearance in court is very important and can impact your credibility. You should be well groomed too. Additional information on this topic is found in the section "The Officer's Appearance in Court," which follows in this chapter.

- **Act professionally.** This means you should do the following:

  o   Be on time. Courts (and judges) have little patience with individuals who appear in court late. Know when you will be expected to testify, and be present at that time.

  o   State only the facts of the case. Your opinions are unimportant. Your job is not to inspire the jury or the judge to convict the defendant. The jury and judge should view you as an impartial arbiter of the facts.

  o   Do not allow your personal feelings or emotions to affect your testimony. Even if the defense attorney asks questions designed to provoke you, you should respond with clear, concise, complete, and correct testimony, thereby not opening yourself up to any attacks from the defense counsel.

  o   Do not provide more information than necessary. Defense attorneys will also attempt to build your ego by asking a series of questions designed to elicit information from you—to get you talking on the witness stand. As a result, you may give the defense counsel more information than he or she needs, and this information may be used by that defense attorney to find faults with your testimony. Answer the questions posed to you, but keep your responses short. The more information you provide, the more likely the defense attorney will be to use it against you.

  o   Take a short pause before answering any questions. You should carefully consider your response to a question before responding. Formulate your concise answer that is consistent with your reports and your prior testimony.

  o   Do not testify for another private security officer. The defense attorney may attempt to have you respond to a question about the officer involved in the incident (e.g., the officer who shot the suspect after the suspect pulled a weapon). Do not guess at the thought process or mental state of that individual. You may have witnessed the incident, but you have no idea what occurred in the mind of the officer involved in the incident.[3]

Law enforcement, corrections, and private security officers must follow the same code of conduct for testifying in court. Some differences exist in what is expected of these officers depending on the location of the case, whether criminal or civil court, and the type of case; however, the need for preparation involving review of reports and previous testimony, having a professional appearance, and acting in a professional manner are all characteristics needed for establishing credibility. Given that cases often pivot on the testimony of these individuals, we must stress the need for preparation and professionalism. The next section of this chapter covers details associated with an officer's appearance in court and stresses the importance of professionalism.

THE OFFICER'S APPEARANCE IN COURT

The courtroom is a somber and ominous environment. Initially, officers have a sense of foreboding regarding their performance in court. As the time passes, officers become more relaxed since their appearances have been regular; they have come to understand how the system operates and what is expected of them. Officers should never become complacent about appearing in court.

Court cases (hearings) are scheduled for the convenience of the judge and the attorneys. Law enforcement officers are seldom consulted regarding scheduling their individual court appearances. Therefore, officers frequently spend a great deal of time in the courtroom waiting for their testimony to be heard. Law enforcement officials who have worked long hours or late hours often succumb to their fatigue and fall asleep in court. While sleeping may not be particularly obtrusive to the workings of the court, it does present a poor first impression to a judge or jury. Prosecutors who have established a sound working relationship with the judge and defense attorneys may assist these individuals by attempting to schedule their cases as early in the day as possible. This early scheduling not only ensures that officers will be fresh during direct and cross-examination but also enables the officer to feel as though he or she has some impact in scheduling.

As was said previously regarding initial first impressions, the appearance of the officer makes a statement about credibility. Officers who are appropriately and neatly attired lend nonverbal credence to their statements. Judges and juries associate truthfulness and competence with individuals who are neatly dressed and who speak clearly and confidently. Some prosecutors require officers to wear their uniforms when appearing in court; others prefer that the officers dress in business attire (jacket and tie). Irrespective of the dress, common courtesy and respect should apply in all situations. Matters before the court are of a serious nature, and therefore, joking or jocularity is inappropriate.

Testifying

When an officer is called to the witness stand to testify, he or she will be placed under oath by a court clerk or other official and will then be asked to take a seat in the witness box by either the judge or the clerk. As a sign of respect, the officer should wait to be seated until he or she is told to do so. The officer should adhere to the rules of nonverbal communication—avoid fidgeting, wildly gesturing, looking around the courtroom, or failing to make eye contact with the appropriate individual—as some nonverbal actions are interpreted as signs of deception or ineptitude. A confident voice is clear and respectful and under no circumstances cocky or arrogant. Questions should be answered with "yes" or "no" unless one is asked to explain or expand on the response by the prosecution or the defense.

The first questions an officer will be asked will be directed toward personal information, such as the officer's name, rank, and current assignment, and then the questions will begin to focus more on the incident and the officer's involvement. The role of the officer is to testify to accounts that he or she has witnessed or facts that he or she has gathered and not to attempt to aid the prosecution or to hinder the defense. The role of the prosecutor is to ensure all pertinent information is solicited from the testifying officer and that any contradictory or confusing statement that has been made

FIGURE 8.1 ■ **Sample Question-and-Answer Testimony From Court Transcript**	

Prosecutor: Would you state your full name for the record, please.

Officer: Officer M. W. Jackson.

Prosecutor: What is your current assignment?

Officer: I am a patrol officer for the Brookhaven City Police Department.

Prosecutor: Officer Jackson, were you on duty the day of April 9, 2017, at 4:00 p.m.?

Officer: Yes, sir.

Prosecutor: Did you have an occasion to respond to 3607 Elmer Trail?

Officer: Yes, sir, I did.

Prosecutor: And officer, upon your arrival, what did you discover?

Officer: Upon my arrival, I spoke with the complainant, Mr. James Hemby, in reference to a larceny. Mr. Hemby directed me to a shed behind his house where he stored his riding lawn mower between uses. I discovered a lock had been broken off the hasp, and the door was open. I looked inside and noted that the shed was empty. Further examination revealed a wallet that was located inside the shed. I picked up the wallet and looked inside. I found a driver's license with the name and address of Harry P. Smith (the defendant), 1616 Mockingbird Lane, Brookhaven, MS 39601.

Prosecutor: Officer, did you determine a value for the missing lawn mower?

Officer: Yes sir, I was advised by the victim that the mower was valued at $2,500.

Prosecutor: Officer, did anyone have permission to take the lawn mower?

Officer: No, sir, according to the victim, no one had permission to take the riding lawn mower.

Prosecutor: Officer, was anything else located at the scene?

Officer: Yes, sir. I dusted the door for fingerprints and located one print on the hasp. I recovered this print and returned it to the identification bureau for comparison in the event that a suspect was developed.

Prosecutor: What were the results of the fingerprint analysis?

Officer: A fingerprint match was discovered by AFIS, and a subsequent analysis by a fingerprint technician revealed that the print recovered from the scene matched a fingerprint belonging to Mr. Harry P. Smith.

Prosecutor: Officer, did you have an occasion to speak with the defendant, Mr. Smith, as a result of this fingerprint match?

Officer: Yes, sir, I did.

Prosecutor: Officer, what if anything did you learn from your conversation with the defendant?

Officer: Mr. Smith stated that he did not know the victim, nor did he know anything about a missing riding lawn mower, and he had never been to 3607 Elmer Trail, nor did he know where it was located.

Prosecutor: Officer, what if anything did you do at this time?

Officer: I advised Mr. Smith that he was under arrest and read him his Miranda rights.

by the defense attorney is rebutted. The role of the prosecutor is to prosecute, and the role of the defense attorney is to defend his or her client.

During testimony, the investigating officer should never feel compelled to alter facts or to make statements that could damage or hinder his or her credibility. Officers should realize that pressure could be exerted by ambitious or overly aggressive prosecutors or by the victim's grieving family. Yet under no circumstances should an officer succumb to pressure to appease or satisfy others. A successful career in criminal justice is predicated on an officer's integrity in court.

After the prosecution and defense have exhausted their questions, the witness must wait to be excused by the court. On occasion, defense attorneys will seek to "trip up" the witness by asking one last question. The witness should remember to remain alert until he or she has left the courtroom. The judge will dismiss or excuse the witness when all questions have been asked and answered. When exiting the courtroom, the witness should proceed directly to the doors and into the hallway without exhibiting any signs of emotion (no smiling, glaring, etc.). Also, the witness should refrain from speaking to any individual as he or she exits the courtroom.

SUMMARY

Testifying in court is a necessary aspect of employment with any criminal justice agency. This part of working in the industry is not generally regarded as the most pleasurable; however, it should not be viewed as a burden. The interests of the community and the agency are best served by truthful, accurate testimony. This type of testimony may best be achieved by being prepared, appropriately dressed, and well mannered. Investigation, arrest, and prosecution are vital links in the process of criminal justice.

Criminal justice professionals must realize that they have fulfilled their responsibility by thoroughly investigating the case and accurately testifying as to those facts in court. The determination of guilt or innocence (the verdict) rests with the judge or the jury, and predicting the outcome is hazardous at best. Therefore, officers must not gauge their success or failure predicated on the decision of the judge or jury. Satisfaction should be derived from knowing that the case was thoroughly investigated and that the facts were accurately stated in court. Therefore, irrespective of the verdict, criminal justice professionals should refrain from expressing joy or disappointment with the subsequent finding of guilt or innocence.

KEY TERMS

Bailiff 168

Bifurcated trials 165

Cross-examination 168

Defendant 166

Defense attorney 165

Deposition 167

Direct examination 168

Discovery 167

Grand jury 167

Hearsay 166

Interrogatories 167

Judge 164

Jury 165

Motions 167

Perjury 167

Plaintiff 166

Preponderance
    of the evidence 166

Prosecutor 165

Recross-examination 168

Redirect examination 168

Rules of admissibility 164

Rules of evidence 164

Voir dire 165

Witness 165

FOR FURTHER REFLECTION AND DISCUSSION

1. Who are the principal actors in a criminal or civil action?

2. What roles do the prosecution and defense play in criminal procedures?

3. What is the process of voir dire?

4. How are depositions and discovery utilized in the trial process?

5. Of what significance is the grand jury?

6. What preparations are necessary for the testifying officer to make the best possible impression on the witness stand?

7. List at least three mistakes witnesses make that impugn their credibility.

8. Should officers conceal their feelings at the outcome (verdict) of a trial? Why, or why not?

9. Given what you have learned in this chapter, do you feel it would be appropriate for a testifying officer to shake the hand of the prosecuting attorney on his or her way out of the courtroom following his or her testimony? Why, or why not?

10. If not directly questioned about an event, should an officer leave out facts or information during his or her testimony that may assist the defense?

ETHICAL ISSUE EXERCISES

1. Should an officer become personally involved with the family of a victim? Why, or why not?

2. If the investigator truly believes that the defendant is guilty, should he or she embellish or enhance facts that may not be strong enough to stand on their own in order to point the finger of guilt at the defendant?

3. Are there any conditions under which an investigator should commit perjury? Explain your answer.

ADDITIONAL TOPICS FOR INVESTIGATION

1. Visit a court proceeding, and observe the testimony of various witnesses. List the strengths and weaknesses of each individual's testimony, and determine whether you believe him or her. What made an impression on you? What made you believe in his or her truthfulness? Write a brief summary of your findings, and present them to the class. Focus on the factors involved in your decision-making processes concerning the veracity of the witnesses.

2. Observe police officers or investigators as they testify in a court setting. Pinpoint any weaknesses you observed. Did one officer testify "better" than another? Why? Do police officers make better witnesses? Why, or why not?

3. Interview one prosecuting and one defense attorney. Ask what defines a good witness. Ask them, in their opinions, what differentiates a good witness from a poor witness. What areas do they seek to exploit or take advantage of in a witness's testimony?

9

TECHNOLOGY AND COMMUNICATION

A New Frontier

When I started my career in law enforcement nearly 35 years ago, the only "technology" we needed was the police radio and the location of the nearest pay phone. Today police radios scan 30 channels and officers typically have in-car video cameras, traffic monitoring radar units, in-car computer data terminals with Internet access, body cameras, a department issued cellphone and, of course, personal cellphones. With all this technology in the cruisers, it's a wonder we don't have more officer-involved crashes than we do.[1]

—Brian Cain and Michael Bostic,
Police Magazine

The criminal justice field has made tremendous strides in the last 40 years, with the most notable developments being in the area of law enforcement and corrections. The process of prosecution or the application of law has undergone societal changes; and court decisions have altered some of the protections afforded offenders and, in some cases, hindered law enforcement. Technological advances in the area of crime detection, investigation, incarceration, and communication have made the greatest impact.

When I began my career in policing, sidearms, nightsticks, and car radios were all the tools required of a patrol officer. The first portable radios were low band frequency, limited range, heavy, and awkward. Communication was limited to the individual officer's local dispatch center. Communication between agencies required phone calls among the various entities, a time-consuming and difficult process. The scenario that follows demonstrates how communication between agencies (interagency communication) was handled in the 1970s and 1980s.

LEARNING OBJECTIVES

After students have completed this chapter, they will be able to do the following:

1. Identify and explain how criminal justice agencies are using technology to improve communication, investigation, prosecution, and incarceration

2. Identify types of social media, and explain how criminal justice agencies are employing social media in their communities and beyond

3. Identify alert systems, and explain their purposes for criminal justice agencies

4. Describe ways in which the use of smartphones and other tools has impacted criminal justice agencies

5. Explain cybercrime, and identify the types of cybercrimes

6. Identify and explain how virtual platforms are impacting training and meetings within criminal justice agencies

A city patrol officer needs information about a possible warrant or summons for an individual in another jurisdiction (county). The officer must contact the city dispatcher, explaining what he or she needs from the county officer. The city dispatcher contacts the county's dispatcher by phone and relays the question. The county's dispatcher contacts his or her officer to confirm possession of a warrant or summons, if such exists. After receiving a response from the officer, the county dispatcher calls the city dispatcher and provides the requested information. The city dispatcher then contacts the patrol officer by radio, advising him or her of the answer to the warrant or summons question.

Today's criminal justice professionals have instantaneous access to information from a variety of sources—local, state, and federal. Vehicles today still use radios, but they are high band frequency, expanded range, light, and easily carried. Most of the technological advances have been positive; however, a few have created potential opportunities for new types of crimes to proliferate, particularly social media programs that have made coordination of terrorist and gang activities easier and more difficult to police. Other technological concerns center on mobile applications on smartphones and tablets that allow users to identify current locations of law enforcement officers (e.g., Waze, a traffic-tracking tool). If people can pinpoint the exact location of a police officer using this type of mobile application, that officer's safety is jeopardized—particularly if an individual is intent on doing harm to members of the law enforcement community.[2]

According to a 2016 Rand study, "The future might be so saturated with data and information that police agencies will need new ways to tag, sort, and share what they know."[3] Thus, how do criminal justice agencies decide what technologies are useful, and how do they balance the cost of purchase and maintenance against the safety of the public and the privacy of the citizens they protect?

TECHNOLOGY AND TODAY'S CRIMINAL JUSTICE AGENCY

As mentioned earlier, technology has changed and provided new opportunities for today's criminal justice agencies to be more proactive and to solve crimes with a higher percentage of accuracy. Some of these technologies are surveillance based while others are designed to provide additional protections for law enforcement officers.[4]

Aviation technology—including both planes and helicopters—aids officers on the ground in locating and apprehending suspects, locating lost children or older citizens who have wandered away from home, and providing an additional layer of safety for officers.

Detection and surveillance technology allows officials to monitor specific individuals for criminal or dangerous behavior and to keep officers and innocent citizens safe. Detection and surveillance technology includes cameras with night vision capability to record in low-light situations, which aids in the identification of offenders and serves as undisputable proof in the prosecution of criminal cases.

Vehicle and body cameras are common in law enforcement agencies. Vehicle and body cameras can be both an aid and a detriment to an officer. These devices provide visual evidence in cases such as driving under the influence (DUI) or driving while intoxicated (DWI), vehicle pursuits, or officer-involved shootings. However, in some instances, these videos reveal improper conduct on the part of the officer or, in the severest cases, unlawful behavior of an officer.

- In 2017, an Orlando, Florida, police officer was captured on video taunting a participant involved in a family dispute and threatening to beat him and take him to jail.[5]

- An example of severe misconduct occurred in 2017 when a Balch Springs, Texas, officer fired at a vehicle fleeing from a party. His shots struck a 15-year-old passenger in the head and resulted in the individual's death.[6] The officer testified that the vehicle was driving toward him at a high rate of speed and posed an imminent threat to his life. The police chief fired the officer on May 2, 2017, for violating policy, although the chief did not specify what policy.[7]

Body armor, once expensive, heavy, and uncomfortable, has become standard issue for most departments. With the advent of Kevlar and other advanced fibers, body armor has become less expensive, lighter, and cooler to wear.

Less lethal technologies, such as pepper spray, Tasers, beanbag rounds, rubber bullets, tear gas, and stun grenades, allow officers to use alternatives to methods that may involve greater risk for harm to the suspect and the officer. These tools are utilized in situations that involve escalating violence. Each tool is designed to be used in a specific order but may be taken out of sequence in the event of imminent danger to life or limb. While these technologies serve a valuable purpose, the first step—or first line of defense—in any situation is for the officer to use the *command voice* to inform citizens of the action you want them to take and how to comply with your commands. If the command voice does not achieve desired results, you move forward with the use of these less lethal technologies.

Crime mapping (software) and **predictive analysis** is another area where the use of statistics provides criminal justice agencies with a more cost-efficient use of resources to increase the likelihood of crime prevention and suspect apprehension. Crime mapping is a software that was created to allow criminal justice agencies to track crimes—types, dates, times, and geographical locations of crimes.

Biometrics has a variety of uses: confirmation of an individual's identity through voice and/or facial features and expedited capture of personal physical features (fingerprints, facial recognition, and retinal scans).

Communication technologies have expanded greatly. Consider the following:

- While vehicle radios are still used, most officers prefer mobile technologies. Thus, smartphones are used to receive photographs, fingerprints, criminal histories, and messages from other individuals involved in an investigation, as well as general messages.

- Message boards over the interstates and major roadways alert motorists to accidents or road hazards.

- **Amber Alerts** or **Silver Alerts** are broadcast on local television and radio stations, as well as via weather alert radios, to notify citizens of missing or kidnapped children or a missing older person.

- Twitter, Snapchat, Instagram, and Facebook all play a role in the process of modern criminal justice communication (and will be covered later in this chapter).

- Mobile phones, smartphones, or cell phones and tablets have also expanded the options for communication within and among criminal justice agencies and among personnel. Cell phones allow agency personnel to make calls; send text messages; take and receive photographs of suspects, victims, and witnesses; and take and receive criminal histories, photo lineups, and GPS (Global Positioning System) locations. Tablets may be used as a supplement to cell phones if a larger screen or added software applications are required.

Most recently, texting and driving (also known as distracted driving) has become a significant problem and has resulted in an increasing number of traffic accidents. In 2016, approximately 40,000 traffic fatalities occurred nationwide, an increase of 6%.[8] Despite the fact that 46 states have laws prohibiting texting while driving, and 14 ban the use of handheld devices while driving, a number of the fatalities that occurred were the result of distractions due to smartphones.[9]

In response to this issue, lawmakers in New York and a number of states are considering ways to make obtaining phone records easier for law enforcement. At present, without probable cause to obtain a warrant, law enforcement officers (and other members of criminal justice agencies) cannot check personal smartphones. Due to the advent of a new roadside technology developed by Cellebrite, called the Textalyzer, however, agencies may be able to determine what drivers were doing at the time of an accident using a process similar to that employed with the breathalyzer.

New York is considering the first-of-its-kind legislation to require drivers involved in accidents to submit their phones to roadside testing via the Textalyzer. The proposed law is meeting with resistance based on privacy issues. However, Cellebrite engineer Lee Papathanasiou has explained that the Textalyzer would capture only taps and swipes to determine if a driver was using the phone, that it would not download content, and that it would merely display a summary of what apps on the phone were open and in use.[10] According to the Centers for Disease Control and Prevention, in the United States, more than 1,153 people are injured and 9 people die each day due to distracted-driving accidents.[11]

While not widely recognized as a specific form of technology, **technology assistance** serves as an invaluable asset for agencies that do not possess the budget to purchase new technology or the expertise to use it successfully or to train individuals in its use. State resources (e.g., the Tennessee Bureau of Investigation [TBI]) or federal resources (e.g., the Federal Bureau of Investigation [FBI]) serve as points of information and scientific analysis. These agencies provide the professional analysis and, when necessary, the professional testimony to interpret the information collected from crime scenes to aid jurisdictions in the prosecution of a suspect.

The Intranet (Organizational Network)

One of the most significant advances in criminal justice technology centers on the use of organizational networks, often referred to in the private sector as intranets.

An **intranet** is a group of connected computers and servers that exchange information and share equipment within a specific organization. Prior to the advent of network typologies, criminal justice agencies relied on clerks, secretaries, or office personnel to retrieve information or data from extensive file cabinets and records centers. This method of maintaining and retrieving data was extremely time-consuming, labor-intensive, and costly.

In the corrections area, the use of intranets offers options that facilitate the manner in which inmates are admitted to the institution and tracked during their incarceration. Again, prior to the implementation of intranets, inmate files were stored in a secure records facility and retrieval involved lengthy and arduous procedures. From a computer offering access to the organizational network, records can be reviewed by authorized correctional personnel in order to confirm identities, to determine the appropriate classification and assignment of inmates, to track inmates' disciplinary problems, to review credit for "good time," and to complete any other administrative functions.

Mobile Data Terminals (MDTs)

The establishment of an organizational intranet allows authorized personnel to access information from a variety of locations. Officers in patrol cars have access to database information via the use of a **mobile data terminal (MDT)**. The mobile data terminal is a screen and keyboard that connects the patrol car to the central computer or server and allows the officer to stay in contact with the dispatch center. The use of the MDT not only enhances the officer's ability to access information but also reduces the need to use the police radio. Furthermore, the use of the MDT provides an additional measure of security because the communication cannot be accessed by the general public, unlike radio communication that is frequently monitored by civilians who possess police scanners.

MDTs allow officers to be dispatched on calls for service without the utilization of the police radio. When a call is received, the MDT makes a noise, either a beep or a buzz. This sound notifies the officer that an incoming call will be received on the terminal. As the call is received, the officer reviews the nature of the call and the address and strikes a function key, which notifies dispatch that the call has been received and that the unit is en route. When the officer arrives at the designated address, another function key is struck to notify dispatch that the officer is on the scene and out of service. In some of the more advanced MDT units, a follow-up tone will notify the dispatcher that the unit is still out of service and may require assistance. This innovation was designed to ensure that dispatchers check on the safety of officers who have been marked out of service for a specified period of time.

Once the officer has handled the call, he or she returns to the unit and prepares an initial offense report. At one point, offense or incident reports had to be prepared by hand and delivered to a supervisor, who reviewed and approved the document. The reports were disseminated to the proper divisions for investigation or storage in records. However, with the development of appropriate software, reports may be generated by utilizing the MDT keyboard to type and send them to a supervisor for review. One caveat, nonetheless: Even though you prepare your reports using the MDT, you still need to adhere to the rules of report writing discussed in earlier chapters.

Once the report is completed and forwarded to the appropriate supervisor, the officer again strikes a function key on the MDT to notify the dispatcher that the unit has cleared from that address and is in service or able to receive a call.

Another vital aspect of the MDT is the ability of the officer to retrieve information while in the field. Frequently officers see suspicious vehicles and want to know to whom the vehicle is registered. By utilizing the MDT, an officer may access the State Division of Motor Vehicle (DMV) records and determine the owner of the vehicle. Additionally, officers may verify the license status of a driver by accessing the DMV records to determine if the driver has a valid operator's license or if his or her privilege to drive has been suspended or revoked.

Officers frequently come in contact with a wide variety of individuals during the course of their patrol activities and will routinely run what is referred to as a "wants and warrants check." The MDT allows them to obtain the status of these individuals locally, statewide, and nationally. Officers can seek information from the Federal Bureau of Investigation's National Crime Information Center (NCIC) through a link from their MDT. They also have the capability of retrieving data from their state system (e.g., Virginia's VCIN [Virginia Crime Information Network]).

Department or Bureau Computers

Much like their MDT counterparts, these computers allow authorized personnel access to a variety of information. The only significant difference is that these computers are located on the desks of officers or supervisors or in a central location that is easily accessible to qualified personnel. Generally, these computers are used to prepare supplemental offense reports (discussed elsewhere in this text). However, they may be used to transcribe the notes from victim, witness, or suspect statements.

Department or bureau computers have expanded capability or access to information unavailable to their MDT counterparts. Access to sensitive information, however, may be limited to certain individuals by issuing passwords for specific levels. An example of sensitive information may be a list of informants or suspected drug dealers that would be contained within the narcotics or vice bureau. An administrative example of sensitive information would be the department budget or salary structure for the department.

Typically, networked computers require users to log on with a username and a password. This username and password are considered to be of an extremely sensitive nature and, therefore, should be kept confidential. Only select administrative personnel should have access to departmental personnel's usernames and passwords.

Electronic Mail (E-Mail)

E-mail, or electronic mail, is a means by which a message, a bulletin, or other information may be distributed to an individual or a group of individuals from a single source. E-mail is the electronic equivalent of the U.S. Postal Service. However, unlike the postal service and the confidentiality assumed in the delivery of a letter, e-mail can and is frequently monitored by other individuals. These individuals may be supervisors or hackers. Either way, you should always be aware that e-mail is not generally secure.

E-mail may be a particularly effective means of disseminating information that needs to be shared with a large group of people immediately, such as changes in the warrant status of current offenders, changes in the current status of search warrants, or any modifications to departmental policy. Additionally, e-mail may be utilized to handle the more mundane aspects of organizational operation, such as the date for change from summer to fall uniforms, shopping vehicles for maintenance, or extra duty assignments. E-mail could also be utilized to submit routine information, such as the number of officers on sick leave, the number of officers on vacation, or the number of officers on special assignment.

If e-mail is adopted as the official channel of intradepartmental or interdepartmental communication, then it holds the same authority and status as any written document containing the same information. The same rules of composition (including grammar and punctuation) that are used to create a written document also apply to e-mail.

Etiquette Guidelines for E-Mail

The use of e-mail as an official communication channel requires a basic understanding of the rules of etiquette for its use.

- Use e-mail only when it is the most efficient channel for communication. Remember that e-mail has permanence. Even deleted e-mails can be retrieved, and lawyers can subpoena e-mails to use as evidence in court. Choose e-mail for short, informal messages that need to be written and read.

- Do not key your e-mail messages in ALL CAPS, as the use of all capital letters is viewed as shouting. If you need to call attention to a word or words, you can enclose it in asterisks (i.e., *all caps*).

- Always include a relevant subject line; change the subject line when the purpose of the message changes; make sure the subject line reflects the purpose of your message and that the subject line is specific (i.e., avoid using "Information," "Question," or "Need Help" as subjects because they are too vague and do not offer your reader the necessary information as to the specific purpose of your message).

- Do not leave the subject line blank. If you want to be effective at e-mail, you need to use subject lines in the same fashion as newspapers use headlines. Your subject line is actually an advertisement for the attention of your recipient. Busy people require specifics in the subject line. If you are requesting some kind of action, tell the reader in the subject line. If you are providing an update, summarize the information in the subject line by using the 140-character Twitter postings as an example. However, you should state your subject in about half of a tweet posting—70 characters or less.

- Address your recipient in a salutation (Dear Skip or Dear Dr. Grubb) or in the opening sentence. Do not use openings such as Hi, Skip; Hello, Skip; or Hey, Skip. Follow simple rules of courtesy in your opening; if you have been given permission to address someone by his or her first name, then do so. If you are writing to people you do not know, address them as Mr., Ms., Rev., or Dr.

- Remember that without facial expressions, some comments may be misinterpreted. Choose your words carefully when writing your e-mails.

- Keep your e-mails to one topic only. Your recipient should not need to focus on more than one purpose for your message, so do not confuse the reader.

- Keep your e-mails short; an e-mail message should cover no more than one screen. If you have to scroll down to read the entirety of the e-mail, your message is too long. You might want to consider preparing your message in a Word format and sending it as an attachment to an e-mail. You would ensure a higher percentage of your e-mail messages get read in their entirety by recipients if you follow the writing guidelines for all messages: Keep them concise, complete, clear, and correct.

- Consider the purpose of your message. Is the purpose to deliver bad news, criticize, or share confidential information? If so, you need to step away from the keyboard and pick up your phone to schedule a face-to-face meeting. You want to think about the response of the recipients. If they will be angry, upset, hurt, or disappointed, you need to select another channel by which to communicate with these individuals. Certainly, the use of e-mail is fast and efficient; but in situations where the information is difficult to share in person, you just want to use e-mail to distance yourself from people. That approach is unacceptable. Electronic messages diminish the impact of a message. So choose carefully what type of messages you are willing to send via electronic means.

- Follow the proper guidelines for creating your message. Analyze your audience (who will be reading my message), write your message, and then proofread and revise your message. Do not hit the "Send" button until you complete all three of these steps, especially the proofreading and revising one. Check your grammar, spelling, and punctuation. Make sure that what you have written is reflective of what you intended to say. Communication is not effective unless the recipient of the communication understands the message the way that you intended it. (Chapter 1 of this text covered this important information.) If you have run-on sentences, sentence fragments, subject–verb disagreement, misplaced modifiers, or other grammatical issues, your message can be confusing to your recipient.

- Avoid using abbreviations or brief forms in your professional messages or texts. You certainly might use "u" or "gr8" in a message or text to your friends; but for work-related messages, stick with the tried and true, and spell out your words; you are not in middle school.

- Verify the e-mail address for your recipient, and ensure that you are sending carbon copies to only those individuals who should receive them. Do not "cc" (carbon copy) everyone. If you are sending sensitive information, you want to ensure that your message goes only to those individuals who are allowed access to that information.

- Create an electronic signature for your e-mail messages. Think of the electronic signature as a substitute for department or agency letterhead (stationery), so include your full name, position, agency or department name, address, phone number, and e-mail information—anything relevant to you and your position.

- If you are angry, do not send an e-mail message (known as flaming). Rather than tempt fate, go to Word and type everything you want to say—in whatever form you want to say it. Type a message that is as lengthy as you need it to be in order to fully vent your anger or frustration. The good news is that since you are in Word and not your e-mail account, you cannot press send once you complete your angry diatribe. After you have finished keying your message, move on to another project. Give yourself a minimum of 2 hours before returning to your message. After you have completed that reasonable waiting period, if you still feel you need to send a message, read what you have written. Select parts of the message you deem to be pertinent. Copy and paste those selected parts of your message into your e-mail. Be forewarned, however: E-mail is nothing more than words on a screen, and no nonverbal communication, such as facial expressions or voice inflections, are present to help defray the impact of those words on the screen. So your recipient may react in a like fashion—angry. The rule of thumb is to exercise caution. If you can avoid angry messages, do so.

- Sarcastic messages follow the same guidelines as angry messages. Avoid them whenever possible. Sarcasm does not translate well to words only. You need the accompanying facial expressions, gestures, and voice qualities to ensure a positive response.

- When responding to an e-mail message that is asking you for information (such as answers to a series of questions), include pertinent parts of the original message in your response. For example, copy and paste the list of questions from the original e-mail message into your response, and key your answers beneath each question. You will remind the recipient of the questions he or she wanted you to answer without the necessity of having to open the original e-mail message to view them.

- Respond to all e-mail messages in a timely fashion. Send a reply as soon as possible but no later than 24 hours after receipt of the message, even if you simply state that you have received the e-mail message and will follow up. If you plan to be away from your workplace and your e-mail program has the capability of an automatic response, then you should set up a response that automatically acknowledges receipt of messages and explains when you will return.

- Keep personal e-mail messages out of your workplace e-mail account.[12]

While e-mail is the most frequently used communication channel, it is not the only technology designed for such use.

Texting

Because of its convenience and the speed at which messages can be sent and received, texting is gaining in popularity. E-mail requires you to log in to your agency or department system. Texting requires only the use of your smartphone.

The downside to texting, however, is that you are limited in what you can send (i.e., no attached documents), and you cannot easily print text messages. With e-mail, you can maintain a record of communication, a trail of correspondence that you can use for legal purposes or simply for departmental or agency records. In addition, you can easily print your e-mail messages from a computer or directly from your smartphone if you are using a departmental or agency network with a wireless printer.

Etiquette Guidelines for Texting

If your agency or department approves the use of texting, you will need to follow a set of etiquette guidelines to ensure appropriate responses.

- Texting is faster than e-mail because of the shorthand (abbreviations) that can be used, but you have to make sure that the recipient has an understanding of all abbreviations in your message. If not, your abbreviations may lead to misunderstandings or cause wasted time while the recipient attempts to translate the message.

- Texting offers greater privacy, especially in agencies and departments where open work spaces are used. You should not default to texting just because it is quieter, however. Some situations call for a phone call or a face-to-face meeting.

- Text messages are not easily tracked or recorded. So if you need a record of this information for future reference, texting is not the best option. E-mail will provide you with that option.

- Do not allow your text messages to cross the line into unprofessional conversations.

- Do not allow yourself to become distracted while texting. Text only in safe locations.

- Do not text while driving. Some states have enacted laws against texting while operating a moving vehicle. Whether your state has enacted such laws or not, you should never text and drive.

- If your agency or department has established an acceptable cell phone use policy, you may find that you are restricted to certain times of the day or certain locations when and where you may text. You may be required to sign an agreement that you will adhere to the organization's policy. Follow the policy guidelines.

Remember that your agency or department establishes the guidelines for the technology you are allowed to employ in your daily work activities. If texting is allowed only among members of your agency or department, you should adhere to that guideline.

TECHNOLOGY IN THE COURTROOM AND IN CORRECTIONS

While many of the technologies previously discussed are used by law enforcement agencies, some of these technologies—and others yet to be discussed—have applications to criminal justice agencies aside from law enforcement. The following section discusses these new and emerging technologies and their applicability to corrections and the courts.

New Technologies in the Courtroom

Nothing is more dramatic than the positive identification of the suspect by an eyewitness in the courtroom. However, this type of identification is frequently exploited and dismissed by defense attorneys. Research has shown that human memory is fallible, and positive eyewitness identification is not always an asset. Historically, suspects have been identified through a variety of means, including the sketch artist. Victims or witnesses would come to police headquarters and provide an artist with details from which a sketch or composite would be created. In some instances, these sketches or composites were remarkably accurate. Unfortunately, in some instances, these sketches or composites were remarkably inaccurate. In cases where DNA was collected, 70% of eyewitness testimony was proven false.[13] Herman E. Kimsey offered the following explanation for why creating a sketch of a suspect from human memory using common language is difficult, if not totally impossible.

> One of the most difficult problems in human communication is that of exactly duplicating in another mind the visual image one has in one's own. Language is not adequate to the job: the range of variant concepts corresponding to each descriptive word, not to mention their inevitable emotional and imaginative colorings, create inaccuracies, distortions, and downright false impressions. Man has therefore had to resort to comparing such an image or its elements with accepted common physical standards, which reach their ultimate precision in the standard units of measurement. This procedure leaves no room for the vagaries of individual interpretation.[14]

Since sketch artists are few in number and not readily available, several attempts were made to create a library of different facial characteristics. Generically, these attempts were marketed as *Identi-Kits*. Initially, these Identi-Kits provided investigators with a means of developing a visual representation of a suspect without having any particular expertise or specialized training in sketching. Original Identi-Kits were transparencies that overlaid each other in order to develop a facial reconstruction of a suspect.[15] The investigator began with a facial shape such as round, oval, or square, and from that point proceeded to the shape of the eyes. Then the shape of the nose and the mouth and the hairline and its relationship to the ears were developed until ultimately a visual representation of the suspect was created.

An improvement on the Identi-Kit came when facial composite sketch software was created. Identi-Kit is a graphics-based application that is available to criminal justice agencies via cloud-based delivery. This tool was designed to be used by investigators, not computer programmers, so it is intuitive to use. A facial reproduction may be electronically created, stored, and printed within a matter of minutes. Furthermore, this image may be distributed very rapidly to local, state, or national authorities to assist in the apprehension or detention of a suspect.[16]

The facial composite sketch software is not the only tool of technology available to the prosecutor in the courtroom. The axiom "A picture is worth a thousand words" is never more true than in a courtroom setting when the prosecutor is trying to describe a crime scene and the relationship that may exist between pieces of evidence. **ScenePD**[17] and **CAD Zone**[18] are two examples of computer software that aid an evidence technician in diagraming a crime scene. Crime scenes presented in court are the result of a scaled final product prepared by a law enforcement evidence technician. Upon arrival at the crime scene, an evidence technician prepares a rough draft of the scene that includes the position of the victim, any evidence, and the layout or design of the area. These technicians formulate a sketch by utilizing a variety of methods, but three of the most prominent are the **grid**, **triangulation**, or **cross-projection**. These methods allow technicians to accurately draw the crime scene and to ensure the relationship between pieces of evidence is factual. Once this diagram is completed, a scaled drawing is constructed by the technician for display in court. ScenePD and CAD Zone allow these technicians to more efficiently and effectively create diagrams of the crime scene.

Other design technologies similar to ScenePD and CAD Zone are utilized in the re-creation of crime scenes and traffic accidents. However, the use of these technologies for court purposes has been limited. Generally, these technologies have found more success in civil proceedings than in criminal trials.

Furthermore, with the increasing availability of body cameras and the proliferation of smartphones, recording of crime scenes has become widespread—for both the good and the bad. A distinct advantage to recording crime scenes is the addition of color and the clarity with which the scene may be presented. Jurors and judges are impressed with being able to view the entirety of a crime scene and the relationship that exists between the evidence and its relative position in a specific location. Recording could eliminate the necessity of transporting the judge and/or jury to the actual crime scene, thereby saving time and money for the local jurisdiction, an important factor to consider given today's high cost of prosecution.

In-car camera systems (also called dash cameras) are being used in law enforcement vehicles to monitor the officer's safety and to serve as a visual confirmation of the officer's observations and the suspect's actions. In many instances, defendants who are charged with driving under the influence plead guilty once they or their attorneys have viewed the officer's recording of the traffic stop. In other cases, suspects have been found guilty by a judge or jury as a result of having viewed the recording. In extreme cases where officers are injured or killed, in addition to serving as evidence in the trial of the suspect, these recordings serve as a graphic training reminder for new officers and seasoned veterans to remain vigilant.

In 2011, a five-county judicial circuit in Missouri deployed a Skype-like system to help judges remotely preside over motions, arraignments, and other legal proceedings without the need to drive across the state to do so. The system selected for the 4th Judicial Circuit included a large-screen, high-definition television and top-mounted video camera for each of the five counties. Cameras were arranged so that one focused on the judge and the other camera on the defendant.[19]

Additionally, videoconferencing is being employed as a means for out-of-state witnesses or experts to offer testimony in civil trials. However, in criminal cases, the Confrontation Clause of the Sixth Amendment of the Constitution still holds sway in the realm of testimony. One case in point is *New Mexico v. Truett Thomas*. Thomas is alleged to have bludgeoned to death a woman named Guadalupe Ashford. State forensic analysts collected DNA samples from her body and the murder weapon (a brick) and found them to match Truett Thomas. The state tried and convicted Thomas for first-degree murder and kidnapping. The issue with this case, however, was that of the testimony of the forensic analyst who matched the DNA samples. The analyst moved out of New Mexico during the time preceding Thomas's trial and did not wish to physically return to the state to testify. The court allowed the testimony via Skype.

As New Mexico's entire case against Thomas hinged on the DNA analyst's work, her testimony was the mainstay of the trial. Without the analyst's work, the state had no case. The New Mexico Supreme Court consequently ruled that courts cannot use Skype to circumvent the Sixth Amendment to the Constitution. Defendants have the right to confront all witnesses against them.[20]

As far as the use of Skype and whether personal sessions are admissible in court—or can be subpoenaed for introduction in a courtroom—the answer is no to recordings of videoconference sessions but yes to certain other information. In 2007, Skype created a Law Enforcement Relations Management (LERM) Team to handle records requests. Skype can provide only the following information via subpoena:

- Registration information provided at the time of account registration

- E-mail address

- IP address at the time of registration

- Financial transactions conducted with Skype in the past year (only billing provider used regarding credit cards is available—e.g., Bitbit and PayPal)

- Destination telephone numbers for any calls placed to the public-switched telephone network (PSTN)

- All services and account information, including any billing address(es) provided, IP address (at each transaction), and complete transactional information[21]

Twice each year, Skype publishes the number of legal demands for customer data it receives from law enforcement agencies from around the globe.[22] These data can be filtered by country and time frame.

Videoconferencing has definitely gained a foothold in criminal justice. Whether using a video camera and specific programs designed for a corrections or court setting or simply employing Skype, criminal justice agencies have seen the benefits of real-time communication that does not require travel or an investment of time beyond the actual virtual meeting or interview. While videoconferencing occasionally experiences issues in connectivity and streaming capability, these problems are small in comparison to the advantages this technology provides. Prior to the use of this technology, communication with experts, witnesses, victims, family members, colleagues, attorneys, mental health staff, and others required scheduling face-to-face meetings in the office, bureau, department, prison, or judge's chamber.

New Technologies in Corrections

Booking suspects in the docket historically involved fingerprinting and photographing. While a visual representation of the suspect was captured, these pictures were not always the best quality. Differences in skin tone, light facial hair, or facial scars were not always discernible. Now, digital cameras and editing software ensure that photographs of suspects are more realistic and representative of the individual. Digital cameras allow a suspect to be photographed from at least three different angles and for this information to be stored in the local computer database. Those facial anomalies previously undetectable can be enhanced to provide a better photograph or description of the subject. Furthermore, these photographs may be altered by means of new software to reflect the addition or removal of mustaches, beards, toupees, glasses, and other features. Since these photographs are stored electronically or digitally, agencies no longer have to budget for costs associated with purchasing, developing, and storing traditional film.

In addition to the digital camera, certain departments are using a **live scan fingerprinting process**. These two new technologies not only improve the processing of incoming suspects but also reduce the possibility that violent or repeat offenders will be released or lost in the system.

In 2003, rural counties in West Virginia experimented with an innovative approach to arraigning suspects. This new approach involved **synchronous transmission** of information. Synchronous transmission of data or information is "real-time" transmission or reception of video images and audio. A suspect in the local jail was taken to an interview room that contained a microphone, video camera, and monitor. The suspect was able to hear, as well as to see, the local magistrate or judge, who advised him or her of the charge and the determination of bail. Local law enforcement agencies were pleased with this adaptation of existing technology because it eliminated the need to transport prisoners over long distances and reduced the probability of an escape attempt. Deputies were reassigned to other duties or placed in the field rather than used for transport details.

Spring forward a decade, and you will see that arraignments are being handled in a variety of ways involving technology. For example, Skype or other virtual platforms for videoconferencing are being employed to cut down on transportation issues and costs, as well as to handle arraignments quickly and more efficiently.

In December 2011, the Niagara County Jail in Lockport, New York, began using a web-based videoconferencing system. This system was implemented to reduce the number of physical visitors the jail must accommodate, such as attorneys, mental health staff, and probation officers. These individuals could engage in online meetings with prisoners without the necessity of traveling to the facility.[23]

In 2013, the Yellowstone County Detention Facility in Montana implemented a remote visitation system for inmates. This visitation system was the first of its kind in Montana and allowed inmates to have 30-minute scheduled visits via webcam with family and friends. The system chosen by the Yellowstone County Detention Facility was not Skype but one offered by Telmate. This system allowed family and friends to link to an inmate through a web browser. The system the inmate uses in the detention facility resembles a pay phone with a screen and is equipped with a camera and telephone for communication. Family and friends must pay $10.50 per session to visit with an inmate. The facility commander explained that this system was beneficial for family and friends because no travel was required, and it was beneficial to the inmates, as the profits from these virtual visit charges went toward the facility's GED program, anger management classes, and other inmate activities.[24]

MOBILE DEVICE APPS

What is an app? **App** is merely an abbreviation for the word *application*. In the world of smartphones and tablets, mobile apps are those programs downloaded to perform a specific function. A plethora of apps are available for both the iOS (Apple) and Android operating systems; however, these programs must be evaluated carefully before deploying them. Many are useful for short periods of time or for specific activities but have little value over the long term.

A review of published research regarding apps used by law enforcement reveals a minimal number of recommended programs.[25] The following list of applications is not comprehensive. Most of these apps work on both the iOS and Android platforms.

Law Enforcement Apps

- **TBL Universal Reporting.** The Thin Blue Line Reporting app allows law enforcement officers to create reports and sync them to the cloud. CJIS and FIPS compliant.

- **Spanish for Police.** Offers more than 200 simple Spanish commands and questions. Has written and audio translations.

- **Net Transcripts.** Officers who have a Net Transcripts account can record and submit dictation and interviews for transcription. This app touts itself as the "nation's leading provider of confidential transcription for law enforcement agencies."

- **NoteM8.** Keeps a local copy of your data, images, and documents. You can also synchronize your local data for sharing with your peers using the NoteM8 Cloud or the Presynct Report Network enterprise server.

- **Video Armor: Police Camera.** Turns your smartphone into a body worn video camera. The app records high-quality video that is automatically tagged with date, time, and GPS location data.

- **Snitch'n.** Allows you to browse police images of wanted criminals, suspects, associates, missing persons, and more.

- **Appriss MobilePatrol.** Improves communication between sheriffs' offices and the communities they serve.

- **PublicEye.** Allows everyone in the department to collaborate from his or her mobile device.

- **U.S. Cop.** Provides resources for street officers, including more than 2,000 pages of accident investigation formulas, training articles, a pill identifier, case law resources, and more.

- **Camera Canvas Tracker.** Addresses difficult tasks associated with canvassing for surveillance cameras.

- **Crashdocs.org.** Designed to be used by officers responding to an accident scene. The responding officer can use a smartphone or cell phone to scan the vehicles' identification numbers and input information about the collision. The officer provides a card to the individuals involved in the accident that contains the web address for access to the accident report (http://www .crashdocs.org). The driver seeking a copy of the accident report must still pay the same fee as that required for "in-person" requests. However, the use of this app and corresponding website provides more convenience for the drivers. According to CarFax, the company behind the app and website, accident reports are normally available on crashdocs.org within 5 to 7 business days after the accident. CarFax sends all monies collected for the accident reports to the corresponding law enforcement agency.[26]

Corrections Apps

Very few applications are available for corrections officers themselves. Those available have a fitness focus rather than anything related to the job.

Some states have deployed mobile applications that track probation and community corrections officers as an overall safety and accountability measure. In addition, a smartphone-based GPS monitoring solution has recently been released that will assist case managers in monitoring offenders. This Telemate Guardian app provides real-time monitoring, reports, and check-in controls, as well as voice and facial detection, and is compatible with both iOS and Android smartphones.[27]

Private Security Apps

Most of the applications available for private security are geared toward corporate staff or security companies themselves. Some of the apps recommended for law enforcement in the previous section would be helpful to private security officers, however, especially Spanish for Police.

An important point to remember about mobile applications is that they are continually evolving. If you do not find one of these apps in your app store, you should not despair, as another one has most likely taken its place in the list of importance.

The next section of this chapter discusses social media. Social media applications are also mobile apps (e.g., Facebook, Twitter, LinkedIn, Instagram, and Snapchat). However, we did not wish to include them in the section on mobile apps, as their importance extends beyond the ease of access via smartphone and tablets.

SOCIAL MEDIA: CRIMINAL JUSTICE'S NEWEST WEAPON

No technology has opened the closed doors of criminal justice agencies to the public more than social media. The advent of Facebook, Twitter, and Instagram has led to opportunities for agencies to become more transparent and community friendly. While many criminal justice agencies have embraced this new technology, still others have failed to recognize its potential to create a bond with the communities they serve.

What is social media? **Social media** is defined as "forms of electronic communication (such as websites for social networking and microblogging) through which users create online communities to share information, ideas, personal messages, and other content (such as videos)."[28] Facebook, Twitter, Instagram, LinkedIn, and Snapchat are examples of social media. Facebook and Twitter are the two dominant social media programs used by criminal justice agencies.

In 2016, the International Association of Chiefs of Police and the Urban Institute created a Social Media Survey designed to gain information about how law enforcement agencies are using social media technology. The survey was distributed to law enforcement officials who manage their agencies' social media accounts in the United States. Demographic data from the survey indicated that 539 law enforcement agencies representing 48 states and the District of Columbia participated in the study. Responses revealed that participating law enforcement agencies use social media for a variety of purposes:

- 91% to notify the public of safety concerns

- 81% for community outreach

- 86% for public relations and reputation management

- 59% for obtaining information to use as evidence[29]

When asked how long their agencies had used social media, 5% of responding law enforcement departments indicated using social media for over a decade; 5% revealed they had adopted it within the last year.

Not all agencies use social media in the same fashion. When asked about management of social media sites, 80% of the responding agencies reported that they have written social media policies that detail how officers use the technology. Still others have policies in the development phase (11%). Also, a majority of respondents (25%) indicated that a public information officer is the person responsible for managing their agency's social media accounts. Use of a public information officer is considered the best option, as this individual serves as a central point of contact for releasing information, for presenting a positive and consistent message to the public, and for serving as an intermediary between the public and the chief administrative officer. The public information officer does not have to be responsible for every communication sent from or posted to agency sites. Rather, he or she can be charged with oversight of social media and agency websites and the personnel who manage them.

The public information officer need not be a sworn member of the agency. He or she could be a civilian with experience in mass communication and the media. Individuals who have previously worked for local television stations as anchors or reporters and who have effective communication skills typically make the best choices for public information officers since they will be interacting with the media and the local community in a myriad of situations requiring the ability to "think on your feet" while not revealing any confidential information.

When asked about content on social media sites, agencies revealed that most respond to user questions on their social media sites (86%). Only 14% indicated that they do not respond to any questions on social media. Most agencies reported responding to questions or comments on a case-by-case basis—both positive and negative questions and comments.

An interesting finding regarding differing tones and strategies used to engage community members was that 29% of responding agencies stated they always or almost always use an informal tone while 26% said they never use or almost never use an informal tone. However, 85% of responding agencies reported using humor at least some of the time while posting.

In many instances, social media is taking the place of community policing—the cop on the beat—by initiating conversations with new generations of technology-savvy individuals while engendering trust and providing vital information to the people these agencies have sworn to serve and protect. In addition, the use of social media helps humanize police departments and shows that the officers are also members of the community they serve. Social media can be an effective way for agencies to highlight officers' accomplishments, make announcements regarding enforcement campaigns, and provide messages about safety. Agencies can also use social media to ask followers for tips on crimes or to provide important warnings or alerts regarding missing children or suspected criminals who may be on the street or in the community.[30]

Participating agencies (84%) indicated adapting to new online trends to be a challenging issue for them, followed closely by measuring the impact of their social media presence (82%) and training personnel to effectively use social media (81%). In this situation, challenges that law enforcement agencies face are no different than those the average citizen or any business, organization, corporation, or foundation faces, particularly in terms of keeping up with and adapting to new online trends.

When asked how many social media accounts participating departments had, the responses varied by size of department and the community population. Larger departments may require the use of several accounts to reach different segments of the population, such as crime victims, abused spouses, and child advocates. A separate account may be created solely for official statements from the chief administrative officer.

Agencies responding to the survey indicated that they believed training would be beneficial to their agencies. The greatest percentage of responses revealed training that focuses on engaging the community to be of the most value to agencies (28%). However, 26% of respondents indicated that training to improve the use of social media would be most valuable to them. Of note as well, 21% of respondents believe that training to protect agencies from liability issues created by social media would be of the most value.[31]

Writing for Social Media

In earlier chapters of this text, we discussed the need for conciseness in the writing process. Nowhere is this more evident than in the social media world, particularly with Twitter. Twitter limits each post to a maximum of 140 characters. Therefore, if you are going to post something, you must remember a few facts in addition to the character limit:

- Recognize the difference between voice and tone. Voice does not change. Tone, however, should vary based on the situation. If a person had a negative experience (left a negative comment), your response should be more sympathetic and understanding.

- Talk with people, not at them. Reply to any "@ mentions," and address both positive and negative feedback. Twitter is a real-time network, so the sooner you respond, the better.

- Keep your tweets conversational.

- Be professional without being overly formal.

- Avoid jargon when possible. Most laypeople do not understand "police" speech.

- Consider how your content will be consumed by your followers. Would they want to retweet it or pass it along to others?

- When possible, incorporate humor, inspiration, and newsworthy content to draw in followers.

You can post a URL for a specific published newspaper or other article. You can also post a link to your agency's website where you are sharing additional information, photos, or video. In order to maintain the 140-character post, however, you will want to use a tool to shorten your URLs. Several tools are available, including the following: Bitly, Goo.gl, tinyURL.com, Ow.ly, Is.gd, AdF.ly, Bit.do, and Mcaf.ee.

When preparing to write for your Facebook page, you do not have to be constrained by a character limit. However, you do not want to stray too far from your point or add too much extraneous material to your posts, as that will deter your audience from reading them. Consider the following suggestions:

- **Listen.** Before you can talk to a community, you have to understand and embrace how they talk about you. Your community should inform your voice and your content (to an extent). Check to see how people talk about your agency, and use that to inform your writing.

- **Write to one action.** You either want your community to like, share, comment, or click your link. Review your post carefully, and determine what you are trying to get your community to do—what action are you trying to spur? If you have more than one action, you may be confusing your readers. Keep it simple.

- **Do not limit your post to writing only.** The best Facebook writers spruce up pictures and infographics with clever copy. Infographics do not need to be long images riddled with stats and graphics. The busier ones tend to be ignored on Facebook. If your infographic takes too much thought or too much time, people will not review it.

- **Be inspiring first.** If you want your community to post photos, you have to show and ask. Show them the types of photos you want to see on your page, and ask them to do the same.

- **Refrain from making your posts feel forced.** Often when you manage an agency's Facebook page, you will have specific messages that you have to work into your content plan: legal notices, warnings, and reminders. These postings are not always a natural fit with the content you normally push out. If you have to post some of these types of messages, push to make sure that you keep them in line with the agency's voice, tone, and overall approach. When you try to force engagement, your writing will seem or feel inauthentic. Your audience will recognize lapses in authenticity, and your engagement will suffer for it.

- **Standard tenets of good writing still apply.** Just because the people who comment on your page fail to use the proper versions of your/you're and there/their/they're does not mean you can. There is nothing new here, as you have read this information throughout this text.

- **Experiment, measure, and respond.** The more chances you take with your writing on Facebook, the more you can use metrics to understand what type of writing works with your community.

- **You are only as good as your next post.** Any writer should continually strive to improve his or her craft. When it comes to writing for any social platform, you can't rest on your laurels. After every post that falls flat, you should ask, "How can I make this better?" Similarly, after every successful post, you should ask, "How can I make this better?"

To see several examples of agencies that effectively use Facebook and/or Twitter, visit the following sites:[32]

Facebook

- https://www.facebook.com/NYPD
- https://www.facebook.com/RoanokeCountyPolice
- https://www.facebook.com/PlacerSheriff
- https://www.facebook.com/PlanoTexasPoliceDepartment
- https://www.facebook.com/SeattlePolice
- https://www.facebook.com/BostonPoliceDepartment

Twitter

- https://twitter.com/FranklinTNPD
- https://twitter.com/salempolicedept
- https://twitter.com/DallasPD
- https://twitter.com/portlandpolice

- https://twitter.com/columbuspolice

- https://twitter.com/cspdpio

Clearly, law enforcement agencies, in an effort to grow closer with their respective communities, are increasingly moving toward the use of technology. While social media does not replace the interpersonal relationships built between the citizens and their protectors, this tool does help agencies reach a broader audience that is very comfortable communicating in this fashion. What will the future bring with respect to communication and technology? We can only wait and see. Our hope is that the relationships between communities and the agencies that serve them strengthen and that these stronger bonds continue with the emerging citizens of the next generations.

The next section in this chapter discusses what some may believe are outdated technologies: bulletin boards and listservs. However, these tools are still in use.

BULLETIN BOARDS

A bulletin board system (BBS) is often called a chat room, where people with similar interests meet online to discuss issues of importance. **Bulletin boards** exist for political activists, hobbyists of all types, collectors, and law enforcement officers, to name a few.

Many law enforcement agencies maintain bulletin board systems as public relations tools but monitor other BBs for unlawful activity. Some ways law enforcement agencies monitor bulletin boards include the following:

- Social site
- Hidden service

- Semantic
- Marketplace profiling

LISTSERVS

Requiring only an e-mail connection, **listservs** are one of the most cost-effective means for networking among criminal justice professionals worldwide. Individuals join a listserv by e-mail. Most often, you are required to e-mail the listserv address and state your desire to subscribe to that service. The listserv will respond by e-mail to your request and advise you that you are now a subscriber. Shortly thereafter, you will begin to receive e-mail from the listserv.

Some listservs are moderated by a list owner who reviews each message and decides whether or not to send it to the subscribers. The list owner can also edit messages before sending them. Examples of listservs that may be of interest to the criminal justice professional would be as follows:

- **BJS, the Bureau of Justice Statistics.** Provides information on crimes and victims, drugs and crime, criminal offenders, and special topics. To subscribe to the listserv, visit the web address for the Bureau of Justice Statics, www.ojp.usdog.gov/bjs.

- **Justice Information Center.** A service of the National Criminal Justice Reference Service. This site is one of the most extensive sources of information on criminal and juvenile justice in the world. It is a collection of clearinghouses supporting bureaus of the United States Department of Justice Office of Justice Programs, the National Institute of Justice, and several other government agencies. To subscribe to the listserv for the Justice Information Center, see their web page at www.ncjrs.org.

The following are some examples of other listservs available for membership, depending on your area(s) of interest and specialization:

- **NIC.** This listserv is the United States' National Institution of Corrections' public forum for the discussion of corrections issues and practices and for the exchange of views and information. It is also intended to facilitate communication between the institute and field practitioners, policy makers, and researchers. Available at https://nicic.gov.

- **National Criminal Justice Reference Service.** Sponsored by the United States Department of Justice, Office of Justice Programs, this electronic newsletter service provides the latest criminal justice news and information. Available at https://www.ncjrs.gov.

- **Yale Prison Project.** Yale University hosts this discussion list on prison issues and topics. Available at https://www.yaleundergraduateprisonproject.org.

- **UNIVPD-L.** A discussion list for sworn law enforcement officers, its purpose is to provide a forum for law enforcement officers to discuss issues of campus safety, crime prevention, and law enforcement as they relate to university and college environments. Available at https://www.listserv.buffalo.edu.

ELECTRONIC JOURNALS

Criminal justice administrators will find a variety of information on a plethora of topics located on the Internet. The most useful tool for gathering and examining information on topics of current interest may well be electronic journals. These journals are generally published by leading authorities in the field or in academia. Some examples of available electronic journals are as follows:

- *Journal of Criminal Justice* (https://www.journals.elsevier.com/journal-of-criminal-justice)
  - ○ "Is a scholarly record of research and opinion on the intersection of crime, criminal justice, and popular culture."

- *Police Quarterly* (https://us.sagepub.com/en-us/nam/police-quarterly/journal201421)
  - ○ "Emphasizes policy-oriented research of interest to both practitioners and academics."

- *American Journal of Criminal Justice* (https://link.springer.com/journal/12103)
  - ○ Is "a multidisciplinary journal devoted to the study of criminal and deviant behavior, the social and political response to crime, and other phenomena related to crime and social justice."

- *Probation Journal* (https://us.sagepub.com/en-us/nam/journal/probation-journal)
  - ○ "Provides a national and international forum for sharing good practice, disseminating high quality criminal justice research and developing debate about the theory and practice of work with offenders."
- Law Enforcement Enterprise Portal (LEEP) (https://www.fbi.gov/services/cjis/leep)
  - ○ "A monthly newsletter which provides law enforcement with a digest of the best relevant information for law enforcement on the Internet."
- *NIJ Journal* (https://www.nij.gov/journals/Pages/welcome.aspx)
  - ○ "The major journal on best practice and latest thinking and research in police science and management."

You can conduct a search for topics of interest, and the results will lead you to other publications, as well as those contained in this list.

LAW ENFORCEMENT AND THE INTERNET

According to the Law Enforcement Directory maintained by PoliceOne,[33] more than 11,000 criminal justice agencies have websites. As an example, in northern California, Placer County residents can file complaints, commendations, and crime reports on the sheriff's department's Internet site; in Roanoke County, Virginia, citizens can click on a map to find out about the latest crimes in their communities.

The Internet is a powerful, versatile law enforcement tool because it offers instant communication, and it crosses jurisdictional barriers. Citizens are able to report crimes, ask questions, and obtain information, all instantaneously. Law enforcement officials are also able to receive information, post pictures of wanted criminals, and communicate with local citizens.

Many websites include active links to federal agencies and state police departments. One of the best-known sites is CopNet (www.copnet.org). CopNet touts itself as a free community service without affiliation to any police agency, government body, or special interest group of any kind, unless clearly stated. CopNet maintains links to international agencies, crime prevention, search and rescue, electronic crime, events, firearms, forensics, list servers, missing, most wanted, seminars, security agencies, traffic, training, fitness, standards, and other sites of interest to the police world. The Federal Bureau of Investigation, the United States Department of Justice, and the International Association of Chiefs of Police also maintain Internet sites for public access.

You need only search the web for police sites, and a myriad become available for you to view—just one click away. In addition to the information mentioned previously, these sites carry information on training, where to get training, how much an officer can expect to be paid, physical standards for officers, and job postings—along with links to completing online applications for those jobs. Training academies that specialize in law enforcement preparation use the Internet as an advertising forum for their programs as well.

Access to the Internet provides criminal justice agencies with another tool to serve their communities more effectively. However, as with many other technological tools, the Internet has a dark side. What is beneficial to criminal justice agencies is also beneficial to criminals. The next section of this chapter will briefly review cybercrime and its ramifications for criminal justice.

CYBERCRIME AND CYBERSECURITY

A chapter on technology would be incomplete without a mention of the crime that is affecting every person who uses any technology to access the Internet for personal or business purposes. Due to the increase in use of the Internet for activities other than research and preparation of documentation, criminals have begun to exploit technology to commit crimes and to harm the safety, security, and privacy of everyone.[34] Titled **cybercrime**, this lucrative new venue for criminals is causing a migration of "traditional" crimes from the physical to the online world, as well as spawning a new set of criminal activity that targets computer networks themselves. Criminal justice agencies are facing technical, legal, and operational challenges in their battle with cybercrime. This section of the chapter will focus on some of these issues and the mechanisms by which agencies are addressing them.

Cybersecurity

Cybersecurity might have previously been more appropriately titled computer security since the value of theft was centered on the actual computer itself.[35] However, would-be thieves are more concerned with the data than the actual equipment since the real value lies in the information that can be stolen and used to the benefit of the thief. A more appropriate definition of cybersecurity may be the protection of the data that lie within the technology itself.

What Are You Trying to Protect?

The most readily identifiable target of value is identity theft. Most individuals attempt to protect their personal information, such as account numbers (ATM PINs and credit card account numbers) and the usernames and passwords associated with debit cards and credit cards. Less recognizable but equally important is the proprietary information associated with businesses—client lists, supplier lists, cost structure, and product information (intellectual, patents, and ingredient lists). Even the United States government is not immune from attacks designed to steal data concerning defense, intelligence, and basic infrastructure designs and protocols.

What Is a Hacker?

A hacker is an unauthorized individual who attempts to gain access to a device or network that he or she is not entitled to use.

What Are the Types of Attacks?

The most common attack may be the denial of service (DoS) or the distributed denial of service (DDos) attack, and the goal of these attacks is to prevent a system or service from functioning normally or to deny the use of access to a specific service or system.

The backdoor and trapdoor attacks were originally designed by software developers to ensure that they could gain access to an application or product in the event that they were unable to gain access through the normal methods.

Sniffing is an attack from someone examining network traffic that passes the network interface card (NIC). Another approach is spoofing, which is making data appear to come from a different source. The last and most publicized is referred to as phishing or pharming attacks. Phishing is the use of fraudulent e-mails or instant messages that appear to be genuine but are designed to trick users into opening and responding to them. Pharming is the impersonation of a website in an effort to deceive a user into entering his or her credentials.

Cybercrime

Cybercrime is of increasing concern to criminal justice agencies. Crimes such as threats, child pornography, fraud, gambling, extortion, and theft of intellectual property are migrating to the online world. To reinforce this information, you need only look to the address of former U.S. assistant attorney general Leslie Caldwell from the Cybersecurity + Law Enforcement Symposium in October 2015, where she talked about the increasing problem with cybercrime and cybersecurity:

> It's no secret that cybercrime poses a significant threat to the privacy and economic security of American consumers and businesses.
>
> Every day hackers are trying to steal the financial information of millions of victims from a computer halfway around the world. Cyber criminals are orchestrating massive disruptions of businesses or electronically spiriting away trade secrets on a daily basis. And, of course, every day we have threats from within: the disgruntled IT manager or the soon-to-be ex-employee, who steals, deletes or otherwise compromises company information.
>
> Indeed, this past year alone we saw a series of extraordinarily invasive and damaging data breaches that victimized some of our nation's largest businesses, as well as the federal government itself, with tens of millions of personal and consumer records being stolen or compromised at a time. All types of businesses were victimized, from banks to retailers, to mom and pop financial firms, to entertainment companies, to restaurant chains, to health care providers. Sadly, according to data from a recent report, there will be more than 32,000 additional victims of online crime by the time we're done with my session this afternoon.
>
> Hackers incessantly target us because barriers to entry are so low and because it is so lucrative. One study released last month estimated that cyber-attacks have cost the global economy at least $315 billion over the past twelve months. A study from this past week stated that hacking attacks cost the average American firm $15.4 million per year. These figures only continue to grow and are just the financial effects. They do not capture the very real—but unquantifiable—personal harm suffered by victims of online crime, such as identity theft and sextortion.[36]

In December 2015, the Department of Justice created a Cybersecurity Unit and staffed it with Computer Crime and Intellectual Property Section prosecutors with extensive experience in the complexities of legal and policy matters associated with cybercrime. This unit was charged with helping the private sector to safeguard consumer data that have been entrusted to it.

In conclusion, cybercrime and the appearance of cybercriminals has presented a new threat to individuals, businesses, and governments around the world.

Criminal justice agencies worldwide must heed the advice of Assistant Attorney General Caldwell; we must "remain committed to bringing perpetrators to justice wherever they may be, disrupting cyber threats, and forging enduring global partnerships across the public and private sectors to ensure that our data, and our economy, are secure and protected from harm."[37] Twenty years ago, a new police officer was given a gun, a flashlight, and a notepad. When that officer retired, the three items would be returned to the police department, and the only intervening equipment expenses would have been replacement bullets, batteries, and note paper. Today, keeping pace with computer criminals means that law enforcement experts in this field must be properly equipped to fight crime on whatever front it presents itself—on the street or on the Internet.

SUMMARY

Criminal justice professionals in both law enforcement and corrections have long been enamored with technology and its potential applications. This fascination has traditionally been limited to specialized weaponry or equipment used in subduing aggressive violators. Tasers and stun guns are two examples of this technology. However, as the sophistication of criminals and criminal behavior has increased, so has the technology with which to detect and apprehend these individuals. Unmanned drones (aviation technology) are being seen more frequently in areas that police officers cannot access. They provide real-time data to crime analysts and criminal justice agencies so that this information can be used to better plan responses. Drones can also be used to capture real-time commission of crimes via video and other images. This information can be especially pertinent for court proceedings.

The organizational intranet, the Internet, and social media serve as primary means of communication to disseminate information among criminal justice agencies and the communities they serve and to help stem the tide of criminal activity. Furthermore, these communication tools assist corrections personnel in maintaining a complete and accurate record of incarcerated individuals and in ensuring that the guilty pay the fullest measure of their debt to society.

Other criminal justice technology, such as MDTs, the live scan fingerprinting process, and synchronous transmission, not only increases the effectiveness of law enforcement and corrections but also helps ensure the public is provided with the best and most cost-effective means available for maintaining a safe community.

The migration of "traditional" crimes from the physical to the online world is increasing. Cybercrime has become more lucrative to the criminal because of the ability to disguise identities, to reach more victims quickly, and to collaborate with other criminals. As computer technology advances with the identification of fingerprints and DNA, so too does the identification of cybercriminals become ever more important. Agencies are constantly searching for officers with new skills in computer investigation and telecommunications. Additionally, governments need to develop global legal structures that will support detection and successful prosecution of offenders. To keep pace with the cybercriminal of today, criminal justice agencies must be properly equipped with cutting-edge software and hardware and also be confident of laws and statutes governing prosecution of cybercrimes.

KEY TERMS

Amber Alerts 181

App 193

Aviation technology 180

Biometrics 181

Body armor 181

Bulletin boards 199

CAD Zone 190

Communication
    technologies 181

FOR FURTHER REFLECTION AND DISCUSSION

1. Compare and contrast an organizational intranet and the Internet.

2. Evaluate the effectiveness of the mobile data terminal (MDT).

3. Are MDT transmissions superior to police radio transmissions? Why, or why not?

4. Compare and contrast the value of ScenePD and CAD Zone and the traditional methods of grid triangulation and cross-projection.

5. Compare and contrast the use of videorecording a crime scene and the traditional method of sketching.

6. List the advantages and disadvantages of installing cameras in law enforcement vehicles. Explain each statement.

7. List the advantages and disadvantages of having a departmental webpage.

8. What are some uses for criminal justice bulletin boards or listservs? How are they useful?

9. Suggest ways in which technology may enhance the effectiveness and efficiency of law enforcement and correctional agencies.

ETHICAL ISSUE EXERCISES

1. Is videorecording an individual suspected of a crime an invasion of privacy?

2. Who should be responsible for retrieving, reviewing, and storing video from law enforcement vehicles?

3. If an officer is accused of wrongdoing that may be captured on the patrol car video, should it be used in an internal affairs investigation?

4. If an officer is accused of wrongdoing, and it is captured on video that is used by internal affairs for departmental disciplinary procedures, could the same video be used in a criminal prosecution?

5. Should individuals who use the computer and the Internet to enter networks and databases to which they have no authorization be punished? Keep in mind that most young "crackers" enter these sites for the challenge rather than to tamper with or remove information.

6. Most of us know that it is wrong to break into our neighbors' houses and steal things or damage their property. Is there a correlation between this behavior and computer hacking and virus dissemination? Why, or why not?

10

CONFLICT RESOLUTION AND OTHER SPECIAL FORMS OF COMMUNICATION

LEARNING OBJECTIVES

After students have completed this chapter, they will be able to do the following:

1. Identify and explain the continuum of various conflict resolution approaches

2. Explain the 12 stages of conflict resolution

3. Compare and contrast the four types of individuals who take hostages

4. Identify and explain the four options utilized by police and corrections officials, including needed equipment

5. Identify characteristics of effective small groups, including task roles and maintenance roles

6. Explain negative roles and the methods for eliminating them from groups

7. Compare and contrast strengths and limitations of group communication

8. Identify and explain influences of cultural values on team and group communication

The typical police officer is trained and prepared to mitigate physical threats, but studies indicate that only about 2% of police–civilian interactions result in physical encounters. The vast majority of conflict events involving officers consist of interpersonal disputes with little actual violence. To successfully navigate the complexities associated with these disputes, officers must have a clear understanding of conflict, must appreciate how their presence changes the conflict dynamic, and must be able to apply various communication and conflict management techniques.[1]

—"Conflict Engagement for Law Enforcement"

The introductory quote offers a truthful and accurate description regarding conflict negotiation. Law enforcement officers become involved in very complex situations since most problems involve individuals who are less-than-skillful communicators and who allow emotions to control their reasoning and decision making. Since emotions are frequently involved in the types of problems in which criminal justice professionals find themselves, **conflict resolution** is an appropriate term to describe the process used to solve these problems.

What problems do criminal justice professionals encounter? On a daily basis, law enforcement officers deal with domestic disorders, neighbor disputes, and traffic. Parole officers are involved with their clients, who have difficulty with their employers, their landlords, and their families. Corrections officers are constantly trying to maintain order in a less-than-ideal communal living arrangement, as well as trying to resolve interpersonal conflicts between inmates. Most of these situations have some elements in common.

Before we discuss conflict resolution, however, we first must address the meaning of conflict and the elements or reasons for conflict.

CONFLICT

Conflict is defined by *Merriam-Webster* as an "antagonistic state or action (as of divergent ideas, interests, or persons)."[2] Conflict can arise because of needs, perceptions, power, values, and feelings or emotions.

Needs

Needs should not be confused with desires. Desires refer to things that we *want*, not need for our overall well-being. If you examine Maslow's hierarchy of needs,[3] you will see that people have an inherent desire to satisfy their needs, starting with the most basic ones and moving up the hierarchy as each type of need is met or fulfilled.

At the bottom of the hierarchy are **physiological needs**. These needs are basic to survival: food, sleep, oxygen, liquids, and shelter. If people are deprived of these basic needs, they seek whichever is missing in order to return to a state of homeostasis (a system in balance). If basic needs are met regularly, they are no longer of concern. A fulfilled need does not motivate a person to any action. A good example of a fulfilled physiological need and how it impacts motivation can be seen from the suggestion that you never go to the grocery store to shop on an empty stomach. If you eat a meal before you shop, you are no longer hungry and are less likely to purchase unnecessary items.

The next level of the hierarchy is safety needs. Once physiological needs are met, a new set of needs emerges, and these are categorized as **safety needs**. These include the need for security, stability, dependency, and protection; freedom from fear, anxiety, and chaos; and need for structure, order, law, and limits. People who come from divorced, dysfunctional, or single-parent homes often get stuck on this level of the hierarchy, as they are always waiting for the next catastrophe (or the "next shoe to drop"). Because of safety needs, children like having a set bedtime and adhering to the traditions surrounding that bedtime. For them, bedtime is predictable and routine; their safety needs are satisfied.

After physiological and safety needs are satisfied, **love or belongingness needs** arise. The love needs involve both giving and receiving love or affection. Maslow offered little scientific information about the belongingness need other than to show its general destructive pattern when children move too often, when people are without roots or are torn away from their family, and when a person is a transient or newcomer and not a native to an area. We have a natural tendency to want to belong to a group. If we feel disoriented and at odds with where we are, our love or belongingness needs are not met. As criminal justice professionals, you need to be aware that psychopaths do not fit the hierarchy of needs, particularly this level, as the need for love or belongingness is nonexistent. The psychopath feels no desire for warmth or affection.

Esteem needs are the next level of the hierarchy. Every person has a need for self-respect or self-esteem and for the esteem of others. Therefore, Maslow classified esteem into two parts. First, individuals desire strength, achievement, adequacy, confidence, independence, mastery and competence, and freedom. Next, we desire respect from others, status, fame and glory, recognition, attention, importance, or appreciation. People brought up in a comfortable, secure environment are more likely to be risk takers than people who have to struggle for existence. Why? Because a person who has never experienced danger or physical want or never experienced separation from loved ones takes for granted the things he or she has. So to achieve a sense of worth, this individual will suffer all manner of hardship, danger, and loneliness—maybe even dying for a cause—to achieve that sense of worth.

The final need, the ultimate goal, is **self-actualization**. Maslow described self-actualization as "the desire to become more and more what one is, to become everything that one is capable of becoming."[4] Self-actualization takes many forms and varies from person to person. In one individual, the desire to be an excellent parent may be self-actualization; in another, self-actualization may be expressed through inventions or paintings. The common thread with the need for self-actualization, however, is that all other needs have been satisfied.

Perceptions

Just as needs are individually based, so too are **perceptions**. Different people interpret situations, things, actions, and reality in different ways. The following can lead to misperceptions and conflict:

- Self-perceptions
- Others' perceptions

- Differing perceptions of situations
- Perceptions of threats

Since we filter everything to which we are exposed through our personal experiences, what we know or understand and what others want us to know or understand are greatly impacted. Perceptions are a barrier to effective communication.

Power

How we define and use power can also impact the frequency and types of conflict that arise. The ways in which we manage power can also determine how we manage conflict. For example, if we try to impose our wishes on others through the use of power, attempt to take advantage of others through the use of power, or make others change their actions through the use of power, conflicts will develop.

Values

The beliefs or principles that we consider to be essential to ourselves and our well-being are our **values**. Our values influence us, and when they are incompatible with others' values—or when our values are not clear—then conflict will ensue. In addition, if we refuse to accept what someone else values—and understand that it is not a preference or choice for that individual—conflict can develop.

Feelings and Emotions

If we ignore others' feelings and emotions, we are sure to have conflict. In addition, if our own feelings and emotions affect how we resolve problems, then conflict will ensue.

Now that we have defined conflict and explained the elements or causes of conflict, we must next examine how to best manage or resolve conflict. An important point to remember is that conflict occurs in all areas of life—in the workplace among colleagues, as well as in the field with suspects, victims, witnesses, inmates, and average citizens. You must develop specific interpersonal skills to help you manage conflict, and these skills were covered in earlier chapters of this text: identifying barriers to communication (e.g., psychological trigger words), developing listening skills, and learning to interpret and understand nonverbal communication. If you focus on what is being said and how it is being said and avoid homing in on trigger words or your own feelings and emotions, you will be better able to manage conflict or to avoid it entirely.

CONFLICT RESOLUTION

Conflict resolution, also referred to as dispute resolution, is a term used to describe a process whereby the parties involved may achieve some measure of success without leaving either party devoid of dignity or respect. Optimally, conflict resolution attempts to create a win/win situation by allowing both parties to gain something in return for giving some consideration to the other party. This description is of the ideal situation, and achieving this goal may be very difficult, if not entirely impossible. Disputes may be handled formally or informally, with the latter being more frequently utilized.

To better illustrate the multiple approaches to conflict or dispute resolution, Christopher Moore created Figure 10.1.[5] With the inclusion of third parties, the likelihood of a win/lose scenario becomes more evident, and the use of coercion or force increases.

Depending on the severity of the dispute and the means available to the parties involved, a continuum or sliding scale may be used. At the most informal end of the scale is the **avoidance of conflict**, where the individuals or parties simply avoid situations that place them in contact with each other. On the opposite end of the continuum is the **extralegal approach** that involves a great deal of persuasion or

FIGURE 10.1 ■ Continuum of Conflict Management and Resolution Approaches

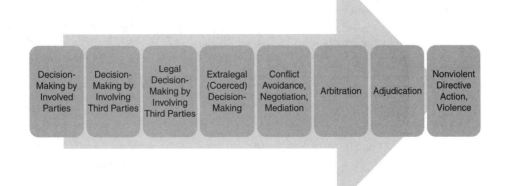

Decision-Making by Involved Parties | Decision-Making by Involving Third Parties | Legal Decision-Making by Involving Third Parties | Extralegal (Coerced) Decision-Making | Conflict Avoidance, Negotiation, Mediation | Arbitration | Adjudication | Nonviolent Directive Action, Violence

coercion and is outside of generally accepted legal standards. Examples of this type of approach are demonstrations and boycotts. The most extreme form of the extralegal approach may be the threat of or use of physical force. Between these two endpoints are the more moderate means of resolution: informal discussion and problem solving, negotiation, and mediation.

- **Informal Discussion and Problem Solving:** Informal discussion and problem solving is one method by which two reasonable parties may come to some agreement and is the approach most frequently used to resolve conflict. Both parties generally make concessions and the dispute is settled; however, the matter may also be dropped for lack of interest or the lack of power to force a solution.

- **Negotiation: Negotiation** involves engaging the opposing parties in a temporary relationship whereby both voluntarily agree to examine the issues and position of the other to bring about a clearer understanding and perhaps a solution to the impasse.

- **Mediation or Arbitration: Mediation** is a progression of the negotiation method. Mediation utilizes a neutral and mutually agreed-upon third party to aid in bringing the parties together to resolve their differences or to resolve "sticking points" to which neither side will concede. These third parties usually have limited or no decision-making authority. Relying on their ability to bring light and reason to the disputants, mediators get involved when the parties can no longer rely on each other to calmly and objectively review the issues and reach a conclusion. Third parties may be involved in other ways. For instance, an individual who is not necessarily impartial but is not actively involved as one of the disputing parties may serve as a mediator in the administrative dispute resolution approach. In this situation, the mediator is attempting to balance the needs of the organization and the needs of the disputants. Governors, county executives, city managers, and mayors may all serve in this capacity in the public sector while chief executive officers (CEOs) and board of directors chairpersons fulfill this role in the private sector.

Mediation is not a new concept; it has an established history in a majority of the world's cultures. Many religions employed the concept of mediation in their respective teachings or doctrines. A contemporary interest in mediation may have occurred as a result of frustration by labor over management practices or the increasing amount of litigation and the staggering costs associated with lengthy court battles. In any event, the use of mediation has grown dramatically in the United States over the last two decades. Mediation is currently experiencing a surge of popularity and implementation. According to Christopher Moore,[6] mediation first begins by building and testing a hypothesis. This process is accomplished by a series of six steps, which encompasses the following:

1. Collect data about the dispute

2. Develop hypothesis about critical situations (faced by parties) and cause of conflict

3. Search for theories that explain conflict, and suggest interventions

4. Select and develop a theory and possible intervention(s) and what the intervention(s) should accomplish

5. Test the hypothesis

6. Accept or reject the hypothesis

This series of six steps leads to the 12 stages initiated by the mediator in an attempt to resolve the conflict. Of these 12 steps proposed by Moore, five occur prior to the beginning of formal mediation and seven occur during the decision-making process. These 12 stages set the foundation for a methodical and successful approach to conflict resolution.

1. Establish a relationship with the disputing parties

2. Select a strategy to guide mediation

3. Collect and analyze background information

4. Design a detailed plan for mediation

5. Build trust and cooperation

6. Begin mediation

7. Define issues, and set an agenda

8. Uncover hidden interests of the disputing parties

9. Generate options for settlement

10. Assess options for settlement

11. Final bargaining

12. Achieve a formal settlement

Arbitration is a further example of a volunteer third party enlisted to aid factions in resolving disputes. In mediation, the parties to the dispute or conflict retain the right to decide whether or not to accept a settlement or agree to a settlement. However, in arbitration, the parties give the power to decide the outcome to the arbitrator. Clearly, this approach is a classic example of a win/lose scenario; however, it does have the benefit of being legally binding and legally enforceable.

While the court has the authority to enforce a decision concerning a dispute between or among parties, the legislatures (state or federal) have the authority to create and enact bills that may force one of the parties to cease action or initiate action in the public's interest. Examples include the elimination of a monopoly, such as AT&T in the 1970s, or the requirement that automobile makers install passive restraint systems (airbags) in new vehicles in the 1990s. Even corporate giants such as Microsoft fear this type of intervention because of the staggering cost involved and the distinct possibility of an unfavorable outcome.

Conflict Resolution in Criminal Justice

The criminal justice system, taking its lead from industry and government, has taken advantage of the benefits provided by the mediation approach. Court officials have implemented mediators in the process of resolving family disputes, such as divorce proceedings and child custody battles. Corrections officials have utilized mediators to bring an end to lawsuits initiated by inmates rather than endure the negative public relations fallout and costs associated with a protracted court battle. However, from both a law enforcement and a corrections perspective, most mediators are summoned as the result of an imminent threat to life or property, such as hostage or barricade situations. These crisis negotiators (mediators) are required to make contact with individuals, determine their demands, resolve tense and hostile standoffs, and preserve life. Individuals involved in these situations fall into four groups: individuals taken by surprise during the commission of a crime, professionals, mentally unstable persons, and terrorists or religious zealots.

When law enforcement or corrections officers are called to the scene of an incident, they have little opportunity to debate confrontation versus negotiation, as the tone of the situation has already dictated how that will go. However, as additional reinforcements arrive on the scene, and the situation escalates, the debate on how to end the confrontation arises. Situations vary, so negotiation, mediation, and conflict resolution should be given equal consideration before defaulting to force. Officers who immediately default to force as the response to a crisis situation are deemed reactionary rather than being recognized as the power in control of the situation. For example, police departments that chose to employ mediation and conflict resolution and other communication skills are viewed favorably, as they are seen as trying to reduce the level of tension.

Attempting to negotiate in a crisis accomplishes two things: It (1) allows law personnel to develop a carefully constructed response and (2) facilitates the placement of key personnel (e.g., special weapons and tactics [SWAT]) and all necessary resources for bringing about a successful conclusion to the situation. In the end, if necessary force becomes the only option, you can say that every effort was made to bring about a successful conclusion through negotiation and mediation; when that failed to resolve the issue, you had to alter the course of your action.

Most hostage situations arise from a rapid response by law enforcement officers to either a robbery in progress call or an alarm call. In either event, the result is the same: innocent clerk and/or bystanders held captive by the shocked and frequently unsophisticated perpetrator. The suspect is agitated and unpredictable, and the hostage(s) is usually in the same mental state, which places everyone involved at great risk. This is not a typical conflict situation faced by most mediators but one which is all too common for criminal justice practitioners.

Mentally unstable individuals frequently take hostages or barricade themselves in an attempt to commit suicide but use officers to complete the act. Referred to by law enforcement professionals as **suicide by cop**, this method allows the individual to accomplish the goal without personally pulling the trigger. While not as agitated as the robber taken by surprise, the mentally unstable perpetrator is still unpredictable and presents a threat to hostages.

The greatest threat to hostage safety is posed by the terrorist or religious zealot. A member of this group is committed to a political cause or a religious ideal. As a result of this commitment, this person is not only not afraid to die but expects to die and earn salvation as a reward for having made a glorious political or religious statement. Most dramatically illustrated on September 11, 2001, by the attack on the World Trade Center in New York City, this type of individual is almost impossible to stop.

Since most mediators are not faced with the type of situations discussed previously, law enforcement and corrections officials need to designate certain members of their organizations to handle these events. Since negotiation, mediation, and conflict resolution skills are not natural talents that each new officer automatically acquires upon entering the criminal justice profession, classes in these areas must be part of the curriculum for in-service training and development for officers. Training is the essential element in establishing a sound foundation for crisis negotiation by criminal justice practitioners. Untrained or poorly prepared personnel, no matter how well intentioned, may irreparably damage the negotiation process. Having written policies and procedures regarding negotiation and conflict resolution are also helpful, as they

- provide guidance in the use of discretion;

- set forth requirements for number of officers responding to disturbance calls;

- provide alternatives to arrest and to resolve problems; and

- enable officers to use alternative resources (e.g., abuse shelters) to aide in responding to situations.

Another step criminal justice agencies can take to ensure the proper approach is taken to conflict resolution and mediation is to form a negotiation team. This specialized team of officers can be trained at greater length and in more specific areas to manage the situations that will arise requiring attempts at conflict resolution and negotiation.

THE NEGOTIATION TEAM

Essential to any successful negotiation is the formulation of a team. While the team may vary in size depending on the size of the agency and the complexity of the situation, the general rule is that the team be composed of as few members as necessary to competently handle the situation; and these members should possess complementary skills. Smaller teams usually ensure better communication and, therefore, are more coordinated in their efforts. In general, small, well-trained teams are more successful in accomplishing positive results.

If possible, the FBI recommends that the crisis negotiation team should consist of three members: the primary negotiator, the secondary negotiator, and the intelligence or liaison negotiator. Each member has a specific role to play and is crucial to a successful outcome. The primary negotiator actually communicates with the suspect and experiences a great deal of physical and emotional stress. This stress is a direct result of constantly evaluating and reevaluating the suspect's mental and environmental position. How agitated is the suspect? Is the suspect becoming more agitated or calmer with the passage of time? How is the suspect relating to the hostage(s)? Does the hostage present a threat to the suspect's safety, or is he or she being docile and compliant? Has anyone been injured or killed at this point in the event? Have containment and control been established? Have an inner and outer perimeter been created?

The secondary negotiator is responsible for monitoring the primary negotiator, as well as keeping notes and offering advice. The intelligence or liaison negotiator interviews people associated with the suspect and gathers other pertinent information. Furthermore, this individual acts as a liaison with the command staff, serving as a conduit for information from both parties. This position is essential since the crisis negotiators are best served by occupying a location away from the command staff.

The intelligence or liaison negotiator role may be expanded or extended to other individuals, which enlarges the size of the team but may facilitate communication with local political leaders and the omnipresent press. If the immediate team needs to be expanded, imperative is the need to include only essential previously trained individuals. The mayor, city manager, or other political leaders may desire to be involved in order to control information released to the press or secure resources necessary for an extended situation. The profile of the situation and the location of the incident may heighten the desire of political executives to become involved. However, some appointed or elected officials may desire to distance themselves from the situation in an effort to minimize any possible negative outcome.

In either event, agencies must have one individual responsible for providing accurate information. This information may come as a briefing to supplemental team members or a news briefing to the press. The intelligence or liaison negotiator may desire to delegate this responsibility to another team member. If at all possible, team membership should be restricted to sworn personnel, with the possible exception of the previously mentioned political leaders and perhaps a mental health consultant. Tactical and traffic considerations may also expand team size.

On occasion, the primary negotiator may need to either position the suspect so that the event may come to a swift conclusion or distract the suspect so that the SWAT team may make an entry. Because of these possibilities, only law enforcement personnel should negotiate with the suspect. Non–law enforcement personnel may be reluctant to perform either of these tasks and are, therefore, unsuitable. Furthermore, one of these well-intentioned individuals (spouse, lover, parent, or friend) may exacerbate the situation.

Since restricting communication to the crisis negotiator is of paramount importance, controlling the telephone is essential. By denying origination (telephone company removes the ability to dial out and restricts access to police only), two objectives are accomplished. The suspect is denied an audience, most frequently the press, and communication is limited to the police negotiator. In some situations, a mobile phone is delivered to the suspect, and landline telephone service (if such is present) to the location is suspended.

Utilities (such as power and water) to the location may also be interrupted for a variety of reasons. Power may be interrupted to prevent the suspect from monitoring the event via television or to cover the entry of a SWAT team. Water may be removed in an attempt to gain surrender from the suspect by creating discomfort or to be restored at a later time as a reward for a concession made by the suspect. In any event, the restoration of services makes an effective bargaining tool.

Tools like these are used to delay or avoid deadlines. Frequently, suspects make deadlines in an attempt to force negotiators into a weakened position. As a general rule, these deadlines are empty threats, and relatively few hostages are harmed as a result of a missed deadline. However, negotiators take these deadlines seriously and seek every opportunity to circumvent them or use them to their advantage. These mental or psychological tactics are part of the crisis negotiator's toolbox. While physical tactics are part of the process, they are more appropriately employed by the command staff in concert with the SWAT team. Even in the best of situations, well-trained professionals may forget or overlook some step or procedure, which may prove to be detrimental at a later time. Therefore, establishing a checklist is essential in order to ensure that procedures are followed and in the proper order.

Hostage and Nonhostage Situations

Well-trained personnel are to distinguish between hostage and nonhostage situations. This is vitally important since hostage situations are less likely to involve injury or death. Hostages are viewed as collateral or as leverage for acquiring a desired outcome. This desired outcome may be as global as the release of political prisoners or the promotion of a cause. Or the outcome may be something as simple as financial gain. In any event, the demands are usually reasonable and have a desired outcome in mind.

Nonhostage situations are more dangerous to the individuals being held since they may be driven by strong emotions on the part of the perpetrator. The desired outcome is not clear and may involve demands that are meaningful only to the hostage taker. Rather than being viewed as an asset in the bargaining process, the hostages are viewed as the agents of some past wrongdoing or misdeed.

Only once the situation has been determined as hostage or nonhostage is negotiation an option. The FBI has listed the following criteria for an event to be classified as negotiable:

1. A need to live on the part of the hostage taker

2. A threat of force on the part of the authorities

3. Demands by the hostage taker

4. Negotiator must be seen by the hostage taker as a person who can hurt the hostage taker but is willing to help

5. Time to negotiate must be available

6. A reliable channel of communication between hostage taker and negotiator must be available

7. The location and communication between hostage taker and negotiator must be secure

8. Negotiator must be prepared for the hostage taker to make decisions

Since officers respond to both hostage and nonhostage situations, options to deal with these events are essential. Four options are generally open to law enforcement or corrections officials. These four options are (1) assault the location, (2) utilize a sniper, (3) utilize chemical agents, and (4) negotiation.

Assaulting the location is highly dangerous and frequently ends in individuals being critically or mortally wounded. Utilizing the sniper is also hazardous since the perpetrator may not be killed immediately or the wrong person may be identified as the perpetrator and killed. Chemical agents may pose health risks to both the suspect and the hostages. Negotiation is both time and labor intensive but has the advantages of promoting good public relations and serving as mitigation in any future civil liability suits.

Correctional Facilities and Hostage Situations

Correctional facilities are not immune to hostage situations, and in fact, they have created some of the most startling headlines over the last 30 years. Attica, Oakdale, and Camp Hill all represent examples of prison riots in which many individuals were killed or injured, and millions of dollars in damage to the institution were sustained. Corrections officials, like their police counterparts, utilize essentially the same team concepts and structured approach. Negotiators in prison settings have some advantages. Generally, all of the participants are inmates or corrections officers. The situation is confined to the institution, and intelligence negotiators usually have access to extensive records on the participants (health, psychological, and disciplinary). Since the hostages may be correctional officers, team members may feel added stress for a successful outcome. Primary and secondary negotiators may experience extreme emotional pressure to ensure their colleagues' safety and gain their freedom.

While the situation may be contained within the confines of the institution, other problems may occur. The assault option may not be employed without a more likely possibility of the loss of staff personnel and a tremendous number of noninvolved individuals. Furthermore, the deployment of snipers and/or chemical agents may exacerbate rather than ameliorate the potential for loss of life since most prison situations generally involve more than the one or two perpetrators present in a police event. In the negotiation option, the team structure is essentially the same, except that higher-ranking government officials will assuredly be involved. Prison riots or correctional situations always garner press coverage, and individual careers are launched or destroyed depending upon the outcome. Therefore, the state commissioner of corrections, the governor, or their federal counterparts are always involved, which may make the negotiation process much more complicated and difficult to control.

Hostage Negotiation Equipment

In order to successfully approach any hostage situation, the proper equipment is essential. The most basic and yet the most important piece of equipment is the negotiator. What characteristics define a competent negotiator? Obviously, the ability to communicate well is vital, but successful negotiators possess several other characteristics. McMains lists the following personality traits:

1. Emotional maturity

2. Good listening skills

3. Straightforward and credible

4. Ability to persuade and use logical arguments

5. Practical intelligence— "street-wise"

6. Ability to cope with uncertainty

7. Ability to be flexible

8. Ability to accept responsibility—sometimes without having the authority

9. Ability to maintain team identity and remain cognizant of the larger issues

10. Total commitment to the negotiation approach and a belief in that philosophy[7]

Formal interviews and a thorough screening process are vital to the selection of these individuals, as they are clearly the most valuable piece of negotiating equipment. In addition to well-trained personnel, routine office supplies are needed. Pens, pencils, paper, and notebooks are all useful items and need to be readily available. Recorders with spare batteries are also helpful. Additional equipment should include cell phones, since they aid in the communication process and keep vital information flowing into and away from the scene. If possible, the team should have a laptop or tablet with Internet access since this allows for a great deal of research to be conducted in a very short amount of time. Some experienced negotiators pack bags with items of personal comfort, such as inclement weather or foul weather gear, extra clothing, medicine (aspirin, antacid, and eye drops), and some staple food items (trail mix, jerky, and protein bars). These bags permit them to maintain the mental and physical energy necessary for any type of extended negotiation. Stress makes enormous mental and physical demands on the negotiator's body, and these demands need to be addressed as soon as possible to keep the negotiator fresh and focused.

Stress for the negotiator comes from a variety of sources. Certainly, conversations with the hostage taker produce stress, but so too do the expectations of political leaders, command personnel, news media, and officers directly involved in the incident. In order to deal with this enormous amount of stress, negotiators will employ several techniques to maintain their emotional and physical well-being. Breathing exercises are effective, and so too are relaxation techniques. If possible, the negotiator should stand and stretch or engage in light exercise, as this will increase the circulation and provide better blood flow to the brain. The increased blood flow allows for better cognition and fights the effects of fatigue.

Once a situation has concluded, a postincident briefing is essential not only to critiquing performance but also to helping alleviate the stress incurred by the negotiator. These briefings should allow the negotiator to vent any feelings, positive or negative, concerning the situation. The negotiator should be meticulous in describing the physical layout of the scene, the emotions associated with the incident, any physical effects from the incident, suggestions for future operations, and any unfinished business associated with the incident.

As mentioned earlier in this chapter, conflict negotiation teams are often a staple of criminal justice agencies. Working as part of a team is difficult, especially in life-threatening, stressful situations. The following portion of this chapter addresses teams and communication skills needed to be part of a successful team.

COMMUNICATION: THE SMALL-GROUP OR TEAM PROCESS

When people work together, performing the same or similar tasks, they bond with each other and develop a sense of solidarity. Criminal justice agencies are no strangers to this phenomenon; in fact, police agencies tend to exhibit a strong solidarity. **Solidarity** refers to "unity (as of a group or class) that produces or is based on community of interests, objectives, and standards."[8]

"Police culture recognizes that officers can only function successfully when they work with colleagues whom they trust."[9] Since law enforcement is fraught with opportunities for mistakes, officers operate as a team—each protecting the others so that no one is falsely accused of inappropriate decision-making.

Small-Group Communication

All people have been involved in group activities at one time or another. For example, through involvement in volunteer programs, organizations, social and religious groups, or some type of committee, you have engaged in group work. Furthermore, as businesses and institutions move progressively toward the preference for work teams, rare will be the case where an individual does not possess a wealth of group experiences. The reliance on team efforts stems from the belief that teams often perform better than do individuals. Here, we can apply the old adage "The minds of many outweigh the mind of one." In essence, the diversity of ideas and creativity that flow from the group communication lead to greater results and increased satisfaction.

A **group** is defined as "two or more figures forming a complete unit in a composition" or "a number of individuals assembled together or having some unifying relationship."[10] An important facet of the definition involves the individuals' interdependence. They must recognize that they need each other and count on each other in order to generate group cohesion or a feeling of group identity. Cohesion will be discussed more fully later in this chapter under the heading of "Effective Small-Group Characteristics."

A **team**, on the other hand, is defined as "a special kind of group that is characterized by different and complementary resources of members and by a strong sense of collective identity."[11] Even though a team shares many characteristics of the group environment (e.g., interaction, interdependence, shared rules, and common goals), it differs from general groups in two ways. First of all, a team consists of individuals who bring specialized knowledge and skills to a common project. Groups, however, are composed of individuals who make contributions to all aspects of the group work. Secondly, a greater sense of interdependence and identity occur in teams than in standard groups. In fact, teams view themselves more as a unit than do ordinary groups. Examples of specialized teams in law enforcement encompass the following: vice, narcotics, intelligence, and SWAT. These same examples are present in correctional institutions where intelligence and emergency response teams (ERTs) are unique elements within that setting. In each of these instances, unit cohesion and interdependence are vital to the safety of the members and to the success of an operation.

Effective Small-Group Characteristics

Research has demonstrated several key components that identify effective small groups:

- They generally have a good working environment.
- They have an optimum number of members.
- They show cohesiveness.
- They are committed to the task.
- They respect the rules.
- They find ways to achieve consensus.
- They are well prepared.
- They meet key role requirements.

The success of the group, however, depends on the members' commitment to the group and on their effective participation in group activities. Members must understand group features and use good communication skills, both verbally and nonverbally. Communication between and within groups is essential to the organization. In law enforcement, for example, vice and narcotics units need to work closely with the intelligence unit in order to obtain the latest information. An important aspect of the uniform division is to ensure that the intelligence unit is supplied with the most recent information concerning suspects they come in contact with in the field (e.g., names, aliases, scars, marks, tattoos, addresses, and associates), so intelligence is aware of the fact that these individuals have been released from correctional institutions or are on parole or have moved to another section of the local jurisdiction.

Number of Members

Arguments abound as to the optimum number of members for a group. Most research, however, has shown that between five and seven members is the ideal size.[12] Problems arise within groups of three to four members due to an absence of specialization or the lack of participation of members. In groups with more than seven participants, those members who are hesitant to actively participate will be even less likely to contribute. In larger groups, where some members are active participants, and others will not or cannot contribute, cohesiveness will not exist, and decisions will seldom be a product of the group process.

Cohesion

"All for one and one for all"—the motto of the Three Musketeers—is a perfect example of cohesion in a group setting. What do we mean by cohesion? **Cohesion** is the degree of members' closeness (sticking together), of members' esprit de corps (pulling for one another), and of group identity. The attractiveness of the group's purpose is one of the qualities that seems most important in developing cohesion. For example, the Fraternal Order of Police builds cohesiveness out of devotion to service or brotherhood. A decision-making group, however, depends on how important the task is to its members to develop cohesiveness.

Many groups engage in **team-building** strategies to assist in their development of cohesion. These activities are designed to help groups work better together. Examples might be composed of such things as merely having the group meet at a location outside its normal setting to engage in tasks to recognize one another's strengths, to share in group processes, and to develop rituals. An important point to remember is that a one-meeting group will be unable to develop cohesiveness. Ongoing meetings are vital to group success.

In law enforcement or corrections, having a group meet outside of its normal business location without the formality of uniforms or rank may place members on a more level plane. The presence of a formal rank structure may inhibit creativity or participation due to a subordinate's reluctance to overshadow or disagree with a superior's ideas or proposals.

Task Commitment

Regardless of how the group task is determined, whether it is assigned to the group or chosen by the group members, all individuals must be committed to the group to achieve success. When members believe the task to be important and that what they are doing matters, they are more inclined to commit to its completion. However, in those times when a task is assigned or a request is made of you to volunteer your time and energy to a task, you have to decide if you want to be part of the group. Without your full commitment to the job or task, you will miss meetings and shirk your responsibilities to the group. Therefore, you would be better suited to decline membership rather than to jeopardize the group's success.

Group Rules

Rules refer to the behavioral guidelines established (or perceived to be established) for conducting group business. In some cases—organizational meetings, for instance—group rules are spelled out in a formal operating guideline, such as parliamentary procedures. Sometimes, group rules simply develop within the context of the meeting or may be adapted from etiquette guidelines. In either event, most group rules develop throughout the course of the project or activity, and they vary from group to group.

Group rules are another mechanism for developing cohesion in the group. Established or implied guidelines assist members in effectively relating to each other. Once the initial anxiety of meeting each other has been surmounted and some guidelines have been developed, group members are able to relax and focus on the task at hand.

One important point to remember regarding group rules is that they are culturally based. Group members' preferences or **norms** will influence the group operations. Norms are learned responses that define or limit appropriate behavior. In essence, what one person may consider appropriate behavior, another may find impolite. As Americans, we have a tendency to interrupt others' speeches to offer our input. Other cultures, however, consider it to be impolite to interrupt another speaking, regardless of the circumstances. Because of our tendency to be **ethnocentric** and to interpret others' behaviors from our own cultural perspective, we must take the opportunity in mixed-culture group settings to discuss rules that will guide individual participation in deliberations and discussions so that each member understands what is expected and permissible and what is not.

Group Consensus

Consensus refers to total group agreement. However, consensus cannot be achieved without the democratic process where each group member interacts and contributes to the discussion and resulting decision. Group members ask questions and use important listening skills and techniques, such as restating, in their own words, what other members have previously said, to summarize or question a point. Typically, one group member will ask if other members are supportive of a decision. At that time, if all group members are in agreement, the decision is reached by consensus. If group members are not in agreement, discussions may continue until all participants have provided input and a new statement has been developed that incorporates different viewpoints. In this case, all group members must participate in the discussion so that the resulting statement represents the entirety of the group position.

In some cases, however, consensus still cannot be reached after many group discussions. In those situations, the group can take a vote of its members. Take the following example:

You are a member of a seven-person group that is examining a change in shift schedule for your police department. The department currently works five 8-hour shifts. The chief has requested that group members explore the possibility of changing the shift schedule to four 10-hour shifts. After lengthy discussions, the group cannot unanimously agree on a decision. Some members are entrenched in the old shift pattern and strongly oppose the new shift concept. Other members strongly favor the new shift change since it will provide them with additional off-duty time. The group, therefore, must vote. While a voice vote is immediate and allows other members of the group to know individual positions, the secret ballot is most often the preferred ballot method. Secret ballots allow group members with less individual resolve to be more candid in their opinions. Since the interests of the entire organization are based on the integrity of the group, the secret ballot is generally more reflective of an individual's true desire. Therefore, your group chooses the option of the ballot vote. When the ballots are tallied and recorded, the vote stands four to three in favor of the new shift. If the vote had been six to one or five to two, the decision would have been given an overwhelming mandate. Since the vote was four to three, questions could arise about support for the proposed change, and further study may be necessary. Nevertheless, since the vote was four to three, the principle of majority rule is the only choice. The decision would be in favor of the shift change.

Preparation

As part of your involvement in a group, your responsibility is to be prepared for group meetings. Preparedness involves reading any materials given to you at or delivered to you after prior meetings. A careful review of this information will make sure you and all other group members are able to participate fully in all discussions. When group members are unprepared or ill-prepared to interact, the whole point of the meeting is wasted.

Another means of preparing for group meetings is to review your personal experiences. In many situations, the group will be charged with responsibilities you have some familiarity with from prior experience. Your own experiences may prove valuable to the group.

Regardless of the topic being discussed, the kind of preparation required will vary. In some cases, library research, surveys, and/or interviews may be required for particular topics. In any event, adequate preparation is the key to a successful group function.

Role Requirements

Each group has two distinct types of roles that need to be filled: task roles and maintenance roles. **Task roles** are those things a group must do in order to fulfill its mission, whereas **maintenance roles** are those necessary group behaviors that keep the group working effectively together. An additional type of role that occurs in groups is problematic and should be avoided—**negative roles**. Negative roles cause the group to suffer, and the work does not get accomplished. This type of group behavior needs to be dealt with in order to minimize disruptions and to maximize meeting efficiency.

Leadership Functions

As we discussed in the foregoing section, task and maintenance roles are vital to the operation of an effective group. Likewise, a group must have a leader or facilitator. You might think that the responsibilities of a leader can be filled by individuals in task and maintenance roles. However, a group leader has jobs that include things such as planning meeting agendas, overseeing group interaction, and summarizing discussions.

Agendas

An **agenda** lists the topics that need to be covered at your meeting. Leaders must prepare the agenda in advance of each meeting and ensure that each group member receives an advance copy so that everyone may be prepared for discussions. Group meetings do occasionally deviate from the printed agenda, but members should recognize that all agenda issues will need to be handled before the project is complete. An agenda helps the group remain focused on the task at hand.

Group Interaction

Leaders oversee meetings in order to ensure that all group members have an opportunity to express opinions or to offer input to the discussion. Additionally, leaders monitor behavior in group meetings so that no individual feels threatened or harassed by other members.

Most individuals bring a wealth of knowledge, skills, and motivation to group meetings. The problem, though, is that without help from a leader, they do not always operate at peak efficiency. To help the group function effectively, leaders must ask appropriate questions to initiate discussion, to focus discussion, to probe for information, or to deal with interpersonal problems. Every group, therefore, needs a leader—not just an individual who has better communication skills than others or who is more sociable or motivated. The group leader is either task-oriented (authoritarian) or person-oriented (democratic) in leadership style. Task-oriented leaders focus on the problem at hand, identifying what needs to be done and how to accomplish it. They tend to exercise control over the group by outlining specific tasks for each group member and by suggesting roles for them as well. Person-oriented leaders, on the other hand, focus on the interpersonal relationships of the group members. They encourage discussions among group members and foster an atmosphere where all individuals feel comfortable in making suggestions. Under a person-oriented leadership style, the group itself ultimately determines what the group does.

Ultimately, leadership means exerting influence and reaching a goal. In examining leadership styles, you can easily see that more work is accomplished under a task-oriented leader. However, motivation and originality are greater under a person-oriented leader. Perhaps the best approach to leadership has been suggested by Fred Fiedler, one of the leading researchers in the field of leadership. "Whether a particular leadership style is successful depends on the situation: (1) how good the leader's interpersonal relations are with the group, (2) how clearly defined the goals and tasks of the group are, and (3) to what degree the group accepts the leader as having legitimate authority to lead."[13]

Limitations and Strengths of Small Groups

Group interaction has both strengths and limitations. As evidenced by the roles discussed in the previous section, disadvantages will appear that influence the group's ability to resolve issues. However, the two most prominent disadvantages of group discussion are time and **groupthink**.

Limitations

Groups have limitations in areas that are not unexpected—time and the desire to agree and move on with decisions, also called groupthink. Establishing meetings when all members can easily attend or remain for the duration of a meeting are just a couple of items that can impact a group. Encouraging decision making from a personal perspective and feeling confident in expressing your opinions are other forms of limitations for the group process.

Time

Decision-making is a time-consuming process for a group. When we function as individuals, we have the opportunity to think through ideas and choose the one best suited for our purposes. In a group, however, discussions must ensue that allow all members to voice opinions and to respond to those of other group members. Describing ideas, clarifying misunderstandings, and responding to questions take substantial time. Additionally, deliberations concerning alternate proposals require time. However, when you desire creativity and thoroughness, a group is the best setting for achieving your goal. In this case, the advantages of group interaction outweigh the disadvantage of time.

Groupthink

Groupthink is an internal group control phenomenon that results when groups are extremely cohesive. In this situation, group members have become increasingly close, less critical of each other's ideas, and less willing to engage in analysis and arguments that are necessary to develop the best outcomes. In essence, they have come to believe that their group is invincible and incapable of making incorrect decisions. As a consequence, group members are less careful in screening and evaluating ideas generated in the group. The result is inferior group outcomes. Symptoms of groupthink include the following:

- Group invulnerability
- Unquestioned morality
- Rationalization of mistakes
- Vilification of opposing groups

- Self-censorship
- False consensus
- Forced conformity
- Blockage of outside information

Prominent examples of groupthink have occurred at the highest level of government in this country from the 1940s to the 1970s: Pearl Harbor, the Marshall Plan, North Korea, the Bay of Pigs, the Cuban missile crisis, Vietnam, and Watergate. Two of the symptoms for groupthink in these cases involved (1) the group's stereotyping of enemy leaders as stupid and evil and (2) the group's absolute belief in its own morality.

In addition, specialized crime units, such as SWAT, and narcotics units can also generate these two symptoms because of the nature of their work and the nature of the criminals they seek to capture. These groups vilify their adversaries so that "they" (the criminals) ultimately become dehumanized. You need only review daily newspapers to read reports of police tactical units who have violated the civil rights of Americans because of their overzealous pursuit of the enemy. Again, this is an example of groupthink in the extreme.

Recommendations for avoiding groupthink include the following:

- encourage ideational conflict;
- assist in the development of the central negative role;
- guard against leader domination of ideas;
- keep consciousness-raising within limits;
- examine the advantages and disadvantages of a proposal; and
- use a problem-solving agenda system.

Strengths

Groups do possess greater strengths than individuals, one of which is the number of available resources. In addition, groups also are typically more creative and possess a greater commitment to decisions than individuals.

Resources

Because of their sheer number of members, groups exceed individuals in the number of ideas, perspectives, experience, and expertise brought to the table. In addressing a problem, group members' differing resources are a key to effectiveness. An example of these resources would be the different backgrounds of the group members (i.e., culture, education, training, and military service).

Thoroughness

Groups tend to create a system of checks and balances for each other. When one member does not understand a particular segment of the issue, another member does; when a member becomes bored, another is interested; when a proposal is developed, and one member sees no gaps or problem areas, another member does. However, discussion and interaction between group members is what makes a group thorough, not just the sheer number of members.

Creativity

Another important factor in group work involves creativity. When group members interact with each other and communicate effectively, they tend to generate ideas. An individual, on the other hand, eventually runs out of ideas. As group members interact and engage with one another, they build on each other's ideas, refine proposals, and see new possibilities in each other's ideas and/or comments. The result is often a greater number of overall ideas and more creative final solutions.

Commitment

Group members have an enlarged commitment to decisions because of two sources: (1) participation in the decision-making process and (2) greater resource allocations. When group members participate in decision-making, they are more committed to a decision, an important fact if group members will also be active in implementing the decision. The other factor, resource allocations, is important because group decisions are more likely to include points of view of individuals involved in the implementation of their suggestions or recommendations.

Time constraints and groupthink are limitations of group processes. However, the advantages of increased creativity, thoroughness, resources, and commitment outweigh any group shortcomings. As long as individuals balance time commitments and refrain from conformity, they will be able to see the value of groups.

Cultures and Groups

For group communication to be effective, it must consider the implications of cultural differences from a verbal and nonverbal perspective. Groups are typically composed of varying individuals from a gender standpoint, as well from a cultural perspective. An important consideration for group interaction is that of understanding individual differences, such as those subsequently outlined.

Individualism

Americans tend to favor **individualism** and often believe that each person is unique and important. Contrast this belief with that of other countries, such as Japan, Colombia, or Pakistan, and you will see a greater emphasis on **collectivism** in those societies. These countries consider everything contributed to be part of the group rather than spotlighting an individual within the group for his or her personal activities—an important element of individualism.

Individual Assertiveness

Individualism also serves as a building block for **assertiveness**. Again, Americans expect people to speak up, assert their ideas, and stand up for their rights. Assertiveness has many focuses: describing feelings, giving valid reasons for beliefs, and suggesting a behavior or attitude we think is fair. While this characteristic is important in the Western world, other cultures (Japan, Thailand, and the Philippines) view this type of behavior as offensive.

Equality

Another Western value is that of **equality**. In group activities, this value influences communication because each individual is considered to have an equal right to speak, and no member is considered to be better than the others. In other cultures, however, hierarchies often exist that define people according to a set of criteria. Male members may speak more, be given more deference, and have their comments given greater respect than those of their female counterparts.

Progress and Change

Progress and change are of importance to Westerners. In fact, Westerners do not see progress as a mere belief or activity; it is a basic mind-set by which they operate. Since progress and change are so important, Westerners tend to focus on the future and to believe they can impact or control everything. No group would feel it had accomplished its mission if the group failed to recommend changes, even if no changes were actually necessary. Societies such as Japan and China revere their history and believe in preserving their traditions. In those settings, group decisions are made relative to sustaining traditions.

Uncertainty and Risk

The United States, Finland, Sweden, and Ireland are countries where citizens accept uncertainty with relative ease. Because Westerners are focused on progress and change, they also are more tolerant of risk. Countries such as Peru, Japan, Greece, and Germany, however, do not easily accept risk or uncertainty.

Informality

Americans and other Westerners tend to be very informal. They greet each other directly and in a relaxed manner. After initial introductions, Americans usually ignore titles and formal rituals in favor of relaxed, casual interaction. Cultures such as those in Japan, Egypt, Turkey, and Germany do not support such informality.

Acknowledging and understanding cultural differences is important to effective group processes. In this age of diversity, we must become cognizant of how our behaviors impact other individuals' behaviors. We should not assume that all group members are the same and everyone follows the same set of cultural norms. Successful communication in your group results from knowing each individual member, valuing each member's contributions and questions, and respecting each person's culture.

SUMMARY

The first part of this chapter deals with the fundamentals of conflict resolution and the approaches to negotiation. In most settings, the art of negotiation is a matter of time, compromise, and posturing. The worst outcome is a loss of personal pride or financial status. Options available to non–criminal justice events usually include avoidance, negotiation, mediation, and arbitration. However, when conflict resolution is applied in the criminal justice setting, the stakes are much higher. The likelihood of serious injury and death are omnipresent. The four options available to criminal justice personnel are (1) assault the location, (2) utilize a sniper, (3) utilize chemical agents, and (4) negotiation.

Hostage negotiation takes a heavy toll on the individual, both emotionally and physically. Hostage negotiators are unique individuals imbued with special personality characteristics. Even in the best situations, every individual involved suffers emotional and physical distress.

Small-group and team communication is vital to the success of an organization. Effective small-group characteristics encompass a good work environment, an optimum number of members, cohesiveness, commitment to task, group rules and consensus, adequate preparation, and appropriate role assignments. Groups, however, possess both strengths and limitations. One limiting phenomenon that occurs as a result of extreme group cohesiveness is that of groupthink. Prominent examples of groupthink have occurred at the highest levels of government in this country from the 1940s to the 1970s. Groups, however, do possess greater strengths than individuals. Groups are typically more creative and possess a greater commitment to decisions than individuals. In addition, groups have a greater number of available resources. These advantages of increased creativity, thoroughness, resources, and commitment, however, far outweigh the group shortcomings of time constraints and groupthink.

KEY TERMS

Agenda 222
Arbitration 211
Assertiveness 225
Avoidance of conflict 209
Cohesion 219
Collectivism 225
Conflict resolution 206
Consensus 220
Equality 225
Esteem needs 207
Ethnocentric 220
Extralegal approach 209

Group 218
Groupthink 222
Individualism 225
Love or belongingness
  needs 207
Maintenance roles 221
Mediation 210
Needs 207
Negative roles 221
Negotiation 210
Norms 220
Perceptions 208

Physiological needs 207
Rules 220
Safety needs 207
Self-actualization 208
Solidarity 217
Suicide by cop 212
Task roles 221
Team 218
Team building 219
Values 208

FOR FURTHER REFLECTION AND DISCUSSION

1. What is the significance of the continuum of conflict management and resolution approaches?

2. What are the 12 stages for a methodical and successful approach to conflict resolution?

3. What are the eight criteria used to classify an incident as negotiable?

4. How do correctional facility hostage incidents differ from law enforcement hostage incidents?

5. Differentiate between the terms *group* and *team*.

6. List five (5) effective small-group characteristics.

7. Discuss the responsibilities of a group leader or facilitator.

8. What are the limitations of small groups?

9. List five (5) symptoms of *groupthink*. In your opinion, which symptom is the worst? Why?

10. List five (5) recommendations for avoiding *groupthink*.

11. What are the strengths of effective small groups?

12. List groups of which you are a member. Discuss your role(s) in each group.

ETHICAL ISSUE EXERCISES

1. The chief and the command staff have studied an issue that is not popular with the line personnel, but their support is necessary for successful implementation of the project. Would it be inappropriate for the chief to select those individuals who support his project as members of a group to study the issue and make a recommendation? Why, or why not?

2. Should group members of higher rank (lieutenant, captain, or major) or status (field training officer, senior officer,

or detective) be allowed to sway or heavily influence group suggestions or recommendations because of their position? If your answer is no, why, since they hold supervisory or senior positions?

3. Given that some negotiations have a power imbalance, would it be inappropriate for the negotiator to provide the weaker party with additional assistance in the negotiation process? Would limiting assistance to the dominant party be appropriate?

4. When officers are confronted with a hostage situation, why negotiate? If negotiation is in progress, why not have the negotiator position the suspect so that a SWAT sniper could end the standoff quickly and save hostages from possible harm?

5. Would it be inappropriate for the commanding officer at the hostage scene to supervise both the SWAT team and the hostage negotiator?

TOPICS FOR FURTHER CONSIDERATION

Directions: Complete each of the following items in an individual capacity and then in a group capacity. Compare your personal responses with the group solutions.

1. The organization is considering removing seniority as an element for consideration in shift assignments or transfers. Individually: What is your opinion? What elements do you think should be discussed considering this change? Would you support this change? Why, or why not?

2. The organization is considering eliminating the use of tobacco as a condition of employment. In an effort to reduce the amount of sick time, the organization is planning to make this requirement mandatory for all members. Is this fair to the members of the organization who are tobacco users and who were hired prior to this mandate? Would you support this change? Why, or why not?

3. The organization is considering changing the assignment of time off (routine days off, vacations, etc.) from a seniority basis to one that accommodates married members with children (Christmas, New Year's Eve, and Thanksgiving). Would this be an equitable solution? Would you support or oppose this change? Why, or why not?

EFFECTIVE COMMUNICATION WITH DIFFERENT POPULATIONS

COMMUNICATION WITH DIVERSE POPULATIONS

Ethnic/Cultural Groups and Children and Youth

11

LEARNING OBJECTIVES

After students have completed this chapter, they will be able to do the following:

1. Identify and explain ethnocentrism

2. Explain the concept of a mosaic culture

3. Explain the shift in demographics related to ethnicity and age

4. Identify factors to consider when interviewing children, adolescents, and adults

5. Identify characteristics associated with gang membership

6. Compare and contrast ways in which you should communicate with diverse cultures

I am a person of colour. It doesn't really matter what colour, but often it does matter to the police. As a woman of colour I feel lucky never to have encountered the negativity of the police, lucky never to have been arrested, lucky never to have experienced any awkward situations with the police but the same cannot be said for my brothers or the men in my family. Let me be clear; not one of them has ever been arrested or charged, but to my dismay all of them have been questioned, stopped, and searched. Why am I using the word "lucky" in a democracy?[1]

—Robyn Spens, "Why Cultural Intelligence Matters for Our Police Forces"

Because America's society is a pluralistic one, communication issues develop involving generation gaps, frames of reference, changing values, and culture. Criminal justice professionals need to be aware of the way racial or ethnic experiences and changing values impact the communication style of each unique group of individuals.

Historically, America has viewed itself as the "Great Melting Pot" where millions of immigrants in the late 19th and early 20th centuries were assimilated into one native culture. This concept, however, has been a misnomer since these immigrants have maintained their distinctive customs, morals, beliefs, and values—their individual **culture**. A more realistic view is that America is a **pluralistic society**.

The dominant Anglo-European culture in America has traditionally imposed its value structure upon immigrants, as well as the native inhabitants of North America. With the arrival of the pilgrims at Plymouth Rock and the Puritans in Massachusetts Bay, Native Americans were subjected to the language and behavioral norms of these new inhabitants, even to the extreme of having the immigrants' religious beliefs imposed on them in a misguided attempt to save their souls from eternal damnation. Even as much as the early American settlers tried to deny their original immigrant status, Americans do not originate from a common stock. America is, in fact, a cornucopia of cultures.

Some scholars suggest that America may be more of a **mosaic**, "in which all races and ethnic groups are displayed in a form that is attractive because of the very elements of which it is made."[2] This mosaic allows each culture to maintain its unique identity and to be appreciated for the distinctiveness of that culture. Therefore, the terms *Mexican American*, *Asian American*, and *African American* are seen as an attempt to establish a foothold in two cultures.

However, this concept of a mosaic is rejected by some individuals. Whoopi Goldberg, a well-known comedian and actor, made the comment that she refused to allow anyone to call her an African American. Ms. Goldberg stated that she had never been to Africa, had no relatives in Africa, and doubted seriously if any person in Africa would be willing to claim her as a relative. She was born in the United States to parents who had also been born in the United States, and she did not see herself as anything other than an American. While her statement lends some support or credence to the belief that Americans have participated in the melting pot concept, this view is rather limited in its approach to multiculturalism.

Just as Ms. Goldberg has expressed her point of view, so too do millions of other Americans. Frequently, their points of view are limited to something known as ethnocentrism. **Ethnocentrism** is the belief that the dominant culture (whether it be American, European, or Asian) is the *only* appropriate culture. Simply put, ethnocentrism is the *refusal to adapt to a different culture even when immersed in that culture*. Ethnocentrism may well be the result of arrogance, fear, and/or ignorance. Many traditional Americans have adopted this limited view, which conflicts with those immigrant Americans who maintain their own ethnocentric views. However, since culture is learned in early childhood and handed down from generation to generation, expecting people to change or remove the rules, values, and attitudes of their culture will only lead to conflict. The better response is to broaden your view of culture and to attempt to be flexible when dealing with cultural differences. After all, culture is inherent in the various regions of the United States, just as it is in the organizations in which we work. Nothing is immune since any shared background creates a culture (e.g., law enforcement in the United States has its own culture—brothers and sisters in blue).

Based on the foregoing information, you can see how important understanding the diversity of our communities is to criminal justice agencies. If we wish to effectively communicate with the people we are sworn to protect and defend, we must know how to reach them. Trying to communicate in just one form will limit the audience you are trying to reach, or using only nonverbal communication that works with Western cultures will fail since nonverbal signals are not identical across diverse groups.

CHARACTERISTICS OF CULTURE

As mentioned earlier, culture is learned from early childhood through exposure to (absorption of) family and society or by being taught culturally accepted behaviors. Culture forms the basis for self-identity, how we tell the world who we are and what we believe.

Cultures have rules, but those rules are logical. While some cultural norms or values may be illogical to an outsider, you can be sure that those rules began with deeply ingrained beliefs. Our culture is also apparent to outsiders based on the things we do—the visible parts of our culture. How we dress, what we say, and our body language and behavior all are visible to others. However, cultures also have invisible characteristics—those things that lie beneath the surface of who we are as a people. Examples might include the following:

- *Beliefs and values* (religion, collectivism, individualism, and worldview)

- *Attitudes and biases* (respect for elders, treatment of minorities, time orientation, attitudes regarding aging/age, gender, occupation, and child rearing)

- *Feeling and fears* (death, personal space, cleanliness, and pain)

- *Upbringing* (rules of conduct, dating practices, touching, courtesy, and facial expressions)

Values form the core of a culture. **Values** are social principles, goals, or standards accepted by persons in a culture; they establish what is proper and improper behavior, as well as what is normal and abnormal. Values are learned by contacts with family members, teachers, and religious leaders.

An important point to remember about culture is that it is dynamic. Cultures change based on advancements in technology, disasters, migration, and wars.

DIMENSIONS OF CULTURE

Social scientists identified five dimensions of culture: context, time orientation, power distance, individualism, and communication style. The most important of these dimensions is context.

Context

According to Edward T. Hall, the cultural anthropologist responsible for this concept, context refers to the environment, stimuli, or ambience of a situation or event.[3] Communication can be greatly impacted based on the context of the culture, whether it is a low-context or a high-context culture. Table 11.1 shows a comparison of how people from low-context and high-context cultures communicate.

North America, Scandinavia, and Germany are considered low-context cultures. Japan, China, and Middle Eastern countries are high-context cultures. As you can see, someone from a high-context culture may not provide the types of responses we are used to, as our culture is low-context—we proceed from point A to point B in a linear fashion.

Time Orientation

The North American culture ascribes great value to time. We see time as being equivalent to money and believe that keeping people waiting is rude. In a

TABLE 11.1 ■ Low-Context Versus High-Context Culture	
Low-Context Culture	**High-Context Culture**
Prefers direct verbal interaction	Prefers indirect verbal interaction
Understands meaning on only *one* level	Understands embedded meanings (at many levels)
Less proficient in reading and understanding nonverbal cues	More proficient in reading and understanding nonverbal cues
Values individualism	Values group membership
Relies on logic	Relies on context and feeling
Says "no" directly	Avoids saying "no" directly; talks around refusal
Communicates with detailed messages using literal meaning (highly structured)	Communicates in simple messages, sometimes ambiguous
Gives authority to written documentation	Understands visual messages easily

high-context culture, however, people do not like to be rushed into decisions or actions. They prefer to slowly and methodically evaluate and deliberate before rendering a decision.

Power Distance

Social psychologist Geert Hofstede introduced the cultural element of power distance.[4] His research involved the development of the Power Distance Index. This index measures how people in societies relate to more powerful individuals. For example, people in high-power-distance countries expect formal hierarchies and embrace authoritarian and paternalistic power relationships. In low-power-distance countries, people feel they are equals and confidently voice their opinions and participate in decision making. Asian cultures are representative of high-power-distance relationships, whereas the Western and Scandinavian cultures embrace the low-power-distance philosophy of democratic, egalitarian, informal interactions.

Individualism Versus Collectivism

Members of low-context cultures are more individualistic. They believe that initiative and drive result in personal achievements. Members of high-context cultures value collectivism, as they value membership in groups, teams, and organizations. They resist independence because it encourages competition and confrontation instead of synergy and teamwork.

Communication Style

Being from a low-context versus a high-context culture impacts the way you use words to communicate. People in low-context cultures (e.g., Americans and Germans) value words. On the other hand, people from high-context cultures place greater value on relationship building than on words. North Americans take words literally, but Latinos enjoy "plays on words"; Arabs and South Americans might speak using poetic figures of speech that should not be taken literally.

The dimensions of culture covered in this section provide a guide for better understanding the role culture plays in people's actions and responses.

How We View Ourselves

Another important facet to consider that is often based on cultural norms and values is how individuals view themselves. Our identities are affected by many orientations; and our attitudes, values, and beliefs most often stem directly from these identity orientations. Table 11.2 lists possible identity orientations, with brief descriptions of each.[5]

Your individual orientations can have a profound impact on your self-concept, which comprises self-esteem and self-image. Your self-concept determines who you are and what you can accomplish. Communication can be impacted by individuals' self-concept, particularly if they believe they will not be heard based on their individual identities or orientations.

Our attitudes are influenced by the culture surrounding us. They can change if our preference for or understanding of something changes. For example, you prefer a Nissan Pathfinder, but someone suggests you try a Toyota Forerunner. So you try the Toyota, and you find you like it better than the Nissan Pathfinder; thus, your attitude changed.

Our beliefs are a different story. Those are usually built over time from previous experiences and personal convictions. You may have very strict religious or political beliefs, not necessarily based on logic or fact, that you deem important to your

TABLE 11.2 ■ Identity Orientations	
Orientation	**How We View Ourselves in Terms of**
1. Gender identity	Gender and what our culture tells us it means to be a man or woman
2. Sexual identity	Sex (e.g., heterosexual, gay, lesbian, bisexual, or transsexual)
3. Age identity	Age (e.g., how someone our age should look and behave)
4. Racial and ethnic identity	Race and ethnicity
5. Physical ability identity	Physical ability (e.g., height, weight, changes across age, and disabilities)
6. Religious identity	Religious affiliation and what that means for our actions and behaviors
7. Class identity	Class (e.g., socioeconomic class) and the norms within and outside of our perceived class
8. National identity	Nationality (e.g., passport affiliation and heritage)
9. Regional identity	Region (e.g., in terms of rural and urban, continent, and geographic location)
10. Personal identity	Personal identity (e.g., could blend all identities but also in minority/majority terms)

Source: Based on Martin, J., & Nakayama, T. (2011). *Experiencing intercultural communication: An introduction* (4th ed.). New York, NY: McGraw-Hill.

self-concept. While beliefs can be changed, you would need very strong evidence and a great deal of time in which to convince someone to change a belief. In fact, some of our belief system is built upon what we observe via television programming or photographs provided by the media. While cultural differences are often greatly exaggerated in television shows or movies, without any direct personal experience to contradict them, we believe the information to be factual.

Values are what shape us into the people we are. Values are more difficult to change than beliefs. Usually, the only way a person undergoes a change in values is because of some type of life experience. For example, someone who believes you have the freedom to cross the street wherever you desire gets hit by a truck while crossing a city street and suffers a closed skull fracture and resulting brain trauma. He or she might change his or her mind about the freedom to cross streets wherever and whenever because of this accident and become an advocate for safer pedestrian walkways and crossovers for busy intersections.

Our personal orientations, values, beliefs, and attitudes make us who we are. Thus, no two people are the same. Therefore, we must learn to practice empathy in our communication with diverse groups of people. **Empathy** is defined as the "ability to share someone else's feelings or experiences by imagining what it would be like to be in that person's situation."[6] Practicing empathy is difficult, as you must suspend your own beliefs, values, and attitudes while assuming those of the other person. You can use the following five steps[7] to help you learn how to practice empathy:

1. Decide to "see" something from the other person's point of view. Because our own personal attitudes, beliefs, and values impose themselves in our communication situations, we must make a conscious decision to keep an open mind to what the other person sees or believes.

2. Be aware of the "filter" we are using to listen. We all have unconscious biases that impact us when we are listening to others. Most often, we are totally unaware that our unconscious biases are impacting us or acting as a filter in these situations. **Unconscious biases** are "social stereotypes about certain groups of people that individuals form outside their own conscious awareness. Everyone holds unconscious beliefs about various social and identity groups, and these biases stem from one's tendency to organize social worlds by categorizing."[8]

3. See the person—not the issue. Affirm the *person* so you create trust in the conversation because you are showing you are willing to listen.

4. Practice active listening. Paraphrase what the individual says and repeat that information so you can be sure you are understanding what he or she is stating.

5. Agree on a way to move forward. Recognize that every person has a unique perspective.

Personal biases, both conscious (explicit) and unconscious (implicit), create problems for engaging and communicating with diverse people. Learning to practice empathy can be helpful in these situations; however, the occasional practice of putting oneself in the shoes of another person will not solve the dilemma of how best to communicate across cultures.

The preceding information provides the foundation for administrators and officers to add the law enforcement, corrections, or security focus to build a strong intercultural communication presence in their communities. The next section of this chapter discusses intercultural communication from the perspective of criminal justice agencies.

CRIMINAL JUSTICE AGENCIES: COMMUNICATING WITH DIVERSE GROUPS

As mentioned in the introduction to this chapter, law enforcement professionals will be communicating with diverse groups of people—persons of varying ethnic and cultural backgrounds—both young and old; male, female, or transgendered; and gay or straight. Since the process of communication is imperfect, individuals must learn to be flexible and make adaptations to their frames of reference, prior opinions, and perceptions. Otherwise, communication will not take place.

We have a natural tendency to interpret behavior from our own cultural point of view and are often blind to our own cultural behaviors. As a criminal justice professional, you should develop an awareness of your own cultural worldview; your attitude toward cultural differences; your knowledge of different cultural practices; and your people skills in this area. In addition, law enforcement officers should develop a level of comfort and professionalism with interacting with people from various cultural backgrounds—whether as a suspect, witness, victim, or coworker. All criminal justice professionals should develop cultural competence so that they effectively interact and communicate with people from all cultures.

Law Enforcement and Immigrant Cultures

Law enforcement faces numerous challenges in working with immigrant communities. Barriers to communication may include the following:

- **Language barriers.** Not every person speaks or understands the same language.

- **Fear.** Not every person came from a country where law enforcement was trustworthy.

- **Federal immigration enforcement's effect on local trust building.** Law enforcement officers may be confused with immigration enforcement officers.

- **Lack of awareness of cultural differences.** This situation occurs on both sides—the police officer may be unfamiliar with the individual's cultural traditions or practices, and the individual may not know how to interact with the officer.

- **Negative experiences with individual officers.** The individual may have experienced a prior incident with an officer that was upsetting or that created distrust or dislike.[9]

To help remove some of these barriers, law enforcement agencies may want to engage in programs designed to build relationships between police and multicultural populations in their communities.

Law enforcement agencies may consider the following strategies for reaching immigrant communities:

- Organizing meetings at local churches or houses of worship. Community meetings should be held in both English and the language that the immigrant community members are fluent in to help establish trust and rapport between police and the community members. Topics may include the following:

    o Common landlord/tenant rights and disputes

    o After-school programs and child-care services

    o Community safety concerns

    o Access to medical services, domestic violence services, and alcohol and drug abuse prevention services

- Providing cultural competence training for police officers. Information to be covered in the training may include

    o misconceptions of police and immigrant populations;

    o statistical data and trends related to working in immigrant communities; and

    o group discussions on past experiences for working with immigrant populations.

- Recruiting volunteer community liaisons. Community volunteers serve as a liaison between police and the people in the community. These individuals assist police by enhancing communication and promoting the reporting of crimes and suspicious activities. Volunteer community liaisons may perform duties such as the following:

    o Provide translation documents for emergency services, important community fliers, and police information pamphlets

    o Assist police with follow-up interviews of victims

    o Assist with community meetings by making PowerPoint presentations[10]

As our communities continue to evolve, criminal justice agencies must also evolve to meet the needs of their community members. Working in these increasingly diverse communities means law enforcement officers need to continually work to build trust and improve relations to ensure fewer crimes and increased public safety.

Law Enforcement and Minority Cultures

Historically, from the police perspective, a pattern of socialized mistrust within minority communities has evolved. Because of this mistrust, police officers are often met with resistance, distrust, dishonesty, and hostility because they are viewed as the enemy and not as an ally. This social mistrust often grew out of the norms and beliefs developed by individuals or a community over time; but with every negative encounter or news story, the relationship continues to deteriorate between law enforcement and the communities they are trying to serve and protect.

Some suggestions or strategies that law enforcement can implement to improve communication in their communities include the following:

- **Critical thinking training.** Officers should be trained to use critical thinking skills and to employ reasonable alternatives to arrest. In other words, avoid resorting to the "by-the-book" approach for every situation and respond to the issues productively.

- **Tactical reviews.** Each law enforcement agency should review all police tactics and the police supervisors using them. The goal is to determine whether the tactics currently deployed for critical incidents are effective or not and whether they are working against efforts to build and maintain community trust. An effective tactic is one that results in a successful conclusion to a situation *without* the loss of life.

- **Media relations training.** Even if a department has a chief information officer (CIO), all officers who may have contact with the media should be trained to effectively respond to community concerns.

- **Examining the role of technology and social media.** Any individual with a smartphone has the capability of recording a police officer's every word and action when interacting with the community. Therefore, when a false or distorted story is published via social media, law enforcement agencies need to respond immediately to rectify the situation. Police officers should use technology and social media to connect with the community and to highlight appropriate police behavior.[11]

Enhancing Communication in Multicultural Communities

If you wish to improve communication—both oral and written—with people from different cultures, you should consider adopting some of the following suggestions:

Oral Communication	Written Communication
Observe eyes (see if the listener is lost—wandering eyes and glazed expression)	Use short sentences and paragraphs
Encourage feedback (ask questions and encourage listener to paraphrase what you said)	Use last names, titles, and other signs of rank or status
Accept blame for any misunderstanding (apologize for not making message clear)	Avoid contractions, idiomatic expressions, figurative clichés, acronyms, abbreviations, and sports references
Avoid the desire to finish the speaker's sentences or fill out ideas; listen and do not interrupt	Avoid words that have multiple meanings
Smile when appropriate, as smiling is a universal sign; just avoid smiling too much, as it may imply insincerity	Use correct grammar
Follow up your face-to-face meeting with something in writing to confirm what was said	Use numbers carefully; date formats and times vary based on culture (including military and paramilitary)

Law enforcement officers can also follow these tips to enhance communication in their diverse communities:

- Be visible in the community. Make positive contact with community members from diverse backgrounds so they see you at times other than when something negative has occurred.

- Leave your negative thoughts inside your vehicle before engaging with your community members. This tip requires a conscious effort on your part, but you are more likely to garner trust and respect if you are positive and nonthreatening.

- Visit your community in a non–law enforcement role so that your community members can see you as much as possible in that "everyday" role.

- Make a conscious effort to treat each situation objectively and to treat all segments of your community fairly.

- Take responsibility for educating members of your community about the role of law enforcement, the police officer, and standard operating procedures in law enforcement.

- Be a change agent in your department or criminal justice agency, and improve the relationships between police and the communities they serve.[12]

The key to successful, effective communication is to practice empathy—set aside your own personal attitudes, beliefs, and values and attempt to view the situation through the eyes of the person with whom you are attempting to communicate. If you can actively listen, observe nonverbal communication of participants, and hold at bay your own unconscious bias, then you will be well on your way to building trust within your communities.

CHILDREN AND YOUTH

America's demographics have shifted rapidly over the last quarter of a century, with the fastest-growing segment of our population now being classified as elderly. However, another large population group is composed of 12- to 17-year-olds. In fact, approximately 23.5 million children fall into this age range (7% of the total U.S. population), with predictions for the year 2027 reaching as high as 26 million teens.[13] This population bulge is even greater than the peak of the baby boom.

In many aspects, our youth are growing up uniquely privileged. They have not had to concern themselves with global war, the draft, or sustained economic poverty. They have access to streaming media, social media, smartphones, and the Internet, which provide them with a tremendous amount of information. This increasingly sophisticated group plans to go to college and have unprecedented opportunities, especially girls. Yet with all these benefits, teenagers still report being increasingly alone and alienated and unable to relate to their parents, teachers, and sometimes peers. In fact, the suicide rate for 10- to 14-year-olds doubled between 2007 and 2014, surpassing the death rate from car crashes in that same age group. Factors leading to this rise in suicide rate are increased pressure to achieve academically, more economic uncertainty, and fear of terrorism and social media.[14]

According to the National Center for Children in Poverty (NCCP),

> the number of poor children in the U.S. grew by 18 percent from 2008 to 2014 (the latest available data), and the number of children living in low-income households grew by 10 percent. More than four in ten U.S. children are living close to the poverty line. In 2014, 44 percent of children under the age of 18 (31.4 million) lived in low income households and 21 percent lived in poor families (15.4 million).[15]

Roughly 15 million American children—nearly one in five—experience poverty and, as a result, are more likely to suffer an array of problems regarding their health, emotional well-being, school readiness, and achievement—and their employability as adults. Growing up in poverty also causes children to engage in risky and criminal behaviors as a means of escaping the life into which they were born.

Child abuse and neglect are at epidemic levels in the United States. During 2015, an estimated 683,000 children (unique incidents) were abused and neglected.[16] Children who are abused and neglected often experience problems later in life involving juvenile crime, poor academic performance, drug and alcohol abuse, domestic violence, and other social ills.

As adults, we hope that children never face tragic outcomes. We want to protect them and keep them free from the pain and the horror of difficult situations. Unfortunately, we do not have that ability. Therefore, communicating with children requires law enforcement professionals to adopt strategies to help them feel safe and secure. Given what a child might have witnessed, he or she needs to know that violence is isolated and he or she will not be harmed. When tragic events occur, children may be afraid that the same will happen to them. Some young children may even think that it already did happen to them. We need to let them know that they are not at risk—if they are not.

The horrific school massacres of the 1990s and 2000s in Littleton, Colorado; Pearl, Mississippi; Sandy Hook, Connecticut; and Santa Monica, California, forced Americans to focus attention on the issues of children, guns, and crime. As of December 2016, since the Sandy Hook massacre in 2012, more than 200 school shooting incidents had occurred, an average of one per week.[17]

During the 1990s, an increase in juvenile violence led many states to change their juvenile justice laws and to place more violent juvenile offenders on trial as adults. Because of tougher laws, violent juvenile crime arrests declined in the 1990s. However, the juvenile arrest rate increased until 2014. "In 2014, law enforcement agencies in the U.S. made an estimated 1 million arrests of persons under the age of 18, 50% less than the number in 2005."[18]

In communicating with child victims of crime, criminal justice professionals should

- identify language ability level of the victim;
- identify the emotional and physical capability of the victim to be interviewed;
- communicate in a compassionate and nonjudgmental manner;

- ensure that the victim is comfortable and understands the purpose of the interview (i.e., the officers needs to learn what happened to hurt or injure the victim);

- adjust language as needed to help the victim understand questions; and

- identify special circumstances and assistance needed to interview a victim with cognitive disabilities.

Definition of Youth

Each state uses its own definition for **youth**. Most states view youth as those individuals who have not yet reached the age of 18. Some states are currently examining the legal issues associated with lowering the age of responsibility or majority to stem the rising trend in violent juvenile crime.

While preschoolers and young children listen to and respect the advice of their parents and older adults, adolescents seem to rely more on their peers for advice and guidance. This shift in information providers creates a chasm between young people and their parents or caregivers. Communication at this stage of development is difficult but not impossible. Adolescents are experiencing a tremendous amount of physical and psychological change that must be considered when attempting to converse. These changes frequently take the form of moodiness or rebellion.

At the same time adolescents are trying to assert their independence, they are regressing to childhood behaviors when they are unsure of themselves or their decisions. Criminal justice professionals should keep in mind that the "attitude" they are receiving may not be the true nature of the young person but rather a manifestation of a stage of development. Therefore, communicating with youth requires just as much, if not more, patience than communicating with the elderly.

To effectively communicate with this age group, criminal justice officials must

- sincerely and genuinely listen;

- establish mutual trust and respect;

- set limits;

- avoid labeling and belittling comments;

- avoid ordering, lecturing, and filibustering;

- avoid mixed messages;

- respect the need for privacy;

- brainstorm and problem solve;

- demonstrate praise; and

- show confidence in decisions or judgments.

Interviewing and Interrogating Juvenile Suspects

Interviewing juvenile suspects requires a different approach than that of interviewing adults. Since adolescents' brains have not yet fully developed (brain development continues well into early adulthood) and the frontal lobes that are responsible for mature thought, reasoning, and judgment are the last to develop, you can safely assume that adolescents will have a different response. In fact, adolescents are much likelier to act on impulse with no regard to the consequences of their actions or decisions.

In 2011, the U.S. Supreme Court[19] ruled that a police officer must take into consideration the age of a child when deciding whether to administer a Miranda warning. In addition, the Supreme Court also recognized biological and development differences when rendering decisions regarding the juvenile death penalty, juvenile life without parole, and the interrogations of juvenile suspects.

The American Academy of Child and Adolescent Psychiatry,[20] based on the Supreme Court decisions, also issued recommendations for interviewing and interrogating juveniles:

- Juveniles should have an attorney present during questioning by police or other law enforcement agencies.

- Juveniles should be allowed to consult with parents prior to and during questioning.

- Police should use terms and concepts appropriate for the individual's age or developmental level when interviewing juveniles.

- Police should provide written material that is geared to the person's grade level and cognitive capacity and not simply rely on reading aloud the information to a juvenile.

- Police should use a simplified Miranda warning developed specifically for use with juvenile suspects.

- All interviews of juvenile suspects should be videotaped.

Interviewing Juvenile Victims and Witnesses

In addition to the guidelines mentioned previously for juvenile suspects, juvenile victims and witnesses have additional rights and options available to them as well. Testifying in open court is one option but not the only one available to juvenile victims and witnesses. Alternatives may include the following:

- Live testimony by two-way closed-circuit television

- Videotaped deposition of juvenile victim or witness

- Guardian ad litem

- Adult attendant

In these instances, juveniles have the right to have their parents, their attorney or the prosecutor, and a guardian ad litem present to protect them from further victimization.[21]

GANGS

As we mentioned earlier, youth tend to look toward their peer group for advice and guidance. Wanting and needing to be part of a group or to belong is perhaps one of the foundations for **gang** membership. A gang is commonly defined as any ongoing organization, association, or group of three or more persons, whether formal or informal, having as one of its primary activities the commission of one or more of the criminal acts . . . which has a common name or common identifying sign or symbol, whose members individually or collectively engage in or have engaged in a pattern of criminal gang activity.[22]

Street gangs are not a recent development, having their roots in the United States in the early 1820s. Irish Americans in New York City established a deviant subculture that engaged in murder, robbery, and muggings. When the United States economy worsened in the early 1930s, gangs appeared across the nation as the chasm between the rich and poor widened. In the 1950s, gangs flourished and this deviant subculture was immortalized in the Broadway play *West Side Story*. In the 1970s, gangs grew as a direct result of the increase in drug trafficking; by the 1980s, gangs grew increasingly more violent, and their economic base was expanded by dealing in weapons and drugs.

Today, street gangs differ from their predecessors in four critical ways:

1. They are larger.

2. They are more organizationally sophisticated.

3. They have full access to powerful weaponry (e.g., shotguns, automatic rifles, handguns, and explosives).

4. They recruit children as young as 7 and 8 years old.[23]

In addition, gangs are expanding their markets from the inner cities to rural communities to bolster shrinking profits from a decreasing base. Gangs have been reported in all 50 states with the typical member being a young male. However, females are also included, not just as associates but as full-fledged members. Furthermore, females have formed gangs of their own and typically exercise the same types of deviant behavior and violence associated with their male counterparts. Nashville, Tennessee, is currently home to five gangs that have expanded their market from larger cities to new territories filled with eager customers: Bloods, Crips, Gangster Disciples, Vice Lords, and Mara Salvatrucha (MS-13). These gangs actively recruit from low-income neighborhoods and neighborhood schools.

Gang Awareness

Every large urban school district is affected by street gang activity; however, youth gangs are not simply a large city or inner-city problem. Nor are they a problem of a particular race or culture. Gang membership crosses all ethnic, racial, and geographic boundaries.[24]

A youth or street gang may be small or large in membership, with subdivisions determined many times by location of the gang or ages of the members. (Sometimes, smaller gangs will be called "sets," "cliques," "posses," or "crews.")

Identification

No single warning sign indicates that a child is behaving in a manner that potentially places the youth at risk of gang involvement.

Gang Recruitment of Youth

Recent research data has identified that the primary age for recruitment into street gangs is 11 to 15 years. This age group is where many gangs actively recruit new members at schools. Gangs in larger cities may recruit children at an earlier age from the neighborhood and from urban primary schools.

Youth gang involvement may begin as early as elementary school. Children as young as 7 and 8 years old are extremely vulnerable and may start acting out, adopting the style and language of a gang, and acquiring the status of a *wannabe*.

Early Involvement Signs

Indicators of a child's or student's possible early involvement with youth gangs are most often present. Changes in behavior or activities are early warning signs and may include the following:

- Falling or poor grades

- Experimental drug use

- Being truant from school

- Affiliating more closely with peers than with family (unwillingness to attend family gatherings or to share regular meals)

- Changing friends (associating with gang members)

- Changing clothes or hair styles

- Keeping late hours

- Developing attitude and behavior problems (rebellious attitude at school and at home)

- Having large sums of money or new expensive items that cannot be explained

The following physical indicators may appear:

- **Graffiti.** Youth gang members will advertise their gang affiliations by writing gang graffiti on their schoolbooks, school bathrooms, school desks, and other school property. They will also write gang graffiti on walls of neighborhood properties adjacent to schools, also known as "marking" their territory. Additionally, gang members will write gang graffiti at their personal residences. Gang graffiti will most certainly be found in the bedroom area of a youth gang member.

- **Youth gang clothing attire.** Clothing continues to be a gang membership indicator; however, not all gang members are obvious in their dress or manner (e.g., Asian gangs are not immediately recognizable by their attire).

- **Hand signs or signals.** Many gang members communicate their affiliation through hand signs. Youth practicing hand signals is an early warning sign of gang affiliation.

- **Gang-style language.** Most street gangs adopt the use of a form of gang slang, and many forms of gang slang exist. Although students who are not gang members may use some gang forms, an excessive amount of gang slang is an indicator of possible gang involvement. Excessive swearing and cursing are also telltale signs of gang involvement.

Signs of Actual Gang Membership

Once involved directly with a street gang, a youth's or student's behavior may change gradually or suddenly. Most likely, it will follow a pattern or process. At school, the youth will promote his affiliation and new status with the gang. The student will most likely become more disrespectful toward teachers, and behavior problems involving defiant issues may increase. However, Asian gang members do not display gang characteristics while in school. They adhere to being respectful to staff, not disrupting activities, and working to maintain their grades and to staying in school.[25]

Indicators of actual gang membership include the following:

- **Monikers.** Gang members pride themselves in being given nicknames, or **monikers**, by the gang. The moniker may highlight a physical characteristic or some personal trait.

- **Attitude.** One of the main activities of gang members is the intimidation of other youth and/or adults. By promoting a defiant and arrogant attitude, gang members obtain a reputation for being tough and aggressive.

- **Tattoos.** Most youth gang members, after initiation or acceptance into the gang, are tattooed, indicating their allegiance and affiliation. These tattoos could be crude or elaborate. Most likely, the gang members' monikers and/or the gang's name will be involved in the tattoo.

- **Fighting.** Once in a gang, children fight others to gain a reputation of being bad.

- **Motivation.** Gang members lack motivation and have no future aspirations.

Communicating With Gang Members

Gang members typically come from economically and socially disadvantaged backgrounds where a breakdown in family and community cohesiveness is present. Youth see the gang as a way to fill the psychological, social, physical, and economic needs that the family and community at large have failed to fill. Gangs provide friendship, security, a sense of purpose, and identity, along with an opportunity to gain wealth.

Youth become involved in gangs for several reasons:

- They may have a need for belonging to something special. Gang membership will provide the recognition, the identity, the attention, the support, and the acceptance of their peers. Many gang youths will join the gang to satisfy the need of belonging.

- Gang membership may be a family tradition. A youth may join a gang because a brother, sister, parent, or relative has or had a gang affiliation.

- The gang lifestyle may be seen as exciting, daring, and dangerous. The potential for violence has a certain level of attraction for many young people.

- A youth may join a gang for physical protection from rival gang members. Some youth will feel they are targets for violence if they do not join a gang. Many of today's gang youth do not believe in themselves outside of their gang structure. They do not see themselves being successful in school or having employment opportunities in their communities.

The key to understanding gang behavior lies in properly identifying the gang's primary objectives and leadership structure. Generally, most youth gangs fall into one of three distinct categories: corporate, territorial, and scavenger.

Corporate gangs focus their attention on making money. They have a clearly defined division of labor. Any activities that gang members participate in are almost exclusively for profit. Corporate gangs tend to have a well-entrenched vertical hierarchy and are likely to participate in group rather than individual violence. The vertical hierarchy of these gangs tends to limit their visibility to law enforcement. It also makes it exceedingly difficult to leave the gang if one wishes.

Territorial gangs tend to focus on the possession of turf, and gang members are very quick to use violence to secure and protect what they see as theirs. This type of gang has a flatter hierarchal structure than corporate gangs, and this results in less control over individual members and a higher rate of gratuitous violence. Because territorial gangs are tied to their turf, they are easier to keep track of, contain, and leave if a member so desires to do.

Scavenger gangs have very little organizational structure, and gang membership is motivated more by a need to belong to a group than anything else. The crimes committed by scavenger gangs tend to be impulsive and often senseless. No objectives and goals are established for the gang, and leadership is very fluid, often depending on who is the most violent that day. Members of scavenger gangs tend to be low achievers who are prone to violence and erratic behavior.

Communication with gang members by criminal justice officials is difficult in the best of situations, if not impossible. Since gangs are closed societies and gang membership breeds suspicion of outsiders, communication and effective dialogue are extremely unlikely. Gang members derive their identity from group acceptance and, therefore, do not seek outsider approval. To attempt to communicate with a gang member, the dialogue must be with the individual—not the gang member. Rapport must be established with the person, devoid of gang personality or identity, in a neutral site or location. If these criteria are met, then a personal relationship may become possible. However, once the individual returns to gang turf or is reunited with the gang, the old identity and mistrust return and the officer is once again an enemy.

The following tips may assist criminal justice professionals to gain and keep the trust of gang-affiliated youth. The guidelines are simple but must be applied consistently.

- **Be reliable.** Most gang-affiliated youth have been let down numerous times.

- **Always look for the positive in the youth.**

- **Be real.** Do not be somebody you're not.

- **Absolutely do not make any promises that you cannot keep.**

- **Be a good role model.** Practice what you preach.

- **Avoid stereotyping.** All youth are not the same.

- **Be aware that every person has different experiences than you.**

- **Listen to the youth.** And he or she will listen to you.

- **Be very aware of your body language.** Remember, gangs do a lot of posturing and may feel threatened by sudden hand movements.

- **Strive to understand the gang member's language.** Do not be afraid to ask, "What does that word mean?"

- **Avoid taking things personally.**

- **Remember, you cannot help those who do not wish to be helped.**

Communication with diverse populations is not an easy task, but it is one that can be accomplished following the guidelines set forth in this chapter. Criminal justice agencies are important to the communities they serve but never more so than when trust can be established and lines of communication opened so that no one is afraid to engage in dialogue with the people who have pledged to serve and protect the members of those communities.

SUMMARY

This chapter focuses on those issues associated with communicating with special groups. These special groups include children and youth and culturally diverse populations. Each group presents its own unique set of problems and solutions. While similarities in communicating with these groups are present, a one-size-fits-all approach will not suffice. Specific techniques exist for overcoming communication barriers with each group, and criminal justice professionals must be aware of them.

Communicating with children and youth presents a unique set of challenges for the law enforcement community. The involvement of youth in gangs creates additional roadblocks to the communication process. Gangs are closed societies, and gang membership breeds suspicion of outsiders. Gang members derive their identity from group acceptance and, therefore, do not seek outsider approval. General rules of thumb to help law enforcement officers gain and keep the trust

of gang-affiliated youths involve such things as looking for the positive in the youth, not making promises that you cannot keep, being a good role model, avoiding stereotyping, listening to the youth, and avoiding taking things personally—among others presented in this chapter.

Cultural sensitivity is a major issue in the 21st century. Police departments that fail to plan for this contingency will find their officers in jeopardy, their departmental reputations in peril, and their municipal or city governments in litigation. Understanding that people from varying cultures hold different viewpoints of and attitudes toward women, ethical standards, and work will help you in the communication process. In addition, as law enforcement professionals, you need to be able to understand variances in greetings and body language between cultures. Learning basic differences in culture will assist law enforcement officials to better communicate with the diverse group of citizens who compose our nation.

KEY TERMS

Corporate gangs 246
Culture 230
Empathy 235
Ethnocentrism 231
Gang 242

Monikers 245
Mosaic 231
Pluralistic society 230
Scavenger gangs 246
Territorial gangs 246

Unconscious biases 235
Values 232
Youth 241

FOR FURTHER REFLECTION AND DISCUSSION

1. Does America live up to its promise of "all men are created equal"? Why, or why not?

2. Is America really a "great melting pot"? Why, or why not?

3. What type of challenges do law enforcement professionals experience when attempting to communicate with young people?

4. How do street gangs differ today from their predecessors?

5. List indicators of a child's or student's possible early involvement in youth gangs.

6. Generally, most youth gangs fall into one of three distinct categories. Identify each category, and compare and contrast them. How are they different? How are they similar?

ETHICAL ISSUE EXERCISES

1. While investigating a violent crime, your information leads you to a gang member as a suspect. You are sure the gang member is guilty of this crime and, upon questioning, discover the suspect has only a limited knowledge of English. Should you seek the services of an interpreter at this point or proceed with the Miranda warning and questioning?

2. You make friends with a young gang *wannabe* and gain his trust. Is it appropriate to use him as a source of information on the gang and a member you suspect of murdering another gang rival?

12

COMMUNICATION WITH SPECIAL GROUPS

Cognitive, Physiological, Psychological, and Emotional Disabilities

It started out as a Peeping Tom call in progress. Two units respond, the suspect is sitting on the porch. As officers approach a teenage boy seems indifferent, like he is in his own little world. Suddenly he reaches for one of the officer's shiny badges. The cops go hands on and suddenly all hell breaks loose. Back up arrives code three which only makes matters worse. The light bars are flashing, sirens wailing, everyone is screaming. The suspect is more than resistant, appears completely oblivious to pain, and is attempting to flee. A responding medic notices a medical bracelet on the suspect's wrist. . . . He is autistic.[1]

—Pamela Kulbarsh,
"Law Enforcement and Autism"

According to the **Americans with Disabilities Act** (ADA), an individual with disabilities is one who has "a physical or mental impairment that substantially limits one or more major life activities, has a record of such an impairment, or is regarded as having such an impairment."[2] The major life activities referenced in this definition, in general, include such things as walking, seeing, hearing, speaking, breathing, learning, thinking, concentrating, bending, lifting, communicating, performing manual tasks, and caring for yourself. Major life activities involving major bodily functions are also covered under this definition. These include "functions of the immune system, normal cell growth, digestive, bowel, bladder, neurological, brain, respiratory, circulatory, endocrine, and reproductive functions."[3]

In 2015, the Centers for Disease Control and Prevention reported that 53 million Americans live with some type of disability. That figure breaks down to 1 in every 5

LEARNING OBJECTIVES

After students have completed this chapter, they will be able to do the following:

1. Identify and explain the various types of disabilities and their impact on the criminal justice system in the United States

2. Discuss how the Americans with Disabilities Act has impacted criminal justice agencies

3. Explain the communication issues inherent in working with individuals with disabilities

4. Explain and demonstrate proper procedures for questioning suspects with disabilities, witnesses, and victims during interviews and interrogations

5. Identify legal requirements for housing and educating juvenile inmates in the correctional system

6. Describe steps necessary for ensuring effective communication with any individual with disabilities

people in the United States. People with mobility impairment (difficulty walking or climbing stairs) account for the largest number (13%), followed by people with cognitive issues (difficulty concentrating, remembering, thinking, and making decisions) (10.6%).[4] Prison populations also have a high percentage of individuals with disabilities. In 2011–2012, approximately 3 in 10 (32%) state and federal inmates and 4 in 10 (40%) individuals incarcerated in local jails reported having at least one disability. The most common disability in each group was cognitive.[5]

The foregoing statistics reveal that as a member of any criminal justice agency, you will be required to engage with individuals with disabilities—whether suspect, witness, victim, inmate, or member of the public. Therefore, you should know what federal laws deem acceptable in the management of and interaction with individuals with disabilities.

LAW ENFORCEMENT AND THE ADA

Members of the law enforcement community have always interacted with persons with disabilities simply because of their involvement with the public. Because law enforcement agencies are programs of state or local governments, they are governed by the ADA Title II Regulations. Title II "prohibits discrimination against people with disabilities in State and local governmental services, programs, and employment."[6] The ADA impacts virtually everything law enforcement officials do, including the following:

- Receiving citizen complaints
- Interrogating witnesses
- Arresting, booking, and holding suspects
- Operating telephone emergency centers (911)
- Providing emergency medical services
- Enforcing laws[7]

In a later section of this chapter, we will review practices that you can use to ensure compliance with the ADA while in the performance of your job in law enforcement. As you will see, many of the suggestions are commonsense approaches to effectively communicating with individuals who have disabilities.

CORRECTIONS AND THE ADA

Corrections officers and probation and parole officers also engage with individuals who report having disabilities. In the case of incarcerated individuals, corrections officers and prison administrators must accommodate those disabilities in accordance with the guidelines set forth under the ADA. While some reasonable accommodations for prisoners with mobility issues involve modifications to cells and the features in those cells (addition of grab bars, wheelchair ramps, and other accommodations), others involve changes to policies, practices, and procedures. For example, inmates with diabetes can have food in their cells to keep blood sugars at appropriate levels despite a rule that specifies inmates are not permitted to have food in their cells except at scheduled times. Additionally, a policy regarding the confiscation of medications from prisoners can be adapted to allow those who have cardiac conditions, epilepsy, or other disabilities requiring self-medication to maintain those medications that do not have abuse potential in their cells.[8] These reasonable accommodation decisions are structured as a top-down process. Prison administrators review and implement the accommodations based on the nature of the individual prisoner's situation and the reasonableness test as per the ADA.

Juvenile Justice

As part of the corrections area, juvenile justice is important to this discussion. On any given day, approximately 60,000 young people are incarcerated in juvenile justice residential or secure care facilities.[9] Correctional facilities where these individuals reside are supposed to provide them with access to a quality education during their incarceration. Therefore, inmates with disabilities should be identified and evaluated. Requirements of Part B of the Individuals with Disabilities Education Act (IDEA) apply to states, state educational agencies, and public agencies in educating these individuals. "Absent a specific exception, all IDEA protections apply to students with disabilities in correctional facilities."[10]

If you work in a juvenile correctional facility, you will need to be able to recognize and understand a variety of disabilities. While you may not be engaged in the teaching and learning process, you will engage with the inmates under your care who have been diagnosed with emotional or behavioral disorders, cognitive disabilities, physiological or physical disabilities, or psychological disabilities. Knowing how to handle a situation that arises out of an inmate's strong response to a minor infraction, knowing what to say to deflect the anger or upset, and being able to employ those communication strategies is important.

The accommodations of most interest to you as part of corrections and communication would be those involving inmates or prisoners with cognitive, psychological, or emotional disabilities or hearing impairment/deafness. Those will be specifically addressed later in the chapter.

PRIVATE SECURITY AND THE ADA

Many private security officers work for security agencies that place them at various agencies, companies, or corporations while others are employed directly by companies, individual artists or officials, or agencies. As private security officers, you may encounter individuals with disabilities during your routine work activities or as part of an incident or accident. Just as employees in any company want to provide excellent service to customers with disabilities, you should strive to do the same in your position as private security. Consider using the following tips for communicating with individuals with disabilities:

- Speak directly to the individuals with disabilities; make eye contact with them; do not speak only to their companions

- Practice patience; give your full attention to the individual, as he or she may have difficulty expressing himself or herself and require additional time to respond

- Ask questions that will help you understand the individual if you are not sure of what he or she is saying; do not pretend that you know what he or she said

- Keep paper and pen or pencil handy in the event you need to communicate with people who are deaf, hearing-impaired, or nonverbal or who have speech difficulties that affect communication

- Know about any assistive communication aids the company has or that are available to you to help you in communicating with hearing impaired or deaf individuals (e.g., large-print materials, assistive listening devices, etc.)

- Sit down when speaking with someone in a wheelchair or who is of short stature so that you are at eye level, if possible, to make the conversation easier

- Identify yourself and others who are with you when attempting to communicate with a person who is blind or who has low vision; use specific words when speaking to the individual to give directions or responses (e.g., do not shake your head "yes" or "no" or point with your fingers or hands to show directions); offer to read any printed material out loud if necessary; let the person know when you are leaving the scene or location

In addition to knowing how to communicate with individuals with disabilities, you would also benefit from knowing how to conduct yourself when interacting with individuals with disabilities in general:

- Do not treat individuals with disabilities with pity or disrespect.

- Be prepared to answer questions regarding accessibility features at your place of employment or your assignment (e.g., does the location have a ramped entrance or level entrance?).

- Ensure that the path of travel is clear for individuals using mobility devices or service animals.

- Recognize that people use service animals for a variety of disabilities. If you are unsure if an animal is a designated service animal, you may ask ONLY two questions:

  ○ Is the dog a service animal required because of a disability?

  ○ What work or task has the dog been trained to perform?[11]

- Realize that a mobility device is a part of the personal space of an individual with disabilities and therefore should not be moved without the permission of the individual.

- Refrain from making assumptions; offer assistance, but wait for the individual to respond; listen, and ask for instructions.

- Respect the individual's wishes.[12]

Remember that you are involved in the customer service industry. The organization for whom you work is expecting you to treat people with courtesy and respect. As a private security officer, you may be the first impression an individual has of a company, organization, association, official, or artist.

Regardless of the criminal justice agency for whom you work, you will interact with individuals with disabilities. Knowing the basic guidelines for navigating the situation will lead to fewer problems, complaints, or lawsuits alleging a violation of the individual's rights. To gain a better understanding of disabilities and their hallmark characteristics, you will need to familiarize yourself with the most commonly occurring disabilities. The next section of this chapter explores disabilities from the cognitive, physiological, psychological, and emotional perspectives.

CATEGORIES, DEFINITIONS, AND EXPLANATIONS

As stated at the beginning of this chapter, 53 million Americans have some type of disability. These disabilities can be cognitive (also termed intellectual or developmental), physiological, psychological, or emotional in nature. Depending on the age of an individual, the disability is most likely either physiological or cognitive. The following section explains each category of disability, offering definitions and explanations for each.

Cognitive (Intellectual/Developmental) Disabilities

Defining cognitive disability is not as simple as you would think because a multitude of intellectual disabilities are covered by this term. People who cannot perform mental tasks that the average person can are said to have a cognitive disability. In simple terms, a disability that affects a person's brain in such a way that makes completing normal tasks harder than it would be for the average person is said to be a cognitive disability. The more severe the cognitive disability, the less independent the person.

People with **cognitive disabilities** have difficulty with memory, attention, problem solving, math calculations, and reading comprehension. They also have difficulty processing emergencies, something of importance to criminal justice professionals who may interact with them. Individuals with cognitive disabilities (also called intellectual and developmental disabilities) are much more likely to have encounters with law enforcement and to have communication issues, some leading to tragic consequences.[13]

Clinical diagnosis of cognitive disability can include the following: **Down syndrome**, **traumatic brain injury** (TBI) and **acquired brain injury**, **autism**, or **dementia**. Less severe cognitive disabilities identified through clinical diagnosis include dyslexia, attention deficit disorder, dyscalculia, and other learning disabilities. The next section of the chapter provides a brief overview of the most frequently occurring cognitive (intellectual or developmental) disabilities and characteristics associated with them that are important for you to know as members of the criminal justice profession, regardless of the specific agency for which you work.

Down Syndrome

"Down syndrome is a genetic disorder caused when abnormal cell division results in extra genetic material from chromosome 21. This genetic disorder, which varies in severity, causes lifelong intellectual disability and developmental delays, and in some people, it causes health problems."[14] Life expectancy rates for people with Down syndrome have increased from estimates in 1985 of 25 years to today's estimate of 60 years. About 6,000 babies are born with Down syndrome each year in the United States. All people with Down syndrome experience mild to moderate cognitive delays. Some of the common physical traits associated with Down syndrome are low muscle tone, small stature, an upward slant to the eyes, and a single deep crease across the center of the palm.[15]

Characteristics of individuals with Down syndrome. In addition to the physical characteristics mentioned previously, individuals with Down syndrome have speech characteristics that occur because of the anatomical differences in tongue size. Therefore, people with Down syndrome have a greater prevalence of stuttering. They also have problems with clear speech. Because they experience repeated ear infections as children, they often develop hearing problems. In fact, hearing loss is common in the Down syndrome population. The loss of hearing affects pronunciation and clear speech. While individuals with Down syndrome have strong social skills, they have difficulty understanding abstract language and conversation and focusing on the overall meaning of a conversation rather than on the meaning of the words themselves.[16] Thus, when you interact with individuals with Down syndrome, you will have to adapt your usual communication approach to one that better matches their abilities.

Traumatic Brain Injury

The Centers for Disease Control and Prevention defines traumatic brain injury (TBI) as "a disruption in the normal function of the brain that can be caused by a bump, blow, or jolt to the head, or penetrating head injury."[17] The most recent data from the United States Department of Health and Human Services reveal that combined rates of emergency room visits, hospitalizations, and deaths resulting from TBI account for a rate of 823.7 per 100,000 (approximately 2.5 million people). This figure has risen sharply since 2008.[18]

Characteristics of individuals with TBI. People living with TBI are not always visible to the average person. In fact, TBI is labeled the invisible disability for this reason. People are perceived as "normal" unless they have a visible scar that denotes some type of head trauma or injury. However, depending on which region and side of the brain was injured, people can have vastly differing changes to their personality and communication skills.

Injuries to the *left side* of the brain might result in the following:

- Difficulties in understanding language (receptive language)
- Difficulties in speaking or verbal output (expressive language)
- Catastrophic reactions (depression and anxiety)
- Verbal memory deficits
- Impaired logic
- Sequencing difficulties
- Decreased control over right-sided body movements

Injuries to the *right side* of the brain might result in the following:

- Visual-spatial impairment
- Visual memory deficits
- Left neglect (inattention to the left side of the body)

- Decreased awareness of deficits

- Altered creativity and music perception

- Loss of "the big picture" type of thinking

- Decreased control over left-sided body movements

Injuries *scattered throughout the brain* (called diffuse brain injury) might result in the following:

- Reduced thinking speed

- Confusion

- Reduced attention and concentration

- Fatigue

- Impaired cognitive (thinking) skills in all areas[19]

Most frequently, people with brain injuries have problems concentrating, paying attention, speaking, learning, remembering, planning, and problem solving. When you encounter people with a TBI, you need to understand that these individuals may

- Be unable to focus or pay attention to more than one thing at a time

- Become restless and easily distracted, thereby having difficulty conversing or sitting for long periods of time

- Take longer to grasp what you and others are saying

- Require additional time to understand and follow directions

- React more slowly (sometimes this occurs when the individual is driving so that he or she cannot react fast enough to stop at traffic lights and stop signs—or other warning signs)

- Ramble or go off topic

- Display difficulty in finding the right word (**aphasia**) or using an incorrect word (**dysphasia**)

- Be unable to read or understand your emotions and other nonverbal messages

- Have difficulty communicating thoughts and feelings using nonverbal communication

- Respond inappropriately to your (or another person's) feelings or to the situation at hand

- Misunderstand jokes or sarcasm

- Have difficulty remembering new information and events (can prove disadvantageous if the individual witnessed a crime, accident, or incident)

- Display false memories ("fill in the gaps" of missing information regarding an event or conversation and recall things that did not actually occur or mesh bits and pieces of information from several events or conversations into one event)

- Have difficulty recognizing when a problem exists

- Have difficulty deciding the best solution for a problem

- Have trouble analyzing information or changing the way they think

- Make quick decisions without thinking about the consequences of an action

- Make poor judgments

- Say hurtful or insensitive things or behave in inconsiderate ways

- Lack awareness of social boundaries and others' feelings (being too personal with people they do not know or not realizing they have made someone uncomfortable)

- Deny they have any cognitive problems (even if those problems are obvious to others)

Individuals who have a TBI often act impulsively and engage in socially inappropriate behavior because of their decreased reasoning abilities and lack of control. Because self-awareness requires people to use complex thinking skills that are weakened following brain injuries, people with TBI cannot reason that if they say or do something inappropriate, then something bad will happen.

Acquired Brain Injuries

"An acquired brain injury is an injury to the brain, which is not hereditary, congenital, degenerative, or induced by birth trauma. An acquired brain injury is an injury to the brain that has occurred after birth."[20] If an acquired brain injury is one that occurs after birth, how does it differ from a traumatic brain injury since any injury to the brain could be called an acquired brain injury? An acquired brain injury is an injury to the brain that is not trauma related. Therefore, examples of acquired brain injuries involve stroke, near drowning, hypoxic or anoxic brain injury, tumor, neurotoxins, electric shock, or lightning strike. Acquired brain injury survivors share many commonalities with traumatic brain injury survivors, particularly in the areas of communication, memory, and judgment or decision-making.

Each year, approximately 795,000 people in the United States have a stroke. To show how acquired brain injury and traumatic brain injury result in similar outcomes, we will look at strokes and how they impact a person's life.

Stroke. Stroke is the third leading cause of death in this country, with approximately 140,000 people dying from stroke each year. Of the 795,000 people having strokes each year, approximately 600,000 of them are having their first stroke.[21] If a stroke occurs in a particular region of the brain and blood flow cannot reach that area, then a particular body function associated with that region of the brain will be impacted. For example, if the stroke occurs toward the back of the brain, some disability involving vision will result. The effects of a stroke are much like traumatic brain injuries in that they are both dependent on the location of the obstruction or trauma and the extent of brain tissue affected. Since one side of the brain controls the opposite side of the body, a stroke affecting one side will result in problems or issues on the other side of the body (e.g., if the stroke occurs in the right side of the brain, the left side of the body—and the left side of the face—will be impacted).

Characteristics of individuals with acquired brain injury of stroke. People recovering from a stroke experience problems in three areas: physical effects, communication challenges, and emotional and behavioral challenges. Because of its impact on the mobility of individuals, stroke could be classified as a movement disorder in the physiological or physical disabilities section. However, because stroke also impacts the cognitive or intellectual area and is classified as an acquired brain injury, we place it in the cognitive disabilities category.

The most common general effects of stroke are as follows:

- Weakness on one side of the body or paralysis on one side of the body

- Difficulty speaking or slurred speech or trouble swallowing

- Fatigue

- Loss of emotional control and changes in mood

- Cognitive changes (e.g., problems with memory, judgment, problem solving, or a combination of these)

- Behavior changes (e.g., personality changes and improper language or actions)

- Decreased field of vision (inability to see peripheral vision) and trouble with visual perception[22]

These same effects are seen among individuals with all types of cognitive disabilities. Despite the official diagnosis of Down syndrome, autism, traumatic brain injury, acquired brain injury, or dementia, individuals with cognitive disabilities share commonalities that require you to learn strategies for interacting and communicating with them.

Autism

"Autism, or autism spectrum disorder, refers to a range of conditions characterized by challenges with social skills, repetitive behaviors, speech and nonverbal communication, as well as by unique strengths and differences. We now know that there is not one autism but many types, caused by different combinations of genetic and environmental influences."[23] Since autism interferes with the typical development of the brain in the areas of social interaction and communication skills, individuals with autism typically have difficulties in verbal and nonverbal communication, social interactions, and leisure or play activities. According to a Centers for Disease Control and Prevention report, autism affects 1 in 68 children in the United States, with the diagnosis being 4.5 times more common in boys than girls.[24]

Characteristics of individuals with autism. Interacting with individuals who have cognitive disabilities requires a modification to processes, procedures, and policies.

You need to understand how these disabilities manifest themselves. For example, a person with autism may

- Have an impaired sense of danger; may not understand danger or consequence

- Be overwhelmed by police presence

- Fear a person in uniform or exhibit curiosity and reach for objects or equipment (e.g., the shiny badge mentioned in the chapter opening quote)

- Not respond to "stop" or other commands

- Not respond to his or her name or verbal commands

- Appear belligerent, argumentative, or stubborn

- Ask "why" or respond "no" to all questions

- Repeat exactly what is said to him or her (parrot questions or statements)

- Avoid eye contact

- Try to walk away, run, or hide

- Toe walk or have a pigeon-toed gait or running style

- Appear psychotic or under the influence of drugs or alcohol

- Not show his or her hands when asked

- Have difficulty judging personal space (e.g., stand too close or too far away)

- Have difficulty interpreting your body language

- Speak in a monotone voice and pronounce words in an unusual fashion

- Ramble about a favorite topic (occurs when a person with autism feels uncomfortable)

- Speak in a blunt, honest fashion (not tactful)[25]

In addition, people with autism may engage in **stimming**. Stimming occurs when the individual flaps his or her hands, rocks, or repeats words. Stimming helps people with autism by providing them with emotional self-regulation, sensory stimulation, and expression. The repetition of words, sounds, or vocalizations is called **echolalia**. For some people with autism, echolalia may include a favorite quote (from a movie or television show), a question, or a verbal command.[26]

Dementia

The Alzheimer's Association defines dementia as follows: "*Dementia is not a specific disease. It's an overall term that describes a wide range of symptoms* associated with a decline in memory or other thinking skills severe enough to reduce a person's ability to perform everyday activities."[27] At least 5 million individuals with age-related dementias reside in the United States; as our population continues to age, these numbers will increase. Estimates for individuals who live past the age of 55 reveal that 1 in 6 women and 1 in 10 men will develop dementia in their lifetime.[28] Alzheimer's disease is the most common form of dementia. However, you should understand that age-related changes and dementia are different. Memory loss that disrupts a person's daily life is a hallmark of dementia.

Characteristics of individuals with dementia. People with dementia have problems in the following areas:

- Poor judgment and decision-making (a chronic problem and not simply making a bad decision on occasion)

- Communication and language (e.g., difficulty having a conversation—more than just forgetting which word to use on occasion)

- Memory (e.g., misplacing things and being unable to retrace steps to find them)

- Inability to manage a budget (more than missing the occasional monthly payment)

- Losing track of the date or season (more than merely forgetting which day it is and remembering later)[29]

Memory problems involve the short-term memory where people plan and prepare meals, keep track of personal possessions (e.g., purse or wallet), remember appointments, pay bills, or travel outside of their neighborhood or community. Dementia progresses at different rates for different individuals and can begin slowly with gradual progression.[30] Therefore, when you encounter an individual over the age of 50 who seems to be experiencing problems in any of the areas referenced previously, you should consider whether the issues are age-related or are symptoms of a greater problem. The person may be in the early stages of dementia and may require assistance.

Cognitive (intellectual or developmental) disabilities share many commonalities related to memory, actions, and responses. In a later section of this chapter, we will discuss ways you can ensure the best possible outcome from interactions with these individuals. The better prepared you are, the less likely you will be to exacerbate a situation. Next, we look at physiological (physical) disabilities and their relationship to communication.

Physiological or Physical Disabilities

"A disability is any condition of the body or mind (impairment) that makes it more difficult for the person with the condition to do certain activities (activity limitation) and interact with the world around them (participation restrictions)." This section focuses on individuals with **physiological or physical disabilities** and what limitations those disabilities impose on these individuals' interactions with others.

Physical disabilities affect a person's vision, movement, hearing, social relationships, and communication. For purposes of this chapter and the relationship to communication and the field of criminal justice, we will focus on hearing impairments or deafness, vision impairments or blindness, and movement disorders.

Hearing Impairment or Deafness

Individuals may experience **deafness** or **hearing impairment**. Not all people who are deaf or hearing-impaired know or use sign language. Some individuals with hearing deficits may be difficult to understand (speech is not clear).

Visual Impairments

Blindness or vision impairment can mean either a complete or partial loss of vision. For some persons, the edges or a part of the visual field might be obscured; some persons might have no central vision, but peripheral vision still exists. Sometimes, a person's visual acuity may change under different light conditions. Many people who are blind use a guide dog or cane to ambulate.

Movement Disorders

Many types of injuries, diseases, and conditions cause **movement disorders** that can affect a person. Some of these disabilities are acquired at birth while others stem from accidents or illnesses later in life. This type of disability can affect basic mobility, coordination and balance, strength and endurance, and other aspects of body function. Many people who have mobility impairments are required to use adaptive equipment of one kind or another, such as canes, walkers, and wheelchairs. Prosthetic devices (artificial arms or legs) and body braces might also be used.

Motor ability and speech may be impacted by muscular or neurological disabilities. Some involuntary or halting movement or limitation of movement in one or more than one appendage, some lisping, and/or indistinct speech or flatness of tone due to lack of fine motor control of the tongue or lips might be present in individuals with these types of disabilities. The severity and functional effects of the disability vary from person to person. Some persons who have significant cerebral palsy or other muscular or neurological disabilities may communicate by writing, typing, or using a communication board or other electronic device.

An upcoming segment of this chapter will address modifications or accommodations you can make or offer to individuals with physical disabilities. Some of these interventions are standard and established by the Americans with Disabilities Act. The next portion of this section addresses psychological (psychiatric) disabilities.

Psychological Disabilities

The term **psychological or psychiatric disabilities** refers to a diverse group of conditions and may include depression, bipolar disorder, generalized anxiety and panic disorder, obsessive compulsive disorder (OCD), social phobia, post-traumatic stress disorder (PTSD), schizophrenia, and eating disorders (anorexia and bulimia).[31] While each condition has a specific definition and behavioral characteristics associated with it, these conditions can impact an individual's ability to communicate in various ways, as you will see in the following descriptions.

Bipolar Disorder

Bipolar disorder was formerly called manic depression because of the intense mood shifts that occur between elevated moods and periods of depression. The elevated moods are referred to as mania or hypomania. People who have bipolar disorder experience intense changes in activity and energy levels as well.

Characteristics of individuals with bipolar disorder. People in the manic phase are easily distracted, irritable, and overly confident. They are also more likely to engage in activities that have long-term negative consequences, such as gambling and shopping sprees. When experiencing depressive episodes, individuals with bipolar disorder can experience intense sadness, guilt, fatigue, and irritability. They may lose interest in activities they previously enjoyed, have sleeping difficulties, and contemplate suicide.[32] Medications are available to assist individuals with bipolar disorder; however, if someone stops taking the medication or has not been diagnosed and treated, you may find communication to be difficult, if not impossible.

Generalized Anxiety and Panic Disorder

Generalized anxiety and panic disorder is characterized by excessive worry about everyday events. While a certain amount of worry is normal, individuals with generalized anxiety and panic disorder are so focused on perceived threats or future threats that they cannot function. Estimates reveal that as many as 18% of Americans suffer from at least one anxiety disorder. Anxiety disorders include generalized anxiety disorder, agoraphobia, social anxiety disorder, specific phobias (natural events, medical, animals, and/or situational), panic disorder, and separation anxiety disorder.

Characteristics of individuals with generalized anxiety and panic disorder. While generalized anxiety and panic disorders encompass six different types with their own set of triggers, they all have a certain response in common: panic attacks. According to the diagnostic criteria listed in the *Diagnostic and Statistical Manual of Mental Disorders* (5th ed.) (*DSM-5*), individuals experiencing panic attacks will have a sudden sense of fear and dread along with four or more of the following mental, emotional, and physical symptoms:

- Accelerated heart rate or heart palpitations
- Excessive sweating
- Trembling
- Smothering sensations or shortness of breath
- Feeling of choking
- Chest pain
- Nausea

- Dizziness
- Chills or hot flashes
- Feeling detached from yourself (being a bystander)
- Fear of losing control or going crazy
- Fear of dying
- Numbness or tingling sensations[33]

Obviously, individuals suffering from a generalized anxiety and panic disorder may prove difficult (or impossible) to communicate with during bouts of panic.

Post-Traumatic Stress Disorder

Most people will experience some type of trauma during their lifetime. **Post-traumatic stress disorder** (PTSD) occurs when an individual has experienced this type of stressful life event. Symptoms of PTSD include the following:

- Reexperiencing the traumatic event

- Avoiding things that remind the person of the event

- Feeling on edge (hypervigilance)

- Having negative thoughts, flashbacks, nightmares, or bursts of anger

- Having difficulty remembering circumstances surrounding the event

- Having an exaggerated startle response

Not every person who experiences a trauma develops PTSD. Certain risk factors have been identified through research as predictors of those who will develop PTSD after a traumatic event.

- Individuals who have experienced a traumatic event are as likely to develop PTSD as are people who had previously diagnosed psychological disorders (e.g., depression or bipolar disorder) or a family history of psychological disorders prior to a traumatic event.

- Individuals who have a preexisting medical condition, such as heart disease or cancer, are more likely to develop PTSD in response to a traumatic event.

- Individuals who experience a life-threatening traumatic event are more likely to develop PTSD.

- Individuals who do not receive emotional support following a traumatic event may be more likely to develop PTSD after a trauma.

- Individuals who are older, with less education and lower incomes, are more likely to develop PTSD after a traumatic event than those who are younger or who have higher incomes.

- Individuals who experience dissociation (feeling cut off from themselves or their surroundings, feeling numb, losing track of time, or feeling as though they are floating outside their bodies) during a traumatic event are more likely to develop PTSD. In a dissociative state, these individuals may have no memories about the event at all.[34]

Characteristics of individuals with PTSD. Individuals with PTSD exhibit certain behaviors that are consistent with arousal and reactivity. They are

- irritable or aggressive behavior;

- reckless or self-destructive behavior;

- hypervigilance;

- exaggerated startle response;

- problems with concentration;

- difficulty falling or saying asleep or restless sleep;

- persistent and exaggerated negative beliefs or expectations about themselves, others, or the world (e.g., *I am bad, Trust no one, The world is a bad place or completely dangerous*);

- persistent, distorted blame of themselves or others about the cause or consequences of the traumatic events;

- persistent fear, horror, anger, guilt, or shame;

- markedly diminished interest or participation in significant activities;

- feelings of detachment or estrangement from others; and

- persistent inability to experience positive emotions.[35]

People with PTSD can have varying responses to situations. You will need to learn the best approaches for communicating with someone who has PTSD and is involved in a situation that calls for law enforcement or another agency intervention.

Schizophrenia

"Schizophrenia is a mental disorder that is characterized by hallucinations (auditory, visual, olfactory, or tactile) and delusions. It is usually treated with a combination of antipsychotic medications and psychotherapy."[36] Positive symptoms for **schizophrenia** include delusions, hallucinations, disorganized thinking, and agitation. These symptoms must be present for at least 1 month with continual signs of disturbance that persists for at least 6 months before a diagnosis of schizophrenia can be made. The typical onset of schizophrenia does not occur until postadolescence, and the peak age for the first psychotic episode is early to mid-20s for males and late 20s for females. Only 0.3% to 0.7% of the population are diagnosed with schizophrenia.[37]

Characteristics of individuals with schizophrenia. Individuals with schizophrenia may exhibit certain behaviors or symptoms. These behaviors and symptoms include

- disorganized speech (e.g., frequently incoherent);

- grossly disorganized or catatonic behavior;

- flattening of emotions (e.g., poor eye contact, reduced body language, and diminished emotional expression);

- brief, empty replies to questions; and

- inability to initiate and persist in goal-directed activities.

As you can see from this symptoms list, communication with an individual who has schizophrenia can be extremely difficult. In addition, a person exhibiting these types of behaviors may automatically be suspected of being impaired due to drugs and/or alcohol.

Emotional (Behavioral) Disorders

Emotional disorders are also called behavioral disorders and are typically associated with children and adolescents. Identifying or diagnosing an emotional or behavioral disorder is difficult, as these types of disorders are not associated with anything going wrong in the brain of the individual. Instead, a combination of factors—biological, environmental, and psychological—affect development and are more likely at the root of these disorders. Because children's behaviors operate on a continuum ranging from troubling behavior to serious emotional problems, they are diagnosed with an emotional or behavioral disorder only when their behaviors occur frequently and are severe. Examples of emotional and behavioral disorders include, among others, adjustment disorders, selective mutism, attention deficit/hyperactivity disorder (ADHD), oppositional defiant disorder (ODD), and conduct disorder.[38] The reason emotional or behavioral disorders are important to this discussion is because you may find yourself working in the juvenile justice area or as a school resource officer or as a university or college campus police officer. In each of these venues, you will be required to uphold federal laws regarding disabilities, under which emotional and behavioral disorders are contained.

Characteristics of individuals with emotional and behavioral disorders. While each of the emotional and behavioral disorders has its own set of identifiers, these disorders have similarities overall in how they manifest themselves. The list that follows includes characteristics from the behavioral and emotional disorders included in the discussion under this topic.

- Truancy

- Vandalism

- Fighting

- Failure to speak in specific social situations where speaking is expected

- Inattention and/or hyperactivity-impulsivity

- Arguing with adults

- Defying or refusing to follow adult directions

- Deliberately annoying people

- Blaming others

- Being spiteful or vindictive

- Bullying or threatening others

- Being physically cruel to animals and people

- Engaging in reckless and risk-taking acts[39]

In 2014, President Obama's My Brother's Keeper Initiative sought to reform the juvenile and criminal justice systems to ensure that incarcerated youth receive educational services to which they are entitled. As part of this initiative,

> Absent a specific exception, all protections provided under the Individuals with Disabilities Education Act (IDEA), including the obligation to identify and evaluate students with disabilities, as well as disciplinary and due process procedures, apply to eligible students with disabilities in correctional facilities and their parents; and agencies and facilities serving youth in correctional

facilities must provide education services comparable to those available to students in community schools.[40]

Thus, you can see that understanding emotional and behavioral disorders plays a significant role in the communication process involving youth with disabilities. In the next section of this chapter, we will look at how you can adapt processes, procedures, and policies to fully engage with individuals with disabilities, whether their disabilities be cognitive, physiological (physical), psychological, or emotional or behavioral. The overarching goal for you will be to ensure that communication is effective and that these individuals receive the care, consideration, and accommodations to which they are entitled under the Americans with Disabilities Act and any other laws governing disabilities in addition to and/or tangential to the ADA.

INTERACTING WITH PEOPLE WITH DISABILITIES

Based on the information covered in the foregoing section of this chapter, you can see that many of the individuals with whom you come into contact have disabilities, because of cognitive, physical, psychological, or emotional disorders, with many of these people having multiple disability diagnoses. If we look at each of the types of disabilities, we see common themes emerge for each category. For example, individuals with cognitive disabilities may have slurred speech or may engage in repetitive behavior or speech patterns because of their disability. Law enforcement officers may view these individuals as being intoxicated or under the influence of drugs.

> **Example:** A police department receives a call from a local restaurant. The manager claims that a customer is causing a disturbance in the restaurant. When the responding officer arrives at the scene, she discovers a 30-year-old woman standing and grimacing. The woman has pulled the table cloth from the table. At first glance, the officer believes the woman has had too much to drink and is behaving aggressively. In fact, the customer is having a seizure.

Individuals with autism or who have a traumatic brain injury may get angry about a perceived misunderstanding or problem. In these cases, law enforcement, corrections, or private security officers might misinterpret the anger as violence and aggression and respond accordingly. Numerous cases have been reported about law enforcement officers failing to properly interact with individuals with Down syndrome or autism. Some of them will be discussed in the next section of the chapter as explanations for changes to existing policies, procedures, and processes based on outcomes of interactions between criminal justice agency personnel and individuals with disabilities.

The following reveals some ways in which law enforcement officers might misconstrue actions of people with physiological or physical disabilities. The actions taken by some individuals with disabilities might be seen as suspicious or involving illegal activity or exhibiting uncooperative behavior.

> **Example:** A police officer approaches a vehicle and asks the driver to step out of the car. The driver, who has a mobility disability, reaches behind the seat to

retrieve her assistive device for walking (without alerting the police officer to her mobility disability and the need for an assistive device, simply assuming that the officer sees the handicap placard/license plate and knows the source of her disability). This action appears suspicious to the officer who may demand that the driver place her hands where he can seem them and who most likely will begin demanding in a very loud voice that the driver open the door and exit the vehicle—all without allowing the driver to identify the reason for reaching behind her seat. You can imagine the possible outcome of this situation based on the confusion of the moment and the driver's failure to comply with the officer's request.

Deaf individuals or those who are blind or visually impaired may not recognize or be able to respond to police directions. Those individuals may erroneously be perceived as uncooperative. In the case of deaf or hearing-impaired individuals, they may not stop when asked or ordered to do so by the officer. Not all hearing-impaired people have or are able to wear hearing devices, and they may rely on the reading lips technique or on sign language. Yelling at deaf or hearing-impaired people will not make them hear you any better, but you can see how that would most likely be the next step in the process if they do not stop when asked to do so. The hearing-impaired person might simply be trying to get closer to the officer to read his or her lips or to produce a card that explains that he or she is hearing impaired or deaf. If the officer does not have the patience to delay any adverse actions, the hearing-impaired or deaf individual may never get the opportunity to explain his or her actions.

Example: An individual is seen in an area where a crime has been reported. The officer on the scene yells "STOP" or "FREEZE" to the individual. The individual, who is deaf and cannot hear the officer, begins walking toward the officers. The officer once again yells "STOP" or "FREEZE," but the individual continues to approach. The officer mistakenly believes that this individual is a suspect in the crime based on his or her proximity to the crime scene and his or her refusal to stop approaching the officer. In fact, the officer sees the individual's behavior as threatening. The officer feels that his or her life is in jeopardy because of the suspect's failure to stop or freeze when ordered to do so. What the officer fails to see (or recognize) are the cues from the suspect. The deaf or hearing-impaired individual is attempting to communicate via nonverbal cues and/or sign language to show the officer that he or she cannot hear what the officer is saying. You can imagine the outcome of this situation if the officer has not received training in recognizing and handling disabilities in potential suspects, witnesses, or victims.

The foregoing examples indicate how easy it is to make assumptions based on individuals' nonverbal behaviors. In each of the scenarios, the nonverbal behavior of individuals with disabilities was perceived by law enforcement professionals to be either threatening, uncooperative, or suspicious.

Real-world examples of issues involving the criminal justice community and individuals with disabilities are much worse than those suggested in these examples.

In January 2013, a 26-year-old man with Down syndrome named Ethan Saylor wanted to go to the movies to see *Zero Dark Thirty*. He and his support person went to the movie. After the movie finished, Ethan and his support person left the theater. His support person went to the parking lot to get the car to drive to the front of the theater to pick up Ethan. Ethan slipped back into the theater while his support person was retrieving the car because he wanted to watch the movie a second time. After being asked to leave the theater by a theater usher, Ethan refused. So the theater manager called security guards for help. According to the lawsuit that was filed in this case, Ethan's support person gave warning to the security guards before their physical encounter with Ethan that Ethan hated to be touched.[41] The security guards (who were off-duty deputies working as security officers) forcibly removed Ethan; during the struggle that ensued, Ethan ended up on the floor and suffered a fractured larynx. His death was later ruled a homicide, the result of asphyxia.

Autopsy reports noted various injuries on Ethan's body: marks on his wrists (from having his hands cuffed behind his back) and fractured cartilage in his larynx that indicated a chokehold had been used. These injuries led to the determination that substantial force was used by the security officers. Dr. Stephen Greenspan, in his review of the case data, stated that Ethan's death was the product of a "perfect storm" of behaviors involving three parties: (1) the security officers (off-duty deputies) and the theater manager; (2) Ethan; and (3) Ethan's 18-year-old support person. In his opinion, Greenspan suggested that the theater manager acted too quickly to call the security officers; then, the officers themselves acted in haste and with excessive force. Ethan, because of his Down syndrome, did not have sufficient social intelligence to prohibit lashing out physically against the security officers. And in the end, this situation began when Ethan's support person left him alone and in harm's way while she went to get the car. However, her behavior does not dismiss the behavior of the other parties. In their actions, you can see anger and frustration, particularly when Ethan became physical. That anger escalated, as did the level of coercion applied to Ethan. Professional officers (those who are properly trained), in Greenspan's opinion, would have recognized that Ethan had a disability and would have responded in a calmer and more clinical fashion.[42]

Could better understanding of individuals with disabilities have prevented this unfortunate outcome in the **Saylor case**? Could training in communication skills with which to interact with individuals with Down syndrome have made a difference? Most likely, if you consider Greenspan's explanation.

A startling fact for any person involved in the criminal justice system to know is that people with autism are 7 to 12 times more likely to encounter police either as victims or as assailants.[43] The following are recent examples involving law enforcement and individuals with autism—incidents where the individual with autism committed a crime or where the law enforcement officers involved misjudged the situation.

- February 2017 (Greenville, SC): Two Greenville police officers faced federal charges of using excessive force when they used a stun gun on Tario Anderson, an individual with autism, during an arrest on Christmas Eve 2014. Anderson was 35 years old, 6'6" tall, and weighed 340 pounds. All charges against Anderson were subsequently dropped.

- February 2017 (Athens, GA): In 2012, Noah McGlawn was accused of attempted murder after randomly shooting and injuring a motorcyclist. McGlawn's lawyer stated that his client had autism. Therefore, McGlawn was unable to understand his action was wrong, and he should be acquitted. The jury found McGlawn guilty of first-degree assault.

- February 2017 (Fouke, AK): A 12-year-old boy with autism was accused of fatally shooting a 21-year-old gas station attendant named Christa Shockley.

- July 2016 (North Miami, FL): A behavioral therapist at a group home (Charles Kinsey) was accidently shot in the leg by a police officer while trying to help a young man with autism who had wandered away from the group home. The officer who fired the shot was trying to shoot the individual with autism because he thought the man was holding a gun. The individual with autism was actually holding a toy truck.

- February 2016 (Mesa, AZ): A transgender person with Asperger's syndrome (a higher-functioning developmental disorder on the autism spectrum) was shot and killed by police who were responding to a suicidal-person call. The individual with Asperger's was wielding a knife at the time of the shooting.[44]

Most recently (April 2017), a man with autism was pepper sprayed in the face by a 53-year-old security guard in a Cub Foods store in Roseville, Minnesota. Apparently, the off-duty security trainer, Timothy Knutsen, had seen the man with autism taking and eating a cookie from the store bakery and was upset by this behavior. Mr. Knutsen reported the customer's behavior to a store employee working the service desk. The individual at the service desk stated that she could not do anything about the man taking a cookie from the bakery unless she saw him eat it. Mr. Knutsen asked to speak with loss prevention. As the service employee went to speak with loss prevention, she saw the customer buying his groceries and then turning to walk back toward the bakery. Mr. Knutsen was closely following the customer at this point. The store surveillance video did not show the incident but revealed the man with autism holding his face and turning in circles while Knutsen left the store. The man with autism told police he decided to walk to the bakery in the store to get a cookie because he had seen a sign saying "free cookie" when some man sprayed him in the face with mace. Knutsen told police that he thought his pepper spray had a safety cap on it that would prevent it from dispensing; but when he put his thumb on the depressor, spray came out.

The unfortunate side of this story—aside from a man with autism being pepper sprayed—is that Mr. Knutsen was not employed by the store, had not been trained in loss prevention, and was merely acting as a private citizen when he attacked the customer with autism at Cub Foods. He made a judgment call that traumatized an individual with a disability. According to Jonah Weinberg, executive director of the Autism Society of Minnesota, for this man to "get out and go shopping on his own may be an incredible feat for him. It could take him a while before he ever goes back there—if he ever does."[45]

As an example of what can occur when interacting with a deaf person, in August 2016, a North Carolina state trooper shot a deaf man, Daniel Kevin Harris. The victim died from his injuries. Howard Rosenblum, CEO of the National Association of the Deaf, released a statement to NBC News in which he said, "There have been too many incidents with tragic consequences between law enforcement officers and deaf people. Too often, officers order deaf people to comply with verbal commands and when they do not, the officers react aggressively."[46]

The foregoing examples are provided to show you how often these types of incidents occur and how the interaction between and among the individuals often leads to unfortunate outcomes because of a failure to understand specific disabilities and how to best communicate with individuals who have those disabilities. Because of the sheer number of incidents involving law enforcement and individuals with disabilities, we are seeing an increased demand for better and more training, particularly in the areas of identification and communication and in methods for de-escalating a situation before it becomes violent.

Addressing the Individual and Not the Disability

Criminal justice agency personnel must understand the ADA and its requirements. Training on the ADA, including both Title II and Title III, will assist with the prevention and/or escalation of situations that have been occurring with increasing frequency. As Oliver Wendell Holmes is purported to have said, "Ignorance of the law is no excuse for breaking it."[47] Therefore, you must have a basic understanding of the ADA, along with sensitivity toward individuals with disabilities and awareness of the variety of disabilities, to ensure equitable treatment of these individuals, whether you are in law enforcement, corrections, or private security.

When you look at the most recent statistics involving victims of violent crime in this country, you will find that between 2010 and 2014, for each age group measured (excluding individuals who are 65 or older), the rate of violent victimization against people with disabilities was at least double the rate of those without disabilities. People with disabilities ages 12 to 15 had a higher rate of victimization than all other age groups except for those 16 to 19 years old.[48]

These data reveal another side to individuals with disabilities, that of victim. You cannot always assume that you will engage with people as perpetrators of a crime, whether those individuals are incarcerated in state or federal facilities or on the street. You will encounter individuals with disabilities as witnesses and victims as well.

First Steps

The first steps in effectively interacting with an individual with a disability might include the following generic actions:

- Be aware that the driver of a vehicle displaying visible signs that a person with a disability may be driving (designated license plate, hang tag, etc.) will or might reach for a mobility device.

- Use hand signals or calling to other people in a crowd to signal for a person to stop to get the attention of a deaf individual.

- Speak clearly and slowly to ensure that an individual understands what is being said.

- Use breathalyzers to obtain accurate results and to reduce the possibility of false arrest of individuals with mobility or neurological disabilities.

- Seek training to help you distinguish behaviors that pose a real risk or threat to health and safety from behaviors that do not when an individual is having a seizure or exhibiting signs of psychotic crisis and needing medical attention.

These actions are generic in nature and can be used at first response to determine the situation at hand. Specific acts for the various types of disabilities follow.

Physiological (Physical) Disabilities

When a law enforcement officer arrests a person in a wheelchair or a corrections officer needs to transport a person in a wheelchair, standard transport practices may be dangerous. The best approach to use in the transport process is to ask the individual what type of transportation he or she can use and how to lift or assist him or her in transferring into and out of a vehicle. The important point to remember is not to harm an individual or to cause damage to his or her wheelchair. Some individuals who use assistive devices, such as crutches, braces, or wheelchairs, might be safely moved in a van or corrections transport.

In the case of an arrest of an individual with a mobility impairment, law enforcement agencies must ensure that he or she has access to the toilet facilities and other amenities provided at the detention facility or jail. Structural changes can be undertaken to ensure officer safety and general security. For instance, grab bars in accessible restrooms can be secured so that they are not removable.

When constructing new prison facilities, all buildings must be made accessible for individuals with disabilities. Correctional and detention facilities also have specific requirements about housing inmates with disabilities. For example, a deaf inmate who communicates only with sign language may need to be housed in a facility where sign language interpreters and other sign language users are present to offer the inmate opportunities to communicate with others.

Visual Impairments

Between 2010 and 2014, 39.4% of violent crimes were committed against a person with vision impairment. For purposes of collecting the data, visual impairment was defined as blindness or serious difficulty seeing, even when wearing glasses.[49] These people may have partial sight, allowing them to get around without much difficulty. However, they require adaptive methods to read and write. You should take the following steps when interacting with an individual with visual impairment or blindness.

Witnesses

- Introduce yourself immediately as a law enforcement officer when you approach victims.

- Have others who are present introduce themselves, including children (if present).

- These introductions let the victim know who is present and where they are situated and help the victim recognize voices during your interview.

- Mention the presence of a dog, cat, or other pet to protect victims from tripping over the animals or being startled by them.

- Tell victims your name, badge number, and the telephone number of your dispatcher when responding to victims who are alone, and support them in verifying your identity.

- Describe the chair and seating arrangements when assisting victims in sitting down, and place their hand (after obtaining permission) on the back or arm of the chair.

- Speak in a conversational tone. (Do not speak loudly.) Most people with blindness or vision impairment are not hearing impaired.

- Identify the person to whom you are speaking when talking with a group of people. Exactly which person you are speaking to may not be apparent to victims who are blind or who have a vision impairment.

- Let victims know when you or other persons step away (and return) during a conversation.

- Avoid lapses of conversation in your interview without first informing victims of why you need to be silent; for example, tell victims that you are writing.

- Project attentiveness, concern, and compassion.

Victims. Remember that victims cannot see your facial expressions or body language to ascertain whether you are listening to them and interested in what they are saying. You should take the following steps to assist visually impaired individuals who are victims of a crime.

- Offer to fill out forms and read aloud written information for victims.

- Explain what printed materials you are providing, and upon request, make the materials available in an alternative format, including large print, saved to a flash drive, audio recording, and braille. This provision of materials in an alternative format is legally required, with few exceptions, by the Americans with Disabilities Act and Section 504 of the Rehabilitation Act of 1973.

- Never separate victims from their **guide dogs** or pet the dogs without permission. These dogs are working animals that must not be distracted.

- Offer your arm, instead of holding the arm of victims, if they want you to guide them in moving about.

- Let victims take your arm from behind, just above the elbow. In this position, they can follow the motion of your body.

- Walk in a relaxed manner and remember that victims will follow at a half-step behind you, so they can anticipate curbs and steps.

- Orient victims to their surroundings, and give cues about what lies ahead when guiding them.

- Close doors to cabinets, rooms, and cars that obstruct their path.

- Warn of hazardous objects around them.

- Before going up or down stairs, come to a complete stop; inform victims about the direction of the stairs, the approximate number of steps, and the location of the handrail.

- Make your warnings and directions specific, such as "in front of you" and "to your left," rather than giving vague references like "at the front of the room" or "beside you."

Deaf or Hearing-Impaired Individuals

The United States Department of Justice publishes a brochure titled "Communicating With People Who Are Deaf or Hard of Hearing: ADA Guide for Law Enforcement Officers."[50] This publication specifies the ADA requirements for effective communication with a deaf or hearing-impaired individual and explains that these individuals are entitled to the same services provided by law enforcement to any other individuals. Practical suggestions for effectively communicating with deaf or hearing-impaired individuals include the following:

- Get the person's attention with a wave of the hand or a gentle tap on the shoulder.

- Face the person, and do not turn away while speaking.

- Try to converse in a well-lit area.

- Do not cover your mouth or chew gum (or eat anything—mints, candy, etc.).

- If a person is wearing a hearing device, do not assume the individual can hear you.

- Minimize environmental noise, background noise, and any other distractions (if possible).

- Speak slowly and distinctly; use gestures and facial expressions to reinforce what you are saying.

- Use visuals when possible (e.g., pointing to printed information on a citation or other document); if video with closed captioning is available, allow the person to view it.

- Write notes, but remember that individuals who use sign language may have limited (or no) English reading and writing skills.

- Use written notes to ask about communication aids or devices that could be helpful in the situation.

- Use a sign language interpreter if available, but ask which language the person uses (America Sign Language and Signed English are the most common); the use of an interpreter is especially important in situations where you are interviewing a witness or engaging in any complex conversation.

- Speak directly to the deaf or hearing-impaired person even when using an interpreter.

- Talk at your normal rate or slightly slower if your normal rate is very fast.

- Avoid using family members of the deaf or hearing-impaired person as interpreters (they could have impartiality issues or simply may not have the vocabulary necessary to interpret the information).

- Use short sentences and simple words.

- Allow only one person to speak (no talking over others).

Other ways that members of the criminal justice community can ensure they comply with the ADA for hearing-impaired or deaf individuals is to learn the basics in American Sign Language and a list of commonly used signs to communicate with deaf or hearing-impaired individuals during an emergency. In addition, you should know what communication aids—auxiliary aids and services—are available to assist people who are deaf or hearing impaired, such as telecommunications devices for the deaf (TDDs), telephone handset amplifiers, assistive listening systems, and videotext displays. TDDs must be available to deaf or hearing-impaired individuals (or those with speech impediments), so they can make outgoing calls. TDDs must also be available to inmates with disabilities under the same terms and conditions as telephone privileges are offered to all inmates. Today's technologies allow for hearing-impaired or deaf individuals to use SMS (text messages), e-mail, or chat to communicate effectively with others in writing.

Criminal justice agencies should have an interpreter available on call. These interpreters must be familiar with law enforcement or other criminal justice agency terms to ensure that communication via sign language is effective.

Cognitive Disabilities

When an individual who has cognitive disabilities is arrested, the arresting officer must modify the procedure for giving Miranda warnings. Law enforcement personnel should use simple words and ask the individual to repeat each phrase of the warnings in her or his own words. The officer should also check for understanding by asking the individual such questions as "What is a lawyer?" and "How might a lawyer help you?" or by asking the individual for an example of what he or she considers a right. Using simple language or pictures and symbols, speaking slowly and clearly, and asking concrete questions are all ways to communicate with individuals who have cognitive disabilities.

As mentioned previously in this chapter, persons with autism have communication difficulties because their disorder makes it hard for them to relate to the outside world. Some examples of the communication difficulties a person with autism might exhibit are as follows:

- May be nonverbal or may only repeat what is said to him or her

- May not respond to "STOP" command, may run or move away, or may cover ears and look away constantly

- May appear argumentative, stubborn, or belligerent; may say "NO" in response to all questions; may ask "Why?" incessantly

- May have difficulty recognizing and repairing breakdowns in communication (for example, asking for clarification or responding to a request for clarification)

- May be poor listener; may not seem to care what you have to say; lack of eye contact may lead you to believe they are not listening

- May have passive, monotone voice with unusual pronunciations (often sounding robotic)

- May have difficulty judging personal space; may stand too close or too far away; may stare at the police officer; may continue to invade your "space"; may not differentiate private body parts

- May not recognize danger or hurt; may approach and talk to strangers; may possess weak help-seeking skills; may not be able to distinguish between minor and serious problems; may not know where or how to get help for problems; may not be able to give important information or be able to answer questions

- Will have difficulty interpreting body language and social cues, such as defensive posture and facial expressions; may not recognize jokes, teasing, and nonverbal or verbal emotional responses

When you encounter a person with cognitive disabilities, you want to be able to recognize the behavioral symptoms and to know contact approaches to avoid situations of risk. In situations involving people with cognitive disabilities (e.g., autism, Down syndrome, TBI, ABI, and dementia), officers should consider the following responses:

- Make sure the person is unarmed, and maintain a safe distance; they may suddenly invade your personal space.

- Evaluate for injury; remember, pain tolerance is high.

- Assess for seizure symptoms or injury; request a paramedic response as appropriate.

- Talk calmly and softly in direct, short phrases: "Stand up now," or "Get in the car."

- Your uniform, gun, and/or handcuffs may frighten him or her; reassure him or her that no harm is intended.

- Indicate a willingness to understand and help.

- Avoid quick motions or gestures.

- Avoid slang expressions.

- Allow for delayed responses to your questions or commands. Repeat or rephrase as needed. Understand that a rational discussion may not take place.

- Consider use of pictures, written phrases and commands, and/or sign language.

- Avoid pointing or waving.

- Check for medical alert tags or an autism handout card.

- Model calm body language and behaviors.

- Get information from caregivers at the scene about how to best communicate with the person and de-escalate his or her behavior.

- Do not stop repetitive behaviors, unless there is risk of injury to yourself or others.

- If possible, decrease sensory stimulation (sirens, flashing lights, and crowds).

- Use geographic containment, and maintain a safe distance until aggression diminishes.

- Remain alert to the possibility of outbursts or impulsive acts.

- Assess for symptoms of psychosis—delusions or hallucinations.

- Do not express anger, impatience, or irritation.

- If possible, allow the person to de-escalate himself or herself without your intervention. Throw him or her a blanket or a towel to allow him or her to self-soothe.

- Touching the person with autism may cause a protective fight-or-flight reaction, especially on the shoulders or near the face. Announce your actions before initiating them.[51]

Other suggestions for interacting with individuals with cognitive disabilities may include the following:

- Talk in direct, short phrases (for example, "Stand up," or "Go to the car").

- Allow for delayed responses to questions, directions, or commands.

- Talk calmly and/or repeat. Talking more loudly will *not* help understanding.

- Model calming body language (slow breathing and keep hands down).

- Use low gestures for attention (avoid rapid pointing or waving).

- Look and wait for responses and/or eye contact. Do not interpret limited or lack of eye contact as deceit or disrespect.

- Never lightly touch or pat on shoulders or near face.

- Avoid standing too near or behind.

- Avoid stopping the individual's repetitive behaviors unless self-injury or potential injury for others is present.

- Evaluate the person for injury. The individual may have a high threshold for pain or may not indicate pain.

- Consider the use of a "YES–NO" sign board, alphabet, simple phrase word board, or picture board.

- Avoid literal or slang expressions (i.e., "I'd give my eyeteeth to know," "spread eagle," or "You think it's cool?").

If an individual is taken into custody for booking and arraignment and the arresting officer believes this person may have a cognitive disability such as autism, the primary rule is to "err on the side of caution."

When dealing with persons with disabilities, law enforcement professionals must keep in mind certain responses and behaviors that are typical of this population, behaviors that can often result in grave legal situations for individuals with disabilities. when the behaviors are not recognized in their full context. Persons with disabilities may exhibit or demonstrate the following:

- An inordinate desire to please authority figures
- The inability to move to abstract from concrete thought
- Watching for clues from interrogators
- The longing for friends
- Relate best with children or the elderly
- Bluffing greater competence than one possesses
- An all-too-pleasant facade
- Abhorrence for the term *mental retardation*
- Real memory gaps
- A quickness to take blame
- Impaired judgment
- An inability to understand rights, court proceedings, or the punishment
- Problems with receptive and expressive language
- Short attention span and uncontrolled impulses
- Unsteady gait and struggling speech
- Exhaustion and surrender of all defenses

Dementia

People with dementia may also exhibit some of the same characteristics as an individual with autism, traumatic brain injury, or acquired brain injury. As members of the criminal justice profession, you need to follow some important rules of etiquette when dealing with older people:

- Carefully identify yourself to the person to avoid confusion.
- When first addressing the person, use his or her courtesy title (Mr., Mrs., Ms., Miss, or rank) and last name. You may use the first name of the individual later if requested by the person to do so.
- Do *not* assume dementia or lack of understanding.
- Watch for signs of a hearing deficiency.
- Speak directly if you need to be heard; do *not* shout.
- Allow extra time for responses.
- Ask the person what will make him or her comfortable.
- Maintain eye contact.

Remember, advanced age may only be one of many special circumstances you may have to consider. Other conditions about which you must be aware are physical and cognitive disabilities. For example, aphasia affects older people, as well as people with both traumatic brain injury and acquired brain injury. A total or partial loss of the power to use or understand words, often because of a stroke or other brain damage, results in aphasia. Expressive aphasics can understand what you say; receptive aphasics cannot. Some suggestions for communicating with individuals who have aphasia are as follows:

- Be patient, and allow plenty of time to communicate with a person with aphasia.

- Be honest with the individual. Let him or her know if you cannot quite understand what he or she is telling you.

- Ask the person how best to communicate. What techniques or devices can be used to aid communication?

- Allow the aphasic to try to complete his or her thoughts, to struggle with words. Avoid being too quick to guess what the person is trying to express or to finish the individual's sentences.

- Encourage the person to write the word he or she is trying to express and read it aloud.

- Use gestures or pointing to objects if helpful in supplying words or adding meaning.

- A pictogram grid can sometimes be used to great advantage. These devices are useful in filling in answers to requests such as "I need" or "I want." The person can merely point to the appropriate picture.

- Use touch to aid in concentration, to establish another avenue of communication, and to offer reassurance and encouragement.

In the elderly, Alzheimer's disease or related disorders may also present problems in the communication process. You should be aware of strategies in aiding communication with persons with Alzheimer's disease or other related disorders.

- Always approach the person from the front, or within his or her line of vision—*no surprise appearances*.

- Speak in a normal tone of voice, and greet the person as you would anyone else.

- Face the person as you talk to him or her.

- Minimize hand movements that approach the other person.

- Avoid a setting with a lot of sensory stimulation, like a big room where many people may be sitting or talking, a high-traffic area, or a very noisy place.

- Maintain eye contact and smile. A frown will convey negative feelings.

- Be respectful of the person's personal space and observant of his or her reaction as you move closer. Maintain a distance of 1 to 1.5 feet initially.

- If the individual is a pacer, walk with him or her, in step with him or her as you talk.

- Use distractions if a situation looks like it may get out of hand.

- Use a low-pitch, slow speaking voice, which older adults hear best.

- Ask only one question at a time. More than one question will increase confusion.

- Repeat key words if the person does not understand the first time around.

- Nod and smile only if what the person said is understood.

The best way to make a good impression is to engage people where "they" are—not where you are. Learning to communicate effectively with individuals having a multitude of disabilities can minimize problems for your agency or department and for you. These accommodations are straightforward and require elements of patience and understanding; they also help to meet the requirements of the Americans with Disabilities Act of 1990, a law that governs all actions and interactions with people with disabilities.

GUIDELINES FOR WRITING ABOUT PEOPLE WITH DISABILITIES

When investigating an incident or accident, you must create a report explaining it. Writing reports was covered in an earlier chapter in this text, so you are aware of the importance of choosing the right words and making sure your writing is clear, concise, complete, and correct. When we add individuals with disabilities into the mix, however, we add an additional component for our writing.

As covered in this chapter, individuals with disabilities deserve respect and care. Describing a person by his or her disability is demeaning and not likely to produce the desired outcome. The following steps can help you as you navigate the writing process:

Ask *first* if the individual is willing to disclose his or her disability. Do not assume that people with disabilities are always willing to disclose them, especially if the information is going to be used in some way to bring attention to them. After you clear this hurdle, you can move on to the next steps.[52]

1. **Emphasize abilities, not limitations in your writing.** Choose language that describes what the person can do—not what he or she cannot do.

USE	DO NOT USE
Person who uses a wheelchair	Wheelchair-bound; confined to a wheelchair
Person who uses a communication device; uses an alternative medium or channel for communication	Is nonverbal; cannot talk

2. Refer to the person first and the disability second.

USE	DO NOT USE
People with disabilities; person with disability	Disabled person; the disabled; handicapped; afflicted; victims; sufferers; invalids; crippled
Man with paraplegia	Paraplegic; paraplegic man
Person with learning disability	Slow learner
Student receiving special education services	Special education student
Person of short stature or little person	Dwarf; midget

3. **Ask the individual for his or her language preferences.** People often identify with their disability and see it as an essential part of who they are. For these individuals, they prefer to be identified with their disability first. This preference is referred to as *identity-first language* (*deaf person* or *autistic person*). Still, others with disabilities prefer to use the *person-first language* (*person with hearing impairment, person who is deaf*, or *person with autism*).

4. **Use neutral language.**

USE	DO NOT USE
Person with epilepsy	Person afflicted with epilepsy; epileptic
Person who has had a stroke	Stroke victim
Congenital disability	Birth defect
Person with a brain injury	Brain damaged; brain injury sufferer
Burn survivor	Burn victim

5. Use language that emphasizes the need for accessibility rather than the presence of a disability. *Handicapped* is an outdated term and should be avoided.

USE	DO NOT USE
Accessible parking	Handicapped parking
Accessible restroom	Disabled or handicapped restroom

6. Do not use condescending euphemisms (*differently abled, challenged, handi-capable,* or *special*). These terms are considered condescending.

7. Do not use offensive language (*freak, retard, imbecile, vegetable, cripple, crazy,* or *psycho*).

8. Include both people with disabilities and people without disabilities in discussions, but do not use words that imply negative stereotypes of the disabilities.

USE	DO NOT USE
People without disabilities	Normal, healthy, able-bodied, or whole
She is a child without disabilities.	She is a normal child.

9. Do not write or indicate that disabilities are illnesses. People with disabilities are not patients. People with disabilities can be healthy even with chronic conditions, such as arthritis or diabetes. So only refer to someone as a patient when his or her relationship with a health care provider is part of your report.

USE	DO NOT USE
A person with or who has diabetes	Suffering from diabetes
HIV-positive status	A victim of AIDS

10. Do not use language that perpetuates the negative stereotypes about psychological (or psychiatric) illnesses.

USE	DO NOT USE
Attempted suicide	Unsuccessful suicide
Died by suicide	Committed suicide
He has a diagnosis of bipolar disorder; he is living with bipolar disorder.	He is (a) bipolar; he is (a) manic-depressive.
She is receiving mental health services.	Mental health patient/case; mentally ill
Person with schizophrenia	Schizophrenic; schizo; psycho
Person with learning disability	Mentally handicapped; retarded; subnormal
Person with substance use disorder; person experiencing alcohol or drug problem	Addict, abuser, or junkie
She has a mental health condition or psychiatric disability.	She is emotionally disturbed, mentally ill, or insane.

11. Do not refer to or label people who have physiological or physical disabilities with outdated or derogatory terms.

USE	DO NOT USE
Sensory impairment	The deaf
Hearing impaired, deaf, or deafened	
Deaf people who use sign language or BSL	Deaf and dumb
Deaf without speech	
Visually impaired, blind, or partially sighted	The blind or visually handicapped

Taking a careful approach to how you discuss individuals with disabilities in your written reports will help demonstrate that you are respectful of these individuals and that you are balanced in your writing because you are using language that is accurate, neutral, and objective. You will not be embarrassed when your reports are introduced into evidence in a court case, and you will not have to defend what you have written as being stereotypical in your description of an individual with a disability or as being unprofessional and rude. You never get a second chance to make a good first impression. Make sure your written documents do not reveal unpleasant traits or characteristics about you.

SERVICE DOGS AND DISABILITIES

Law enforcement interaction with people who have **service dogs** is governed by the Americans with Disabilities Act as well. Moreover, Title II of the ADA provides specific obligations that police officers have regarding people who are visually impaired or blind and who use guide dogs. Title II prohibits discrimination against these individuals while providing police services to the public.

Since police officers can be dismissed or demoted for unlawful use of deadly force against a guide dog, departments should provide training or appoint a special needs liaison to offer guidance on ADA and guide dogs.[53]

Identifying individuals with disabilities is the first step to properly communicating and interacting with them. While the thought of going through a checklist may seem daunting, the Tennessee Department of Intellectual and Development Disabilities, as part of its IDD and Community Policing Training for Tennessee Law Enforcement Officers, created a handy checklist just for that purpose. The checklist is found next and may be used to assess situations and to determine ways to handle them to reduce risk to those involved, including you.

CHECKLIST FOR INTERACTION WITH INDIVIDUALS WITH DISABILITIES[54]

Actions	Checks
Determine if a person may have a disability. Does the person	
Have an appearance that signals a disability (e.g., Down syndrome, Fragile X, or other)?	
Have a caregiver?	
Display age-inappropriate behavior?	
Live with parents or relatives?	
Fail to respond to requests or commands?	
Respond slowly to requests or commands?	
Have difficulty coming up with solutions to his or her problem?	
Have difficulty repeating to you what you have requested?	
Have difficulty or no ability to communicate?	
If the person encountered is suspected of having a disability, did I	
Advise the dispatcher as soon as the situation permits?	
Require the individual to obtain legal counsel before questions him or her?	
Take extra precautions in making a *Terry Stop* to ensure that the person understands his or her right to leave?	
If a physical altercation appears possible, did I	
Request Emergency Medical Service or Crisis Intervention Team support?	
Use appropriate judgment in determining the level of risk involved?	
Try verbal reduction techniques designed to de-escalate the crisis?	
In making a decision to restrain a person, did I consider	
The risk that the restraint might cause an escalation in behavior?	
The risks of positional or aspirational asphyxiation?	
Weight	
Communication problems	
Ability to observe the person's face	
Increased risk of Gastro-Esophageal Reflux	
Increased risk of placing the person in a prone or supine position	
Increased risk of placing pressure on the neck, back, or chest	

		Ways to reduce risk?	
		Using alternatives to prone or supine restraint (e.g., standing, seated, or side immobilization)?	
		Ensuring I have the ability to see signs of distress on the person's face?	
		Monitoring breathing and color no less frequently than every 60 seconds?	
		Taking actions to help the person calm down while in restraint?	
		Releasing the person from restraint if signs of difficulty breathing or discoloration are noted?	
		Minimizing the duration of the restraint?	

SUMMARY

In this chapter, you were introduced to various types of disabilities: cognitive, psychological (psychiatric), physiological (physical), behavioral, and emotional. You learned ways in which to identify an individual with disabilities based on specific traits. And you also learned ways in which to interact with individuals with disabilities based on the type of disability. Considering the number of people in the United States who live with disabilities, you will meet many individuals with disabilities as part of your work with criminal justice agencies. You must be prepared by knowing what the Americans with Disabilities Act of 1990 covers and how it impacts your job and the agency for which you work. We discussed many of the facets of the ADA in this chapter, particularly as they relate to Title II and Title III.

One of the most salient points in this chapter is that knowing the characteristics of individuals with disabilities can help you to de-escalate situations and reduce the risk involved in those interactions. This chapter explained what can happen—and what has occurred—between members of law enforcement, corrections, and private security agencies when they interact with individuals with disabilities without knowing how to manage the situation. Deaths have occurred, and lawsuits have been filed against criminal justice agencies and specific officers therein. We cannot stress enough the importance of effectively communicating with people with disabilities. You cannot simply assume you know what people will do or how they will act. You must be prepared by being fully aware of specific characteristics and potential actions that will be taken by individuals with disabilities, especially when they feel threatened or afraid.

Many criminal justice agencies have in-house training for their officers to help reinforce the information we have provided in this chapter. With the number of people with disabilities continuing to escalate, these agencies have recognized that they can no longer assume that their officers will recognize and understand. Too many lives have been lost and too many lawsuits have been filed against officers and agencies for failure to follow the ADA and for failure to change their processes and procedures to include citizens with disabilities.

KEY TERMS

Acquired brain injury 253
Americans with Disabilities
   Act 249
Aphasia 255

Autism 253
Bipolar disorder 260
Blindness 260
Cognitive disabilities 253

Deafness 260
Dementia 253
Down syndrome 253
Dysphasia 255

FOR FURTHER REFLECTION AND DISCUSSION

1. Why is it important to know what the Americans with Disabilities Act is and what it covers?

2. How does the ADA affect your role in the criminal justice system?

3. List five (5) ways to properly interact with individuals who have a cognitive disability.

4. List five (5) tips for interviewing a deaf or hearing-impaired witness to a crime.

5. List five (5) ways you can help de-escalate an episode involving an individual with Down syndrome.

6. What behaviors do people with traumatic brain injuries exhibit? How can you effectively interact or communicate with individuals with TBI?

7. What characteristics do people with autism display?

8. How do you differentiate between an individual who is impaired by alcohol or drugs and one who has a cognitive disability?

ETHICAL ISSUE EXERCISES

1. You are interrogating a victim who has a physical disability. How far must you go to accommodate this individual?

2. As the officer responding to a call, if you injure someone who has a cognitive disability who failed to respond to your commands, are you responsible or liable for that injury or those injuries?

3. Why should I be concerned about individuals with cognitive disabilities? Why is that my concern?

4. Should we be able to track individuals with cognitive disabilities who have the police respond frequently to their location or residence?

5. Should every contact with a person with a disability be documented and entered into a separate database so he or she can be readily identified? Why, or why not? Explain your response.

ENDNOTES

CHAPTER 1

1. Glennon, J. (2010, February 22). Communication skills and your survival. *PoliceOne*. Retrieved from https://www.policeone.com/patrol-issues/articles/2008039-Communication-skills-and-your-survival

2. Fox, H. (2015, July 21). Here are some top leadership traits that will carry us far in our profession. *CorrectionsOne*. Retrieved from https://www.correctionsone.com/column/articles/8685690-8-skills-of-successful-correctional-officers/

3. Maliwat, J. (2013, January 8). Effective communication for security officers. *Security Matters*. Retrieved from https://securitymatters.com.ph/effective-communication-for-security-officers-8480

4. Blarr, M. (2017, January 20). More cases involving suspended Auburn corrections officer dismissed. Retrieved from http://auburnpub.com/news/local/more-cases-involving-suspended-auburn-corrections-officer-dismissed/article_c6b91ce0-77f7-5aff-a193-5cdf0f29fec1.html

5. Cardon, P. (2016). *Business communication: Developing leaders for a networked world* (2nd ed.). New York: McGraw-Hill.

6. Lahiff, J. M., & Penrose, I. M. (1997). *Business communication: Strategies and skills* (5th ed.). Upper Saddle River, NJ: Prentice Hall.

7. *Pittsburgh Post Gazette*. (1997, February 13). p. A.

8. United States Department of Justice, Office of Public Affairs. (2017, January 13). Justice Department announces findings of investigation into Chicago Police Department: Justice Department finds a pattern of civil rights violations by the Chicago Police Department. Retrieved from https://www.justice.gov/opa/pr/justice-department-announces-findings-investigation-chicago-police-department

9. Mehrabian, A. (1971). *Silent messages*. Belmont, CA: Wadsworth.

10. Mausehund, J., & Timm, S. (1994). Teaching strategies for nonverbal skills. *Delta Pi Epsilon Instructional Strategies: An Applied Research Series, 10*(3).

11. Guffey, M. E., & Loewy, D. (2018). *Business communication: Process and product* (9th ed.). Belmont, CA: Cengage Learning (p. 128).

12. Who told you that? (1985, May 23). *Wall Street Journal*, 33.

13. Guffey & Loewy (2018).

14. Haney, W. V. (1992). *Communication and interpersonal relations: Text and cases* (6th ed.). Burr Ridge, IL: Richard D. Irwin.

15. Guffey & Loewy (2018).

16. Guffey & Loewy (2018).

17. Fry, R. (2015, May 11). *Millennials surpass Gen Xers as the largest generation in U.S. labor force*. Washington, DC: Pew Research Center, FactTank, News in the Numbers.

18. Fry (2015).

19. *Gen Z: New research and findings on the generation after Millennials*. (2016). Austin, TX: Center for Generational Kinetics.

20. Williams, A. (2015, September 18). Move over Millennials; here comes Generation Z. *New York Times*. Retrieved from https://www.nytimes.com/2015/09/20/fashion/move-over-millennials-here-comes-generation-z.html

21. *Gen Z* (2016).

22. Fry (2015).

23. University of Missouri Extension. (n.d.). Meet the generations. Retrieved from extension.missouri.edu/extcouncil/documents/ecyl/Meet-the-generations.pdf

24. University of Missouri Extension (n.d.).

25. University of Missouri Extension (n.d.).

26. Fry (2015).

27. University of Missouri Extension (n.d.).

28. University of Missouri Extension (n.d.).

29. Taylor, P., & Gao, G. (2014, June 5). *Generation X: America's neglected "middle child."* Washington, DC: Pew Research Center, FactTank, News in the Numbers.

30. Arnold, E. (n.d.). Robert Capa Remembered. *The Independent* (UK). Retrieved from http://www.independent.co.uk/arts-entertainment/robert-capa-remembered-1358188.html

31. Taylor & Gao (2014).

32. Blakemore, E. (2015, November 9). The latchkey generation: How bad was it? ITHAK: JSTOR Daily. Retrieved from https://daily.jstor.org/latchkey-generation-bad

33. University of Missouri Extension (n.d.).

34. University of Missouri Extension (n.d.).

35. Millennials in adulthood: Detached from institutions, networked with friends. (2014, March 7). Retrieved from http://www.pewsocialtrends.org/2014/03/07/millennials-in-adulthood

36. University of Missouri Extension (n.d.).

37. University of Missouri Extension (n.d.).

38. Beall, G. (2016, November 5). 8 key differences between Gen Z and Millennials. *Huffington Post*. Retrieved from http://www.huffingtonpost.com/george-beall/8-key-differences-between_b_12814200.html

39. Hartman Group. (2016, March 31). New kids on the block: A first look at Gen Z. *Forbes*. Retrieved from https://www.forbes.com/sites/thehartman-group/2016/03/31/new-kids-on-the-block-a-first-look-at-gen-z/#8b59abe1bab6

40. Johnson, W. (2015, May 25). Why today's teens are more entrepreneurial than their parents. *Harvard Business Review*. Retrieved from https://hbr.org/2015/05/why-todays-teens-are-more-entrepreneurial-than-their-parents

41. Beall (2016).

42. Dorsey, J. (2016). *Gen Z tech disruption: 2016 National Study on Technology and the Generation After Millennials*. Austin, TX: Center for Generational Kinetics. Retrieved from http://genhq.com/gen-z

43. Dorsey (2016).

44. Williamson, J. (2016, January 20). Millennials who? Why you need to get to know Generation Z. Retrieved from http://sodexoinsights.com/millennials-who-why-you-need-to-get-to-know-generation-z

45. Quicke, S. (2015, October 6). Get ready because generation z is coming. *ComputerWeekly*. Retrieved from http://www.computerweekly.com/microscope/news/4500254953/Get-ready-because-generation-z-is-coming

46. Corporate Culture. (2016). Encyclopedia, Business Terms. Inc.com. Retrieved from http://www.inc.com/encyclopedia/corporate-culture.html

47. Muir, W. K. (1977). *Police: Streetcorner politicians*. Chicago, IL: University of Chicago Press.

48. Espinoza, C., Ukleja, M., & Rusch, C. (2010). *Managing the Millennials: Discover the core competencies for managing today's workforce*. Hoboken, NJ: John Wiley & Sons.

49. Schein, E. H. (2004). *Organizational culture and leadership*. San Francisco, CA: Jossey-Bass.

50. Frost, M. W. (2011). How the Millennial generation will influence future law enforcement leadership. Franklin Pierce University. ProQuest Dissertations Publishing, No. 3473428.

51. Cantor, C. (2016, November 29). Too much self-esteem may be keeping Millennials single. *Psychology Today*. Retrieved from https://www.psychologytoday.com/blog/modern-sex/201611/too-much-self-esteem-may-be-keeping-millennials-single

52. Sanders, D., & Stefaniak, A. (2008, November 17). To protect and serve: What Generation Y brings to law enforcement and how police agencies can benefit. *Policy Perspectives*. Retrieved from gardner.utah.edu/_documents/publications/workforce/pp-to-protect-and-serve.pdf

53. Murphy, S. A. (2007). *Leading a multigenerational workforce*. Washington, DC: AARP. Retrieved from http://assets.aarp.org/www.aarp.org_/articles/money/employers/leading_multigenerational_workforce.pdf

54. Murphy (2007).

55. Murphy (2007).

56. McDermott, P. J., & Hulse, D. (2012, February). *Focus on training: Interpersonal skills training in police academy curriculum*. Retrieved from https:///leb.fbi.gov/2012/february/focus-on-training-interpersonal-skills-in-police-academy-curriculum

57. O'Connell, S. W. (1979). *The manager as communicator*. New York, NY: Harper & Row Publishers (p. 25).

CHAPTER 2

1. Borelli, F. (2009). Think before you speak. Retrieved from https://www.poam.net/train-and-educate/2010/think-before-you-speak/

2. Marshall, T. A., & Vincent, J. (1998). Improving listening skills: Instructional module for business communication classrooms. Methods, activities, evaluations, and resources. Published in conjunction with Dr. Mary Ellen Guffey, ITP South-Western College Publishing.

3. Lake, R. (2015, September 17). Listening Statistics: 23 Facts you need to hear. Retrieved from https://www.creditdonkey.com/listening-statistics.html

4. Nichols, R. G., & Stevens, L. A. (1957, September). Listening to people. *Harvard Business Review*. Retrieved from https://hbr.org/1957/09/listening-to-people

5. Verderber, R. F., Verderber, K. S., & Sellnow, D. D. (2010). *Communicate!* (13th ed.). Boston, MA: Wadsworth.

6. What is a mnemonic device? (1998–2017). Mnemonic Devices Memory Tools. Retrieved from https://www.mnemonic-device.com/what-is-a-mnemonic-device

7. Wood, J. T. (2009). *Communication in our lives*. Boston, MA: Wadsworth/Cengage Learning (pp. 79–80).

8. Aldag, R. M., & Kuzuhara, L. (2015, February 11). *Creating high performance teams: Applied strategies and tools*

for managers and team members. London, UK: Routledge (pp. 152–153).

9. Johnson, I. W., & Pearce, C. G. (1990, March). Assess and improve your listening quotient. *Business Education Forum*, 22–27.

10. Joki, K. (2015, August 14). Five ways to write better text messages. *Grammarly*. Retrieved from https://www.grammarly.com/blog/five-ways-to-write-better-text-messages

11. Derning, D. R. (1973, March). The true measure of police/public relations. *Police Chief*, 8.

12. Brake, M. (1978, October). Establishing a public information officer. *FBI Law Enforcement Bulletin*, 22–25.

13. Surette, R. (1995). Public information officers: A descriptive study of crime news gatekeepers. *Journal of Criminal Justice, 23,* 325–336.

14. Statement, A. (1997, April). LAPD blues. *Public Relations Tactics, 4*(4).

15. Motschall, M., & Cao, L. (2002). An analysis of the public relations role of the police public information officer. *Police Quarterly, 5*(2), 152–180.

CHAPTER 3

1. Winton, R. (2016, March 4). Lack of knife always dogged O. J. Simpson murder investigation. *Los Angeles Times*. Retrieved from http://www.latimes.com/local/lanow/la-me-ln-knife-oj-simpson-murder-case-20160304-story.html

2. Galle, W., Nelson, B., Luce, D., & Villere, W. (1997). *Business communication*. Irwin-McGraw Hill.

3. Mausehund, J., & Timm, S. (1994, September). Teaching strategies for nonverbal skills. *Instructional Strategies: An Applied Research Series*. Little Rock, AR: Delta Pi Epsilon.

4. Goleman, D., & Freedman, J. (1982). *What psychology knows that everyone should*. Lexington, MA: Lewis Publishing.

5. Goleman & Freedman (1982).

6. Cockcroft, L. (2008, August 20). Liars are exposed by blinking. *The Telegraph*. Retrieved from http://www.telegraph.co.uk/news/2589073/Liars-are-exposed-by-blinking.html

7. Fast, J. (2002). *Body language* (Rev. ed.). New York, NY: M. Evans and Co. (p. 3).

CHAPTER 4

1. Weiss, D. C. (2013, January 17). Is it pleaded or pled? *ABA Journal*. Retrieved from http://www.abajournal.com/news/article/is_it_pleaded_or_pled

2. Lightning. (1888, October 15). Directory of Mark Twain's maxims, quotations, and various opinions. Retrieved from http://www.twainquotes.com/Lightning.html

3. McAdams, M. (2008, August 28). A spelling test. Retrieved from http://web.archive.org/web/20080105055617/http://www.sentex.net/~mmcadams/spelling.html

CHAPTER 5

1. Smith, D. (2013, March 12). You said what? *Police Magazine*. Retrieved from http://www.policemag.com/channel/careers-training/articles/2013/03/you-said-what.aspx

2. Dwyer, K. K., & Davidson, M. M. (2012, April–June). Is public speaking really more feared than death? *Communication Research Reports, 29*(2), 99–107. Retrieved from https://www.researchgate.net/publication/271993200_Is_Public_Speaking_Really_More_Feared_Than_Death

3. Guffey, M. E., & Loewy, D. (2018). *Business communication: Process and product* (9th ed.). Belmont, CA: Cengage Learning.

4. Westside Toastmasters. (n.d.). The 6 main purposes of presentations. Retrieved from http://westsidetoastmasters.com/resources/powerspeak/lib0026.html

5. Guffey & Loewy (2018).

6. McGraw-Hill Public Speaking. (1998). Speaking to an audience. Retrieved from http://www.mhhe.com/socscience/comm/new-home/tutorial/speak/method.htm

7. Pierce, W. L., Professor Emeritus, Adult Education, The University of Southern Mississippi (Personal Communication).

8. Guffey & Loewy (2018).

9. Investopedia. (2017). Demographics. Retrieved from http://www.investopedia.com/terms/d/demographics.asp

10. Guffey & Loewy (2018), p. 525.

11. Effective use of PowerPoint: Online tutorial. (n.d.). Retrieved from https://www.baruch.cuny.edu/tutorials/powerpoint/slide2.htm

12. United States Department of Health and Human Services, National Institutes of Health, National Eye Institute. (2017). Facts about colorblindness. Retrieved from https://nei.nih.gov/health/color_blindness/facts_about

13. Dvorsky, G. (2012, October 10). The neuroscience of stage fright and how to cope with it. Retrieved from http://io9.gizmodo.com/5950544/the-neuroscience-of-stage-fright----and-how-to-cope-with-it

14. Phillips, G. M. (1991). *Communication incompetencies: A theory of training oral performance behavior.*

Carbondale: Southern Illinois University Press. ERIC Number: ED330000.

15. Cho, M. (2013, April 30). What happens to our brain when we have stage fright: The science of public speaking. Buffer. Retrieved from https://blog.buffer-app.com/what-happens-to-our-brains-when-we-have-stage-fright-the-science-of-public-speaking

16. Guffey & Loewy (2018).

17. Guffey & Loewy (2018).

18. Bernsen, R. (2016, August 9). Media: Getting in front of the story. *Police Magazine*. Retrieved from http://www.policemag.com/channel/careers-training/articles/2016/08/media-getting-in-front-of-the-story.aspx

19. Indiana State Police. (2017). Chief public information officer. Retrieved from http://www.in.gov/isp/3201.htm

20. Davis, P. (2017). The public information officer and today's digital news environment. Federal Bureau of Investigation. Retrieved from https://leb.fbi.gov/2010/july/the-public-information-officer-and-todays-digital-news-environment

21. Stephens, D. W., Hill, J., & Greenberg, S. (2011, September). *Strategic communication practices: A toolkit for police executives*. Washington, DC: United States Department of Justice, Community Oriented Policing Services. Retrieved from http://www.cops.usdoj.gov

22. Federal Bureau of Investigation, LEEDA. (2017). Media and public relations. Retrieved from http://fbileeda.org/page/MediaPubRel_Landing#

23. Color Matters. (n.d.). Blue: The meanings of blue. Retrieved from https://www.colormatters.com/the-meanings-of-colors/blue

24. Baer, D. (2014, November 17). 17 tactics for reading people's body language. *Entrepreneur*. Retrieved from https://www.entrepreneur.com/article/239840

25. Duarte. (n.d.). Persuasive speech: Chunk information into bite-sized pieces. Retrieved from http://www.duarte.com/persuasive-speech-chunk-information-into-bite-sized-pieces

CHAPTER 6

1. Toers-Bijns, C. (2012, February 13). Report writing for correctional officers. Retrieved from http://corrections.com/news/article/30175-report-writing-for-correctional-officers

2. Choose a precise conjunction or preposition to indicate cause and effect. (2017, April). *EditPros News*, 21(4). Retrieved from http://www.editpros.com

3. Provost, G. (n.d.). *Gary Provost quotes. Quotable quote*. Retrieved from http://www.goodreads.com/quotes/373814-this-sentence-has-five-words-here-are-five-more-words

4. Lanham, R. A. (2006). *Revising prose* (5th ed.). New York, NY: Pearson.

5. Paragraph. (2017). *Merriam-Webster dictionary*. Retrieved from https://www.merriam-webster.com/dictionary/paragraph

6. Hacker, J., & Sommers, N. (2015). *A writer's reference* (8th ed.). Boston, MA: Bedford/St. Martin's.

7. Correctional Officer Training HQ. (2014, May 31). Guide to correctional officer incident report writing. Retrieved from http://www.correctionalofficertraininghq.com/correctional-officer-report-writing/

8. Shanks, R. (2014, July 8). How to write a report like a corrections officer. *CorrectionsOne.com News*. Retrieved from https://www.correctionsone.com/column/articles/7357589-How-to-write-a-report-like-a-corrections-officer/

9. Police: Private police and industrial security. (2002). Retrieved from http://www.encyclopedia.com/law/legal-and-political-magazines/police-private-police-and-industrial-security

10. Police: Private police and industrial security. (2002). Retrieved from http://www.encyclopedia.com/law/legal-and-political-magazines/police-private-police-and-industrial-security

11. U.S. Bureau of Labor Statistics, Occupational Employment Statistics, Occupational Employment and Wages. (2016, May). Security guards. Retrieved from https://data.bls.gov/cgi-bin/print.pl/oes/current/oes339032.htm

12. Police: Private police and industrial security—Legal authority. (n.d.). Retrieved from http://law.jrank.org/pages/1687/Police-Private-Police-Industrial-Security-Legal-authority.html

13. Sparkman, C. (2014). How to write a daily activity report that matters. Retrieved from http://www.officerreports.com/blog/how-to-write-a-daily-activity-report

14. Miksen, C. (2017). How to effectively write reports as a security officer. Retrieved from http://work.chron.com/effectively-write-reports-security-officer-20169.html

15. Rikhter, V. (n.d.). How security guards can write incident reports in 5 easy steps. Retrieved from http://blog.zenput.com/security-guards-mobile-forms-incident-reports

16. Security Guard Training IHQ. (2014). How to write an incident report: Basic fundamentals you need to know. Retrieved from http://www.securityguardtrainingihq.com/how-to-write-a-detailed-incident-report-security-guard-training-security-guard-training-ihq

17. Gregory, A. H., Compos, N. S., Vertefeuille, L., & Zambruski, G. (2011). A comparison of US police interviewers' notes with their subsequent reports. *Journal of Investigative Psychology and Offender Profiling, 8*(2), 203–215.

18. Haire, L. (2017). Records life cycle: Definition & stages. Retrieved from http://study.com/academy/lesson/records-life-cycle-definition-stages.html

19. State of Connecticut, Division of Criminal Justice. (2012). Records retention schedule. Retrieved from https://ctstatelibrary.org/wp-content/uploads/2015/06/13-2-2-DCJ.pdf

CHAPTER 7

1. Hoffman, C. D. (2005, August). Investigative interviewing: Strategies and techniques. Naples, FL: International Foundation for Protection Officers. Retrieved from www.ifpo.org/wp-content/uploads/2013/08/interviewing.pdf

2. Buckley, J. P. (n.d.). The Reid technique of interviewing and interrogation. Retrieved from https://law.wisc.edu/fjr/clinicals/ip/wcjsc/.../buckley_chapter_on_reid_technique.doc

3. Nicholson, L. G. (2000). *Security investigations: A professional's guide.* Boston, MA: Butterworth Heinemann.

4. *Miranda v. Arizona,* 384 U.S. 436 (1966). Retrieved from https://www.law.cornell.edu/supremecourt/text/384/436

5. *Lynumn v. Illinois,* 83 S. Ct. 917 (1963). Retrieved from http://supreme-court-cases.insidegov.com/l/1954/Lynumn-v-Illinois#The%20Case&s=167Jdt

6. *Spano v. New York,* 360 U.S. 315 (1959). Retrieved from https://supreme.justia.com/cases/federal/us/360/315/

7. *Arizona v. Fulminante,* 499 U.S. 279 (1991). Retrieved from http://caselaw.findlaw.com/us-supreme-court/499/279.html

8. What are your Miranda rights? (2017). Retrieved from http://www.mirandawarning.org/whatareyourmirandarights.html

9. Leo, R. A. (2009). False confessions: Causes, consequences, and implications. *Journal of the American Academy of Psychiatry and the Law Online,* 37(3), 332–343. Retrieved from http://jaapl.org/content/37/3/332#ref-7

10. Kassin, S. M., & Gudjonsson, G. H. (2004). The psychology of confessions: A review of the literature and issues. *Psychological Science in the Public Interest,* 5(2), 33–67. Retrieved from http://journals.sagepub.com/doi/10.1111/j.1529-1006.2004.00016.x

11. Leo (2009).

12. Leo (2009).

13. Leo (2009).

14. Drizin, S., & Leo, R. (2004). The problem of false confessions in the post-DNA world. *North Carolina Law Review, 82,* 891–1007. Retrieved from https://scholar.google.com/scholar? q=THE+PROBLEM+OF+FALSE+CONFESSIONS+IN+THE+POST-DNA+WORLD&hl=en&as_sdt=0&as_vis=1&oi=scholart&sa=X&ved=0ahUKEwiDlq2Dt-TVAhVC3IMKHS61DvwQgQMIJDAA

15. Leo (2009).

CHAPTER 8

1. York, G. (2016, May 17). Are you prepared for court? 4 keys to courtroom demeanor for correctional officers. *CorrectionsOne.* Retrieved from https://www.correctionsone.com/careers/articles/179688187-Are-you-prepared-for-court-4-keys-to-courtroom-demeanor-for-correctional-officers/

2. Wells, M. (2016, November 22). 6 tips for preparing correctional officers for courtroom testimony. *CorrectionsOne.* Retrieved from https://www.correctionsone.com/corrections-training/articles/243073187-6-tips-for-preparing-correctional-officers-for-courtroom-testimony/

3. Going to court is a big deal. (2012, September 26). Retrieved from http://securityofficerhq.com/blog/2012/09/26/Going-To-Court

CHAPTER 9

1. Cain, B., & Bostic, M. (2015, December 8). How technology is changing law enforcement: The latest high-tech innovations offer benefits and challenges for crime fighters. *Police Magazine.* Retrieved from http://www.policemag.com/blog/technology/story/2015/12/how-technology-is-changing-law-enforcement.aspx

2. Cain & Bostic (2015).

3. Irving, D. (2016, January 7). *How will technology change criminal justice?* Santa Monica, CA: RAND Corporation. Retrieved from https://www.rand.org/blog/rand-review/2016/01/how-will-technology-change-criminal-justice.html

4. Law enforcement equipment and technology. (2014, March 28). Washington, DC: National Institute of Justice, Office of Justice Programs. Retrieved from https://www.nij.gov/topics/law-enforcement/technology/Pages/welcome.aspx

5. Harris, D. (2017, February 22). Video shows Orlando cop berating man during disturbance call. *Orlando Sentinel.* Retrieved from http://www.orlandosentinel.com/news/breaking-news/os-jose-sanchez-orlando-police-20170221-story.html

6. Blackburn, B. (2017, May 1). Great kid killed in officer-involved shooting in Balch Springs. WFFA. Retrieved from http://www.wfaa.com/news/local/15-year-old-boy-killed-in-officer-involved-shooting-in-balch-springs/435409090

7. Balch Springs officer terminated after death of Jordan Edwards. (2017, May 3). WFFA. Retrieved from http://www.wfaa.com/news/balch-springs-officer-terminated-after-shooting-and-killing-15-year-old-jordan-edwards/436130282

8. Schaper, D. (2017, April 27). "Textalyzer" aims to curb distracted driving, but what about privacy? NPR Now. Retrieved from http://www.npr.org/sections/alltechconsidered/2017/04/27/525729013/textalyzer-aims-to-curb-distracted-driving-but-what-about-privacy

9. Gronewold, A. (2017, May 14). New York eyes "Textalyzer" to combat distracted driving. USA Today. Retrieved from https://www.usatoday.com/story/money/2017/05/14/new-york-eyes-textalyzer-combat-distracted-driving/101689750/

10. Schaper (2017).

11. Kravets, D. (2016, April 11). First came the Breathalyzer, now meet the roadside police "Textalyzer." ARS Technica: Law & Disorder. Retrieved from https://arstechnica.com/tech-policy/2016/04/first-came-the-breathalyzer-now-meet-the-roadside-police-textalyzer

12. Hemby, K. V. (2014). Professionalism in the digital age. Belmont, CA: Cengage. (On-demand publication).

13. Innocence Project. (2017). Eyewitness misidentification. Retrieved from https://www.innocenceproject.org/causes/eyewitness-misidentification

14. Identi-Kit. (1995, September 18). Central Intelligence Agency. Retrieved from https://www.cia.gov/library/center-for-the-study-of-intelligence/kent-csi/vol4no1/html/v04i1a03p_0001.htm

15. Identi-Kit (1995).

16. Identi-Kit. (2017). Quickly create amazingly clear facial composite sketches. Retrieved from http://identikit.net.

17. ScenePD. (2017). Retrieved from http://en.freedownloadmanager.org/Windows-PC/ScenePD.html

18. CAD Zone. (2017). Retrieved from http://www.faro.com/en-us/products/faro-software/faro-cad-zone/overview

19. Heaton, B. (2012, January 19). Missouri courts stay connected with video conferencing. Government Technology Magazine. Retrieved from http://www.govtech.com/public-safety/Missouri-Courts-Stay-Connected-With-Video-Conferencing.html?utm_source=embedded&utm_medium=direct&utm_campaign=Missouri-Courts-Stay-Connected-With-Video-Conferencing

20. Stern, M. J. (2016, July 11). New Mexico Supreme Court: Courts can't use Skype to get around the Constitution. Slate/Future Tense. Retrieved from http://www.slate.com/blogs/future_tense/2016/07/11/new_mexico_supreme_court_rules_on_skype_and_the_confrontation_clause.html

21. Skype. (2007). Responding to law enforcement records requests. Retrieved from http://www.slate.com/blogs/future_tense/2017/07/07/third_circuit_affirms_the_constitutional_right_to_record_police_officers.html

22. Microsoft. (2016). Law enforcement requests report. Retrieved from https://www.microsoft.com/en-us/about/corporate-responsibility/lerr

23. Heaton, B. (2012, March 5). Web chats help streamline operations at New York jail. Government Technology Magazine. Retrieved from http://www.govtech.com/public-safety/Web-Chats-Help-Streamline-Operations-at-New-York-Jail.html

24. News Staff. (2013, December 13). "Skype" for jail: Video chat moves inmate visits online. Government Technology Magazine. Retrieved from http://www.govtech.com/public-safety/Video-Visitation-with-Inmates-in-Montana-Jail.html

25. Police iPhone Apps. (2017). PoliceOne. Retrieved from https://www.policeone.com/police-iphone-apps

26. Campbell, D. (2017, August 17). Brookhaven Police Department makes accident reports available online. Daily Leader. Retrieved from http://m.dailyleader.com/2017/08/17/brookhaven-police-department-makes-accident-reports-available-online

27. Telmate Guardian offers innovative smartphone-based, GPS monitoring solution for community corrections. (2017, July 15). PRWEB. Retrieved from http://www.prweb.com/releases/2015/04/prweb12658452

28. Social media. (2017). Merriam-Webster. Retrieved from https://www.merriam-webster.com/dictionary/social%20media

29. Kim, K., Oglesby-Neal, A., & Mohr, E. (2017, February). 2016 law enforcement use of social media survey. Washington, DC: Urban Institute/International Association of Chiefs of Police. Retrieved from www.urban.org/research/publication/2016-law-enforcement-use-social-media-survey

30. Roufa, T. (2017). The use of social networking in law enforcement. The Balance. Retrieved from https://www.thebalance.com/social-networking-and-law-enforcement-974548

31. Kim, Oglesby-Neal, & Mohr (2017).

32. 50 most social media friendly police departments in America's largest cities. (2017). MPH Programs List. Retrieved from http://mphprogramslist.com/50-most-social-media-friendly-police-departments

33. Law Enforcement Directory. (2017). PoliceOne. Retrieved from https://www.policeone.com/law-enforcement-directory

34. Chertoff, M. (2001, June 12). Statement before the Subcommittee on Crime, Committee on the Judiciary, U.S. House of Representatives, June 12, 2001. Retrieved from http://www.cybercrime.gov/cybercrime61201_MChertoff.htm

35. Conklin, W. A., White, G., Williams, D., Davis, R., & Cothren, C. (2010). *Principles of computer security: Comp TIA security+ and beyond* (2nd ed.). New York, NY: McGraw-Hill.

36. Caldwell, L. R. (2015, October 16). The threat today. Remarks prepared for Cybersecurity + Law Enforcement: The Cutting Edge Symposium. Retrieved from https://www.justice.gov/opa/speech/assistant-attorney-general-leslie-r-caldwell-delivers-remarks-cybersecurity-law

37. Caldwell (2015).

CHAPTER 10

1. Law Enforcement Learning. (2017). Conflict engagement for law enforcement. Retrieved from https://lawenforcementlearning.com/course/conflict-engagement-for-law-enforcement

2. Conflict. (2017). *Merriam-Webster*. Retrieved from https://www.merriam-webster.com/dictionary/conflict

3. Maslow, A. H. (1954). A theory of human motivation. In *Motivation and personality*. New York, NY: Harper & Row. Retrieved from http://pages.ucsd.edu/~nchristenfeld/Happiness_Readings_files/Class%207%20-%20Maslow%201954.pdf

4. Maslow (1943).

5. Moore, C. W. (1986). *The mediation process: Practical strategies for resolving conflict*. San Francisco, CA: Jossey-Bass.

6. Moore (1986).

7. McMains, M. J., & Mullins, W. C. (2001). *Crisis negotiations: Managing critical incidents and hostage situations in law enforcement and corrections*. Cincinnati, OH: Anderson Publishing.

8. Solidarity. (2017). *Merriam-Webster*. Retrieved from https://www.merriam-webster.com/dictionary/solidarity

9. Palmiotto, M. J. (2000). *Community policing: A policing strategy for the 21st century*. Gaithersburg, MD: Aspen Publishers (p. 42).

10. Group. (2017). *Merriam-Webster*. Retrieved from https://www.merriam-webster.com/dictionary/group

11. Wood, J. T. (1997). *Communication in our lives*. Belmont, CA: Wadsworth Publishing (p. 265).

12. Wood (1997).

13. Van Vliet, V. (2013). Fred Fiedler. Retrieved from https://www.toolshero.com/toolsheroes/fred-fiedler

CHAPTER 11

1. Spens, R. (2015, March 27). Why cultural intelligence matters for our police forces. Professional Passport. Retrieved from http://www.professional-passport.com/blog/globalization-of-our-citizenry-demands-a-culturally-intelligent-police-force

2. Shusta, R. M. (2015). *Multicultural law enforcement: Strategies for peacekeeping in a diverse society* (6th ed.). Boston, MA: Pearson.

3. Hall, E. T., & Hall, M. R. (1990). *Understanding cultural differences*. Yarmouth, ME: Intercultural Press (pp. 183–184).

4. Hofstede, G. (2001). *Culture's consequences: Comparing values, behaviors, institutions, and organizations across nations* (2nd ed.). Thousand Oaks CA: Sage. Retrieved from https://geert-hofstede.com/national-culture.html

5. Martin, J., & Nakayama, T. (2011). *Experiencing intercultural communication: An introduction* (4th ed.). New York, NY: McGraw-Hill.

6. Empathy. (2017). *Cambridge dictionary*. Retrieved from http://dictionary.cambridge.org/us/dictionary/english/empathy

7. Inam, H. (2016, December 13). Five steps to practice empathy. Transformational Leadership. Retrieved from http://www.transformleaders.tv/five-steps-to-practice-empathy/

8. Navarro, J. R. (n.d.). Unconscious bias. San Francisco: University of California, San Francisco, Office of Diversity and Outreach. Retrieved from https://diversity.ucsf.edu/resources/unconscious-bias

9. Gokey, C., & Shah, S. (Eds.). (2016). *How to serve diverse communities. Police perspectives: Building trust in a diverse nation, no. 2*. Washington, DC: Office of Community Oriented Policing Services. Retrieved from https://www.vera.org/publications/police-perspectives-guidebook-series-building-trust-in-a-diverse-nation

10. Gokey & Shah (2016).

11. Gokey & Shah (2016).

12. Cultural diversity. (2009). *Texas Commission on Law Enforcement, course curriculum materials and updates, course no. 3939, training supplement*. Retrieved from https://www.tcole.texas.gov/training-instructor-resources

13. Forum on Child and Family Statistics. (2017). Child population: Number of children (in millions) ages 0–17 in the U.S. by age, 1950–2015 and projected 2016–2050. Retrieved from https://www.childstats.gov/americaschildren/tables/pop1.asp

14. McNeill, J. M. (2017, July 16). Suicides rise among middle schoolers. *The Tennessean*.

15. National Center for Children in Poverty. (2016, March). Nearly half of American children living near poverty line. Retrieved from http://www.nccp.org/topics/childpoverty.html

16. National Children's Alliance. (2017). National statistics on child abuse. Retrieved from http://www

.nationalchildrensalliance.org/media-room/media-kit/national-statistics-child-abuse

17. Miller, H. (2016, December 14). There have been over 200 school shooting incidents since the Sandy Hook massacre. *Huffington Post*. Retrieved from http://www.huffingtonpost.com/entry/school-shootings-since-sandy-hook_us_58503d99e4b04c8e2bb232eb

18. Office of Juvenile Justice and Delinquency Prevention. (2015, December 13). Juvenile arrests. *OJJDP statistical briefing book*. Retrieved from http://www.ojjdp.gov/ojstaffbb/crime/qa05101.asp?qaDate=2014

19. Kelly, J. (2011, June 16). Supreme Court gives juveniles protection in police interrogations. Juvenile Justice Information Exchange. Retrieved from http://jjie.org/2011/06/16/supreme-court-gives-juveniles-protection-police-interrogations/

20. American Academy of Child and Adolescent Psychiatry. (2013, March 7). Policy statements. Retrieved from https://www.aacap.org/aacap/Policy_Statements/2013/Interviewing_and_Interrogating_Juvenile_Suspects.aspx

21. Child victims' and child witnesses' rights. (18 U.S. Code §3509). Ithaca, NY: Cornell Law School Legal Information Institute. Retrieved from https://www.law.cornell.edu/uscode/text/18/3509

22. California Penal Code Section 186.22.

23. Los Angeles Police Department. (2017a). Introduction to gangs. Retrieved from http://www.lapdonline.org/top_ten_most_wanted_gang_members/content_basic_view/23466

24. Los Angeles Police Department (2017a).

25. Los Angeles Police Department. (2017b). Pre-teens and gangs: Telltale signs. Retrieved from http://www.lapdonline.org/top_ten_most_wanted_gang_members/content_basic_view/23472

CHAPTER 12

1. Kulbarsh, P. (2013, February 15). Law enforcement and autism. Command/HQ Online Exclusive. Retrieved from http://www.officer.com/article/10880086/law-enforcement-and-autism

2. Americans with Disabilities Act. (1990, July 26). Section 12.102 Definition of disability. U.S. Department of Justice, Civil Rights Division. Retrieved from https://www.ada.gov/pubs/adastatute08.htm#12102

3. Americans with Disabilities Act (1990).

4. CDC: 53 million adults in US live with disability. (2015, July 30). Centers for Disease Control and Prevention CDC Newsroom. Retrieved from https://www.cdc.gov/media/releases/2015/p0730-us-disability.html

5. Bronson, J., Maruschak, L. M., & Berzofsky, M. (2015, December). *Disabilities among prison and jail inmates*

2011–12 (NCJ249151). Washington, DC: U.S. Department of Justice, Office of Justice Programs, Bureau of Justice Statistics. Retrieved from http://www.bjs.gov/content/pub/pdf/capd0912st.pdf

6. Americans with Disabilities Act Title II Regulations. Part 35 Nondiscrimination on the basis of disability in state and local government services. (2016, August 11). Retrieved from https://www.ada.gov/regs2010/titleII_2010/titleII_2010_regulations.htm

7. U.S. Department of Justice, Civil Rights Division. (2008, December 1). Commonly asked questions about the Americans with Disabilities Act and law enforcement. Retrieved from https://www.ada.gov/policeinfo.htm

8. U.S. Department of Justice, Civil Rights Division. (2008).

9. Department of Justice, Office of Justice Programs, Juvenile Justice and Delinquency Prevention. (2014, August). *Juveniles in residential placement, 2011* (p. 3). Available at http://www.ojjdp.gov/pubs/246826.pdf

10. U.S. Department of Education, Office of Special Education and Rehabilitative Services. (2014, December 5). Dear colleague letter on the Individuals with Disabilities Education Act for students with disabilities in correctional facilities. Retrieved from https://www2.ed.gov/policy/gen/guid/correctional-education/index.html

11. U.S. Department of Justice, Civil Rights Division. (2011, July). Service animals. ADA 2010 Revised Requirements. Retrieved from https://www.ada.gov/service_animals_2010.htm

12. U.S. Department of Health and Human Services, the ADA National Network. (2016). Customer service quick tips for front line staff serving customers with disabilities. Retrieved from http://adata.org/factsheet/quick-tips-customer-service

13. National Down Syndrome Society. (2012). Law enforcement training. Retrieved from http://www.ndss.org/Advocacy/Legislative-Agenda/Community-Integration/Law-Enforcement-Training

14. Mayo Clinic. (2014, April 19). Down syndrome definition. Retrieved from http://www.mayoclinic.org/diseases-conditions/down-syndrome/basics/definition/con-20020948

15. National Down Syndrome Society. (2012). Down syndrome fact sheet. Retrieved from http://www.ndss.org/Down-Syndrome/Down-Syndrome-Facts/

16. American Speech-Language-Hearing Association. (2017). Communication characteristics: Selected populations with an intellectual disability. Retrieved from http://www.asha.org/Practice-Portal/Clinical-Topics/Intellectual-Disability/Communication-Characteristics--Selected-Populations-With-an-Intellectual-Disability

17. Centers for Disease Control and Prevention. (2017). Traumatic brain injury and concussion. Retrieved from https://www.cdc.gov/traumaticbraininjury/index.html

18. Centers for Disease Control and Prevention. (2016, January 22). Rates of TBI-related emergency department visits, hospitalizations, and deaths—United States, 2001–2010 traumatic brain injury, data and statistics. Retrieved from https://www.cdc.gov/traumaticbraininjury/data/rates.html

19. Brain Injury Association of America. (2015). Living with brain injury. Retrieved from http://www.biausa.org/living-with-brain-injury.htm

20. Brain Injury Association of America. (2017). About brain injury. Retrieved from http://www.biausa.org/about-brain-injury.htm

21. The Internet Stroke Center. (2017). Stroke statistics. Retrieved from http://www.strokecenter.org/patients/about-stroke/stroke-statistics

22. American Stroke Association. (2017). Let's talk about changes caused by stroke. Retrieved from http://www.strokeassociation.org/STROKEORG/LifeAfterStroke/RegainingIndependence/PhysicalChallenges/Physical-Challenges-After-Stroke_UCM_308548_SubHomePage.jsp

23. Autism Speaks. (2017b). What is autism. Retrieved from https://www.autismspeaks.org/what-autism

24. Centers for Disease Control and Prevention. (2017). Autism spectrum disorder: Data and statistics: Prevalence. Retrieved from https://www.cdc.gov/ncbddd/autism/data.html

25. Autism Speaks. (2017a). Information for law enforcement. Retrieved from https://www.autismspeaks.org/family-services/autism-safety-project/first-responders/law-enforcement

26. National Autism Association. (n.d.). What is echolalia? Retrieved from nationalautismassociation.org

27. Alzheimer's Association. (2017b). What is dementia? Retrieved from http://www.alz.org/what-is-dementia.asp

28. Louisiana State University System, Institute for Dementia Research and Prevention at Pennington Biomedical Research Center. (2017). FAQ: What is dementia? Retrieved from http://idrp.pbrc.edu/faq.htm

29. Alzheimer's Association. (2017a). 10 warning signs of Alzheimer's disease: Early detection matters. Retrieved from http://www.alz.org/what-is-dementia.asp#memory-loss-symptoms

30. Alzheimer's Association (2017b).

31. University of Texas at Austin: Division of Diversity and Community Engagement, Services for Students with Disabilities. (2017). Psychological disabilities. Retrieved from http://diversity.utexas.edu/disability/psychological-disabilities-2

32. Cherry, K. (2017, April 13). A list of psychological disorders. Retrieved from https://www.verywell.com/a-list-of-psychological-disorders-2794776

33. Cherry (2017).

34. Boudoukha, A. H., Ouagazzal, O., & Goutaudier, N. (2016). When traumatic event exposure characteristics matter: Impact of traumatic event exposure characteristics on posttraumatic and dissociative symptoms. *Psychological Trauma: Theory, Research, Practice, and Policy, 9*(5), 561–566. doi:10.1037/tra0000243

35. Anxiety and Depression Association of America. (2016, April). Symptoms of PTSD. Retrieved from https://www.adaa.org/understanding-anxiety/posttraumatic-stress-disorder-ptsd/symptoms

36. Grohol, J. M. (2017). Schizophrenia. *Psych Central.* Retrieved from https://psychcentral.com/disorders/schizophrenia

37. Bressert, S. (2017). Schizophrenia symptoms. *Psych Central.* Retrieved from https://psychcentral.com/disorders/schizophrenia/schizophrenia-symptoms

38. The PACER Center. (2006). What is an emotional or behavioral disorder? Retrieved from www.pacer.org/parent/php/PHP-c81.pdf

39. The PACER Center (2006).

40. Correctional Education Guidance Package. (2015, January 7). Highlights from guidance. Retrieved from https://www2.ed.gov/policy/gen/guid/correctional-education/index.html

41. Greenspan, S. (2013, November 13). The preventable death of Ethan Saylor: When three people are incompetent, tragedy results. *Psychology Today.* Retrieved from https://www.psychologytoday.com/blog/incompetence/201311/the-preventable-death-ethan-saylor

42. Greenspan (2013).

43. The Autism Site. (2017). This devastating scenario reminds us how important autism training is for police. Retrieved from http://blog.theautismsite.com/autism-and-police

44. Autism Society of Indiana. (2017). Individuals with autism in the criminal justice system. Retrieved from http://www.autismsocietyofindiana.org/individuals-autism-criminal-justice-system

45. Heaphy, R. (2017, April 27). Police report: Autistic man pepper-sprayed in face for eating cookie. Fox 9. Retrieved from http://www.fox9.com/news/251233898-story

46. Stelloh, T. (2016, August 22). North Carolina trooper fatally shoots deaf man after traffic stop. NBC News. Retrieved from http://www.nbcnews.com/news/us-news/north-carolina-trooper-fatally-shoots-deaf-man-after-traffic-stop-n636221

47. Holmes, O. W. (2013). *The common law* (pp. 47–48). Retrieved from http://www.gutenberg.org/files/2449/2449-h/2449-h.htm

48. U.S. Department of Justice, Office of Justice Programs, Bureau of Justice Statistics. (2015). Crime against persons with disabilities, 2010–2014 statistical

tables. Retrieved from https://www.bjs.gov/content/pub/pdf/capd0914st.pdf

49. U.S. Department of Justice, Office of Justice Programs, Bureau of Justice Statistics. (2015).

50. U.S. Department of Justice, Civil Rights Division, Disability Rights Section. (2006, January). Communicating with people who are deaf or hard of hearing: ADA guide for law enforcement officers. Retrieved from https://www.ada.gov/lawenfcomm.htm

51. Kulbarsh, P. (2013, February 15). Law enforcement and autism. Command/HQ Online Exclusive. Retrieved from http://www.officer.com/article/10880086/law-enforcement-and-autism

52. ADA Knowledge Translation Center, ADA National Network. (2015). Guidelines for writing about people with disabilities. Retrieved from https://adata.org/fact-sheet/ADANN-writin

53. Decker, D. M. (2014, November). *Attention: Law enforcement officers. Interacting with people who use guide dogs. Facts you should know.* Imperial, MO: Guide Dog Users, Inc. Retrieved from http://guidedogusersinc.org/wp-content/uploads/2014/11/attention-law-enforcement-officers.pdf

54. State of Tennessee, Department of Intellectual & Developmental Disabilities. (2015, April). DIDD services and investigation processes training for Tennessee law enforcement officers. Retrieved from http://tn.gov/didd/topic/law-enforcment-training

INDEX

ABOUT THE AUTHORS

Dr. Robert E. Grubb retired as sergeant, Roanoke City Police Department, in 1991. He has personal experience with the information covered in the text. As part of his training opportunities, Dr. Grubb engages in discussions with current agency personnel to ascertain their needs with regard to communication skills development. So he is continually seeking and receiving data that support the use of this type of text in both educational and training facilities. He was the criminal justice program coordinator at Cumberland University, criminal justice program director at Columbia State Community College, and an award-winning associate professor at Marshall University, where he served as the department chair, graduate director, and internship director. He is currently pursuing an additional degree in information systems, with an emphasis in digital security, at Middle Tennessee State University.

Dr. K. Virginia Hemby is a certified hospitality educator (CHE) and a certified online instructor (COI) and has taught business communication at the university level for the past 22 years. She worked as a legal secretary for 10 years prior to earning her doctorate. Dr. Hemby's areas of specialization are business communication; professional meeting, event, exhibition, and convention (MEEC) management; training and development; and office and administrative management. She is currently a professor of marketing at Middle Tennessee State University and director of Raiders' Closet, a nonprofit project established to provide professional attire to MTSU students in need to be used for interviews for postgraduation jobs. Students are allowed to keep any suit and accessories secured from Raiders' Closet at no cost to them. Dr. Hemby created Raiders' Closet in 2012 in response to students' comments that they were unable to afford to purchase suits to wear for interviews. She was honored by MTSU as the recipient of the 2016–2017 Public Service Award for her work with Raiders' Closet.